Through the process of writing this book,
I have experienced crossing a river on
dry land. It is truly a memorial to me and
my family, forever and always.

To Florence (Myoung Jin), Johana, and Joe.
You are my past, present, and future.

Contents

Preface

Data mining is a rapidly emerging concept in the area of computational intelligence. It is rather new and intellectually stimulating, whereas its applications are diverse, advanced, and practical.

This book presents practical issues in the design and implementation of data mining systems. A practical approach is adhered to such that the concepts and techniques presented can be applied not only to the examples in the book, but also to many of the real-world data mining applications. It provides a highly readable and systematic exposition of the fundamental concepts of data mining with a coherent presentation of practical design examples.

■ Purpose

This book is intended to serve as an introduction to the field of data mining. The subject matter has been approached from a practical point of view to promote discussions on various topics relevant to practical and intelligent data mining systems. Various aspects of data mining systems are touched upon to present a concept of intelligence that can be embedded into database systems.

This book will provide the readers with an understanding of the concept, the nature, and various techniques and algorithms needed for intelligent data mining systems. The main objective is to illustrate how these techniques and algorithms can be exploited, integrated, and used to design intelligent data mining systems. Students who complete a course using this text will have the ability to understand the design concerns and constraints of a real-world application, the different types of methods and approaches that yield intelligent systems, and the role that the modern intelligent database designer plays in achieving practical and useful solutions to intelligent data mining systems design problems. Ultimately, the concepts and techniques presented in each chapter should motivate the reader to move beyond the current coverage level since the reader will be exposed to an effective design approach fully revealing and exploiting the basic and essential properties of intelligent data mining systems design.

■ Intended Readers, Usage, and Curricula

Increased emphasis is given to databases with intelligent and advanced features in our modern computer science curricula. Familiarity with the concept of data mining systems becomes a necessary and essential asset to a number of other scientific disciplines such as medicine, business management, biology, and sociology.

I have attempted to make the material understandable by an educated layman who is interested in learning a wide variety of techniques for data mining systems and intelligent database design. This book is designed to be especially useful for undergraduate seniors or graduate students who have completed an introductory database design principles course and want to further learn various methods and techniques related to data mining systems. It is intended to give these students a working-level familiarity with concepts and techniques necessary to fit their acquired relational database design skills into a larger framework consistent with the practical needs of data mining systems design. The material focuses on the practical needs of various application areas and takes into account the currently existing curricular structure of graduate and undergraduate courses.

At a graduate level, this text can be used for a sequence in database systems course. After being exposed to basic concepts of a wide variety of topics in data mining systems, the reader may choose an area of special interest for advanced study. At the undergraduate level, this text is appropriate for an advanced-level database course to expose students to emerging and advanced topics. For both graduate and undergraduate students, this text will serve as the source for providing a wealth of ideas on development projects for real-world applications.

The material in this book can be used either in a quarter- or semester-oriented course. A ten-week quarter course might include the materials of chapters 1, 2, 3, 4, 5, and 7 to cover fundamentals of data mining. The remaining chapters (6 and 8) can be added to a fifteen-week semester course for extended coverage of the concepts with the introduction of fuzzy logic, expert systems, and neural networks. A carefully formed moderate-scale design project could be added to the coverage depending on the structure of the course, the intended focus, and audience.

Computer and IT professionals interested in learning about the concept and nature of data mining systems, as well as those already familiar with the field, should find this book beneficial, informative, and thought provoking. The techniques and examples on a wide variety of topics will enable database practitioners to delve into the system development issues.

■ Significant Features

A number of features make this book unique from others that are already available:

1. An abundance of illustrations for easy interpretation and understanding of concepts and applied techniques,

2. A balanced introduction to data mining with equal emphasis on concepts, techniques, applications, and design aspects of this technology,

3. Inclusion of practical, real-world application examples throughout the chapters for design-oriented illustration of ideas and concepts,

4. A wide variety of topics that can be understood with no prerequisites except for the basic knowledge of introductory database design and implementation,

5. Provision of background knowledge for advanced and extended study and research of selected topics, and

6. Project-oriented approach toward the design and implementation of intelligent databases with a wealth of real-world and practical project suggestions.

■ Course Coverage and Organization

The primary purpose of this book is to provide a basis for understanding the nature of intelligence that can be embedded into database systems as a scientific discipline concerned with the mechanisms and limits involved in acquiring, representing, and applying knowledge. This book focuses on three main themes: theory, practice, and projects. Most chapters of this book are devoted to the discussion on the topics related to these themes.

The first part of each chapter presents the basic concept and algorithms of a technique for understanding the nature of intelligence that can be incorporated into database systems. In addition, a number of carefully selected illustrative examples of practical applications are included in the chapters to motivate the reader to recall important concepts concerning the chapter contents. The essence of this book is highlighted in the following brief description of chapter topics.

Chapter 1 provides an introduction to the brief history of evolution of databases, current and future trends, main ideas, and concepts of intelligent database design and its applications. The subsequent material is divided into several conceptually diverse areas throughout the text within a cohesive overall framework. It is organized in such a way that even readers who are not familiar with intelligent database design concepts will be able to comprehend. Chapter 2 focuses on various techniques for association rules. Mining of basket data, attribute-oriented induction method, association rules in hypertext databases, and quantitative association rule mining are covered. Chapter 3 discusses various topics on classification such as Prism, Induct, REP, IREP, RIPPER, Cart, ID3, C4.5, C5.0, and decision trees, whereas Chapter 4 introduces various ways the system performs statistical data mining. Chapter 4 also describes the topics of conditional probability, equality tests, coefficient of correlation, contingency tables, and linear regression. Chapter 5 covers rough sets and Bayes' theorem, which are other important set-theoretic data mining methods. In Chapter 6, the neural networks are discussed as an important branch of data mining. The topics discussed in the chapter include back propagation model, bi-directional associative memory model, learning vector quantization model, and probabilistic network model. Chapter 7 introduces clustering in data mining. Many algorithms in clustering such as hierarchical algorithm, partition algorithm, and density search algorithm are described in depth. The book concludes with Chapter 8 with the introduction to fuzzy logic for data mining.

■ Chapter Bibliography

The material for this book came from many sources including the most pertinent literature on the subject, personal lecture notes, and various project development experiences. References are not cited in the chapter discussions, but rather cited in selected bibliographic note sections at the end of each chapter since the intent is to produce primarily a book that integrates concepts, techniques, and applications. The most pertinent bibliographic references are cited. I apologize to the authors, if any, of the works that I failed to acknowledge due to lack of awareness on my part.

■ Acknowledgments

There are many people who have contributed directly and indirectly to the completion of this book. It is not possible to thank all of them here, but there are some names that deserve special recognition. I particularly thank my graduate students at Texas A&M University—Commerce for contributing a great deal of time and effort to some of my original manuscript writing. Special thanks goes to Zaoya Wang, Youwen Li, Cheung Lung Ni, Jianwei Li, Duan Li, Wei Zhang, Samathi and Ekapol Wongnapapan for their time and effort in collecting and reviewing an extensive list of references as well as practical examples to illustrate data mining algorithms presented in each chapter. They also helped me refine the manuscript.

Dr. Keith McFarland, the former President of Texas A&M University—Commerce, motivated me during the early stages of the book writing process. Professor Murat M. Tanik at the University of Alabama at Birmingham has gladly reviewed the manuscript and provided valuable input to improve the content. Encouraging words and confidence from John Kocur enabled me to continue on whenever I felt like giving up. My research team at the Intelligent Cyberspace Engineering Lab (ICEL – http://icel.tamu-commerce.edu) has been a driving force for topic formation and presentation in every chapter as well as for collecting information on data mining products and applications provided in the appendix.

My family has always been extremely supportive in this endeavor. My wife, Myoung Jin (Florence) has always been understanding and patient with my late work hours and curtailed family time. She has been my best friend, mentor, comforter, and supporter. My daughter Johana and my son Joe have always been my hope, future, and reason for my diligent work to complete this book. My parents and parents-in-law have been close at hand with daily wisdom and support, right from the start. Encouraging words from my brother Jong Chuhl has often energized me to continue the writing process.

Special thanks goes to Tim Anderson, the acquisitions editor at Jones & Bartlett Learning, for his support and guidance. I also express sincere gratitude to Tiffany Sliter, my production editor, and the entire production team for their excellent work on manuscript revisions. Melissa Potter also assisted me a great deal, for which I am thankful.

Foreword

Amazing growth in the generation of data and information requires amazing techniques and methodologies to deal with it. Among many approaches to exert an intellectual control over this growth, data mining shines as one of the most successful techniques. It is of a class of techniques that can be considered a significant part of the general area of computational intelligence.

The impact of the printing press was immense due to the fact that it allowed storing concepts and notions in a static form for the generations to come. Humanity, insofar as scientific achievements, did not accomplished any significant progress until its advent during the 17th century. In a mere four hundred years we have achieved significant scientific insight into the fundamental principles governing nature and ourselves. Although it is significant, this level of knowledge is practically nothing compared with what we will achieve in the next hundred years. The reason for this expected future explosion of knowledge is the recent invention and establishment of computational elements, which we are calling computers. These computers—combined with sophisticated algorithms and techniques such as data mining—allow us to store not only data but also "processes," which are dynamic pieces of knowledge. In other words, the second and dynamic process-oriented information revolution, after the invention of the printing press, is unfolding in front of our eyes.

Perhaps more importantly, they allow the integration of data generated by numerous disciplinary activities. Disciplines by their very nature are not set up to systematically share data among each other. As a result of this phenomenon, we are generating mountains of data in each discipline without the benefit of connecting them. Computational intelligence techniques in general and data mining techniques, particularly as transdisciplinary activities, are attempting to fill this immense need. The Society for Design and Process Science (SDPS)—the very first transdisciplinary society—has benefited from professor Suh's participation and contributions over the years. Many of these contributions, as I see throughout the book, have matured and grown into real-life applications.

Dr. Sang Suh has been adding value not only to SDPS but also to this field since the early 1990s. Ultimately, his conscientious efforts produced a comprehensive, practical, and timely manuscript that we can not only enjoy reading, but also reap a practical benefit in the form of design and implementation of data mining systems.

I am greatly honored to be given the opportunity to write the foreword to such an important transdisciplinary book.

Murat M. Tanik, PhD, Professor
ECE Dept., University of Alabama—Birmingham, AL
Executive Board Member
Society for Design and Process Science, http://www.sdpsnet.org/

Foreword

To begin this foreword, I offer two anonymous quotations. The first is: "If there is artificial intelligence, there must also be artificial stupidity." The second is: "We need artificial intelligence because of a scarcity of the natural kind." The intent of the first is to remind us that, simply because we can do something, that does not mean we should. The second is not really an indictment of mankind, but of the alarmingly accelerated rate of the increase in human knowledge, which has outpaced our capacity to absorb it, much less put it to good use without substantial help.

We have watched the first decade of the 21st century come and go. The path to the computer technology we enjoy today is strewn with monumental mistakes and short-sightedness. (Can you say "Y2K"?)

Trying to shape a better future, in a better manner, is what drives Dr. Suh, as it has driven me, through over 30 years as a technical communicator, and now 14 years as a senior software engineering consultant, including intelligent aids for C4ISR systems, medical and healthcare applications, and currently with AllStates Technical Resources, providing enterprise document management and JDEdwards-to-SAP data and reporting bridges for one of the largest domestic and international engineering and construction companies in the industry.

After a successful career as an award-winning technical communicator, publishing over 13,000 pages of technical documents, I looked for another opportunity: one where I might make an even more dramatic impact. While looking for that opportunity, I first met Dr. Suh at Texas A&M University—Commerce who was teaching a wide range of Computer Science- and Engineering-related technical courses at both academic and professional levels.

Great teachers must have great communication skills, but a teacher is far more than a gifted communicator. Dr. Suh is a great teacher, because he is all of the things that contribute to the making of such, especially his dedication, enthusiasm, encouragement, and inspiration. He is the chief reason why I submitted derivative papers to six international Computer Science conferences. His energy and enthusiasm inspired me to a level of effort I did not know I had (especially since my full-time job was taking 60+ hours per week). He fully deserves the credit for a rare first submittal acceptance by DEXA in 1995 which was held in London, England.

Dr. Suh brings all of these skills and a vast wealth of knowledge to this book. My hope is that it will be used to educate and inspire the next generation of software system professionals. My belief is that the quality of this book is more than up to that task. I look forward to the next 20 years as many realize the potential of computers to become man's dedicated and tireless servants, magnifying his view and amplifying his capacities.

John Kocur
Senior Software Engineering Consultant
AllStates Technical Resources, a Division of BE&K
Birmingham, AL

CHAPTER 1

Introduction to Data Mining

■ 1.1 TRADITIONAL DATABASE MANAGEMENT SYSTEMS

A traditional Database Management System (DBMS) provides generic software tools and environments that support the development of a database application. A DBMS environment supports the two main functions of database development and operations: data definition and data manipulation. During the data definition stage of database development, the structural components of a database—such as table structures, primary keys, and the number of tables for the database—are determined. The tasks of data manipulation include data storage, data modification, and data retrieval through the use of queries. This concept is depicted in Figure 1.1. Other tools of a DBMS include utilities, report generators, form generators, development tools, design aids, and transaction managers.

In Figure 1.1, the application developers are those who perform logical database design and database programming for physical database development. They design Entity Relationship Diagrams (ERDs), define and construct relational tables, determine primary and foreign keys of each table, and specify data types. Database refinement and maintenance tasks are also performed by application developers. They select a particular software product from a particular vendor that can provide all the necessary tools for the design requirements.

Any DBMS software product should provide all functions of data definition and data manipulation. In addition, a DBMS software product should provide data security and integrity functions. Through these functions, the DMBS can monitor user queries, and any attempts to violate security and

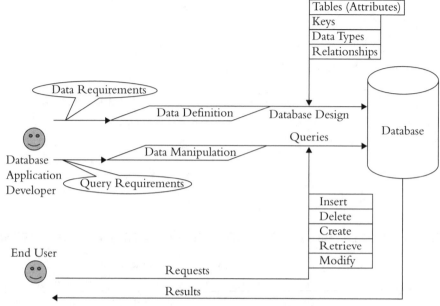

integrity constraints will be denied. The data dictionary is another function that must be supported by the DBMS. The data dictionary contains metadata, which is data about data, and generally contains various data schemas and mappings, security and integrity constraints, and virtually anything about data that can be useful to a database developer for development and maintenance. Data recovery and concurrency functions must also be supported by the DBMS together with performance-tuning functions, since all DBMS functions should be performed as efficiently as possible.

The task of end users is to simply submit requests. Queries allow users to insert, delete, create, retrieve, and modify data in databases. Hence, user requests are submitted as database queries to a database through the DBMS, which in turn returns the result of the query execution. The efficiency of a database system is often measured by the convenience and the ease of query writing and data manipulation. Users feel more comfortable when it is easier for them to manipulate the system and write the desired queries. Therefore, the system should allow users to access all parts of the database and to form queries as easily as possible. Once the queries are formed and submitted, it is the task of the DBMS to interpret the query and execute it.

A DBMS software component is often available to allow queries to be specified in a flexible manner, such as "forms" or Query By Example (QBE).

The presentation of query results is another area that affects usability. Analysis and interpretation of query results is needed if they are to be meaningful. DBMS software products often provide "report" capabilities to help users with the interpretation of query results. However, there is still one potential issue, namely confirming their validity. If a query returns incorrect results, it must be decided whether the query was wrongly formed or the database contains invalid data. Although many commercially available software products support integrity constraints, the task of proving the correctness of query results has been a major challenge in database application system development.

In general, the effectiveness of database applications depends on the type and accuracy of the data in the database, the flexibility and convenience of user queries, clear and accurate interpretation of query execution results, and validation of query results. If the data in a database is incorrect, then regardless of the query, the result is also incorrect. Data cleansing, noise reduction, and noise removal methods may partially solve this problem, but any missing and/or invalid data must be replaced with correct data in order for the correct result to be obtained. Furthermore, convenient tools for query generation minimizes potential problems and errors. The interpretation of query results is also a very important task because this information will be used for decision making. Finally, providing justification of query results is also very important because it gives confidence and assurance to the user regarding the accuracy of the resulting data.

■ 1.2   KNOWLEDGE DISCOVERY IN DATABASES

The rapid and constant growth of databases in business, government, and science has far outpaced our ability to interpret and make sense of this data avalanche, creating a need for a new generation of tools and techniques for intelligent and automated analysis of databases. These tools and techniques are the subject of the rapidly emerging field of data mining and Knowledge Discovery in Databases (KDD).

KDD is a process that takes a large amount of unprocessed and raw data stored in a data warehouse, transforms it into meaningful patterns,

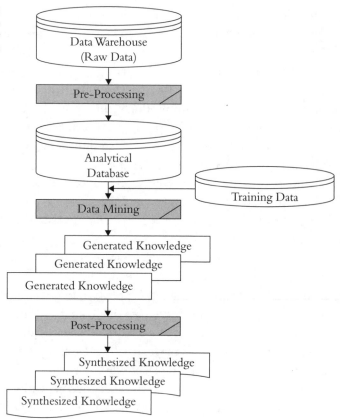

and presents them in a form that can easily be interpreted and understood. KDD is a three-step process, as illustrated in Figure 1.2.

The first step is the pre-processing stage, which takes as input a database from the data warehouse with raw data. During pre-processing, the database is cleaned, converted, and prepared for analytical processing in the next step, data mining. During the data-mining step of the KDD process, specific algorithms are applied to extract potentially useful patterns from the raw data. This is the heart of the KDD process because it identifies and exposes interesting and useful patterns and rules hidden in the database. During the data-mining stage, either an entire database or a sample containing a training dataset is used as input to the analytical processing. If the target database is extremely large, it may take too long to process all of the data, and a training dataset should be used instead of the entire dataset to reduce the time needed for data mining. The training dataset is obtained during pre-processing, and it often contains useful information for data analysis. This dataset can also be used by the data-mining algorithms as a model of the raw data.

Once a certain amount of knowledge is generated by the data-mining stage, the generated pieces of knowledge have to be converted into a form more suitable for interpretation by end users in a post-processing stage. The main purpose of post-processing is to synthesize the generated knowledge into useful and usable information for strategic decision making by end users. During the post-processing stage, irrelevant patterns are eliminated, and relevant patterns are further summarized into more understandable and meaningful expressions. The synthesized knowledge is then usually integrated with or embedded into other systems to help improve the decision-making process.

■ 1.2.1 Pre-Processing

Once the target database has been selected, it has to be cleaned up during the pre-processing stage by eliminating incomplete data and outliers and by filling in missing data. After the dirty data is cleansed, the database has to be prepared for data mining. Depending on the particular data-mining algorithm used, the database might have to be trimmed by being sliced either vertically or horizontally. Occasionally a training dataset of samples may have to be used because the large size of the target database would require an extensive amount of processing time. The collection of data tables prepared during pre-processing constitutes the analytical database. Eventually this analytical database is passed on to the next stage of data mining.

Another task performed during pre-processing is the retrieval of attribute properties from the data dictionary. The attribute-property information helps determine the appropriateness of an attribute for use with a data-mining algorithm. Certain algorithms accept only numeric attributes or only categorical attributes, whereas others can accept a combination of attribute types. Some algorithms deal only with non-key attributes because key attributes generally do not contribute to the identification of patterns and rules hidden in tables.

An additional task of the pre-processing stage is the enforcement of the input requirements of the data-mining algorithm. The raw data in the data warehouse has to be prepared according to the expectations of the data-mining algorithm used. Sometimes information in addition to the raw data may need to be provided for the execution of the algorithm. Sometimes multiple tables are required by the algorithm. It is the ultimate task of the pre-processor to prepare the input data for use by the data-mining algorithm.

■ 1.2.2 Data Warehousing

Data warehousing is the process of storing as much data as possible (relevant to the task) and retrieving any part or all of it for analysis. It involves the merging of data, the cleaning up of data errors, and the storing of historical information about the data. It is often expensive, and it is a very time-consuming process.

■ 1.2.3 Post-Processing

In predictive data mining, the post-processing step evaluates the discovered models that can be used for the prediction of future processes. In descriptive data mining, on the other hand, the post-processing step evaluates the discovered patterns and presents them in a way that can be easily interpreted and understood by end users. During post-processing, the discovered patterns are interpreted and visualized after any redundant and irrelevant patterns are removed. The useful patterns are presented to end users in a more natural and logical manner. In addition, post-processing helps the decision-making process by converting the generated knowledge into synthesized knowledge. It also checks for and resolves any potential conflicts with previously believed or previously extracted knowledge. The data-mining results synthesized through post-processing are generally integrated with other systems to improve the decision-making processes.

■ 1.3 DATA-MINING METHODS

While KDD refers to the overall process of transforming raw data into useful knowledge, data mining is a large part of this process. Data mining involves the application of specific algorithms to databases to extract potentially useful knowledge.

Data mining is a tool used in various business sectors that provides effective, strategic assistance for decision making. The kind of information produced by a data-mining system depends on the information needs of the organization using the system. A great variety of information can be extracted from databases using different algorithms. An efficient system is often considered to be one that provides the most assistance to the decision-making process. Simple, blind application of data-mining algorithms can lead to the discovery of meaningless and useless "knowledge" from databases. Hence, data-mining systems have to be carefully customized to fit the individual needs of the intended users.

Sophisticated analytical methods are used for the extraction of mission-critical information from databases. Different algorithms render different types of information. Users are often required to receive extensive training because they have to choose appropriate information to develop the most effective business strategies.

The dynamics of datasets (including size, dimensionality, noise, distributed nature, and diversity) often make data-mining applications difficult to develop. These properties can also make formal problem specifications more difficult to create. Furthermore, solution techniques must deal with the simplification of large volumes of data-mining results and the meaningful interpretation and user-friendly presentation of those results.

While the scope of data-mining applications is extremely wide, typical goals of data-mining applications include the thorough detection, accurate interpretation, and easy-to-understand presentation of meaningful patterns in data. Effective implementations that satisfy these goals use data-mining algorithms employing techniques from a wide variety of disciplines such as artificial intelligence, database development, statistics, and mathematics. Clustering, classification, neural networks, associations, and fuzzy theory are a few examples of algorithmic categories. In the following sections, several data-mining techniques are discussed.

■ 1.3.1 Association Rules

An association rule in a transactional database takes the form $X \Rightarrow Y$, where X and Y are sets of items appearing in transactions. An example of such a rule might be that a customer purchasing a tomato and lettuce will also get salad dressing with 80% likelihood. Data mining in a transactional database is used to find all such rules. Generally, these rules are valuable for cross-marketing, attached mailing applications, add–on sales, catalog design, store layout, and customer segmentation based on purchasing patterns.

The formal definition of the problem of data mining for association rules can be stated as follows: Let Z be a set of items that can be purchased, and let D be a set of transactions for a given period. Let $T \in D$ and $T \subseteq Z$. A unique identifier called a TID is assigned to each transaction. Mining for association rules refers to the process of extracting rules of the form $X \Rightarrow Y$ from databases containing raw data, where $X, Y \subseteq Z$, and $X \cap Y = \varnothing$. There are two factors that affect the significance of the association rules extracted: support and confidence. We say that rule $X \Rightarrow Y$ has support s in transaction set D if $s\%$ of the transactions in D contain $X \cup Y$. On the other hand, we say that rule $X \Rightarrow Y$ holds in transaction set D with confidence c if $c\%$ of transactions in D that contain X also contain Y.

Given the set of transactions D, the goal is to generate all association rules with support and confidence that are greater than a minimum support (called *minsup*) and a minimum confidence (called *minconf*). Generally, both *minsup* and *minconf* are specified by users. The transaction set D can be represented in a flat data file or as a relational table.

Chapter 2 outlines a number of data-mining techniques dealing with association rule extraction. The topics discussed include the Apriori algorithm, attribute-oriented rule induction, association rules in hypertext databases, quantitative association rules, compact association rule mining, and time-constrained association rules.

■ 1.3.2 Classification Learning

Classification learning is a learning scheme that generates a set of rules for classifiying instances into predefined classes from a complete set of independent examples, and then predicts the classes or categories of novel instances according to the generated rules.

The purpose of classification learning is to predict classes of instances, in contrast to other methods. Association learning predicts not only classes but also the attributes used in inducing the classes. In clustering, the classes are not predefined, but rather are unknown at the point of learning, and defining and identifying classes in the database is part of the learning task in clustering. In numeric prediction or regression, the classes are not discrete categories, but continuous numeric values. Regression learning uses techniques very similar to classification learning and is sometimes considered a subtype of classification learning. Therefore, a typical application of classification learning requires the following characteristics: (1) predefined classes, (2) discrete classes (except in regression learning), (3) a sufficient amount of data (at least as many as the number of classes), and (4) attribute values that are flat rather than structured data such that the values are fixed and each attribute has either a discrete or numeric value.

Among the many algorithms used for classification learning, three major approaches toward inducing classification rules are found. The first approach uses a top-down, "divide and conquer" technique to induce knowledge rules by organizing all instances of the dataset into a "decision tree" based on a series of test outcomes on each attribute. The "divide and conquer" approach recursively selects one attribute at a time to partition the dataset into subsets based on the outcome of a test until pure subsets are obtained (i.e., all members are classified as belonging to only one class). The process of tree creation is in fact the process of heuristically searching for all possible classification rules. The classification rules can be directly generated from the tree by traversing paths from the root to each leaf.

The second approach uses a top-down, "separate and conquer" or "covering" technique to take each class in turn and to directly induce a set of rules, each covering as many instances of the class as possible (and excluding as few instances of other as possible) without erecting the tree first. After a rule is induced, the covered instances are excluded or separated from the dataset. The "separate and conquer" approach takes only one class at a time and performs all the tests to quickly purify the subset, while both subsets may not be pure in the "divide and conquer" approach. Since there are some limitations in the representation of the classified rules, this process is less accurate than the "divide and conquer approach," but it is faster because it does not follow the heuristic tree-searching procedure.

The third approach, the "partial-decision tree approach," is a combination of both the "divide and conquer" and "separate and conquer" approaches and produces rules by the induction of corresponding partial decision trees and separates the covered instances from further induction.

The goal of these approaches is to accurately and efficiently induce classification knowledge from datasets. In Chapter 3, the three classification-learning methods given above are illustrated by algorithms and by examples of how each algorithm is applied, and the advantages and disadvantages of each are compared.

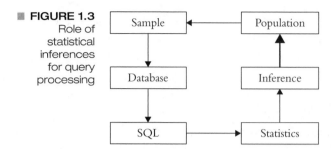

■ **FIGURE 1.3**
Role of
statistical
inferences
for query
processing

■ 1.3.3 Statistical Data Mining

Statistics provide a useful tool for data mining, and they can be used to analyze or make inferences about data to discover useful patterns from a dataset. The database is integrated with statistical functions to draw statistical conclusions about the dataset in the database. Figure 1.3 shows an illustration of the role of statistical inferences in query processing. The population is a collection of objects from which new facts and patterns are extracted. It may contain either known objects or unknown objects. If the population is unknown, then a sample dataset has to be used to derive any facts or trends about the population. If the population is known, on the other hand, the entire population can be used for statistical processing. If the volume of the known population is very large, a sample dataset can be used for statistical processing. Without a database, statisticians perform statistical processing to make inferences about the population from the sample directly, but the sample dataset can usually be handled in a more efficient manner using SQL-like queries.

In traditional database query processing, data is retrieved using SQL-like queries with built-in database functions or operators to find the exact values of interest. Once a database is integrated with statistical functions, statisticians face two major problems. One is that the structure or format of the data or variables retrieved does not match the statistical variables or functions. The other is that the built-in functions provided by the database systems may not support the statistical calculations that need to be performed.

Statistical query processing can be performed as a two-step process. The first step involves statistical processing and the second step involves the

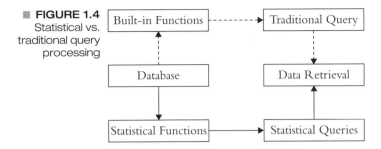

traditional query-processing operation. The transition from the first step to the second step may involve calling functions in other software to meet the needs of the statistical variables or functions in the traditional queries. This fact is illustrated in Figure 1.4. In Chapter 4, several statistical approaches are presented with examples using the data in a house sales database to do statistical analysis, interpretation, and implementation.

■ 1.3.4 Rough Sets for Data Mining

Data mining and knowledge discovery have become increasingly important topics in database discussions. In many applications, the size of the database grows rapidly as transactions continue to occur on a day-to-day basis. These databases can be analytically exploited to discover concepts, patterns, and relationships. But real-life databases often contain data that is imprecise, incomplete, and noisy, which makes it difficult for many data-mining techniques to extract knowledge from the data. Therefore, there is a strong need for a knowledge discovery technique that can identify patterns under noisy conditions.

To deal with uncertain or inaccurate data for knowledge extraction, Bayes' theorem and rough sets are the two known methods widely used for data analysis. Bayes' theorem is based on probability theory. Hence, the interpretation of data analysis is based on the computation of conditional probabilities. Rough-set theory, on the other hand, employs rigorous mathematical techniques for discovering regularities in data and is particularly useful for dealing with ambiguous and inconsistent data. Unlike other methods, such as the fuzzy-set theory of Zadeh and various forms of neural network methods, rough-set analysis requires no external parameters and uses only the information present in the obtained data. These two techniques have been successfully applied to medical data analysis, decision making in business, industrial design, voice recognition, image processing, and process modeling and identification.

For applications with a great deal of invalid data, it is often difficult to know exactly which features are relevant, important, and useful for the given tasks. Furthermore, certain attributes in the dataset may be undesirable, irrelevant, or unimportant. Some tuples may even contain redundant information. The number of attributes used by practical applications is often greater than 20, and the number of tuples is often greater than several hundred thousand or even more. As the size of databases and the number of attributes grows, effective data analysis techniques such as rough sets and Bayes' are needed to simplify the knowledge extraction process.

In Chapter 5, Bayes' and rough-set theories are introduced as effective methods for analyzing large amounts of data to discover knowledge from a database. The application of Bayes' and rough-set approaches to various data samples in different fields is discussed to describe the process of automated discovery of rules from a database. In rough-set analysis, important and useful information is generated through the removal and separation of redundant tuples and irrelevant attributes.

■ 1.3.5   Neural Networks for Data Mining

Most traditional DBMSs store data in the form of structured records. When a query is submitted, the database system searches for and retrieves records that match the user's query criteria. Artificial neural networks offer an attractive approach for the realization of intelligent query processing in large databases, especially for data retrieval and knowledge extraction based on partial matches. Traditional data analysis techniques make predictions about the future based on a sequence of rules generated from past data, and knowledge is obtained from a database in the form of rules. The traditional system makes predictions and creates classifications based on these rules which contain empirical knowledge.

Neural networks are different. They do not need to identify empirical rules in order to make predictions. Instead, a neural network generates a net by examining a database and by identifying and mapping all significant patterns and relationships that exist among different attributes. The net then uses a particular pattern to predict an outcome.

The neural net tries to identify an individual mix of attributes that reveals a particular pattern. This process is repeated using a lot of training data, consequently making changes to the weights of the data for more accurate pattern matches. The model is normally built without the need for interactive human participation because the neural network can automatically identify these patterns.

The patterns that exist among the attributes in the database can be identified, and the influence of each attribute can be quantified. Neural networks simply concentrate on identifying these patterns without human guidance, whereas in traditional systems the database and any predictions on it can only be described through the rules that exist behind them.

To support the pattern-generation process of neural networks, three different types of datasets are classified and used as shown below:

Training set: The training set is used for training and for teaching the network to recognize patterns. The training process is done by adjusting the weights according to the input data.

Validation set: A set of examples is used to tune the parameters of a classifier by choosing the number of hidden nodes or hidden layers in a neural network. This set is called a validation set.

Test set: The test set is used to test the performance of a neural network. It consists of a set of examples used only to assess the performance of a fully specified classifier.

Since our goal is to build a network with the best performance based on new data, the simplest approach to the comparison of different networks is to evaluate an error function using the data that is different from the data used for training. Various networks are trained through the minimization process of an appropriate error function defined with respect to a training dataset. The performance of the networks is compared based on the evaluation results of the error function applied to an independent validation set. The network giving the smallest error rate when tested with the validation set is selected. Finally, the performance of the selected network is confirmed by measuring its performance in relation to the third independent set of data called a test set.

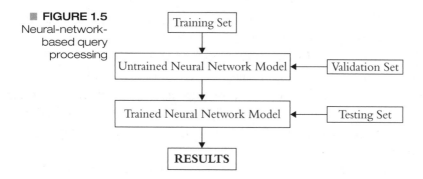

■ **FIGURE 1.5**
Neural-network-
based query
processing

Figure 1.5 shows the role and the relationship of the training set, the valida-tion set, and the test set. First, the training set is used to build an untrained neural network model and to train it. The validation set is then used by the network to validate the trained neural network model and to determine the appropriate number of hidden layers and nodes. After the trained network model is built and validated, the results can be generated in response to the test sets provided. In Chapter 6, various neural network models are presented as tools for data mining and are illustrated with a number of different datasets as examples.

■ 1.3.6 Clustering for Data Mining

Clustering can be used as a data-mining method to group together items in a database with similar characteristics. This methodology on how to group data items is based on the similarities among them. A cluster is a set of data items grouped together according to common properties and is considered an entity separate from other clusters. Hence, a database can be viewed as a set of multiple clusters for simplified processing of data analysis. One advantage of clustering is that the clusters can be profiled according to specific objectives of data analysis so that high-level queries can be formed to achieve objectives such as "identifying critical business values" or "discovering interesting patterns from the database."

As the amount of data stored and managed in a database increases, the need to simplify the vast amount of data also increases. Clustering is defined as the process of classifying a large group of independent data items into smaller groups that share the same or similar data properties. Due to the role of clustering in classifying and simplifying data, it has been extensively studied and has been demonstrated as a tool for any system dealing with massive amounts of data.

A cluster is a basic unit of a classification of initially unclassified data based on common properties. Understanding the various characteristics of clusters will help us to understand the details of the algorithms used for cluster analysis. Unfortunately, explicitly defining a cluster is somewhat difficult due to the diverse goals of clustering, and there is no universal definition. There are many definitions because different researchers define it differently. The following is a list of a few:

- A cluster is a set of entities that are alike and entities from different clusters that are not alike.
- A cluster is an aggregation of points in the test space such that the distance between any two points in the cluster is less than the distance between any point within the cluster and any other point outside the cluster.
- Clusters may also be described as connected regions of a multidimensional space containing a relatively high density of points.
- A cluster is a group of contiguous elements of a statistical population.

Considering these definitions, we can see that even if the clusters consist of entities, points, or regions, the components within the clusters are more similar in some respects than are other components outside of the clusters. A cluster can be considered a set of entities that are more similar in certain aspects within the cluster than the entities classified into other clusters. This definition deals with two important points. One is that similarity can be reflected with distance measures, and the other is that classification suggests the objective of clustering. Therefore, clustering can be defined as a process of identifying those data groups that are similar and of building a classification among them. Hence, the main objective of clustering is to identify a group of data that meets one of the following two conditions:

1. Groups whose members are very similar (similarity-within criterion)
2. Groups that are clearly separated from one another (separation-between criterion)

In Chapter 7, basic clustering concepts and techniques are presented and discussed. Procedures for handling data clusters for data mining are also demonstrated with practical examples. Several different clustering algorithms and methods are examined and compared in four different categories.

■ 1.3.7 Fuzzy Sets for Data Mining

Most of us have had some contact with conventional logic, in which a statement is either true or false with nothing in between. Although this principle of true or false has dominated Western logic for the last 2,000 years, the idea that things are either true or false does not apply in most cases. For example, is the statement "I am rich" completely true or false? The answer is probably neither true nor false since the question we need to consider is how rich *is* rich. A man with a million dollars may or may not be a rich man depending on with whom he is compared. This idea of gradations of truth is familiar to every one of us who faces decision making of any kind.

A fuzzy subset of some universe U is a collection of objects from the universe in which each object is associated with a degree of membership. The degree of membership is always a real number between 0 and 1. It measures the extent to which an element is associated with a particular set. A degree of membership 0 for an element of a fuzzy set is given to an element that is not in an ordinary set, whereas the membership value 1 is given to the elements that are in an ordinary set. Consider the fuzzy set defined as follows:

A = {1/RED, 0.3/BLACK, 0.6/PINK, 0.5/YELLOW, 1/BLUE, 0/GREEN}.

This fuzzy set indicates that:

1. Members RED and BLUE are in the fuzzy set.
2. Member GREEN is not in the fuzzy set.
3. Members B, C, and D are in the fuzzy set with partial membership values of 0.8, 0.2, and 0.7, respectively.

Mathematically speaking, a fuzzy set is a general case of an ordinary set. A fuzzy set is a set without a crisp boundary, which means the transition from "does belong to the set" to "does not belong to the set" is gradual. This gradual transition is characterized by a membership function that gives the fuzzy set flexibility in modeling commonly used linguistic expressions such as "the water is cold" or "the weather is hot." The membership degree of a fuzzy set depends on the problem that needs to be solved and on the information that is to be retrieved. The membership functions can be as simple as a linear relation or as complicated as an arbitrary mathematical function. Furthermore, membership functions can be multidimensional.

Unlike conventional set theory, which uses Boolean values of either 0 or 1, fuzzy sets have a function that admits a degree of membership in the set from complete exclusion, which corresponds to 0, to absolute inclusion, which corresponds to 1. While conventional sets have only two possible values, 0 and 1, fuzzy sets do not have this arbitrary boundary to separate members from nonmembers.

Fuzzy logic can be used to naturally describe our everyday business applications because it presents us with a flexible method to get a high-level abstraction of problem representation. In the real world, problems are often vague and imprecise, so they cannot be described in the conventional dual (true or false) logic ways. On the contrary, fuzzy logic allows a continuous gradation of truth values ranging from false to true in the description process of application models.

In Chapter 8, basic fuzzy-set theory is described. Information retrieval based on a fuzzy set is described as a data-mining example. Furthermore, problem representation with linguistic variables is presented from the viewpoint of fuzzy information retrieval. Problem-solving approaches related to fuzzy information retrieval are also described and reviewed.

■ 1.4 INTEGRATED FRAMEWORK FOR INTELLIGENT DATABASES

The data warehouses of our current market are growing exponentially in number and size, and there are very few tools on the market that fully decipher and process this information into useable information with the ease of use of natural language queries against an array of optimized data-mining algorithms. The majority of tools on the market look into the past, and they effectively use the rear-view-mirror analogy to help decision makers make decisions regarding their future. Data-mining tools are usually used by technically oriented statisticians. Herein lies the gap in time, relevance, technical proficiency, and direct access with which managers are currently faced.

A search mechanism that can find patterns or irregularities in highly data-intensive and ill-structured environments can play a very crucial role in the discovery of information essential for effective management and decision making in a very time-critical operational and strategic environment.

An intelligent database system goes beyond traditional database systems in that it deals not only with structured data but also with unstructured data such as images, audio clips, movie clips, and hypertexts. It is often integrated with knowledge-based systems and automatic knowledge discovery systems that help convert data into knowledge. A main function of an intelligent database is to provide faster and more automatic access and service to users, even with partial and incomplete data. When user requests are clearly specified, the system's task can be focused and narrowed down for easier and faster retrieval of expected results. On the other hand, requests can be vague and ambiguous when users do not have explicit goals but are simply interested in finding any patterns and/or regularities in data. In that case, filtering of found patterns and regularities may be necessary to determine their usefulness. Intelligent databases can be defined as systems that do the following:

- Manage information in a natural way, making that information easy to store, access, and use
- Provide faster and automatic service to partial and incomplete user requests
- Can handle huge amounts of information in a seamless and transparent fashion, carrying out tasks using appropriate sets of information management tools

From the definitions above, we can see that any database system considered intelligent must deal with partial and incomplete input data and requests and must provide effective ways to manage databases to store, retrieve, modify, access, and use data for appropriate decision making.

In this section, an integrated framework for intelligent databases, called an Embeddable Intelligent Information Retrieval System (EI^2RS), is presented. This framework is used for an embeddable component of intelligent database systems that carries out the task of knowledge extraction from a series of databases containing highly structured or poorly-structured data. A diagrammatic view of the individual components of the EI^2RS structure is shown in Figure 1.6.

The EI^2RS framework can accept two types of input. One input comes from front-end managerial users of the system, and the other input comes from either computer sensors or data packages from various databases. The inputs from front-end users are generally in the form of requests framed in a semi-natural English-language format. The front-end interface accepts these user queries as input and returns the results of the analytical processing performed by the Knowledge Extraction Engine (KEE).

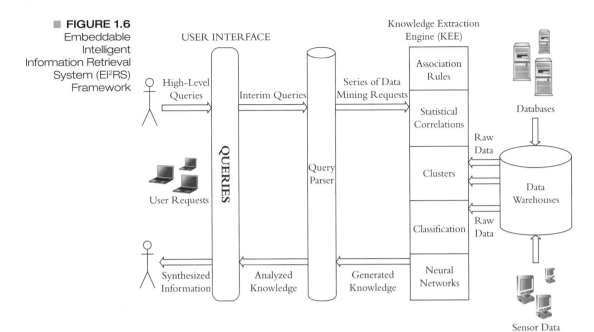

■ **FIGURE 1.6** Embeddable Intelligent Information Retrieval System (EI²RS) Framework

The role of the EI²RS is to more effectively generate synthesized information and to provide it to decision makers by utilizing the effectiveness and efficiency of optimized data-mining algorithms against either sensor-input data or against nontechnical natural-language queries. The main function of the KEE is to support this role by extracting and synthesizing knowledge and/or information gathered from various databases and input sensors. The KEE applies various data-mining techniques such as classification, association rule mining, clustering, statistical correlation, and neural networks to perform the data analysis and synthesis process. Among the many techniques available for data mining, an optimal one is selected and applied by KEE to extract knowledge from raw data and to synthesize it for further processing.

The processing of EI²RS components is as follows. As can be seen from Figure 1.6, it first accepts either a series of user requests or a collection of sensor data as input. The user requests are then processed by a query parser, which will in turn generate a series of internal requests to be used for the selection and execution of data-mining algorithms. These algorithms are applied to extract knowledge from raw data. The KEE will accept data from either input sensors or from various databases. Then it performs an intensive data analysis process using the optimally selected data-mining algorithms to generate useful, expected, or requested knowledge. The knowledge generated by the KEE is processed further by the query parser and is presented to the end user as synthesized information. This synthesized information will eventually be used for effective decision making.

■ 1.5   PRACTICAL APPLICATIONS OF DATA MINING

In this section, four applications are presented to illustrate the potential implications of data mining. A brief description is given for each application. Next, the implication of data mining in each application is given. The impact and advantages in each application are also illustrated. A list of natural-language queries possible in the specific application is provided to illustrate the potential application of data-mining methods. The various data-mining techniques (described in Chapters 2 through 8) are techniques that can be used to solve these natural-language queries.

■ 1.5.1   Healthcare Services

Data mining has been used intensively and extensively by many healthcare organizations and can greatly benefit all parties involved. For example, data mining can help healthcare insurers detect fraud and abuse, can help healthcare organizations make customer-relationship management decisions, can help physicians identify effective treatments and best practices, and can help patients receive better and more affordable healthcare services. In general, applications of data mining in healthcare services include, but are not limited to, the following:

• Modeling health outcomes and predicting patient outcomes
• Modeling clinical knowledge of decision support systems
• Bioinformatics
• Pharmaceutical research
• Business intelligence such as management of healthcare, customer-relationship management, and the detection of fraud and abuse
• Infection control
• Ranking hospitals
• Identifying high-risk patients
• Evaluation of treatment effectiveness

1.5.1.1 *Implications of Data Mining in Healthcare Applications*

The large amount of data generated by healthcare transactions is too complex and voluminous to be processed and analyzed by traditional methods. Data mining provides the methodology and technology to transform these mounds of data into useful information. For example, data-mining algorithms such as the Apriori algorithm can be used to generate sets of association rules to identify relationships among different types of diseases, individual living environments, individual living habits, and individual body indices such as blood pressure, body mass index, and weight.

1.5.1.2 *Natural Language Queries*

a. How likely is it that a man whose age is more than 60 years old, whose weight is more than 200 pounds, and who has been diagnosed with high blood pressure will have a stroke?

b. How likely is it that an adult whose age is more than 70 years old, whose weight is more than 200 pounds, who has been told by a doctor that both blood pressure and blood cholesterol are high, who is not used to eating vegetables and is not currently taking blood pressure medication will have a heart attack?

c. How likely is it that an adult whose age is more than 70 years old and who has had a stroke will have a heart attack?

d. How likely is it that an adult who is not used to eating fruit and vegetables and does not exercise everyday will be overweight?

e. How likely is it that a man who drinks alcoholic beverages and smokes more than 20 cigarettes every day will be diagnosed with high blood pressure?

f. What are the notable characteristics of patients with a history of at least one occurrence of stroke?

g. Which medications generally have a better curative effect for stroke?

h. According to the current health status of this patient, how long is the patient likely to live?

i. According to current risk factors of a patient, what kind of treatment is likely to make him or her live longer?

j. What hospitals provide patients the best recovery rate, if he or she has a stroke, heart attack, or diabetes?

k. What are the diabetes risk factors for a male senior citizen?

■ 1.5.2 Banking

In today's world, traditional banking has changed for many reasons. Gone are the days when conducting simple surveys would enable banks to make necessary changes in their various marketing, business-process, and customer-relationship strategies. While the emergence of new banks has provided strong competition among them, it has also made it unrealistic for them to rely on only their internal procedures to stay profitable in the market.

Streamlining business procedures, improving customer relationships, detecting fraudulent characters and providing security at all levels of service, and taking other measures to improve business builds trust among not only major players of the market, but also among employees.

1.5.2.1 Implications of Data Mining in Banking

The implementation of data-mining procedures has enabled banks to improve services as described above. At all levels of service, data mining provides the historical data needed to make decisions about the implementation of future strategies. For example, coupling data mining with security involves identifying and flushing out all suspicious individuals before they get away with a crime. Credit-card companies can mine their transaction databases and look for spending patterns that might indicate transactions with a stolen card.

In marketing, data mining helps to detect any changes in customer behavior and to identify factors that may have left customers disgruntled or that may have brought in more customers. These facts will eventually enable banks to make changes that will generate assets.

1.5.2.2 Natural Language Queries

a. What potential factors will draw major industries and investors to the bank?

b. What are the main factors that leave customers unsatisfied and eventually lead them to close their accounts?

c. What are the potential types of loans that might bring profit for the bank?

d. What are the behavioral banking patterns of customers who are the most loyal and profitable for the bank?

e. What information-processing methods often leave customers disgruntled?

f. What are the most effective marketing strategies for bringing in the most customers?

g. What incentives will increase customer satisfaction?

h. What employee-hiring practices can reduce the number of customer complaints?

i. What methods are commonly used to commit fraud against the bank?

j. How easily will employees embrace new banking procedures?

k. How has the change and/or introduction of new information-processing methods affected the overall performance and/or functioning of the bank?

■ 1.5.3 Supermarket Applications

While the success stories of countless retail industries have invariably changed the way traditional businesses were once looked upon, at the same time, they have also brought to light a new range of situations a retail company might encounter. Important decisions have to be made concerning the targeted customer base, transportation of commodities to local shops, estimation of future demands, and marketing strategies, while maintaining low costs and high profits.

1.5.3.1 Implications of Data Mining in Supermarket Applications

Some of the issues faced by a supermarket management team are these: how to increase profits, what items sell faster on certain days, and at which times of year most transactions occur. The management team might also want to know, for example, how likely a customer who purchases a game controller will end up buying a game for the console as well.

To answer these questions and make these decisions, management needs to know a lot about not only the customers coming into the store but also their transaction history. A customer profile can include not only a customer's item preferences but also their age group, ethnic background, gender, occupation, and education. People in a certain age group, for example, might be more interested in certain items than those not in that age group.

Two important decision-making factors in supermarket applications, where data mining is crucial, are transportation of commodities and manufacturing. The cost of commodities is derived largely from the way they are transported to local stores and affects the sale price of those commodities. There is almost always a trade-off in speedy transportation and price of goods. Hence, in designing data-mining algorithms, certain factors must be taken into account about how the sale of an item will be affected and how it will be transported.

When defining the price of a particular commodity, it makes sense to take a look at the targeted customer base, the overall impression of the company, and the sale of other commodities launched by the company. Data-mining methods not only help a company evaluate overall performance but also identify crucial factors that must be considered when deciding the price of a new commodity.

1.5.3.2   *Natural Language Queries*

a. What items in the store are popular among teenagers?

b. Do certain branches of the store sell a particular type of item more than others?

c. If an item is purchased by a customer, what other items are likely to be purchased at the same time?

d. At what time of the year are certain products more likely to be sold?

e. Do customers who buy portable MP3 devices also buy ear-bud type headphones, too?

f. How different are the buying patterns of urban customers from rural customers in terms of certain items?

g. Do the buying patterns of customers in certain age groups differ from those in other age groups in terms of frequency and amount of purchase?

h. How likely is it that an item will sell fast enough to make a good profit this year and next?

i. What items are likely to be removed from the shelves or replaced by other items?

j. If a person buys a fishing pole, how likely is it that he will buy fishing tackle and a hunting knife as well?

k. What kind of items should be stocked during holiday seasons such as Christmas, Easter, or Thanksgiving so that even if there is a sale, profits can still be maintained?

l. How likely is it that vegetarian customers will buy non-vegetarian products?

■ 1.5.4 Medical Image Classification

Breast cancer represents the second leading cause of cancer deaths in women today, and it is the most common type of cancer in women. The image classification method used for breast cancer diagnosis is based on digital mammograms. They help detect breast cancer by dividing tumors into two categories: normal and abnormal.

Normal mammograms characterize a healthy patient. Abnormal mammograms include both benign cases with mammograms showing a tumor that is not formed by cancerous cells, and malignant cases with mammograms from patients with cancerous tumors. Digital mammograms are among the most difficult medical images to read due to low contrast and differences in types of tissue. Important visual clues of breast cancer include preliminary signs of masses and calcification clusters. Unfortunately, in the early stages of breast cancer, these signs are very subtle and varied in appearance, making diagnosis difficult. The development of automatic classification systems will assist specialists with early diagnosis of breast cancer.

1.5.4.1 Implications of Data Mining in Medical Image Classification

Association-rule mining has been extensively investigated and presented in the data-mining literature. Association-rule mining typically aims at discovering associations between items in a transactional database. Hence, it can be used to discover association rules among the features extracted from the mammography database and the category to which each mammogram belongs. The association rules are constrained such that the antecedents of the rules are composed of a conjunction of features from the mammogram, while the consequents of the rules are always the category to which the mammogram belongs. In other words, a rule would describe frequent sets of features per normal and abnormal (benign and malignant) based on an association-rule discovery algorithm.

After all the features are merged and put in a transactional database, the next step is to apply the association-rule mining algorithm to find the relevant association rules in the database. Once the association rules are found, they are used to construct a classification system that categorizes the mammograms as normal, malignant, or benign. In any learning process for building a classifier, there are two steps involved with the classification performed by association rule mining. The first one deals with the training of the system, and the second one deals with the classification of the new images.

During the training phase, the Apriori algorithm is applied to the training data to extract the association rules. During this phase, appropriate support values are used to generate the rules. In the classification phase, the low and high thresholds of confidence are set to reach the maximum recognition rate for the rules selected. Neural networks can also be used to train the system, but the advantage of using an association-rule-based classifier is that it requires less time for training.

1.5.4.2 Natural Language Queries

a. What are the physical characteristics of women who have a higher chance of getting breast cancer?

b. What is the likelihood that a tumor looks like a normal tissue?

c. How likely is it that smoking is a leading cause of breast cancer in women?

d. What are effective ways of preventing breast cancer?

e. Does the region where women live affect their chances of getting breast cancer?

f. What is the probablity that a female child born to a mother suffering from breast cancer will be affected by breast cancer tumors?

g. How likely is it that breast cancer is hereditary?

h. What is the probablity that breast cancer is caused by nutritional habits such as caffeine consumption?

i. What is the probablity that breast cancer tumors will cause other cancer tumors to grow?

j. Does breast cancer have anything to do with body weight?

k. What is the likelihood of women over 75 years of age getting breast cancer?

l. How early should breast cancer be detected to prevent it from getting worse?

■ 1.6 CHAPTER SUMMARY

This chapter began with a brief description of a traditional DBMS, which provides generic software tools and environments that support the development of a database application. The standard functions of a traditional DBMS were described to illustrate the various functions of data definition and manipulation processes in data management. However, a traditional DBMS can only support retrieval operations on data that is physically stored in the database. It does not generally go beyond what an SQL query can offer.

Today's data avalanche has created a need for a new generation of tools and techniques for intelligent and automated analysis of databases. These tools and techniques are the subject of the rapidly emerging field of data mining and Knowledge Discovery in Databases (KDD). KDD is a process that takes a tremendously large amount of unprocessed and raw data that is stored in a data warehouse and transforms it into meaningful patterns and presents them in a form that can easily be interpreted and understood. KDD is a three-step process: pre-processing, data mining, and post-processing.

In Section 1.3, various data-mining methods were described. Data mining involves the application of specific algorithms to databases to extract potentially useful knowledge. Although the scope of data-mining applications is extremely wide, typical goals of data-mining applications are the thorough detection, accurate interpretation, and easy-to-understand presentation of meaningful patterns in data. To effectively satisfy these goals, data-mining algorithms employ techniques from a wide variety of disciplines such as artificial intelligence, databases, statistics, and mathematics. Clustering, classification, neural networks, associations, and fuzzy theory are a few examples of algorithmic categories briefly described in this chapter. Further details of each technique are given in the subsequent chapters of the book.

An intelligent database system goes beyond a traditional database system in that it deals with not only structured data but also with unstructured data such as images, audio clips, movie clips, and hypertexts. It is often integrated with knowledge-based systems and automatic knowledge discovery systems that convert data into knowledge. A main function of an intelligent database is to provide fast and automatic access and service to end users, even with partial and incomplete data. When user requests are clearly specified, the system's task can be focused and narrowed down for easier and faster retrieval of results. On the other hand, sometimes users do not have explicit goals, but are simply interested in finding patterns and regularities from a database. In that case, filtering of results may be necessary to determine the usefulness of the results.

In Section 1.4, an integrated framework for intelligent databases, called an Embeddable Intelligent Information Retrieval System (EI^2RS), was presented. This framework is used as an embeddable component of an intelligent database system to carry out the task of knowledge extraction from a series of databases containing highly structured or poorly-structured data.

In the final section of this chapter, four practical applications of data mining were provided to illustrate potential implications of data mining. For each application, a brief description was first given. Then, the implication of data mining in each application was described. The impact and advantages of data mining in each application was illustrated. A list of natural-language queries that are possible in the specific application was provided to illustrate potential applications of data-mining methods.

2

Association Rules

■ 2.1 INTRODUCTION

Many large retail organizations are interested in instituting information-driven marketing processes, managed by database technology, that enable them to develop and implement customized marketing programs and strategies. These organizations collect and store massive amounts of sales data, also referred to as *basket data*. Each record in the basket database consists of a transaction date and a list of items in the transaction. This data can be used for decision making through the process of synthesis and analysis of the records in the basket database. In this section, we will consider the problem of discovering association rules in a large basket database.

■ 2.2 MINING OF ASSOCIATION RULES IN MARKET BASKET DATA

An association rule in a basket database takes the form $X \Rightarrow Y$, where X and Y each are a set of some items appearing in transactions. An example of such a rule might be that a customer purchasing bread and milk will also get cheese with 90% likelihood. Mining for association rules in the basket database is used to find all such rules. Generally, these rules are valuable for cross-marketing, attached mailing applications, add-on sales, catalog design, store layout, and customer segmentation based on purchasing patterns.

The formal definition of association-rule mining can be stated as follows:

Let $Z = \{i_1, i_2, \ldots, i_n\}$ be a set of items, and let D be a set of transactions, where $T \in D$ and $T \subseteq Z$. A unique identifier called a TID is assigned to each *transaction. An association is an implication of the form $X \Rightarrow Y$, where X, Y $\subseteq Z$, and $X \cap Y = \emptyset$. Two factors affect the significance of association rules: support and confidence. We say that the rule $X \Rightarrow Y$ has support s in the transaction set D if s% of the transactions in D contain $X \cup Y$. On the other hand, we say that the rule $X \Rightarrow Y$ holds in the transaction set D with confidence c if c% of the transactions in D that contain X also contain Y.*

Given a set of transactions D, the problem of mining association rules is to generate all association rules that have support and confidence greater than a minimum support (called *minsup*) and a minimum confidence (called *minconf*), respectively. Both *minsup* and *minconf* are normally specified by users. The set of transactions D could be represented as a flat data file, as a relational table, or as the result of a relational expression. The association rules that we consider are probabilistic in nature and are distinct from functional dependencies. A functional dependency $X \Rightarrow A$ implies an additional functional dependency $X + Y \Rightarrow A$ through redundancy. However, the presence of an association rule $X \Rightarrow A$ does not necessarily imply that the rule $X + Y \Rightarrow A$ also holds in the database because the latter may not satisfy the *minsup*. Similarly, the presence of two association rules $X \Rightarrow Y$ and $Y \Rightarrow A$ does not necessarily mean that the association $X \Rightarrow A$ holds because the latter may not satisfy the *minconf*.

■ 2.2.1 Apriori Algorithm

The problem of discovering all association rules can be broken down into two parts as follows:

1. Find all sets of items that have support values greater than the minimum support. These itemsets are called large itemsets. All others are called small itemsets.

2. Use the large itemsets to generate the desired rules. A simple algorithm for this task is as follows. Find all non-empty subsets of every large itemset L. For every such subset A, generate a rule of the form $A \Rightarrow (L - A)$ if the ratio of support(L) to support(A) is at least *minconf*. All subsets of L must be considered to generate rules with multiple consequents.

Algorithms for discovering large itemsets make multiple passes over the data. In the first pass, large itemsets of size one are generated. These itemsets are individual items with support at least *minsup*. In each subsequent pass, we use the large itemsets found in the previous pass. This seed set of large itemsets is used to generate new, potentially large itemsets called candidate itemsets. The support for these candidate itemsets is counted during the passes over the data. At the end of each pass, we determine which candidate itemsets are actually large. These large itemsets are used in the next pass. This process continues until no new large itemsets are found.

The Apriori algorithm generates candidate itemsets using the large itemsets found in the previous pass without considering the transactions in the database. The rationale behind this principle is that any subset of a large itemset must be large. Therefore, the candidate itemsets of size K can be generated by joining two large itemsets of size $(K - 1)$ and deleting those that are not large. A description of the Apriori algorithm is given in Figure 2.1. In this algorithm, we assume that the items in each transaction and the items within each itemset are kept in lexicographic order. A count field is associated with each itemset to store the support for the itemset. The count field is initialized to zero when the itemset is first created.

In Figure 2.1, two set notations, L_k and C_k, are used. L_k is the set of large k-itemsets (i.e., those itemsets of size k with *minsup*). C_k is the set of candidate k-itemsets (i.e., potentially large itemsets of size k). Each member of both sets has two fields associated with it: itemset and support count. The first pass of the algorithm counts the occurrences of each individual item to determine the large 1-itemsets. Each subsequent pass k consists of two parts.

■ **FIGURE 2.1**
Apriori algorithm

```
L₁ = {large 1-itemsets};
for (k=2; L_{k-1} ≠ Ø; k++) do
    begin
        C_k = apriori-gen(L_{k-1}); // new candidates
        forall transactions t∈D do
            begin
                C_t=subset(C_k, t);
                forall candidates c∈C_t do
                    c.count++;
            end
        L_k={c∈C_k| c.count ≥ minsup}
    end
answer = ∪_k L_k;
```

In the first part, L_{k-1}, the large itemsets generated in the previous pass are used to generate C_k, the large candidate k-itemsets. The apriori-gen( ) function is used for this purpose. In the second part, each itemset in C_k is counted in all transactions in the database. Only those itemsets with support that is at least *minsup* are collected to generate L_k.

■ 2.2.2 Apriori-gen( ) Function

The apriori-gen( ) function takes an argument L_{k-1} to generate C_k, the set of potentially large k-itemsets. In other words, C_k is a superset of the set of all large k-itemsets. The function consists of two steps. First, join operations are performed to join L_{k-1} with L_{k-1}. In the next step, we perform pruning to delete all itemsets $c \in C_k$ such that some $(k-1)$-subset of c is not in L_{k-1}. The algorithm is as follows:

```
(join step)
insert into C_k
select p.item_1, p.item_2, ..., p.item_k-1, q.item_k-1
from L_k-1 p, L_k-1 q
where p.item_1 = q.item_1, ..., p.item_k-2 = q.item_k-2, p.item_k-1
< q.item_k-1

(prune step)
forall itemsets c∈C_k do
    forall (k-1)-subsets s of c do
        if ( s ∉ L_k-1) then delete c from C_k;
```

For example, let L_3 be $\{\{1\ 2\ 3\}\ \{1\ 2\ 4\}\ \{1\ 3\ 4\}\ \{1\ 3\ 5\}\ \{2\ 3\ 4\}\}$. After the join step, C_4 will be $\{\{1\ 2\ 3\ 4\}\ \{1\ 3\ 4\ 5\}\}$. After the prune step, the itemset $\{1\ 3\ 4\ 5\}$ will be deleted from C_4 because $\{3\ 4\ 5\}$, $\{1\ 4\ 5\}$, and $\{1\ 3\ 4\}$ are not in L_3. Therefore, the final value of C_4 will be $\{1\ 2\ 3\ 4\}$.

■ 2.2.3 Apriori Example

Consider the database in Figure 2.2 and assume that the *minsup* is 3. Calling apriori-gen( ) with L_1 produces C_2, which contains six candidate itemsets. Four out of these six itemsets are chosen as large itemsets to be included in L_2. The apriori-gen( ) is called again with L_2 to generate C_3, which contains only one candidate itemset $\{1, 3, 4\}$. The candidate $\{1, 3, 4\}$ in C_3 turns out

TID	Items
1	1, 3, 4
2	1, 2, 3, 4
3	2, 4
4	1, 2, 4
5	1, 3, 4, 5

Database

Itemset	Support
{1}	4
{2}	3
{3}	3
{4}	5

L_1

Itemset	Support
{1, 2}	2
{1, 3}	3
{1, 4}	4
{2, 3}	1
{2, 4}	3
{3, 4}	3

C_2

Itemset	Support
{1, 3}	3
{1, 4}	4
{2, 4}	3
{3, 4}	3

L_2

Itemset	Support
{1, 3, 4}	3

C_3

Itemset	Support
{1, 3, 4}	3

L_3

to be large and is the only member of L_3. When we generate C_4 with L_3, it turns out to be empty, and we terminate.

■ 2.2.4 AprioriTid Algorithm

The AprioriTid algorithm is very similar to the Apriori algorithm in that both algorithms use the apriori-gen( ) function. In the Apriori algorithm, the database D is used to count support on every pass when C_k is generated. In AprioriTid, however, the database D is not used after the first pass. Rather, the set C_k' is used for counting support. Each member of the set C_k' is of the form <TID, $\{X_k\}$>, where each X_k is a potentially large k-itemset present in the transaction associated with TID. For $k = 1$, C_1' is the database D with each item i replaced by the itemset $\{i\}$. For $k > 1$, C_k' is generated by the algorithm shown in Figure 2.3. The member of C_k' corresponding to a transaction t is < t.TID, $\{c \in C_k \mid c$ is contained in $t\}$ >. If transaction t does not contain any candidate k-itemset, C_k' will not have any entry for this transaction. Thus, the number of entries in C_k' may be smaller than the number of transactions in the database. Especially for large values of k, each entry in C_k' may be smaller than the corresponding transaction because very few candidates may be contained in the transaction. For small values of k, however, each entry in C_k' may be larger than the corresponding transaction because the entry includes all candidate k-itemsets contained in the transaction.

■ **FIGURE 2.3**
AprioriTid algorithm

```
L₁ = {large 1-itemsets};
C'₁ = database D
for (k=2; Lₖ₋₁ ≠ Ø; k++) do
    begin
        Cₖ=apriori-gen(Lₖ₋₁); // new candidates
        C'ₖ=Ø
        forall entries t ∈ C'ₖ₋₁ do
            // determine candidate itemsets in Cₖ contained
            // in the transaction with t.TID
            begin
                Cₜ={c∈Cₖ | (c-c[k]) ∈ t.set-of-itemsets ∧
                               (c-c[k-1]) ∈ t.set-of-itemsets};
                forall candidates c ∈ Cₜ do
                    c.count++;
                if (Cₜ ≠ Ø) then C'ₖ += <t.TID, Cₜ>;
            end
        Lₖ={c∈Cₖ | c.count ≥ minsup}
    end
answer = ∪ₖLₖ;
```

Applying AprioriTid to the example in Figure 2.2 will construct C'_1, C'_2, and C'_3 as shown in Figure 2.4. The actual sequence of the generated tables resulting from the application of AprioriTid is $C'_1 \Rightarrow L_1 \Rightarrow C_2$ (itemsets) $\Rightarrow C'_2 \Rightarrow C_2$ (support) $\Rightarrow L_2 \Rightarrow C_3$ (itemsets) $\Rightarrow C'_3 \Rightarrow C_3$ (support) $\Rightarrow L_3$. Notice that there is no entry in C'_3 for the transactions

■ **FIGURE 2.4**
C'_k (k = 1, 2, 3) from AprioriTid algorithm

TID	Set-of-Itemsets
1	{{1} {3} {4}}
2	{{1} {2} {3} {4}}
3	{{2} {4}}
4	{{1} {2} {4}}
5	{{1} {3} {4} {5}}

C'_1

TID	Set-of-Itemsets
1	{{1 3}{1 4} {3 4}}
2	{{1 2}{1 3} {1 4} {2 3}{2 4} {3 4}}
3	{{2 4}}
4	{{1 2}{1 4}}
5	{{1 3}{1 4} {3 4}}

C'_2

TID	Set-of-Itemsets
1	{{1 3 4}}
2	{{1 3 4}}
5	{{1 3 4}}

C'_3

with TIDs 3 and 4 because they do not contain any itemset in C_3. The candidate $\{1, 3, 4\}$ in C_3 turns out to be large and is the only member in L_3. We terminate the algorithm since C_4 is empty after applying Apriori-gen( ) with L_3.

■ 2.3 ATTRIBUTE-ORIENTED RULE GENERALIZATION

The Apriori algorithm discussed in Section 2.2 deals mainly with market basket data in which each record consists of a set of transaction items. The size of each record varies because each record contains a variable-length list of items purchased in each transaction. This method may not be appropriate for knowledge discovery in relational databases where each record is represented in terms of a fixed number of attributes. Furthermore, the records in a relational database are not a variable-length itemset, but instead are instances of a relation consisting of the same number of attributes. To extract generalized data from actual data in relational databases, a machine-learning technique integrated with database operations should be adopted.

In this section, we present an attribute-oriented induction method for knowledge discovery in relational databases. This approach is used to generate different types of knowledge, including characteristic rules, discrimination rules, and data evolution regularities. A characteristic rule is an assertion that characterizes a concept that is satisfied by all or the majority of cases in a target class under consideration. For example, the symptoms of a disease can be described by a characteristic rule. On the other hand, a discrimination rule is an assertion that discriminates a concept in the target class from other concepts in the contrasting classes. For example, to distinguish cardiovascular diseases from other kinds of disorders, a discrimination rule would be used to summarize their distinctive features. The data evolution regularity of the characteristic rules summarizes the characteristics of the changed data, whereas the discrimination rules summarize the features that discriminate the instances of target data from the contrasting ones. If a generated rule is associated with a quantitative measurement, it is called a quantitative rule.

The key to this approach is *tree ascension for attribute generalization*, which applies set-oriented database operations. This approach can be extended to knowledge discovery in other kinds of databases, such as nested relational databases, deductive databases, and databases containing noisy data and irregularities.

Furthermore, the generated rules can be used for intelligent query processing, cooperative query answering, and semantic query optimization.

■ 2.3.1 Concept Hierarchies

Since a database may consist of multiple relations, each with a varying number of attributes, containing a huge amount of data, not all the data in the database may be relevant to a specific learning task. Rule induction in databases relies mainly on generalization. To derive a characteristic rule by generalization, the task-relevant data are collected into a class called the *target* class, whereas to derive a discrimination rule, the data are collected into two classes, the *target* class and the *contrasting* class.

Concept hierarchies are used to represent appropriate background knowledge and to control the generalization process. A concept taxonomy represents different levels of concepts according to a general-to-specific ordering. The values of each attribute in the database correspond to the most specific concepts, and the null description, denoted as "ANY," corresponds to the most general concepts in the hierarchy. The generated rules are generalized according to the concept hierarchies and should be given in a simple and explicit form, which is desirable to most users. Figure 2.5 shows a concept hierarchy table for a typical university database.

In Figure 2.5, $A \subset B$ indicates that B is a generalization of A. From this concept hierarchy table, we can generate a concept tree for status as shown in Figure 2.6. The concept hierarchies can be specified either explicitly by knowledge engineers and/or domain experts or implicitly by database schema. For example, a hierarchical relationship such as "city $\subset$ province $\subset$ country" can be attached to a relation containing "city," "province," and "country" attributes. From the relation, the information that "Dallas is a city of Texas which in turn is a state of the U.S.A." can be obtained.

Some concept hierarchies can be discovered semi-automatically or automatically through the careful analysis of the attribute domains. For numerical domains, a discrete concept hierarchy can be automatically constructed based on database statistics. For example, one may discover that a grade point average falls between 0 and 4, and therefore classify the GPA domain into the following four categories: {0.0–1.99}, {2.0–2.99}, {3.0–3.49}, and {3.5–4.0}. For domains with discrete values, a statistical method can also be used. For example, the country-of-origin for most students is scattered among

FIGURE 2.5
A concept hier-
archy table for a
university database

```
{biology, chemistry, computing, ..., physics} ⊂ science
{civil, electrical, ..., mechanical} ⊂ engineering
{engineering, science} ⊂ ANY-major
{freshman, sophomore, junior, senior} ⊂ undergraduate
{master's, Ph.D.} ⊂ graduate
{undergraduate, graduate} ⊂ ANY-status
{Austin, Dallas, ..., Houston} ⊂ Texas
{Jacksonville, Miami, ..., Tampa} ⊂ Florida
{Texas, Florida} ⊂ U.S.A.
{Pusan, Seoul, ..., Taegu} ⊂ Korea
{Beijing, Nanjing, ..., Shanghai} ⊂ China
{China, Japan, Korea, ..., Switzerland} ⊂ foreign
{foreign, U.S.A.} ⊂ ANY-place
{0.0-1.99} ⊂ poor
{2.0-2.99} ⊂ average
{3.0-3.49} ⊂ good
{3.5-4.00} ⊂ excellent
{poor, average, good, excellent} ⊂ ANY-grade
```

FIGURE 2.6
A concept tree for
status

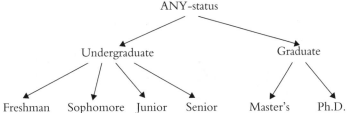

foreign countries and concentrated on the United States, so we may be able
to categorize the concept of the attribute into "domestic" and "foreign." The
concept hierarchy for an attribute can be modified based on database statistics,
and it can be discovered and refined based on its relationship with other attributes. Furthermore, different hierarchies may be constructed from the same
set of attributes, according to different viewpoints or preferences.

From a logical viewpoint, each tuple in a relation is a logical expression in conjunctive terms. Similarly, a data relation may be characterized by a large set of disjunctions of such conjunctive terms. Users may specify the preferred generalization threshold, that is, the maximum number of disjuncts of the resulting expression. For example, if the threshold value is 5, the final generalized rule will consist of at most five disjuncts. The generalization threshold controls the complexity of the rule. A large threshold value may lead to a complex rule with many disjuncts, whereas a small threshold value leads to a simple rule with few disjuncts that may result in an overly general rule and loss of valuable information.

■ 2.3.2 Basic Strategies for Attribute-Oriented Induction

Seven basic strategies are suggested to perform attribute-oriented induction in relational databases. These strategies are applied to an initial relation that results from preprocessing the original databases. Pre-processing involves identifying the learning task, consulting the concept hierarchy to extract the set of primitive attribute sets in the relation, and forming the initial relation on which the induction can be performed. Consider the student relation in Figure 2.7 which contains information on 100 graduate students and 100 undergraduate students. The relation consists of five attributes: *id_no, status, major, origin*, and *GPA*.

■ **FIGURE 2.7**
The relation
student in a
university database

Id_no	Status	Major	Origin	GPA
1	Master's	Civil	Houston	3.5
2	Junior	Biology	Dallas	3.7
3	Junior	Electrical	Jacksonville	2.6
4	Master's	Physics	Miami	3.9
5	Ph.D.	Biology	Beijing	3.3
6	Sophomore	Chemistry	Austin	2.7
7	Senior	Computing	Tampa	3.5
8	Ph.D.	Biology	Shanghai	3.4
...	...	...	...	...
197	Sophomore	Electrical	Fort Worth	3.0
198	Ph.D.	Computing	Tampa	3.8
199	Master's	Biology	Nanjing	3.2
200	Freshman	Mechanical	Plano	3.9

■ **FIGURE 2.8**
The initial relation
for induction

Id_no	Major	Origin	GPA	Vote
1	Civil	Houston	3.5	1
4	Physics	Miami	3.9	1
5	Biology	Beijing	3.3	1
8	Biology	Shanghai	3.4	1
...	...	...	...	...
198	Computing	Tampa	3.8	1
199	Biology	Nanjing	3.2	1

Assume that the learning task is to generate characteristic rules for graduate students with respect to *id_no, major, origin*, and *GPA* using the default hierarchy in Figure 2.6 and the default threshold value of 3. To begin the preprocessing we consult the concept hierarchy to retrieve the corresponding primitive attribute set from the *student* relation. The retrieved primitive attribute set is {Master's, Ph.D.}. Then the data about the graduate students are projected upon *id_no, major, origin*, and *GPA* to retrieve the initial data relation. The initial relation for the induction obtained as the result of preprocessing is shown in Figure 2.8. Notice that a special attribute called *vote* is attached to each tuple in the relation with the initial value set to 1. Once this initial relation is obtained, we then apply the following seven basic strategies in sequence.

Strategy 1: Generalization on the Smallest Decomposable Components

To avoid overgeneralization, the least commitment principle (commitment to the minimally generalized concept) is enforced to ensure that the smallest possible opportunity for generalization is considered. Hence, we perform the generalization on the smallest decomposable components (or on attributes) rather than on larger sets of decomposable components or attributes.

Strategy 2: Attribute Removal

If there is a large set of distinct values of an attribute and there is no higher-level concept associated with the attribute, the attribute cannot be generalized to a higher-level concept, and thus we eliminate the attribute from the generalization. For example, from the initial relation in Figure 2.8, we find after examining the task-relevant attributes in sequence that there is no higher-level concept on the attribute *id_no*. Thus, we remove the *id_no* attribute from the generalization because a graduate student cannot be characterized by the attribute *id_no*.

Strategy 3: Concept Tree Ascension

The substitution of an attribute with a higher-level concept makes the tuple cover more cases than the original one, and thus generalizes the tuple. If there is a higher-level concept for an attribute in the concept tree, the substitution of the attribute with the higher-level concept should be performed by ascending the concept tree one level at a time to enforce the minimal generalization. This follows the least commitment principle and reduces the chances of overgeneralization. At this point, we add the special attribute *vote* to incorporate the quantitative information into the generalization process.

Strategy 4: Vote Propagation

The *vote* information in the generalized tuple indicates the total number of tuples generalized in the initial relation. Therefore, to keep the correct vote, when merging multiple tuples together, the vote counts should be accumulated in the process. After eliminating the attribute *id_no* and generalizing the relation in terms of the remaining three attributes, we get the generalized relation in Figure 2.9.

Strategy 5: Threshold Control on Each Attribute

The number of distinct tuples in the generalized relation must be less than or equal to the threshold value. If the number is larger than the threshold value, it means that one attribute contains more distinct values than the threshold, and thus further generalization must be performed.

■ **FIGURE 2.9**
A generalized relation

Major	Origin	GPA	Vote
Engineering	Texas	Excellent	35
Science	Florida	Excellent	10
Science	Texas	Excellent	30
Science	Korea	Good	10
Science	China	Good	15

Strategy 6: Threshold Control on Generalized Relations

If the total number of tuples in the generalized relation of the target is greater than the generalization threshold value, further generalization on the relation should be performed. The size of the generalized relation is further reduced by generalizing the relation on selected attributes and merging the identical tuples together. The generalization process continues until the total number of distinct tuples in the relation is less than or equal to the threshold value. As criteria for selecting attributes for further generalization, we may consider the following:

- Preference of a larger reduction ratio on the number of tuples or the number of distinct attribute values
- Simplicity of the final generalized rules
- Explicit selection and control of the attribute by users or experts

The third criterion above is based on the rationale that different rules can be discovered by following different paths, which may lead to multiple generalized relations for further examination. Experts and users may interactively filter out trivial and redundant rules and keep useful and interesting rules. Since the relation in Figure 2.9 contains five tuples, which is greater than the generalization threshold of 3, further generalization is performed. In this case the attribute *origin* is chosen since it has four distinct values. Ascending one level up in the concept hierarchy tree results in the relation shown in Figure 2.10. This final generalized relation meets the generalization threshold requirement since the number of tuples in the relation is 3. A characteristic rule can be retrieved by converting this relation to a simple logical formula, as follows, which justifies the need for strategy 7.

Strategy 7: Rule Transformation

Each tuple in the final generalized relation is transformed into conjunctive normal form, and these are combined into a formula in disjunctive

FIGURE 2.10 Further generalization of the relation

Major	Origin	GPA	Vote
Engineering	U.S.A.	Excellent	35
Science	U.S.A.	Excellent	40
Science	Foreign	Good	25

Major	Origin	GPA	Vote
ANY	U.S.A.	Excellent	75
Science	Foreign	Good	25

normal form. The final relation in Figure 2.10 can be simplified as shown in Figure 2.11.

We can convert the final generalized relation to the following characteristic rule, which characterizes all of the data in the target class (i.e., the graduate student class).

Characteristic rule:
A graduate student is either a U.S. student with an excellent GPA with 75% probability, or a foreign student with a good GPA with 25% probability.

This rule above corresponds to the following quantitative rule:

$$\forall (x) \; graduate(x) \rightarrow (\text{place-of-origin}(x) \in \text{U.S.A.} \wedge \text{GPA}(x) \in \text{excellent}) \; [75\%] \vee$$
$$(\text{place-of-origin}(x) \in \text{foreign} \wedge \text{GPA}(x) \in \text{good}) \; [25\%]$$

■ 2.3.3 Basic Attribute-Oriented Induction Algorithm

Based on the strategies discussed in the previous section, we now summarize the attribute-oriented induction algorithm below:

Algorithm: Basic attribute-oriented induction in relational databases
Input: A relational database, the learning task, the preferred concept hierarchy (optional), and the preferred form to express the learning result (such as a generalization threshold).
Output: A characteristic rule generated from the database.
Method: The basic attribute-oriented induction method consists of the following four steps:

Step 1: Collect the task-relevant data.
Step 2: Perform basic attribute-oriented induction as follows:

```
begin {basic attribute-oriented induction}
   for each attribute Aᵢ (1 ≤ i ≤n, n = the number of
attributes) in the generalization relation GR do {
```

```
while (# of distinct values in Aᵢ) > threshold do {
  if there is no higher-level concept for Aᵢ in the
concept hierarchy table
  then remove Aᵢ
  else
              (1) substitute the values of Aᵢ with its
                  corresponding minimally generalized
                  concept;
              (2) merge the identical tuples;
  }


while (# of tuples in GR) > threshold do {
        (1) selectively generalize attributes;
        (2) merge the identical tuples;
  }
}
end {the end of basic attribute-oriented induction}
```

Step 3: Simplify the generalized relation.

Step 4: Transform the final relation into a logical rule. □

The basic attribute-oriented induction algorithm extracts a characteristic rule of the form *learning_class* (*x*) → *condition* (*x*) from the initial relation. This rule covers all of the positive examples in the database and hence forms a necessary condition for the learning (generalized) concept. However, it may not cover data in other classes that also meet the specified condition.

■ 2.3.4 Generation of Discrimination Rules through Attribute-Oriented Induction

Discrimination rules distinguish concepts of one class (the target class) from those of another class (the contrasting class). Therefore, common concepts that exist in both classes should be detected and removed from the description of the discrimination rules. A discrimination rule can be obtained by simultaneously generalizing both the target class and the contrasting class and removing the conditions that exist in both classes from the final generalized rules. Consider a discrimination rule that distinguishes *graduate* classes from *undergraduate* classes in the *student* relation in Figure 2.7. Let's assume that the generalization process (through attribute removal and concept tree

■ **FIGURE 2.12**
A generalized
relation

Class	Major	Origin	GPA	Vote	Mark
Undergraduate	Science	Florida	Excellent	15	
	Engineering	Florida	Average	20	
	Science	Texas	Average	60	
	Science	*Texas*	*Excellent*	*35*	*m1*
	Engineering	Texas	Average	50	
	Engineering	Alabama	Excellent	20	
Graduate	Engineering	Texas	Excellent	35	
	Science	Alabama	Excellent	10	
	Science	*Texas*	*Excellent*	*30*	*m1*
	Science	Korea	Good	10	
	Science	China	Good	15	

ascension on both classes) results in the generalized relation in Figure 2.12. Note that the tuples marked with *m1* in both classes are overlapping tuples. They indicate that *Texas*-born, *science* major students with *excellent* grades may be either *graduate* or *undergraduate* students. These overlapping rules must be eliminated in the generalization process to generate an effective discrimination rule. Thus, we need an additional strategy to handle the overlapping tuples when generating discrimination rules.

Strategy 8: Handling Overlapping Tuples

The tuples that are shared by both the target and the contrasting classes are called *overlapping* tuples. The overlapping tuples must be marked and eliminated from the final discrimination rules.

Assuming a threshold value of 3, the relation in Figure 2.12 is not the final discrimination rule because both classes have more than three generalized tuples. Hence, we continue with further generalization on the attribute *origin*. The resulting relation is shown in Figure 2.13. From the relation we notice that the overlapping marks are inherited because the generalized concepts overlap in both classes. The total number of unmarked tuples in both the target and contrasting classes is less than the specified threshold value of 3, so we stop the process.

The unmarked tuple in the target (graduate) class yields the following qualitative discrimination rule, which excludes all overlapping disjuncts. The rule states that if a student is born in a foreign country, has a good GPA, and

■ FIGURE 2.13
A final
generalization
relation

Class	Major	Origin	GPA	Vote	Mark
	Science	U.S.A.	Excellent	50	m1
	Engineering	U.S.A.	Average	70	
Undergraduate	Science	U.S.A.	Average	60	
	Engineering	U.S.A.	Excellent	20	m2
	Engineering	U.S.A.	Excellent	35	m2
Graduate	Science	U.S.A.	Excellent	40	m1
	Science	Foreign	Good	25	

is a science major, (s)he is a graduate student. A qualitative discrimination rule provides a sufficient condition, but not a necessary condition, for a tuple (an object) to be in the target class, since the rule may not cover all the positive examples of the target class in the database. In other words, the tuples that meet the condition are in the target class, but some tuples in the target class may not satisfy the condition. Thus, the rule is represented in the form *learning-class*(x) ← *condition*(x) as follows.

$$\forall(x)\ graduate(x) \leftarrow major(x) \in science \wedge origin\ (x) \in foreign \wedge GPA(x) \in good$$

In many cases, it is necessary to associate each disjunct in the generalized relation with a quantitative measurement (called *d-weight*) to derive a quantitative rule from the final generalized relation. The *d-weight* for a concept q is defined as the ratio of the number of original tuples in the target class covered by q to the total number of tuples in both the target and the contrasting classes covered by q. The formal definition of the *d-weight* of the concept q in a class C_i is given as follows. Note that the *d-weight* values are in the range [0–1].

$$d\text{-}weight = votes\ (q \in C_i) / \sum_{i=[1..k]} votes(q \in C_i)$$

Using this *d-weight* formula, we can derive the following quantitative discrimination rule for graduate students in the database. The *d-weight* for the first tuple is 35/(35 + 20) = 63.64% and is 40/(40 + 50) = 44.44% for the second tuple. Note that any unmarked tuples have 100% *d-weight* value.

$$\forall(x)\ graduate(x) \leftarrow$$

$$(major(x) \in science \wedge origin\ (x) \in foreign \wedge GPA(x) \in good)\ [100\%]\ \vee$$

$$(major(x) \in engineering \wedge origin\ (x) \in U.S.A. \wedge GPA(x) \in excellent)\ [63.64\%]\ \vee$$

$$(major(x) \in science \wedge origin\ (x) \in U.S.A. \wedge GPA(x) \in excellent)\ [44.44\%]$$

The quantitative rule above presents the quantitative measurements of the graduate students' properties in the target class (graduate class) with that of the contrasting class (undergraduate class). The 100% *d-weight* value illustrates that the generalized tuple is in the target class only. All other *d-weight* values show the possibility of the generalized tuple in the target class.

■ 2.4 ASSOCIATION RULES IN HYPERTEXT DATABASES

A hypertext system is a database in which each page is connected to other pages through a set of page links that allows nonsequential access to relevant information. Navigation in a hypertext system is highly dependent upon each individual user's familiarity with the system, preferences, domain-knowledge level, and the specific piece of information that is being searched. Internet businesses such as online bookstores and online general merchandise stores rely heavily on hypertext databases. The success of such websites depends on the quality of the database services since on the Web it only takes a mouse click for a customer to move to a competitor's site. Therefore, it is crucial to analyze users' behavioral patterns when browsing web pages and to understand their preferences. This data can help design the best hypertext system to achieve the highest profit and cost savings.

Mining for access patterns in a Web-like environment may be viewed as a generalization of association rules in the context of flat transactions. Server log files contain information that characterizes user access to the server, including user identification, the sequence of the requested pages, and the date and time of access. In this section we formalize the concept of composite association rules in a hypertext system in the context of a directed graph by generalizing the concept of association rules with confidence and support. From the server log data, user navigation sessions can be reconstructed to build a weighted directed graph that summarizes it. The graph represents the user view of the hypertext system and delineates the domain for mining user patterns. Each node in the graph denotes a page visited by the user, and an arc in the graph denotes a link traversed by the user. Initially, weight on each arc is set to zero, and its value is incremented by one every time the user traverses the arc. Therefore, the weight on each arc represents the frequency of the user's traversing along that particular link.

This model does not represent a user's individual site visits, but rather, it summarizes a collection of sessions. Therefore, the generated weighted graph is intended to represent the navigation patterns of a single user or a group of users with similar interests. In the following section, we present a formal model of a simple hypertext system in terms of a weighted directed graph.

■ 2.4.1 Formal Model

The formal model for a hypertext system is given as a weighted directed graph $G = (N, E)$, where N is a set of nodes and E is a set of arcs, each connecting a pair of nodes. A node represents a page, while an arc (A, B) represents a link between a pair of pages. In the arc, A is called the source node, and B is the target node. For simplicity, we can assume that there is at most one link between any two nodes. The graph is weighted, and the weight on each arc represents the number of times the user traverses the link. To discuss the problem of mining association rules in a hypertext system, we start with the following assumptions:

1. The hypertext system contains only elementary pages that represent a single concept or idea.
2. Every node connected by a link refers to a page as a whole, not to a subset of the page or its contents.
3. The hypertext system does not contain any loop in which the source node coincides with the target node.
4. There is at most one link between any two nodes.

Initial interaction of the user with the hypertext system starts with the selection of a link on a page among all those available. User preferences among the available links in the pages of the system can be represented as a trail, which is an alternating sequence of nodes and arcs. A trail is $(v_1, e_1, v_2, e_2, ..., e_{n-1}, v_n)$ such that $v_i \in N$, $1 \leq i \leq n$, and every $e_i = (v_i, v_{i+1}) \in E$, $1 \leq i \leq n - 1$ is distinct. For simplicity, a trail $(v_1, e_1, v_2, e_2, ..., e_{n-1}, v_n)$ will be referred to as $(v_1, v_2, ..., v_n)$ since the graph does not contain two links with the same source and target node by assumption.

We now define a composite association rule in the hypertext system as follows. A composite association rule is a statement such as "When a user browses the hypertext system, he is likely to traverse a trail $A_1, A_2, ..., A_n$ with a certain probability." It can be expressed as $[(A_1 \rightarrow A_2) \wedge (A_2 \rightarrow A_3) \wedge ... \wedge (A_{n-1} \rightarrow A_n)]$, where $A_i \in N$ $(1 \leq i \leq n)$ and $\{(A_i, A_{i+1}) \mid i = 1, 2, ..., n - 1\} \in E$. The above expression means that when a user traverses a hypertext system, he will follow the trail $(A_1, A_2, ..., A_n)$ with a certain confidence. The validity of the rules is supported by two factors called *confidence* and *support* as defined below.

Confidence

Let a rule $r = [(A_1 \rightarrow A_2) \wedge (A_2 \rightarrow A_3) \wedge \cdots \wedge (A_{n-1} \rightarrow A_n)]$. Then the *confidence* of the rule r, written as C_r, is defined as the product of the confidences of all the corresponding single rules, that is $C_r = \prod_{i=1}^{n-1} C(A_i \rightarrow A_{i+1})$, where $C(A_i \rightarrow A_{i+1})$ is

$$\frac{|(A_i, A_{i+1})|}{\sum_{\{x|(A_i, x)\in E\}} |(A_i, x)|}.$$

In the last equation, $|(A_i, A_{i+1})|$ the number of times the link (A_i, A_{i+1}) is traversed and $\sum_{\{x|(A_i, x)\in E\}} |(A_i, x)|$ is the number of times the user traversed any link having A_i as the source node.

Support

The composite association rule $r = [(A_1 \rightarrow A_2) \wedge (A_2 \rightarrow A_3) \wedge \cdots \wedge (A_{n-1} \rightarrow A_n)]$ holds with *support* S_r, where S_r represents the average number of times the links of the rule were traversed over the average number of times all of the links in the graph were traversed., $S_r = X/Y$ where

$$X = \frac{\sum_{i=1}^{n-1} |(A_i, A_{i+1})|}{n-1}, \qquad Y = \frac{\sum_{\{i|(x_i, x_{i+1})\in E\}} |(x_i, x_{i+1})|}{|E|},$$

and $|E|$ is the total number of links in E. In the equation, $|(A_i, A_{i+1})|$ is the number of times the link (A_i, A_{i+1}) is traversed. The values of this *support* tend to distribute around the value of 1, that is, the rules with a *support* value greater than 1 consist of the links that were traversed more than average. Furthermore, we define the *monotonic support*, S_m, of a composite association rule as the minimum *support* value among all the single rules that constitute the composite rule.

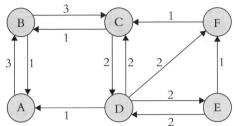

FIGURE 2.14
A weighted
directed graph

Now, let's consider the weighted directed graph in Figure 2.14. Let the rule r be $(B \rightarrow C \rightarrow D)$. Then

$$C_{(B \rightarrow C \rightarrow D)} = \frac{3}{3+1} \times \frac{2}{2+1} = 0.5 \quad \text{and} \quad S_{(B \rightarrow C \rightarrow D)} = \frac{\frac{3+2}{2}}{\frac{21}{12}} = 1.43.$$

With an appropriate *support* value, we can capture rules that are globally frequent, but the rules may contain some links that are below the support threshold. From the trail $B \xrightarrow{3} C \xrightarrow{2} D \xrightarrow{2} E \xrightarrow{1} F$ in the example in Figure 2.14, we get

$$S_r = \frac{\frac{8}{4}}{1.75} = 1.14$$

Note in this case that the minimum support value among all the single rules constituting the composite rule is 0.57 since $S_{B \rightarrow C} = \frac{3}{1.75} = 1.71$, $S_{C \rightarrow D} = \frac{2}{1.75} = 1.14$, $S_{D \rightarrow E} = \frac{2}{1.75} = 1.14$, and $S_{E \rightarrow F} = \frac{1}{1.75} = 0.57$. If we assume a support threshold value of 1, this trail is a rule only with the nonmonotonic definition.

■ 2.4.2 Algorithms for Generating Composite Association Rules

In this section, two algorithms for mining composite association rules in hypertext databases are presented. In these algorithms, we assume the nonmonotonic definition of support in which the support value cannot be used as a pruning criterion. The algorithms will generate the set of Candidate Rules (CR), that is, the set of all trails with *confidence* above the threshold. From this CR set, only the trails with *support* above the threshold value are generated and included in the composite rules set. We now define some useful concepts needed to describe the algorithms that follow.

A **neighbor** *link of a given trail* $t = (v_1, v_2, \ldots, v_n)$ *is a link that can be appended to the trail, t, yielding a trail that satisfies the properties of trails given in Section 2.4.1. A* **backward neighbor** *is a link* (x, v_1)*, where x* $\in N, x \neq v_n, (x, v_1) \in E,$ *and* $(x, v_1) \notin t.$ *A forward neighbor is a link* (v_n, x)*, where* $x \in N, (v_n, x) \in E,$ *and* $(v_n, x) \notin t.$

The first algorithm presented is a modified Depth-First Search (DFS) algorithm, a special case of a directed-graph DFS. For each link in the graph, a DFS tree is constructed. Each branch in the tree corresponds to a candidate rule, and therefore each DFS tree generates all possible candidate rules that have the root link as the first link. Furthermore, each branch exploration will identify a new trail, which is its own independent list of visited links. The branch exploration will stop when it finds a node whose links are already marked as visited or when the *confidence* value of the corresponding trail drops below the threshold value *C*. In the algorithm, given a trail *t*, we use *forw_neigh(t)* to refer to its next nonvisited forward neighbor and *last_link(t)* to refer to the last link in *t*. Given a trail *t* and a link *a*, *t + a* denotes the concatenation of *t* and *a*.

```
Modified DFS(G, C) Algorithm


begin
    for each {e∈ E, C_e ≥ C}
        EXPLORE(e, C_e)
    end for
end


EXPLORE(trail, C_trail) Algorithm
begin
    CR: = CR ∪ trail; //CR is the candidate rule set and
initially empty
    for each {f: = forw_neigh(trail)}
        if (C_f × C_trail ≥ C) then
        EXPLORE(trail + f, C_f × C_trail)
    end for
end
```

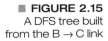
FIGURE 2.15
A DFS tree built
from the B → C link

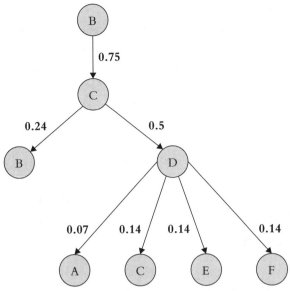

The modified DFS (MDFS) algorithm above considers every link in the graph G and expands it in the same manner that the DFS method does. Let's consider the link $B \rightarrow C$ among the 12 distinct links. Assuming the support threshold $S = 1.0$ and the confidence threshold $C = 0.3$, the MDFS algorithm generates a DFS tree as shown in Figure 2.15.

Each branch of the tree corresponds to a candidate rule. From the tree we observe the following:

$$C_{B \rightarrow C} = 0.75$$
$$C_{B \rightarrow C \rightarrow B} = 0.24 \text{ (stop)}$$
$$C_{B \rightarrow C \rightarrow D} = 0.5$$
$$C_{B \rightarrow C \rightarrow D \rightarrow A} = 0.07 \text{ (stop)}$$
$$C_{B \rightarrow C \rightarrow D \rightarrow C} = 0.14 \text{ (stop)}$$
$$C_{B \rightarrow C \rightarrow D \rightarrow E} = 0.14 \text{ (stop)}$$
$$C_{B \rightarrow C \rightarrow D \rightarrow F} = 0.14 \text{ (stop)}$$

Among the seven trails, only two trails meet the confidence threshold of 0.3. All other trails are dropped from further exploration. Furthermore, both rules meet the support threshold of 1 since $S_{B \rightarrow C} = \frac{3}{1.75} = 1.71$ and $S_{B \rightarrow C \rightarrow D} = \frac{2.5}{1.75} = 1.43$. Therefore, EXPLORE($B \rightarrow C$, 0.3) generates two trails $\{B \rightarrow C, B \rightarrow C \rightarrow D\}$. The process can be repeated with all other links of the graph in Figure 2.14 to generate all trails meeting the support and confidence thresholds.

The other algorithm for mining composite association rules in hypertext databases is called an Incremental Step Algorithm (ISA). In this algorithm, we take advantage of the property that states that every subtrail of a trail with confidence above the threshold itself has confidence above the threshold. This could mean that a trail with n links can be obtained by combining the trails with $n-1$ links. The algorithm starts with the trails with one link, CR_1, that have confidence above the threshold C. It recursively builds the trails with n links, CR_n, from the set of the trails with $n-1$ links, CR_{n-1}. The algorithm is given as follows:

ISA(G, C) Algorithm

```
begin
    for each {e ∈ E, C_e ≥ C}
        CR₁:= CR₁ ∪ e;
    end for
    i=1;
    repeat
      for each r ∈ CR_i;
          for each {x ∈ CR_i; x ≠ r ∧ (x[j] = r[j+1], 1 ≤ j
              ≤ i)}
          if C_r × C_last_link(x) ≥ C then
              CR_{i+1} = CR_i ∪ (r + last_link(x) );
          end for
      end for
      i++;
    until (CR_{i+1} = ∅)
end
```

From Figure 2.14, we find that $CR_1 = \{B \rightarrow C, A \rightarrow B, C \rightarrow D, C \rightarrow B,$ $F \rightarrow C, E \rightarrow F, E \rightarrow D\}$, $CR_2 = \{B \rightarrow C \rightarrow D, A \rightarrow B \rightarrow C, F \rightarrow C \rightarrow D,$ $F \rightarrow C \rightarrow B, E \rightarrow F \rightarrow C\}$, $CR_3 = \{A \rightarrow B \rightarrow C \rightarrow D\}$, and $CR_4 = \emptyset$. From these sets, we can check the support values for each rule to choose only the rules with support above the threshold. For example, since $S_{A \rightarrow B \rightarrow C \rightarrow D} = 1.52$, the rule $A \rightarrow B \rightarrow C \rightarrow D$ could be considered a meaningful rule.

■ 2.5 QUANTITATIVE ASSOCIATION RULES

Data mining in a market basket database is used to find all association rules that satisfy user-specified minimum support and minimum confidence constraints. This problem can be conceptually viewed as finding all associations among the "1" values in a relational table in which all the attribute values are Boolean. The value "1" for the value of an attribute for a given record means that the item corresponding to the attribute is present in the transaction corresponding to the record. The value "0" means exactly the opposite. This problem, often referred to as the "Boolean association rules" problem, is less general than the mining of association rules in relational tables that include richer data types for the attributes. These attributes can be either quantitative, such as age and income, or categorical, such as gender, marital status, and zip code. Boolean attributes can be considered a special case of categorical attributes.

In this chapter, the problem of mining association rules over quantitative and categorical attributes in a relational table is described. This rule-mining problem is referred to as the "quantitative association rules" problem. For illustration purposes, Figure 2.16 shows a "student" table with three nonkey attributes. "Age" and "Courses" are quantitative attributes, whereas "Gender" is a categorical attribute. A quantitative association rule present in the table is <Age: 20..29> ∧ <Gender: M> ⟹ <Courses: 1..2>.

■ 2.5.1 Mapping of Quantitative Association Rules

There are many algorithms for finding Boolean association rules, and a couple of them were introduced in Section 2.2. These algorithms can be used to mine quantitative association rules if a relational table with quantitative or categorical attributes can be mapped to a table with Boolean

■ **FIGURE 2.16**
Example of quantitative association rules

Record#	Age	Gender	Courses	Sample Rules	Support	Confidence
1	21	M	1	<Age: 20..29> ∧ <Gender: M> ⟹ <Courses: 1..2>	25%	100%
2	24	F	2			
3	25	F	3	<Courses: 3..4> ⟹ <Gender: F>	37.5%	100%
4	29	M	2			
5	30	F	3			
6	32	M	2			
7	34	M	2			
8	39	F	3			

■ FIGURE 2.17
Mapping to Boolean association rules problem

Record#	Age: 20..29	Age: 30..39	Gender: F	Gender: M	Courses: 1	Courses: 2	Courses: 3
1	1	0	0	1	1	0	0
2	1	0	1	0	0	1	0
3	1	0	1	0	0	0	1
4	1	0	0	1	0	1	0
5	0	1	1	0	0	0	1
6	0	1	0	1	0	1	0
7	0	1	0	1	0	1	0
8	0	1	1	0	0	0	1

values. This mapping will be straightforward if all attributes in the table are categorical or quantitative with only a few possible values. Instead of having only one field for the attribute, as many fields as there are attribute values are created. The value of the field corresponding to <attribute$_m$, value$_n$> will be 1 if the attribute$_m$ has value$_n$ in the original record and 0 otherwise. If the size of the domain for the attribute values is large, one simple approach is to partition the values into intervals and map each <attribute, interval> pair to a Boolean attribute.

Figure 2.17 shows the mapping of the three nonkey attributes of the student table shown in Figure 2.16. The categorical attribute *gender* has two Boolean attributes <Gender: F> and <Gender: M>. The *courses* attribute is not partitioned into intervals since the number of values for the attribute is small. Instead, each value is mapped into a separate Boolean field. Finally, the third attribute *age* is partitioned into two intervals <Age: 20..29> and <Age: 30..39>.

Two problems are noted with this approach when applied to quantitative attributes. First, if the number of partitioned intervals for a quantitative attribute is large, the support for any single interval can be low. Hence, some rules involving this attribute may not be found due to not satisfying the minimum support. The other problem is that whenever the values are partitioned into intervals, some information may be lost. This information loss increases as the interval sizes become larger. For example, in Figure 2.17, the rule <Courses: 3> $\Rightarrow$ <Gender: F> has 100% confidence. But when the *courses* attributes are partitioned into two intervals such that 2 courses and 3 courses are placed into the same interval, then the closest rule is <Courses: 2..3> $\Rightarrow$ <Gender: F>, which has only 57.1% confidence.

These two problems create the following conflicting situations: (1) large intervals may generate rules that do not satisfy minimum confidence, and (2) small intervals may generate rules that do not satisfy minimum support. These situations can be resolved by considering all possible continuous ranges over the values of the quantitative attribute or over the partitioned intervals since the latter problem (*minSup* problem) disappears by combining adjacent intervals or values. Although the *minConf* problem is still present, the information loss is reduced by increasing the number of intervals that avoid the *minSup* problem. This implies that the number of intervals must be increased while simultaneously combining adjacent intervals. This causes the following two problems:

1. Time complexity of $O(n^2)$: When there are n values or intervals, there are on average $n(n + 1)/2$ ranges. Hence, the number of items per record will sharply increase, which in turn increases execution time.

2. Many rules problem: The number of rules will increase: if a value or an interval has minimum support, any range containing this value or interval will also have the minimum support. Many of the generated rules will not be of interest.

A solution exists to realize faster execution time and fewer intervals to mitigate execution time. This is achieved by combining adjacent values or intervals. The process of combining intervals stops when their combined support exceeds a user-specified maximum support value, with the exception that any single interval or value is still considered, even though its support value exceeds the maximum support. On the other hand, information loss can be reduced by creating more intervals, thus mitigating the *minConf* problem. Hence, a special measure is needed to decide whether or not to partition a quantitative attribute and how many partitions there should be if it is partitioned. In the following sections, an approach to these problems is discussed.

■ 2.5.2 Problem Decomposition

The problem of mining quantitative association rules is to find all quantitative association rules from a given set of records that have support and confidence greater than the user-specified minimum support and confidence. To address the problem of quantitative association rule mining, some terminology is introduced first as follows:

$A = \{a_1, a_2, \ldots, a_m\}$, is a set of attributes.

P is a set of positive integers.

A_V denotes the set $\{<x, v> \in A \times P\}$.

A_R denotes the set $\{<x, l, u> \in A \times P \times P \mid l \leq u$ if x is quantitative; $l = u$ if x is categorical\}.

For any $X \subseteq A_R$ attributes(X) is the set $\{x \mid <x, l, u> \in X\}$.

From the above definitions, it should be noted that either a pair $<x, v> \in A_V$ or a triple $<x, l, u> \in A_R$ represents an item. $\hat{X}$ is a generalization of X (i.e., X is a specialization of $\hat{X}$) if attributes(X) = attributes($\hat{X}$) and $\forall x \in$ attributes(X)$\{<x, l_1, u_1> \in X \wedge <x, l_2, u_2> \in \hat{X} \Rightarrow l_2 \leq l_1 \leq u_1 \leq u_2\}$. For the uniform treatment of categorical and quantitative attributes, the categorical attribute values are mapped into a set of consecutive integers. If the quantitative attributes are not partitioned into intervals, the values are mapped to consecutive integers with the order of the values preserved. If they are partitioned into intervals, then the intervals are mapped to consecutive integers with the order of values preserved. Now the problem of mining quantitative association rules can be solved with the following five steps:

1. Determine the number of partitions for each quantitative attribute.
2. Perform mapping for categorical or quantitative attributes.
3. Find the support for each value of categorical and quantitative attributes.
4. Generate association rules by using the frequent itemsets.
5. Determine the interesting rules to keep in the output.

For example, consider the *student* table shown in Figure 2.18, which assumes 25% minimum support and 50% minimum confidence. The table contains one categorical attribute, *gender*, and two quantitative attributes, *age* and *courses*. The *age* attribute is partitioned into four intervals. After mapping to consecutive integers using tables (b) and (c), the table looks as shown in table (d). Table (e) shows sample frequent itemsets, and (f) shows a couple of sample rules.

■ 2.5.3 Partitioning of Quantitative Attributes

In this section, we address when quantitative attributes should be partitioned and how many partitions should be created. When rules are generated

■ **FIGURE 2.18**
Example of problem decomposition

(a) The *student* table

Record#	Age	Gender	Courses
1	21	M	1
2	24	F	2
3	25	F	3
4	29	M	2
5	30	F	3
6	32	M	2
7	34	M	2
8	39	F	3

(b) Partition & mapping for *age*

Interval	Mapping integer
20..24	1
25..29	2
30..34	3
35..39	4

(c) Mapping for *gender*

Value	Integer
F	1
M	2

(d) After mapping attributes

Record#	Age	Gender	Courses
1	1	2	1
2	1	1	2
3	2	1	3
4	2	2	2
5	3	1	3
6	3	2	2
7	3	2	2
8	4	1	3

(e) Sample frequent itemsets

Item sets	Support
{<Age: 20..29>}	4
{<Age: 30..39>}	4
{<Gender: F>}	4
{<Gender: M>}	4
{<Courses: 1..2>}	5
{<Courses: 3..4>}	3
{<Age: 30..39>, <Gender: F>}	2

(f) Some sample rules

Rules	Support	Confidence
<Age: 30..39> ∧ <Gender: F> ⟹ <Courses: 3..4>	25%	100%
<Gender: F> ⟹ <Courses: 3..4>	37.5%	75%

considering all ranges over the partitions of quantitative attributes instead of raw values, information loss will occur. Since partitioning will cause loss of information, a special measure called *partial completeness* is used to control the amount of information lost by partitioning. Partial completeness measures how far the generated rules over the partitions are from the rules generated

Itemset Number	Itemsets	Support
1	\<Age: 20..29\>	10%
2*	\<Age: 30..40\>	12%
3*	\<Age: 20..40\>	18%
4	\<Courses: 0..1\>	10%
5*	\<Courses: 0..3\>	12%
6	\<Age: 20..29\> and \<Courses: 0..1\>	8%
7*	\<Age: 20..40\> and \<Courses: 0..3\>	12%

over the raw values of the quantitative attributes. The definition of partial completeness is given below assuming that $K \geq 1$, that C is the set of all frequent itemsets in D, and that $P \subseteq C$.

P is K-complete with respect to C if

1. $X \in P$ and $X' \subseteq X \Rightarrow X' \in P$, and $\forall X \in C, \exists \hat{X} \in P$ such that
2. $\hat{X}$ is a generalization of X and support$(\hat{X}) \leq K \times$ support(X), and
3. $\forall Y \subseteq X, \exists \hat{Y} \subseteq \hat{X}$ such that $\hat{Y}$ is a generalization of Y and support$(\hat{Y}) \leq K \times$ support(Y)

For example, if the table shown in Figure 2.19 is assumed to contain the frequent itemsets C, then the itemsets 2, 3, 5, and 7 would form a 1.5-complete set, since for any subset X, either 2, 3, 5, or 7 is a generalization with support at most 1.5 times the support of X. However, the itemsets 3, 5, and 7 do not form a 1.5-complete set, since the itemset 3 is the only generalization of the itemset 1 among the set (3, 5, and 7) and 18% is more than 1.5 times 10%.

Given the partial completeness level desired by the user and the minimum support, the number of partitions required can be calculated by the following formula, assuming equi-depth partitioning.

Number of intervals $= (2 \times n)/[m \times (K - 1)]$, where n is the number of quantitative attributes, m is the user-provided minimum support, and K is the partial completeness level. From the formula, it can be noted that the support of each base interval must be at most $[m \times (K - 1)]/(2 \times n)$ for the frequent itemset to be K-complete.

■ 2.6 MINING OF COMPACT RULES

As the size of the database increases, it gets more difficult to analyze larger amounts of data by finding all possible semantic relationships among them. Hence, the rule-mining focus can be on deriving rules with full confidence. As described in the previous sections, these rules are derived based on the dependencies between a target attribute and other condition attributes. A problem with this plain rule-mining approach arises when many rules are derived or many condition attributes are involved in the antecedent of each rule. Hence, for the efficient use of the rules, it is important to be able to derive rules that are compact.

In this section, a new concept, called a Semantic Association Relationship (SAR), is introduced, which will facilitate the extraction of compact association rules in a database. Through the use of the SAR, the number of attributes involved in the antecedent of each rule and the number of derived rules can be reduced, thus simplifying the complexity of the rules and the dependencies between the attributes.

■ 2.6.1 Semantic Association Relationships

Diminishing the number of distinct values in each attribute makes data easier to characterize in terms of rules. Domain knowledge in the form of the Domain Concept Hierarchy (DCH) is used for this purpose. The DCH is a hierarchy structure that provides a general-to-specific structure of the domain knowledge relevant to an attribute. It is a multilevel abstraction of domain knowledge in which the most specific values (i.e., the terminal nodes in the hierarchy) are domain elements of an attribute, and the remaining values in the hierarchy are domain concepts. This hierarchy is generally specified by domain experts.

The DCH can be either an IS-A hierarchy or a taxonomy for a non-numerical attribute. "A department manager is an employee" is an example of an IS-A hierarchy through which an instance of an object can be specified, whereas "there are many cities in a state" is an example of a taxonomy. The elements of a numerical attribute can be divided into groups, each of which is represented by a concept.

SARs are associations between domain elements and concepts in attributes. They are another important factor that contributes to the reduction of distinct values in attributes. For example, suppose that from a relation called *employment*, a rule "if occupation is medical doctor, then salary is high" is derived. In this rule, "medical doctor" is a domain element of attribute *occupation* and "high" is the concept specified in the DCH for the attribute *salary*. Hence, a semantic association from "Occupation is medical doctor" to "Salary is high" can be derived.

■ 2.6.2 Generalization Algorithm

Generalization is necessary when there are a large number of distinct values for each attribute in a relation. When each attribute contains a large number of distinct values, the derived rules from the relation may not be useful because the rules may be complex or the rules may characterize few tuples. To derive compact rules from reduced relations, the learning process should go through a generalization process that ascends from specific values to higher-level concepts by climbing the DCH so that the number of distinct values is reduced. The generalization process can be performed on each attribute in an initial relation that is formed by joining a target attribute with the condition attributes from a base relation.

The generalization process for an attribute A can be summarized in three steps as follows:

Step 1: Let R be the ratio of the number of distinct values of attribute A to the total number of tuples in the initial relation R. If R is greater than the generalization threshold GH, go to the next step. Otherwise, the generalization on attribute A terminates.

Step 2: If there are no more higher-level concepts for the values of attribute A in the DCH, remove attribute A from R since there is a large set of distinct values that cannot be generalized. Otherwise, replace all values of attribute A with a higher-level concept by ascending one level of the DCH.

Step 3: Repeat steps 1 and 2 until R is less than or equal to GH.

The above process can be applied to all attributes in an initial relation to generalize the entire relation. When going through the generalization steps above, a set of tuples may be generalized by the same tuple. For example, the *gautomobile* relation shown in Figure 2.20 may be the result of the generalization process performed on a relation *automobile*.

Id	Car	MPG	Weight	Drv-Ratio	Horsepower	Displace	Cyl
1	Buick Estate	Low	High	Medium	High	High	8
2	Ford Country	Low	High	Medium	Medium	High	8
3	Chevy Malibu	Low	Medium	Low	Medium	High	8
4	Chrysler LeBaron	Low	Medium	Low	High	High	8
5	Chevrolet	High	Low	High	Low	Low	4
6	Toyota Corona	Medium	Low	High	Low	Low	4
7	Datsun 510	Medium	Low	High	Low	Low	4
8	Dodge Omni	High	Low	Medium	Low	Low	4
9	Audi 5000	Medium	Low	High	Low	Low	5
10	Volvo 240 GL	Low	Medium	High	High	High	6
11	Saab 99 GLE	Medium	Low	High	Medium	Low	4
12	Peugeot 694 SL	Low	Medium	High	Medium	High	6
13	Buick Century	Medium	Medium	High	Low	Medium	6
14	Mercury Zephyr	Medium	Medium	High	Low	Medium	6
15	Dodge Aspen	Low	Medium	Medium	Low	Medium	6
16	AMC Concord D/L	Low	Medium	Medium	Medium	High	6
17	Chevy Caprice	Low	Medium	Low	High	High	8
18	Ford LTD	Low	Medium	Low	High	High	8
19	Mercury Grand	Low	Medium	Low	High	High	8
20	Dodge St Regis	Low	Medium	Low	High	Medium	8

■ 2.6.3 Learning Process

The learning process first begins with the recording of the tuple numbers for the same attribute value of a single attribute and for each combination of attribute values of two different attributes by scanning the generalized relation once. For example, the single-attribute subtables for the two attributes *MPG* (miles per gallon) and *weight* can be created as shown in Figure 2.21.

The single-attribute subtables can be expanded further with more attributes. For example, consider the three attributes *MPG*, *weight*, and *horsepower*. Two-attribute subtables involving these three attributes can be created as shown in Figure 2.22.

■ **FIGURE 2.21**
Single-attribute
subtables for *MPG*
and *weight*

MPG	
High	5, 8
Medium	6, 7, 9, 11, 13, 14
Low	1, 2, 3, 4, 10, 12, 15, 16, 17, 18, 19, 20

Weight	
High	1, 2
Medium	3, 4, 10, 12, 13, 14, 15, 16, 17, 18, 19, 20
Low	5, 6, 7, 8, 9, 11

An event can be defined to be an attribute–value pair. For example, an event $X = (MPG, low)$ describes an event named X, namely, the attribute *MPG* has "low" as its value. A frequency function F maps one or more of these events into the frequency of these events appearing in the generalized relation. For example, $F(X) = 12$. On the other hand, a probability function P maps one or more of these events into the probability of these events occurring in the generalized relation. Hence, $P(X) = F(X)/N$, where N is the total number of tuples in the generalized relation. If we let $Y = (weight, high)$, $P(X)$ and $P(Y)$ are equal to $12/20$ and $2/20$, respectively.

Semantic Association Degrees (SADs) are degrees of semantic associations between domain elements or concepts, which are generally specified by database designers. Suppose that there are two events C and T. A degree D associated with "if C then T" is a SAD from C to T in which C is a condition event and T is a target event. D can be represented as $P(T \mid C) = P(C, T)/P(C) = F(C, T)/F(C)$. Furthermore, D can be extended with more condition events: $C_1, C_2, C_3, \ldots, C_k$. Hence, $P(T \mid C_1, C_2, C_3, \ldots, C_k) = F(C_1, C_2, C_3, \ldots, C_k, T)/F(C_1, C_2, C_3, \ldots, C_k)$. $F(C_1, C_2, C_3, \ldots, C_k)$ can be obtained as $Card\{TS(C_1, C_2) \cap TS(C_2, C_3) \cap \cdots \cap TS(C_{k-1}, C_k)\}$, where $Card$ denotes the cardinality of a set and $TS(A, B)$ is a tuple set in which the two events A and B both appear simultaneously in the generalized relation.

For example, let $C_1 = (weight, low)$, $C_2 = (MPG, medium)$, and $C_3 = (horsepower, low)$ be condition events and $T = (drv\_ratio, high)$ be a target event. Then $P(T \mid C_1, C_2, C_3) = F(C_1, C_2, C_3, T) / F(C_1, C_2, C_3) = Card\{TS(C_1, C_2) \cap TS(C_2, C_3) \cap TS(C_3, T)\}/Card\{TS(C_1, C_2) \cap TS(C_2, C_3)\} = Card\{\{6, 7, 9, 11\} \cap \{6, 7, 9, 13, 14\} \cap \{5, 6, 7, 9, 13, 14\}\}/Card\{\{6, 7, 9, 11\} \cap \{6, 7, 9, 13, 14\}\} = 1$. This semantic association can be used to generate a rule "if $(weight = low)$ and $(MPG = medium)$ and $(horsepower = low)$, then $(drv\_ratio = high)$." This rule is supported by the tuple set $\{6, 7, 9\}$.

Weight / MPG	High	Medium	Low
High	—	—	5, 8
Medium	—	13, 14	6, 7, 9, 11
Low	1, 2	3, 4, 10, 12, 15, 16, 17, 18, 19, 20	—

Horsepower / MPG	High	Medium	Low
High	—	—	5, 8
Medium	—	11	6, 7, 9, 13, 14
Low	1, 4, 10, 17, 18, 19, 20	2, 3, 12, 16	15

Horsepower / Weight	High	Medium	Low
High	1	2	—
Medium	4, 10, 17, 18, 19, 20	3, 12, 16	13, 14, 15
Low	—	11	5, 6, 7, 8, 9

■ 2.6.4   Learning Algorithm

In this section, the steps to derive rules using SADs are described with an example. First, it is assumed that there are k condition attributes $(CA_1, CA_2, ..., CA_k)$ and a Target Attribute (TA) in the generalized relation. The steps to derive the rules are as follows:

Step 1 (First iteration):
Compute the SAD from each condition event to the target event.

Step 2 (Iterations 2 through k):
For each subsequent iteration i ($2 \le i \le k$), compute the SAD from each combination of $j - i + 1$ condition events $CE = \{(CA_i, ca_i), (CA_{i+1}, ca_{i+1}), ..., (CA_j, ca_j)\}$ to each target event with the following strategies:

Strategy 1:
If the SAD from CE to a target event (TA, ta) is 1, derive the following rule R_1 with full confidence (100%): "If (CA_i, ca_i) and (CA_{i+1}, ca_{i+1}) and ...

(CA_j, ca_j), then (TA, ta)." Furthermore, do not combine this CE with any other events since the sets of tuples corresponding to these combined CEs must be subsets of the set of tuples corresponding to the rule R_1. It is also noteworthy that the SADs from the CE to other target events must be 0.

Strategy 2:

If the SAD from CE to a target event (TA, ta) is 0, do not compute SADs from any combination containing the CE to the target event (TA, ta) in later iterations. TS_R is a tuple set supporting the rule R. Assume that $R_1, R_2, \ldots, R_{t-1}$ are previously derived rules.

Strategy 3:

When a new rule R_t is derived, if $TS_{R_1} \cup TS_{R_2} \cup \cdots \cup TS_{R_t}$ contains all tuples in the generalized relation, terminate this algorithm. On the other hand, if all tuples in which the target event (TA, ta) appears in the generalized relation are contained in $TS_{R_1} \cup TS_{R_2} \cup \cdots \cup TS_{R_t}$, do not compute the SAD from any condition event combination to the target event (TA, ta).

Strategy 4:

If TS_{R_i} $(1 \leq i \leq t - 1)$ is a proper subset of TS_{R_t}, then discard R_i.

Strategy 5:

If TS_{R_t} is a subset of $TS_{R_1} \cup TS_{R_2} \cup \cdots \cup TS_{R_{(t-1)}}$, then discard R_t.

For example, consider the generalized relation *gautomobile* shown in Figure 2.20. The relationships between the target attribute *drv_ratio* and the three condition attributes *weight, horsepower*, and *MPG* are used to derive compact rules about the attribute *drv_ratio* from the relation. In the first iteration, the SADs from each condition event to the target event are obtained as shown in Figure 2.23. In the figure, the SAD from (*MPG, medium*) to the target event is 1. Hence, the rule "IF (*MPG = medium*) THEN (*drv_ratio = high*)" is derived and recorded as rule 1. This rule covers tuples 6, 7, 9, 11, 13, and 14. In the subsequent iteration, the event (*MPG = medium*) is removed from forming any other combination of condition events.

Continuing the algorithm in the next iteration to obtain SADs from a combination of two condition events to the target event yields the table in Figure 2.24. From the table, five rules with full confidence are derived and recorded as rules 2, 3, 4, 5, and 6 as follows:

Rule 2: IF (*MPG = low*) and (*weight = high*) THEN (*drv_ratio = medium*)

Rule 3: IF (*MPG = low*) and (*horsepower = low*) THEN (*drv_ratio = medium*)

FIGURE 2.23
SADs from *MPG*, *weight*, and *horsepower* to *drv_ratio*

MPG Drv_ratio	High	Medium	Low
High	1/2	1/2	0
Medium	1	0	0
Low	1/6	1/3	1/2

Weight Drv_ratio	High	Medium	Low
High	0	1/2	1/2
Medium	1/3	1/6	1/2
Low	5/6	1/6	0

Horsepower Drv_ratio	High	Medium	Low
High	1/7	1/7	5/7
Medium	2/5	1/5	2/5
Low	1/2	1/2	0

Rule 4: IF (*weight* = *high*) and (*horsepower* = *medium*) THEN (*drv_ratio* = *medium*)

Rule 5: IF (*weight* = *high*) and (*horsepower* = *high*) THEN (*drv_ratio* = *medium*)

Rule 6: IF (*weight* = *low*) and (*horsepower* = *medium*) THEN (*drv_ratio* = *high*)

Note that rule 2 is supported by tuples 1 and 2, rule 3 is supported by tuple 15, rule 4 by tuple 2, rule 5 by tuple 1, and rule 6 by tuple 11. In Figure 2.24, the × marks in the table indicate that the SADs need not be computed because the condition event combinations corresponding to them include the condition events corresponding to the value 0 in the table in Figure 2.23.

Continuing the algorithm with an additional condition event, the table in Figure 2.25 is obtained. In the table, no rules with full confidence are found. All the rules that can be generated from the table are ones with partial confidence. Hence, the algorithm to generate compact rules with full confidence terminates at this point.

FIGURE 2.24
SADs from two condition events to *drv_ratio*

MPG	Weight	Drv_ratio		
		High	Medium	Low
High	Low	1/2	1/2	×
High	Medium	0	0	×
High	High	×	0	×
Low	Low	0	0	0
Low	Medium	1/5	1/5	3/5
Low	High	×	1	0

MPG	Horsepower	Drv_ratio		
		High	Medium	Low
High	Low	1/2	1/2	×
High	Medium	0	0	×
High	High	0	0	×
Low	Low	0	1	×
Low	Medium	1/4	1/2	¼
Low	High	1/7	1/7	5/7

Weight	Horsepower	Drv_ratio		
		High	Medium	Low
High	Low	×	0	×
High	Medium	×	1	0
High	High	×	1	0
Medium	Low	2/3	1/3	×
Medium	Medium	1/3	1/3	1/3
Medium	High	1/6	0	5/6
Low	Low	4/5	1/5	×
Low	Medium	1	0	0
Low	High	0	0	0

FIGURE 2.25
SADs with three condition events

MPG	Weight	Horsepower	Drv_ratio		
			High	Medium	Low
High	Low	Low	1/2	1/2	0
Low	Medium	Medium	1/3	1/3	1/3
Low	Medium	High	1/6	0	5/6

■ 2.7   MINING OF TIME-CONSTRAINED ASSOCIATION RULES

Some databases, such as website traffic logs, contain sequential and timing information. For example, the rules generated from web log databases need to indicate sets of pages visited together in a certain order. This information can be used to forecast the next set of pages a visitor might frequent. In the generation of association rules considered so far, timing and sequential data has not been taken into account. To indicate timing and sequential constraints in association rules, the association rule generation algorithms presented in the previous sections need to be extended.

■ 2.7.1   Time-Constrained Association Rules

In this section, we extend the association rule framework by introducing time constraints. For this purpose, traditional databases need to be augmented with a time stamp, which indicates sequence and timing of events. Suppose that we have a relation as shown in Figure 2.26. It should be noted that only the timing within a transaction is considered important, and hence the first item in every transaction is always timestamped at 0.

The support and confidence used in the previous sections are extended as follows, where $I = \{i_1, i_2, i_3, \ldots, i_n\}$ is a universe of all possible descriptive items. Assume that $X, Y \subseteq I$, and $X \cap Y = \varnothing$.

$$forward\_sup(X \Rightarrow Y) =$$

$$\frac{\text{number of transactions containing } X \cup Y, \text{ where } time(X) \leq time(Y)}{\text{total number of transactions}}$$

■ FIGURE 2.26
A relation with a time stamp

Transaction Numbers	Items	Time Stamp
T_1	B A	0 4
T_2	A B G D	0 2 5 9
T_3	C B A F G	0 3 5 12 45
T_4	A B C D	0 5 9 19
T_5	B F G	0 7 36
T_6	A B G D	0 6 12 28
T_7	F G A B	0 4 7 8

$$forward\_conf(X \Rightarrow Y) = \frac{forward\_sup(X \Rightarrow Y)}{sup(X)}$$

From the example relation, $forward\_sup(A \Rightarrow B)$ = 4/7 = 57% and $forward\_conf(A \Rightarrow B)$ = 4/6 = 66.7%. Notice that the first and third transactions are not counted because A is preceded by B. Furthermore, $forward\_conf(F \Rightarrow G)$ = 100%, which means F is always visited in combination with G, whereas $forward\_conf(D \Rightarrow G)$ = 0%, from which it is deduced that D is never visited before G. Combining the above two measures gives more meaning to the association rules and gives us better insight into the data. Similarly, it is possible to define backward support and confidence measures as follows:

$$backward\_sup(X \Rightarrow Y) = $$
$$\frac{\text{number of transactions containing } X \cup Y, \text{ where } time(X) \geq time(Y)}{\text{total number of transactions}}$$

$$backward\_conf(X \Rightarrow Y) = \frac{backward\_sup(X \Rightarrow Y)}{sup(X)}$$

Therefore, both forward and backward measures of support and confidence can be generalized as the following definitions:

$$time\_sup(t_1, t_2)(X \Rightarrow Y) = $$
$$\frac{\text{number of transactions containing } X \cup Y, \text{ where } t_1 \leq time(Y) - time(X) \leq t_2}{\text{total number of transactions}}$$

$$time\_conf(t_1, t_2)(X \Rightarrow Y) = \frac{time\_sup(t_1, t_2)(X \Rightarrow Y)}{sup(X)}$$

In the definitions above, t_1 and t_2 are integers that are used to define a timing window and $t_1 \leq t_2$. From these generalized definitions, the following can be observed with $t_i \leq t_j$:

1. $time\_sup(t_j, t_k)(X \Rightarrow Y) \leq time\_sup(t_i, t_k)(X \Rightarrow Y) \leq sup(X \Rightarrow Y)$
2. $time\_sup(t_k, t_j)(X \Rightarrow Y) \leq time\_sup(t_k, t_j)(X \Rightarrow Y) \leq sup(X \Rightarrow Y)$
3. $time\_conf(t_j, t_k)(X \Rightarrow Y) \leq time\_conf(t_i, t_k)(X \Rightarrow Y) \leq conf(X \Rightarrow Y)$
4. $time\_conf(t_k, t_j)(X \Rightarrow Y) \leq time\_conf(t_k, t_j)(X \Rightarrow Y) \leq conf(X \Rightarrow Y)$

From the definition of $time\_sup$ and $time\_conf$ above, it can be observed that for $t_1 = -\infty$ and $t_2 = +\infty$, $time\_sup(t_1, t_2)(X \Rightarrow Y)$ and $time\_conf(t_1, t_2)(X \Rightarrow Y)$

converge to normal $sup(X \Rightarrow Y)$ and $conf(X \Rightarrow Y)$. Furthermore, for $t_1 = 0$ and $t_2 = +\infty$ they converge to *forward_sup* and *forward_conf* and for $t_1 = -\infty$ and $t_2 = 0$ they converge to *backward_sup* and *backward_conf*.

■ 2.7.2 Properties of Time Constraints

From the definitions of *time_sup* and *time_conf*, two special measures called *support_ratio* and *confidence_ratio* can be defined as follows:

$$support\_ratio\ (t_1, t_2)(X \Rightarrow Y) = \frac{time\_sup(t_1, t_2)(X \Rightarrow Y)}{sup(X \Rightarrow Y)}$$

$$confidence\_ratio\ (t_1, t_2)(X \Rightarrow Y) = \frac{time\_conf\ (t_1, t_2)(X \Rightarrow Y)}{conf\ (X \Rightarrow Y)}$$

It should be noted that both ratios are within the range of 0 to 1 because *time_sup* and *time_conf* are always smaller than normal *sup* and *conf*. Given the fact that both X and Y appear in the transaction, both ratios express the conditional probability of X and Y within the time window defined by t_1 and t_2.

In a real-life situation, an item may appear more than once. For example, in web navigation a visitor may access web pages more than once. In that case, the time difference between two items is not unique. Consider the case in Figure 2.27 in which some items appear more than once.

To calculate the *time_sups* of two items that appear multiple times, there are several measures that can be used. For example, to calculate $time\_sup(t_1, t_2)$ $(A \Rightarrow B)$, a transaction can be counted if

1. $t_1 \leq time(B) - time(A) \leq t_2$ is valid for all occurrences of A and B;
2. $t_1 \leq time(B) - time(A) \leq t_2$ is valid for at least one occurrence of A and B;
3. $t_1 \leq average[time(B) - time(A)] \leq t_2$ is valid; and
4. $t_1 \leq time(\text{first occurrence of } B) - time(\text{first occurrence of } A) \leq t_2$ is valid.

■ **FIGURE 2.27**
Transaction with multiple occurrences of some items

Time	0	4	7	10	12	15	19
Items	A	B	A	B	C	A	C

■ 2.7.3 Potential Applications

The main goal of web mining is to extract useful knowledge from web-server databases containing data about the behavior of customers. The potential application of the discovery of time-constrained association rules is the mining of a website visitor's navigational patterns. On the data collected about a visitor's activities, a slightly modified version of the Apriori algorithm can be used with values for t_1 and t_2 to define a time window.

In market basket analysis, our first application of association rules, there was no ordering of items since all of the items were placed in a basket and were paid for. It was actually impossible to detect the order in which customers picked the items from the shelves. However, random checks can be performed to gain worthwhile information to improve sales. Marketers can see how customers wander through the store to determine a customer's pattern of moving from shelf to a shelf. However, it's not so easy to see why (say) eggs and wine are frequently sold together. It may be that the wine was the primary reason for shopping and eggs were picked up while passing by. The use of time-constrained association rule mining can provide useful tips for answering some of these questions.

■ 2.8 CHAPTER SUMMARY

Association-rule mining in databases was discussed in this chapter. The problem of discovering all association rules in market basket data was described in the first section. The Apriori algorithm was used for association-rule mining in market basket data. In the next section, the attribute-oriented rule induction method was presented. A concept hierarchy was used to mine characteristic and discrimination rules in a database. The third section dealt with association rules in hypertext databases. In this section, hypertext systems were modeled as weighted graphs. Finding a set of web pages connected by a link was the focus of the discussion. The mining of association rules over quantitative and categorical attributes was described in the next section. Next, the problem of mining compact rules was discussed. In this section, a new concept called the semantic association relationship was defined and was used to facilitate the extraction of compact association rules. The chapter concluded with a discussion on mining time-constrained association rules, an extension of the association-rule framework, which was illustrated by introducing time constraints.

■ 2.9 EXERCISES

1. Use the database table in Figure 2.28, which contains ten market transactions. Use the Apriori algorithm to complete the association rule generation process. Experiment with different values of support and confidence to observe how they control the number of association rules
   generated.

2. Consider the weighted directed graph shown in Figure 2.29. Generate
   all possible composite association rules meeting the support values of
   1.0, 1.5, and 2.0.

3. The database table shown in Figure 2.30 contains a dataset with the following five attributes: *color* (yellow, purple), *size* (large, small), *act* (stretch, dip),

■ FIGURE 2.28
Table for Apriori
example

TID	Items
1	1, 3, 4, 5, 6, 7, 9, 10
2	2, 4, 5, 7, 8, 9, 10
3	1, 2, 3, 4, 10
4	2, 4, 5, 6, 7, 10
5	1, 3, 4, 5, 7, 8
6	3, 5, 7, 8, 9, 10
7	1, 3, 4, 8, 9, 10
8	2, 5, 6, 7, 8, 9
9	1, 3, 4, 5, 6, 7, 10
10	1, 2, 3, 4, 5, 7, 8, 9, 10

■ FIGURE 2.29
A weighted
directed graph

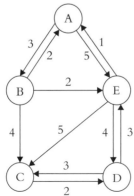

■ FIGURE 2.30
Balloon table

Color	Size	Act	Age	Inflated
Yellow	Small	Stretch	Adult	T
Yellow	Small	Stretch	Child	T
Yellow	Small	Dip	Adult	T
Yellow	Small	Dip	Child	T
Yellow	Large	Stretch	Adult	T
Yellow	Large	Stretch	Child	F
Yellow	Large	Dip	Adult	F
Yellow	Large	Dip	Child	F
Purple	Small	Stretch	Adult	T
Purple	Small	Stretch	Child	F
Purple	Small	Dip	Adult	F
Purple	Small	Dip	Child	F
Purple	Large	Stretch	Adult	T
Purple	Large	Stretch	Child	F
Purple	Large	Dip	Adult	F
Purple	Large	Dip	Child	F

age (adult, child), and *inflated* (T, F). Follow the method used in Section 2.6 for generating compact rules to derive all rules with full confidence.

4. The major-salary table in Figure 2.31 shows 30 instances of IT professionals in terms of four attributes: *age*, *education*, *major* (computer science, electrical engineering, management information science, decision science), and *salary*. Construct conceptual hierarchies for *age*, *edu*, *major*, and *salary*. Generate interesting learning tasks for deriving discrimination and characteristic rules from the table. Use the AO induction method to derive either discrimination or characteristic rules based on the learning tasks generated.

5. Figure 2.32 shows a contact lenses table that contains information about contact lens prescriptions (hard lenses, soft lenses, and no contact lenses). From the table, derive quantitative association rules by mapping tables to Boolean association rules.

■ **FIGURE 2.31**
Major–salary table

ID	Age	Edu	Major	Salary	ID	Age	Edu	Major	Salary
1	35	Ph.D	EE	70K	16	34	B.S	MIS	58K
2	45	B.S	EE	60K	17	36	Ph.D	EE	64K
3	55	B.S	CS	65K	18	34	Ph.D	CS	70K
4	28	M.S	EE	45K	19	56	M.S	CS	72K
5	32	B.S	DS	46K	20	52	B.S	EE	65K
6	31	B.S	EE	44K	21	37	M.S	CS	62K
7	42	B.S	EE	55K	22	42	Ph.D	MIS	70K
8	29	M.S	DS	41K	23	42	M.S	CS	69K
9	35	Ph.D	CS	72K	24	38	Ph.D	MIS	73K
10	39	Ph.D	CS	75K	25	45	M.S	CS	65K
11	41	Ph.D	CS	75K	26	49	M.S	CS	67K
12	32	B.S	DS	43K	27	36	Ph.D	MIS	69K
13	54	M.S	CS	68K	28	28	M.S	EE	46K
14	37	M.S	EE	56K	29	36	B.S	EE	46K
15	35	Ph.D	DS	67K	30	32	Ph.D	CS	77K

■ **FIGURE 2.32**
Contact lenses
table

ID	Age	Spectacle	Astigmatic	Tear Production	Contact lens
1	21	Myope	No	Reduced	None
2	24	Myope	No	Normal	Soft
3	20	Myope	Yes	Reduced	None
4	26	Myope	Yes	Normal	Hard
5	27	Hypermetrope	No	Reduced	None
6	22	Hypermetrope	No	Normal	Soft
7	28	Hypermetrope	Yes	Reduced	None
8	27	Hypermetrope	Yes	Normal	Hard
9	38	Myope	No	Reduced	None
10	32	Myope	No	Normal	Soft
11	36	Myope	Yes	Reduced	None
12	37	Myope	Yes	Normal	Hard
13	33	Hypermetrope	No	Reduced	None
14	32	Hypermetrope	No	Normal	Soft
15	39	Hypermetrope	Yes	Reduced	None
16	34	Hypermetrope	Yes	Normal	None
17	52	Myope	No	Reduced	None
18	51	Myope	No	Normal	None
19	50	Myope	Yes	Reduced	None
20	54	Myope	Yes	Normal	Hard
21	52	Hypermetrope	No	Reduced	None
22	55	Hypermetrope	No	Normal	Soft
23	58	Hypermetrope	Yes	Reduced	None
24	54	Hypermetrope	Yes	Normal	None

■ 2.10   SELECTED BIBLIOGRAPHIC NOTES

The Apriori and AprioriTid algorithms described in Section 2.2 are from [Agrawal 1994]. General survey and comparisons of various association-rule mining algorithms are given in [Hipp 2000]. [Agrawal 1994] and [Manilla 1994a] give new and improved methods for discovering association rules. Generalized association-rule mining is discussed in [Srikant 1995], whereas [Denwattana 2001] gives a parameterized algorithm for association-rule mining. Temporal constraints in association-rule generation are from [Li 2003], [Lee 2001], and [Ting 2003]. Detailed algorithms and strategies for mining attribute-oriented associations described in Section 2.3 are directly from [Han 1992] and [Hwang 1995]. [Brin 1997] discusses the problem of generalizing association rules to correlations, whereas the mining of regression rules and trees is shown in [Sher 1998].

Special hashing techniques are used to improve the efficiency of association-rule mining in [Ozel 2001] and [Park 1997]. Generating navigation patterns of users on hypertext-based web pages is an important application area of association-rule mining. Section 2.4 addresses this issue. The method of rule generation proposed is from [Borges 1998]. Preserving data privacy in mining of association rules is covered in [Evfimievski 2002] and [Rizvi 2002]. Special constraints other than minimum support and confidence are used in [Bayardo 1999] and [Yen 2001].

Special techniques for mining of special patterns from data are proposed in [Monge 1996], [Pei 2001], [Michail 2000], [Nahm 1986], and [Nahm 2002]. For induction used as the primary tool for knowledge extraction, see [Moshkovich 2002], [Wu 1999], and [Stefanowski 1994]. Relating association rules with weights is discussed in [Cai 1998], whereas [Pôssas 2000] and [Hong 1999] address the issue of generating association rules from quantitative data. The method for generating quantitative association rules presented in Section 2.5 is from [Srikant 1996]. Memory-adaptive association-rule mining is discussed in [Nanopoulos 2004]. For predictive association-rule discovery, see [Megiddo 1998].

For efficient algorithms for association-rule mining in large databases, see [Savasere 1995], [Agrawal 1993], and [Han 1999]. [Cheung 1996] and [Dehaspe 1995] discuss the mining of association rules in distributed databases and multiple relations. For parallel mining of association rules, see [Agrawal 1996]. The algorithm presented in Section 2.6 for generating compact rules is proposed in [Yen 1995]. The chapter concluded with a discussion of time-constrained association-rule mining. The material presented in this section is proposed in [Huysmans 2004]. [Liu 1998] discusses the integration of classification with association-rule mining. The application of association rules for protein-protein interaction networks is proposed in [Besemann 2004], whereas its application to remotely sensed data is discussed in [Dong 2000]. Concepts of decision rules and decision trees are used in [Quinlan 1987] and [Shan 1993] to generate rules from databases. Association-rule mining is combined with formal concept analysis in [Deogun 1998]. For approximate rule mining, see [Nayak 2001].

■ 2.11 CHAPTER BIBLIOGRAPHY

[Agrawal 1993] R. Agrawal, T. Imielinski, and A. Swami: "Mining Association Rules Between Sets of Items in Large Databases," *ACM SIGMOD*, pp. 207–216, Washington, 1993.

[Agrawal 1994] R. Agrawal and R. Srikant: "Fast Algorithms for Mining Association Rules," *Proceedings of the 20th VLDB Conference*, Santiago, Chile, 1994.

[Agrawal 1996] R. Agrawal and J. C. Shafer: "Parallel Mining of Association Rules," *IEEE Transactions on Knowledge and Data Engineering*, Vol. 8, No. 6, pp. 962–969, 1996.

[Agrawal 2001] C. Agrawal and P. Yu: "A New Approach to Online Generation of Association Rules," *IEEE Transactions on Knowledge and Data Engineering*, Vol. 13, No. 4, pp. 527–540, 2001.

[Bayardo 1999] R. Bayardo, R. Agrawal, and D. Cunopulos: "Constraint-Based Rule Mining in Large, Dense Databases," *Proceedings of the 15th International Conference on Data Engineering*, 1999.

[Besemann 2004] C. Besemann, A. Denton, and A. Yekkirala: "Differential Association Rule Mining for the Study of Protein-Protein Interaction Networks," *Proceedings of the 4th Workshop on Data Mining in Bioinformatics (BIOKDD)*, Seattle, WA, pp. 1–9, 2004.

[Borges 1998] J. Borges and M. Levene: "Mining Association Rules in Hypertext Databases," *International Conference on KDD*, pp. 149–153, 1998.

[Brin 1997] S. Brin, R. Motwani, and C. Silverstein: "Beyond Market Baskets—Generalizing Association Rules to Correlations," *SIGMOD*, pp. 265–276, 1997.

[Cai 1998] C. H. Cai, A. Fu, C. H. Cheng, and W. W. Kwong: "Mining Association Rules with Weighted Items," *Proceedings of IEEE International Database Engineering and Applications Symposium (IDEAS)*, United Kingdom, pp. 68–77, 1998.

[Cheung 1996] D. W. Cheung, V. T. Ng, A. W. Fu, and Y. Fu: "Efficient Mining of Association Rules in Distributed Databases," *IEEE Transactions on Knowledge and Data Engineering*, Vol. 8, No. 6, pp. 911–922, 1996.

[Dehaspe 1995] L. Dehaspe and L. De Raedt: "Mining Association Rules in Multiple Relations," *Proceedings of 7th International Workshop on ILP*, Vol. 1297 of LNCS, pp. 125–132, 1995.

[Denwattana 2001] N. Denwattana and J. R. Getta: "A parameterized algorithm for mining association rules," *Proceedings of the 12th Australasian Database Conference*, pp. 45–51, Queensland, Australia, 2001.

[Deogun 1998] J. Deogun, V. Raghavan, and H. Sever: "Association Mining and Formal Concept Analysis," *Proceedings of the 6th International Workshop on Rough Sets, Data Mining and Granular Computing*, Vol. 1, pp. 335–338, 1998.

[Dong 2000] J. Dong, W. Perrizo, Q. Ding, and J. Zhou: "The Application of Association Rule Mining to Remotely Sensed Data," *Proceedings of the ACM Symposium on Applied Computing*, pp. 340–45, Vol. 1, 2000.

[Evfimievski 2002] A. Evfimievski, R. Srikant, R. Agrawal, and J. Gehrke: "Privacy Preserving Mining of Association Rules," *Proceedings of 8th ACM SIGKDD International Conference on Knowledge Discovery and Data Mining (KDD)*, 2002.

[Han 1992] J. Han, Y. Cai, and N. Cercone: "Knowledge Discovery in Databases: An Attribute-Oriented Approach," *Proceedings of the 18th VLDB Conference*, Vancouver, *British Columbia, Canada*, 1992.

[Han 1999] J. Han, Y. Fu: "Mining Multiple-Level Association Rules in Large Databases," *IEEE Transactions on Knowledge and Data Engineering*, Vol. 11, No. 5, pp. 1–8, 1999.

[Hipp 2000] J. Hipp, U. Guntzer, and G. Nakaeizadeh: "Algorithms for Association Rule Mining—A General Survey and Comparison," *ACM SIGKDD Explorations*, Vol. 2, No. 1, pp. 58–64, 2000.

[Hong 1999] T. P. Hong, C. S. Kuo, S. C. Chi: "Mining Association Rules from Quantitative Data," *Intelligent Data Analysis*, Vol. 3, pp. 363–376, 1999.

[Huysmans 2004] J. Huysmans, B. Baesens, C. Mues, and J. Vanthienen: "Web Usage Mining with Time Constrained Association Rules," *Proceedings of the 6th International Conference on Enterprise Information Systems (ICEIS)*, Porto, Portugal, pp. 343–348, 2004.

[Hwang 1995] H. Hwang and W. Fu: "Efficient Algorithms for Attribute-Oriented Induction," *International Conference on KDD*, 1995.

[Lee 2001] C. H. Lee, C. R. Lin, and M. S. Chen: "On Mining General Temporal Association Rules in a Publication Database," *ICDM*, pp. 337–344, 2001.

[Li 2003] Y. Li, P. Ning, X. S. Wang, and S. Jajodia: "Discovering Calendar-based Temporal Association Rules," *Data and Knowledge Engineering*, Vol. 44, No. 2, pp. 193–218, 2003.

[Liu 1998] B. Liu, W. Hsu, Y. Ma: "Integrating Classification and Association Rule Mining," *Proceedings of International Conference on Knowledge Discovery in Databases*, pp. 80–86, 1998.

[Mannila 1994a] H. Mannila, H. Toivonen, A. Verkamo: "Efficient Algorithms for Discovering Association Rules," *Proceedings of AAAI Workshop: Knowledge Discovery in Databases*, pp. 181–192, 1994.

[Mannila 1994b] H. Mannila, H. Toivonen, and A. Verkamo: "Improved Methods for Finding Association Rules," *Proceedings of AAAI Workshop: Knowledge Discovery in Databases*, 1994.

[Megiddo 1998] N. Megiddo and R. Srikant: "Discovering Predictive Association Rules," *Proceedings of the 4th International Conference on Knowledge Discovery in Databases and Data Mining*, pp. 274–278, New York, 1998.

[Mehta 1996] M. Mehta, R. Agrawal, and J. Rissanen: "SLIQ: A Fast Scalable Classifier for Data Mining," *EDBT*, pp. 18–32, 1996

[Michail 2000] A. Michail: "Data Mining Library Reuse Patterns Using Generalized Association Rules," *International Conference on Software Engineering*, pp. 167–176, 2000.

[Monge 1996] A. E. Monge and C. P. Elkan: "The Field Matching Problem: Algorithms and Applications," *Proceedings of the 2nd International Conference on Knowledge Discovery and Data Mining*, pp. 267–270, 1996.

[Moshkovich 2002] H. M. Moshkovich, A. Mechitov, and D. L. Olson: "Rule Induction in Data Mining: Effect of Ordinal Scales," *Expert Systems with Applications*, Vol. 22, pp. 303–311, 2002.

[Nahm 1986] U. Y. Nahm and R. J. Mooney: "Mining Soft-Matching Rules from Textual Data," *IJCAI*, pp. 979–986, 2001.

[Nahm 2002] U. Y. Nahm and R. J. Mooney: "Mining Soft-Matching Association Rules," *Proceedings of the CIKM*, pp. 681–683, McLean, VA, 2002.

[Nanopoulos 2004] A. Nanopoulos and Y. Manolopoulos: "Memory-adaptive Association Rules Mining," *Information Systems*, Vol. 29, No. 5, pp. 365–384, 2004.

[Nayak 2001] J. R. Nayak and D. J. Cook: "Approximate Association Rule Mining," *FLAIRS Conference* (http://ranger.uta.edu/~cook/pubs/flairsj01.pdf), pp. 259–263, 2001.

[Ozel 2001] S. A. Ozel and H. A. Guvenir: "An Algorithm for Mining Association Rules Using Perfect Hashing and Database Pruning," *Proceedings of the 10th Turkish Symposium on Artificial Intelligence and Neural Networks (TAINN)*, A. Acan, I. Aybay, and M. Salamah (Eds.), Gazimagusa, T.R.N.C. pp. 257–264, 2001.

[Park 1997] J. S. Park, M. S. Chen, and P. S. Yu: "Using a Hash-Based Method with Transaction Trimming for Mining Association Rules," *IEEE Transactions on Knowledge and Data Engineering*, pp. 813–825, Vol. 9, No. 5, 1997.

[Pei 2001] J. Pei, A. K. H. Tung, and J. Han: "Fault-Tolerant Frequent Pattern Mining: Problems and Challenges," *Proceedings of the 2001 ACM-SIGMOD International Workshop on Research Issues on Data Mining and Knowledge Discovery (DMKD)*, Santa Barbara, CA, 2001.

[Pôssas 2000] B. Pôssas, W. Meira Jr., M. Carvalho, and R. Resende: "Using Quantitative Information for Efficient Association Rule Generation," *SIGMOD Record*, Vol. 29, No. 4, pp. 19–25, 2000.

[Quinlan 1987] J. R. Quinlan: "Generating Production Rules From Decision Trees," *Proceeding of the IJCAIS*, pp. 304–307, 1987.

[Rizvi 2002] S. Rizvi and J. Haritsa: "Maintaining Data Privacy in Association Rule Mining," *Proceedings of the 28th VLDB Conference*, Hong Kong, China, 2002.

[Savasere 1995] A. Savasere, E. Omiecinski, and S. Navathe: "An Efficient Algorithm for Mining Association Rules in Large Databases," *Proceedings of the 2nd VLDB Conference*, Zurich, Switzerland, pp. 432–444, 1995.

[Shan 1993] N. Shan and W. Ziarko: "An Incremental Learning Algorithm for Constructing Decision Rules," *Proceedings of the International Workshop on Rough Sets and Knowledge Discovery*, Banff, Canada, pp. 326–334, 1993.

[Sher 1998] B. Y. Sher, S. C. Shao, and W. S. Hsieh: "Mining Regression Rules and Regression Trees," *PAKDD*, pp. 271–282, 1998.

[Srikant 1995] R. Srikant and R. Agrawal: "Fast Algorithms for Mining Association Rules," *Proceeding of the 21st VLDB Conference*, Zurich, Switzerland, 1995.

[Srikant 1996] R. Srikant and R. Agrawal: "Mining Quantitative Association Rules in Large Relational Tables," *SIGMOD*, pp. 1–12, 1996.

[Stefanowski 1994] J. Stefanowski and D. Vanderpooten: "A General Two-Stage Approach to Inducing Rules from Examples," *Rough Sets, Fuzzy Sets and Knowledge Discovery*, pp. 317–325, 1994.

[Wu 1999] X. Wu and D. Urpani: "Induction by Attribute Elimination," *IEEE Transactions on Knowledge and Data Engineering*, Vol. 11, pp. 805–812, 1999.

[Yen 1995] S. Yen and A. Chen: "An Efficient Algorithm for Deriving Compact Rules from Databases," *Proceedings of the 4th International Conference on Database Systems for Advanced Applications (DASFAA)*, pp. 364–371, Singapore, 1995.

[Yen 2001] S. Yen and A. Chen: "A Graph-Based Approach for Discovering Various Types of Association Rules," *IEEE Transactions on Knowledge and Data Engineering*, Vol. 13, No. 5, pp. 839–845, 2001.

[Ying 2003] L. Yingjiu, P. Ning, X. S. Wang, and S. Jajodia: "Discovering Calendar-based Temporal Association Rules," *Data and Knowledge Engineering*, Vol. 44, No. 2, pp. 193–218, 2003.

CHAPTER 3

Classification Learning

■ 3.1 INTRODUCTION

Classification learning is a learning scheme for categorizing unseen examples into predefined classes based on a set of training examples. The learning algorithm generates a set of classification rules from a complete set of independent examples of instances and their corresponding categories, and then the generated rules are used to predict the classes or categories of novel instances.

The purpose of classification learning is to predict the classes of instances, in contrast with other methods. Association learning predicts not only classes but also attributes that are used in inducing the classes. In clustering, the classes are not predefined but are unknown at the point of learning, and the learning task is to define and identify the classes in the database. In numeric prediction or regression, classes are composed not of discrete categories but of continuous numeric values, but otherwise regression learning uses techniques very similar to classification learning and is sometimes considered a subtype of classification learning.

A typical application of classification learning requires the following characteristics: (1) predefined classes, (2) discrete data domains (except in regression learning), (3) a sufficient amount of training data, with at least as many examples as the number of classes, and (4) attribute values that are flat rather than structured data such that the values are fixed and each attribute has either a discrete or a numeric value.

Among the many algorithms used for classification learning, three major approaches to defining classification rules are found. The first approach uses a top-down, "divide and conquer" technique to induce knowledge rules by organizing all instances of the dataset into a "decision tree" based on a series of outcomes of tests peformed on each attribute. The "divide and conquer" approach selects one attribute and partitions the dataset into subsets based on the outcome of a test, then recursively applies the process to the partitions until pure subsets are reached (all members are classified to only one class). This process of tree creation is in fact the process of heuristically searching for all possible classification rules. The classification rules can be directly generated from the tree by traversing through the paths from the root to each leaf. Several sophisticated systems have been developed during the last two decades. The most notable ones are **Cart** [Breiman 1984], **ID3** [Quinlan 1979, 1983, 1986], and its successors **C4.5** [Quinlan 1993] and **C5.0** [Quinlan 1997].

The second approach uses a top-down "separate and conquer" or "covering" technique that takes each class in turn and directly induces a set of rules, each covering as many instances of the class as possible (and excluding as few instances of other classes as possible) without erecting the tree first. After a rule is induced, the covered instances are excluded or separated from further induction. The "separate and conquer" approach is concerned with only one class at a time, and performs all the tests to quickly purify the subset, whereas both subsets may not be pure in the "divide and conquer" approach. Since there are some limitations in the representation of the classified rules, this process is less accurate than the "divide and conquer" approach, but faster because it does not follow the heuristic tree-searching procedure. Systems such as **Prism** [Cendrowska 1987], **Induct** [Gaines 1995], **IREP** [Furnkranz 1994], and **RIPPER** [Cohen 1995] use this approach.

The third approach, the "partial decision-tree" approach [Frank 1998], is a combination of the "divide and conquer" and "separate and conquer" approaches. It produces rules by inducing partial decision trees and separating the covered instances from further induction.

The goals of these approaches are to accurately and efficiently induce classification knowledge from a dataset. In this chapter, we will compare the three approaches mentioned above by introducing algorithms for each approach, with examples of how each algorithm is applied, and examine the advantages and disadvantages of each one.

Before we delve into the details of each algorithm, the representations of the knowledge extracted by the data-mining procedures are introduced. Each algorithm will use one of these forms to represent learned concepts or intermediate results.

■ 3.2 KNOWLEDGE REPRESENTATION

Two major kinds of knowledge representation are used in classification learning: the decision tree and the classification rule.

■ 3.2.1 Classification Rules

Classification rules are the simplest representation of classification knowledge. Each classification rule is composed of a condition, which includes one or more tests, and a conclusion, which associates an instance with the class to which it belongs. Knowledge rules are expressed in the form "if the attribute X is xxx and the attribute Y is yyy, etc., then the instance Z belongs to class zzz." To each class there corresponds a set of relevant attribute values. After the complete set of rules generated from a dataset is sorted by the classes, they constitute a rule list used to represent the complete classification information over the dataset.

Classification rules are simple, straightforward, and easy to understand. The limitation of classification rules is that they cannot resolve conflicting information. If more than one rule have the same condition but specify different classes for the instance, additional attributes are required to resolve the contradiction and form a new knowledge rule.

■ 3.2.2 Decision Trees

The decision trees shown in Figure 3.1 represent the integrated classification knowledge of a system. Each internal node represents a test over one or more attributes and corresponds to the condition of a classification rule. Each branch represents an outcome of the test. The leaf nodes indicate the classes corresponding to the conclusions of the classification rules. To identify an instance, move from the root down to the leaves according to the test results of successive internal nodes. The leaf arrived at shows the class if belongs to.

Classification rules and decision trees represent the same knowledge and are therefore interchangeable in most instances. We can directly generate rules from a simple tree. However, for a complex tree, the process of conversion is not that easy. Although classification rules are simpler and easier to understand than decision trees, there are potential problems with conflicting information. Moreover, decision trees give an integrated, complete view of classification information for the domain. On the other hand, classification

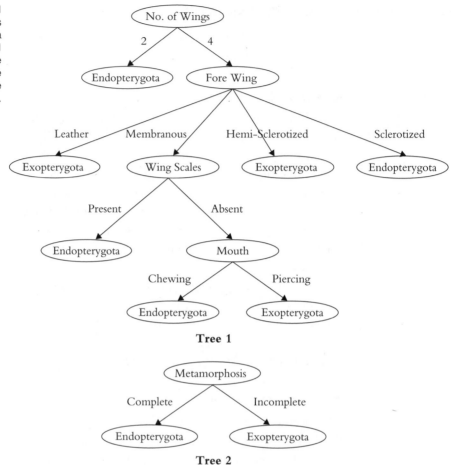

FIGURE 3.1
Decision trees derived from data in Table 3.1. Tree 1 is a random tree and tree 2 is a tree induced from the ID3 algorithm.

rules are the ultimate representation of the knowledge used in all algorithms for classification learning, whereas decision trees are only used in the "divide and conquer" and "partial decision tree" algorithms as an intermediate tool.

■ 3.3   SEPARATE-AND-CONQUER APPROACH

The "separate and conquer" or "covering" technique takes each class and creates rules that cover as many instances of this class as possible while excluding as few instances of other classes as possible. This approach examines only one class at a time. For each class, it builds a rule by selecting and adding tests to the rule until all the subset of instances covered by the rule are "pure" (e.g., all members belong to only one class). The covered subset of instances is then excluded from further processing. The rule-generation process continues until no more unclassified instances are left in the dataset. The advantage of this approach is time efficiency as a result of the following two characteristics: first, it creates knowledge rules directly without inducing an intermediate decision tree; secondly, it immediately excludes instances covered by a newly created rule from further induction.

The criteria used for test selection and the standard of "purity" vary among different algorithms using this approach. For example, in the Prism algorithm, it is assumed that the accuracy of a rule can be measured by the proportion of correct predictions it makes over the entire set of instances covered by the rule. A candidate rule is refined by selecting and adding tests that maximize this quantity until the rule reaches 100% purity or there are no more tests. In the Induct algorithm, the test selection is based on information gain, and this algorithm is robust against noisy data.

■ 3.3.1 Prism

This simple and straightforward covering algorithm works by first picking a class from the dataset for which to create a new rule having the class as its conclusion, and selectively adding tests to the condition of the rule, striving for maximum number of instances covered and 100% accuracy. The accuracy of a test is measured by the ratio of the number of positive instances p to the total number of instances covered by the rule t: p/t. The positive instances covered by the new rule then are removed from the dataset for further rule generation. Then, negative instances should remain in the dataset to await a later iteration of the process. This process continues until no more instances remain to be covered.

Let's consider a simple database in Table 3.1 as an example and show how the algorithm is applied to generate classification rules. This database contains information on morphological characteristics and suborders of ten insects. The purpose of this learning task is to create rules that associate insects to the right suborders according to their characteristics.

Let's randomly pick the suborder *Endopterygota* as the class of the first rule: "If ?, then the suborder is *Endopterygota*." Since the new rule initially has no tests in its condition part, it is not useful yet. It covers six instances. The

■ **TABLE 3.1 Morphological characteristics and suborders of some insects**

Name	No. of Wings	Forewing	Wing Scales	Mouth	Meta-morphosis	Hind Leg	Abdomen Needle	Suborder
Fly	2	Membrane	Absent	Sponging	Complete	Walking	Absent	Endopterygota
Wasp	4	Membrane	Absent	Chewing	Complete	Walking	Present	Endopterygota
Bee	4	Membrane	Absent	Chewing	Complete	Walking	Present	Endopterygota
Beetle	4	Sclerotized	Absent	Chewing	Complete	Walking	Absent	Endopterygota
Butter-fly	4	Membrane	Present	Siphoning	Complete	Walking	Absent	Endopterygota
Moth	4	Membrane	Present	Siphoning	Complete	Walking	Absent	Endopterygota
True Bug	4	Hemi-Sclerotized	Absent	Piercing	Incomplete	Walking	Absent	Exopterygota
Aphid	4	Membrane	Absent	Piercing	Incomplete	Walking	Absent	Exopterygota
Grass hopper	4	Leather	Absent	Chewing	Incomplete	Jumping	Absent	Exopterygota
Cock-roach	4	Leather	Absent	Chewing	Incomplete	Walking	Absent	Exopterygota

question is which *attribute* = *value* tests need to be added to the rule. The decision is made based on the accuracy of each possible test. For example, the accuracy of the test *number of wings* = 4 is measured by the ratio of the number of correct instances (p)—the number of instances satisfying the test—to the total number of instances (of any class) satisfying the test (t). We select the test with the highest accuracy, that is, p/t value. From Table 3.1, a list of the p/t values for each test is shown below:

Characteristics	**p/t**
No. of wings 2	*1/1*
4	*5/9*
Forewing membranous	*5/6*
sclerotized	*1/1*
hemi-sclerotized	*0/1*
leather	*0/2*

Wing with scales present	*2/2*
absent	*4/8*
Mouth sponging	*1/1*
chewing	*3/5*
siphoning	*2/2*
piercing	*0/2*
Hind leg walking	*6/9*
jumping	*0/1*
Abdomen needle present	*2/2*
absent	*4/8*
Metamorphosis complete	*6/6*
incomplete	*0/4*

From this list, we see that seven candidates are tied at a p/t value of 100%: *no. of wings 2, wing sclerotized, wing with scales present, mouth sponging, mouth siphoning, abdomen needle present*, and *metamorphosis complete*. However, because *metamorphosis complete* covers the most instances, we choose it as the first test to be added to the rule, yielding the following rule:

"If metamorphosis is complete, then the insect is in the suborder Endopterygota."

Do we need to add more terms to the new rule? Let's test the purity of the subset covered by the rule. In our case, the purity of the above rule is 100%. Therefore, no more terms need to be added. After the rule is formed, all six instances covered by the rule are then removed from the dataset for further processing. There are now four instances left in the dataset. Using the same strategy, we create the following additional rule:

"If metamorphosis is incomplete, the insect is in the suborder Exopterygota."

This second rule covers all four instances left in the dataset. So, no more rules are needed.

As this example shows, Prism works in three steps to build a classification rule:

1. First, it identifies the attribute-value pairs with the highest p/t ratio as candidate tests to add to the condition term of the rule.
2. If there is a tie among several tests, the test that covers the most positive instances will be selected.

3. After the accuracy of the rule reaches 100% or there are no more attributes left, the process of adding additional tests to the condition term of the rule stops, and the positive instances covered by the rule are removed from the dataset.

The Prism algorithm is summarized in Figure 3.2 below:

■ **FIGURE 3.2**
The Prism rule-
generation
algorithm

```
For each class C
   Initialize E to the instance set
   While E contains instances in class C
      Create a rule R with an empty condition that predicts class C
      Until R is perfect (or there are no more attributes to use) do
         For each attribute A not mentioned in R, and each value V,
            Consider all possible tests A = V for the condition of R
            Calculate p/t values for all possible tests A = V
            Select A and V to maximize the accuracy p/t
            (break ties by choosing the condition with
             the largest p/t ratio)
         Add A = V to R
      Remove the positive instances covered by R from E
```

In real-world applications, data is not always as sound and clean as in our example, especially in large databases. In these circumstances, the 100% accuracy requirement of the rule cannot be satisfied. The Prism algorithm cannot handle this situation and potentially useful information might be ignored. In some applications, a certain level of error is allowed for predictions.

To overcome the over-fitting difficulty in the Prism algorithm, Gaines and Compton [Gaines 1995] proposed a new system called Induct, which uses probability to measure the degree of "goodness" of rules.

■ 3.3.2 Induct

The Induct algorithm inherited the idea of "separate and conquer" from Prism. Unlike Prism, the Induct algorithm does not use 100% accuracy as the measure of "goodness" for rules. Instead, it uses probability to measure the worth of a rule. Moreover, an additional post-pruning process is conducted after "perfect" rules are formed to trim off the over-fitted conditions according to the probability measures.

The key difference in Induct is the use of a probability measure to measure the "goodness" of a rule instead of the accuracy p/t, which is used in the Prism algorithm. This is the probability that a randomly chosen rule will have accuracy the same as or higher than a given rule. If the odds are high for a randomly created rule to have better accuracy than the rule being tested, then the rule being tested is probably not a reliable one.

In general, the probability measurement agrees with the accuracy measurement of Prism: a rule with higher accuracy usually has a lower probability measure. The difference is that the probability is sensitive to not only the accuracy but also the coverage of the rule. A rule with high accuracy may still have a high probability measure if its coverage is very narrow. For example, consider the perfect rule "If wing is membranous and wing scales are present, then the suborder is *Endopterygota*." Given the data in Table 3.1, the accuracy of this rule is 2/2 or 100%, while the overall coverage of the dataset is 6/10. This rule covers two positive cases. The probability of a randomly chosen rule being at least as good as this rule is 0.33 (the details of the probability measure calculation will be explained below). When we loosen the condition of this rule by removing the last test, "wing scales are present," the rule's coverage increases to five positive instances out of six (accuracy of 83%). Although the accuracy dropped from 100% to 83%, the probability measure further drops to 0.071, since the new rule covers six instances instead of two.

To calculate the probability of a random rule having at least the same accuracy as the rule being tested, we first derive the probability of a random rule having an exact number of positive instances, i. This rule has the accuracy i/t, where t is the total number of instances the rule covers. For a better rule or a more accurate rule to be generated, the number of positive instances predicted must be greater than i. If the rule being tested covers t instances and i instances are positive, there exist $t - i$ possible "better" rules. The sum of the probabilities of all such "better" rules and of the rule with exactly i positive instances is the probability of a randomly generated rule having accuracy of at least i/t.

The probability of a rule that covers t instances and has exactly p positive instances in class c is expressed as follows:

Given Pr[*of t instances selected at random, exactly p instances are in class c*], *then the probability of a randomly generated rule having the same or better accuracy than i/t can be expressed as*

$$M(R) = \sum_{n=i}^{t} \text{Pr[of } t \text{ instances selected at random, exactly } n \text{ instances are in class } c]$$

■ **FIGURE 3.3**
Relationship
among various
factors used
in probability
measurement

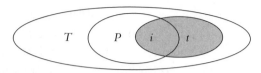

T : total number of instances in the dataset
t : total number of instances covered by the condition of rule R
P : total number of positive instances belonging to class c in the dataset
i : total number of positive instances covered by the condition of rule R

First, let's see how to derive the probability of a randomly chosen rule having exactly i positive instances when it covers t instances. As shown in Figure 3.3, the dataset has T total instances, of which P instances belong to class c. A randomly generated rule covers t instances, of which i instances belong to class c. We are selecting i instances of class c from the positive subset of the dataset with P instances and, at the same time, choosing $t - i$ instances from the rest of the instance set which contains $T - P$ instances. Therefore, the probability of a randomly selected rule R with i positive instances of class c can be expressed as follows:

$$\Pr[\text{of } t \text{ instances selected at random, exactly } i \text{ instances are in the class } c] = \frac{\binom{P}{i}\binom{T-P}{t-i}}{\binom{T}{t}}$$

The probability distribution is hypergeometric. We assume that the selection is done "without replacement." For example, suppose that we derived a rule "If *tear production* rate is **not** *reduced* and *age* is *presbyopic* and *prescription* is *hypermetrope*, then the *recommended contact lens* is *none*" from the contact lens dataset in Table 3.2. The probability of the rule occurring randomly is calculated as follows with $T = 24$, $P = 15$, $t = 2$, and $i = 1$.

$$\Pr[\text{of 2 instances selected at random, exactly 1 is in class } \textit{none}] = \frac{\binom{15}{1}\binom{9}{1}}{\binom{24}{2}} = 0.49$$

From the equation above, we see that the probability of a random rule with accuracy 1/2 is 0.49. Thus, the probability of a randomly chosen rule that will do as well as or better than the above rule R is calculated as the sum of the probabilities of the random rules with one positive instance (accuracy 1/2) and two positive instances (accuracy 2/2), with $T = 24$, $P = 15$, $t = 2$, and $i = 1, 2$.

$$M(R) = \sum_{i}^{t} \Pr[\text{of two instances selected at random, exactly } i \text{ instances are in class } \textit{none}] = \sum_{i=1}^{2} \frac{\binom{15}{i}\binom{9}{2-i}}{\binom{24}{2}} = 0.49 + 0.38 = 0.87$$

The Induct algorithm is a two-stage process. The first stage is the rule-formation stage, which is adopted from the Prism algorithm. The second stage is the post-pruning stage. In the second stage, Induct trims off the tests of each rule one by one, in reverse order, until the probability measure increases. After this post-pruning process, the rules will no longer be over-fitting.

The procedure for rule generation and trimming, which is used to generate a good rule set, is summarized in Figure 3.4:

▨ FIGURE 3.4 Rule generation algorithm with probability measurement

```
Initialize T to be the instance set;
repeat
   do
      for each class C for which T contains an instance
         (1) use the basic covering algorithm to create a perfect rule
             for class C;
         (2) calculate the probability measure M(R) for the rule;
         (3) calculate the probability measure M(R-) for the rule with
             the final condition removed;
         (4) if M(R-) < M(R), remove the final condition from the rule;
         (5) repeat steps (3) and (4) until M(R-) > M(R);
         (6) add the rule to the rule set;
         (7) remove all the instances covered by the rule from T.
      done
until T is empty;
```

Let's take Cendrowska's contact lens example to illustrate Induct's performance on a test dataset [Cendrowska 1987]. This dataset is shown in

■ **TABLE 3.2 The contact lens data**

Age	Spectacle Prescription	Astigmatism	Tear Production Rate	Recommended Contact Lens
Young	Myope	No	Reduced	None
Young	Myope	No	Normal	Soft
Young	Myope	Yes	Reduced	None
Young	Myope	Yes	Normal	Hard
Young	Hypermetrope	No	Reduced	None
Young	Hypermetrope	No	Normal	Soft
Young	Hypermetrope	Yes	Reduced	None
Young	Hypermetrope	Yes	Normal	Hard
Pre-presbyopic	Myope	No	Reduced	None
Pre-presbyopic	Myope	No	Normal	Soft
Pre-presbyopic	Myope	Yes	Reduced	None
Pre-presbyopic	Myope	Yes	Normal	Hard
Pre-presbyopic	Hypermetrope	No	Reduced	None
Pre-presbyopic	Hypermetrope	No	Normal	Soft
Pre-presbyopic	Hypermetrope	Yes	Reduced	None
Pre-presbyopic	Hypermetrope	Yes	Normal	None
Presbyopic	Myope	No	Reduced	None
Presbyopic	Myope	No	Normal	None
Presbyopic	Myope	Yes	Reduced	None
Presbyopic	Myope	Yes	Normal	Hard
Presbyopic	Hypermetrope	No	Reduced	None
Presbyopic	Hypermetrope	No	Normal	Soft
Presbyopic	Hypermetrope	Yes	Reduced	None
Presbyopic	Hypermetrope	Yes	Normal	None

Table 3.2. It contains the relationships between the characteristics of patients and their appropriate contact lens types.

The process of applying the Induct algorithm to this dataset starts with selecting a class. Since the class "*recommended contact lens = none*" covers 15 instances, which is more than the number covered by any other class, we select it as the first class for which to generate new rules. The list of accuracy (p/t) values of the tests for the class is given below:

Tests	***p/t***
Age is *young*	4/8
Age is *pre-presbyopic*	5/8
Age is *presbyopic*	6/8
Spectacle prescription is *myope*	7/12
Spectacle prescription is *hypermetrope*	8/12
Astigmatism is *no*	7/12
Astigmatism is *yes*	8/12
Tear production rate is *reduced*	12/12
Tear production rate is *normal*	3/12

From the list, the test with highest accuracy value (p/t) is "*tear production rate reduced*," which is 12/12. Therefore, the initial condition term of the rule should be "tear production rate reduced." Since the accuracy (p/t) value is 100%, we do not need to add more tests to the rule. Therefore, the first rule generated is

"If tear production rate is reduced, then the recommended contact lens is none."

After the instances covered by the above rule are excluded, the dataset is reduced as shown in Table 3.3. In the reduced dataset, there are still three instances of the class "*none*." More rules need to be created for the class *none*. A new list of accuracy (p/t) values is calculated to continue the process.

Tests	***p/t***
Age is *young*	0/4
Age is *pre-presbyopic*	1/4
Age is *presbyopic*	2/4
Spectacle prescription is *myope*	1/6
Spectacle prescription is *hypermetrope*	2/6
Astigmatism is *no*	1/6
Astigmatism is *yes*	2/6
Tear production rate is *normal*	3/12

From the list, "*age is presbyopic*" has the highest p/t value. Therefore, we choose "*age is presbyopic*" as the initial condition term of the second new rule. Since the p/t value is not 100%, we continue to add more terms to the rule.

TABLE 3.3 Contact lens dataset after the first rule is created

Age	Spectacle Prescription	Astigmatism	Tear Production Rate	Recommended Contact Lens
Young	Myope	No	Normal	Soft
Young	Myope	Yes	Normal	Hard
Young	Hypermetrope	No	Normal	Soft
Young	Hypermetrope	Yes	Normal	Hard
Pre-presbyopic	Myope	No	Normal	Soft
Pre-presbyopic	Myope	Yes	Normal	Hard
Pre-presbyopic	Hypermetrope	No	Normal	Soft
Pre-presbyopic	Hypermetrope	Yes	Normal	None
Presbyopic	Myope	No	Normal	None
Presbyopic	Myope	Yes	Normal	Hard
Presbyopic	Hypermetrope	No	Normal	Soft
Presbyopic	Hypermetrope	Yes	Normal	None

The two tests "*prescription is hypermetrope*" and "*astigmatism is yes*" have the same p/t values and the same coverage. We can randomly choose "*prescription is hypermetrope*" to add to the condition of the rule. Now the p/t value for the combined terms is 1/2. The new rule is still not pure. The next candidate test would be "*astigmatism is yes.*" The p/t value after combining the three conditions is 1/1. Since the accuracy is 100%, no other condition is needed. The new rule covers only one instance. The second rule is the following:

> *"If age is presbyopic and prescription is hypermetrope and astigmatism is yes, then the recommended contact lens is none."*

Next, we drop the instance covered by this rule from the reduced dataset. It is important to point out that when more condition terms are added to a rule, at maximum only one test value can be used for the same attribute. For example, if the term "*age is presbyopic*" has already been selected, the term "*age is young*" cannot later be added to the rule, even if its p/t value is higher than any other test's, since the effect of combining the two test terms for the same attribute broadens rather than restricts the scope of the rule.

■ **TABLE 3.4 Contact lens dataset after all the instances associated with class "*none*" are removed**

Age	Spectacle Prescription	Astigmatism	Tear Production Rate	Recommended Contact Lens
Young	Myope	No	Normal	Soft
Young	Myope	Yes	Normal	Hard
Young	Hypermetrope	No	Normal	Soft
Young	Hypermetrope	Yes	Normal	Hard
Pre-presbyopic	Myope	No	Normal	Soft
Pre-presbyopic	Myope	Yes	Normal	Hard
Pre-presbyopic	Hypermetrope	No	Normal	Soft
Presbyopic	Myope	Yes	Normal	Hard
Presbyopic	Hypermetrope	No	Normal	Soft

By repeating this procedure as described above, two more rules are generated for the class "*recommended contact lens is none*":

1. *"If age is presbyopic and prescription is myope and astigmatism is no, then the recommended contact lens is none."*

2. *"If age is pre-presbyopic and prescription is hypermetrope and astigmatism is yes, then the recommended contact lens is none."*

After these rules are induced for the class "*none*," the dataset is reduced as shown in Table 3.4.

Next, we take *soft* as the next class for which to induce rules. The tests and their accuracy (p/t) values for the class are listed as follows:

Tests	*p/t*
Age is *young*	2/4
Age is *pre-presbyopic*	2/3
Age is *presbyopic*	1/2
Spectacle prescription is *myope*	2/5
Spectacle prescription is *hypermetrope*	3/4
Astigmatism is *no*	5/5

Astigmatism is *yes*	0/4
Tear production rate is *normal*	5/9

The test *"Astigmatism is no"* has the highest accuracy value. So, we select it as the first term of the new rule:

> *"If astigmatism is no, then the recommended contact lens is soft."*

It is the only conditional term needed for the new rule because the accuracy (p/t) ratio is 100%. After all the instances covered by the new rule (five total) are excluded from the reduced dataset, four instances are left in the dataset, as shown in Table 3.5.

Next, we take class *hard* which is the only class left in the dataset. The tests and their accuracy (p/t) values for the class are listed as follows:

Tests	***p/t***
Age is *young*	2/2
Age is *pre-presbyopic*	1/1
Age is *presbyopic*	1/1
Spectacle prescription is *myope*	3/3
Spectacle prescription is *hypermetrope*	1/1
Astigmatism is *yes*	4/4
Tear production rate is *normal*	4/4

From the list, the two tests *"astigmatism is yes"* and *"tear production rate is normal"* have the highest p/t ratios and coverage. We select *"astigmatism is yes"*

■ **TABLE 3.5 Contact lens dataset after all rules associated with classes *none* and *soft* are inducted**

Age	Spectacle Prescription	Astigmatism	Tear Production Rate	Recommended Contact Lens
Young	Myope	Yes	Normal	Hard
Young	Hypermetrope	Yes	Normal	Hard
Pre-presbyopic	Myope	Yes	Normal	Hard
Presbyopic	Myope	Yes	Normal	Hard

as the first term of the new rule. Since the p/t value of the test is 100%, the new rule for class *hard* is as follows:

"If astigmatism is yes, then the recommended contact lens is hard."

Since the new rule covers all four instances left in the reduced dataset, the process of rule formation is finished. In summary, six rules are induced from the contact lens dataset by the procedure. The following are the rules listed in the sequence they were created:

<Generated rule list>

Class: none

1. *"If tear production rate is reduced, then the recommended contact lens is none";*
2. *"If age is presbyopic and prescription is hypermetrope and astigmatism is yes, then the recommended contact lens is none";*
3. *"If age is presbyopic and prescription is myope and astigmatism is no, then the recommended contact lens is none";*
4. *"If age is pre-presbyopic and prescription is hypermetrope and astigmatism is yes, then the recommended contact lens is none."*

Class: soft

5. *"If astigmatism is no, then the recommended contact lens is soft."*

Class: hard

6. *"If astigmatism is yes, then the recommended contact lens is hard."*

The rule list represents the complete classification information of the contact lens dataset. It can be used to diagnose and make correct recommendations for patients. To identify an instance for the correct class, the rules are considered in turn from the beginning of the list and compared against the attributes of the instance until a matching rule is found. It is very important that rules in the rule list be applied in the same sequence as they were created. Because of the exclusion process, the rules produced later are induced without the knowledge of the instances covered by the previous rules. If we apply the rules created later first, the identified class may be incorrect. For example, if a case has the same attributes as those in row 23 of Table 3.2 and we use the last (sixth) rule in the rule list first, the answer will be *hard* instead of the correct class *none*.

Notice that each of the above rules in the list has an accuracy of 100%. They are potentially over-fitted. Next, we are going to post-prune the rules as introduced with Induct. Rules 1, 5, and 6 have only one conditional term and will not be considered in the pruning process. Rules 2, 3, and 4 have three conditional terms each. We will use the probability measure as the criterion to greedily trim off the over-fit conditions of these rules. Let's start with rule 2. As stated above, rules cannot be used independently. The real meaning of rule 2 is as follows:

> "If tear production rate is **not** reduced and age is presbyopic and prescription is hypermetrope and astigmatism is yes, then the recommended contact lens is none."

From Table 3.2, the P, T, p, t values and the probability (Pr) are as follows:

$$T = 24, \qquad P = 15, \qquad t = 1, \qquad i = 1$$

$$M(R) = \sum_{i=1}^{t} \Pr[\text{of } t \text{ instances selected at random, exactly } i \text{ are in class } none] = \sum_{i=1}^{t} \frac{\binom{P}{i}\binom{T-P}{t-i}}{\binom{T}{t}} = 0.625$$

After trimming off the last conditional term "*astigmatism is yes*," the P, T, i, t values and the probability (Pr) are as follows:

$$T = 24, \qquad P = 15, \qquad t = 2, \qquad i = 1$$

$$\Pr = 0.870$$

Since this probability is much higher than the previous value, according to the Induct algorithm the post-pruning process should stop here, and the original rule should be kept.

How does probability change if we continue to trim off additional terms? After trimming off the second to the last condition term "*prescription is hypermetrope*," the P, T, p, t values and the probability (Pr) are the following:

$$T = 24, \qquad P = 15, \qquad t = 4, \qquad p = 2$$

$$\Pr = 0.870$$

After trimming off the third to the last term "*age is presbyopic*," the P, T, p, t values and the probability (Pr) measure are as follows:

$$T = 24, \qquad P = 15, \qquad t = 12, \qquad p = 3$$

$$Pr = 1.00$$

As seen in the example above, the original rule has the lowest probability value. Therefore, we abandon the trimmed rules and keep the original one. The same principle can be applied to rules 3 and 4. No conditional terms are pruned off from these rules. Therefore, the rule list remains the same.

■ 3.3.3 REP, IREP, RIPPER

The preceding procedure for generating rules leads to over-fitted rules since it uses the same dataset to generate and evaluate the rules ([Pagallo 1990], [Brunk 1991], and [Cohen 1995]). Reduced Error Pruning (REP) and other algorithms such as Incremental Reduced Error Pruning (IREP) [Furnkranz 1994] and RIPPER [Cohen 1995] were proposed to correct this problem. These algorithms split the dataset into two parts: the growing set and pruning set. The growing set is used to form the over-fitted rules, while the pruning set is used to prune and evaluate these rules. The procedures for these algorithms are as follows:

1. First, the training dataset is randomly partitioned into two subsets, a growing set and a pruning set. Usually the growing set contains 2/3 of the instances.
2. Next, the rule-growing step is carried out to form an over-fitted rule.
3. Then, the rule is immediately pruned by deleting conditions in the reverse order until no deletion improves the prediction of the rule.

The error measurements are different from one algorithm to another. The probability measurement described in Induct could be used here. However, a success ratio V, which is a simpler measurement, is used in IREP:

$$V = (p + (N - n))/T,$$

where p is the number of positive instances covered by the rule, N is the total number of instances not belonging to this class in the pruning dataset, n is the number of negative (wrong) instances covered by the rule, and T is the total number of instances in the dataset. The algorithm maximizes the success ratio for the rule. The problem with this measurement is that it cannot tell the difference between the two rules that identify the same number of correct instances with different error rates. For example, a rule A that covers 3,000 positive instances with 2,000 negative instances will have the same success ratio as that of another rule that covers 1,001 positive instances with 1 negative instance. In fact, the error rate of the latter is much smaller than the former. Therefore, the probability measurement is probably a better choice for improving the prediction accuracies of rules, although it involves more computation.

The IREP algorithm is summarized in Figure 3.5.

■ FIGURE 3.5
IREP
rule-generation
algorithm

```
initialize T to be the instance set;
repeat
   do
      (1) split T into a growing set and pruning set;
      (2) use the basic covering algorithm to create a
          perfect rule from the growing set;
      (3) prune the perfect rule against the pruning set;
      (4) if the error rate of the pruned rule exceeds 50%
          then
             return rule set;
          else
             add the rule to rule set;
             remove the instances covered by the rule from
             both the growing set and pruning set;
          endif
   until T is empty;
   return rule set;
```

A disadvantage of the REP-type algorithms is that certain important information is prevented from being used in the growing rules because some instances are split into the pruning set. Moreover, some wrong rules may be preserved since the pruning set may not contain enough information to detect the error because it has only one-third of the instances of the whole dataset.

The algorithm is fast and efficient, but not as accurate as a decision tree. The accuracies of predicting classes for unseen instances using existing rules can be improved through a global optimization step on the rule set by revising and replacing individual rules with the method introduced in RIPPER.

RIPPER slightly modifies the strategy used in REP and IREP to form and prune individual rules. In addition, RIPPER adds an additional optimization step to improve the prediction accuracy of the rule set by revising, deleting, or replacing the pruned rules. During the optimization process, for each rule produced from IREP, two alternative rules are constructed: (1) a replacement rule and (2) a revision rule. The former is formed by growing from the empty condition list and then pruning the conditions to minimize the error rate for the whole rule set, not just for one rule. The latter is formed by adding conditions greedily to the original rule until the global error rate increases. The final decision about whether the rule set should include the original rule, the replacement rule, the revision rule, or none, is made based on the Minimal Description Length (MDL) heuristic, which will be explained later in the section on C4.5. The final step in the optimization is to form additional rules to cover the remaining instances left out of the above optimization process.

The rule sets produced by RIPPER are significantly more accurate than those produced by REP and IREP, and are competitive with those of C4.5 without seriously affecting the algorithm's efficiency [Cohen 1995].

■ 3.4 DIVIDE-AND-CONQUER APPROACH

The divide-and-conquer approach is one of the most reliable approaches in classification learning based on using decision trees to induce classification information. The decision tree recursively selects attributes to test and splits the dataset into subsets according to the outcome of the test until a subset is obtained that contains instances of only one class. The prediction based on the integrated decision tree is more complete and accurate than the one based on the independent knowledge rules generated by the separate-and-conquer approach. Several systems have been implemented using this approach. Notable ones among them are ID3 and its successors C4.5 and C5.0 and Cart.

In the following sections, the ID3 algorithm will be presented and explained along with an example to demonstrate the application of the method.

Then, it will be compared with its successors, which are modified versions with additional features.

■ 3.4.1 ID3

The underlying strategy of ID3 is to develop a decision tree recursively from top to bottom by using the information gain measure of each attribute as the criterion to select the attribute to test when splitting the dataset into subsets.

As previously discussed, the leaves in the decision tree represent the classes, and the internal nodes represent the attribute-based tests, which are connected with the branches that represent the outcomes of each test. Only one test is used for each branch. The process of identifying the class of an instance starts from the root of the tree and follows branches down the appropriate path according to the outcome of the tests (internal nodes) until a leaf is reached. The leaf is the class to which the instance belongs.

More than one decision tree can be derived from the same dataset depending on the sequence in which attributes are tested. The topologies of some trees are simpler than others. From our insect dataset in Table 3.1, two possible trees can be derived, as shown in Figure 3.1. It is obvious that tree 1 is more complex than tree 2, even though they both classify the insects into the correct suborder. Of course, the simpler decision tree is the better one because it requires the fewest steps to reach the correct conclusion.

Now, the question is how to build the simplest tree. The tedious way is to explore all possible trees, then choose the simplest one among them. A better way is to build the simplest tree using certain strategies. The strategy of ID3 is to choose the attribute with the smallest information gain and use it as the next test to split the dataset. This strategy guarantees that the tree built is the shortest.

Next, we introduce the concept of information gain and how it is applied in the ID3 algorithm to build decision trees.

Information

Let T be the set of instances to be classified and $\{C_1, C_2, ..., C_k\}$ be the set of classes. If S is any set of instances, let $Freq(C_j, S)$ stand for the number of instances in S that belongs to class C_j. We will also use the standard notation

$|S|$ to denote the number of instances in the set S. If we select one instance at random from S, the probability of the instance belonging to class C_j is $Freq(C_j, S)/|S|$ and the information it conveys is $-\log_2[Freq(C_j, S)/|S|]$ bits. Then, the overall expected information needed to assign instances in S into classes is the sum of the weighted average information conveyed by each class:

$$Info(S) = -\sum_{j=1}^{k} [Freq(C_j, S)/|S|] \times \log_2 [Freq(C_j, S)/|S|] \text{ bits}$$

where k is the number of classes. $Info(S)$ describes the distribution evenness of instances among the classes. If the instances are evenly distributed, $Info(S)$ has the maximum value. If the distribution of the instances is so askew that one class has all the instances and the rest have none, then $Info(S)$ is zero. In classification learning, $Info(S)$ is used to measure the class diversities of the subsets split by the attribute. We favor knowledge rules that split the subsets with less class diversity.

Now let us consider the information measurement after the dataset T has been partitioned in accordance with the test results on an attribute X that has n possible values. First, T is divided into n partitions: $T_1, T_2, ..., T_i, ..., T_n$. For each subset T_i, we can calculate its information measurement, $Info(T_i)$, by using the previous formula. The expected information measurement of the test on the attribute X is the weighted sum of all these values, expressed as follows:

$$Info_X(T) = \sum_{i=1}^{n} [|T_i|/|T|] \times Info(T_i)$$

which measures the average class purity of the subsets with respect to the test attribute X, where n is the number of possible values of X. The smaller $Info_X(T)$ is, the less diversified (in terms of the classes) the subsets split by the attribute X are. If $Info_X(T)$ is 0, no more testing and further splitting are necessary for the subsets split by attribute X.

Information Gain

Another form of information measurement is Information Gain, which is the total information of dataset T minus the information of the test attribute X:

$$Gain_X(T) = Info(T) - Info_X(T)$$

where $Info(T)$ is a constant for each dataset. Contrary to $Info_X(T)$, the bigger the value of $Gain_X(T)$, the less pure the subsets are. When building a decision tree, ID3 examines all candidate attributes and chooses an attribute X with maximal $Gain_X(T)$ or minimal $Info_X(T)$ as the branching test. And then the same process is recursively used to construct the decision tree until each of the subsets of the test belongs to one class. At this point, there is an attribute X with $Info_X(T)$ value of 0.

As an illustration, let's use our insect dataset in Table 3.1 to demonstrate how ID3 is applied to building a decision tree. The information that the dataset contains is represented by $Info(T)$, which can be obtained as shown below:

Two classes are $C_1 = Endopterygota$, $C_2 = Exopterygota$, and their frequencies are $Freq(C_1, T) = 6$, $Freq(C_2, T) = 4$ with $|T| = 10$.
Then,

$$Info(T) = -[6/10] \times \log_2[6/10] - [4/10] \times \log_2[4/10] = 0.971 \text{ bits}$$

The information gain of the attribute *number of wings* is

$T_1 = 2 \text{ } wings$, $T_2 = 4 \text{ } wings$, $|T_1| = 1$, $|T_2| = 9$, $Freq(C_1, T_1) = 1$,
$Freq(C_2, T_1) = 0$, $Info_{no. wing}(T_1) = 0$
$Freq(C_1, T_2) = 5$, $Freq(C_2, T_2) = 4$
$Info_{no. wing}(T_2) = -5/9 \times \log_2[5/9] - 4/9 \times \log_2[4/9] = 0.991$
$Gain_{no. wing}(T) = Info(T) - [1/10 \times Info_{no. wing}(T_1) + 9/10 \times Info_{no. wing}(T_2)]$
$\qquad = 0.971 - [0 + 9/10 \times 0.991] = 0.079$

The information gain of the attribute *metamorphosis* is

$T_1 = complete$, $T_2 = incomplete$, $|T_1| = 6$, $|T_2| = 4$
$Freq(C_1, T_1) = 6$, $Freq(C_2, T_1) = 0$, $Info_{meta}(T_1) = 0$
$Freq(C_1, T_2) = 0$, $Freq(C_2, T_2) = 4$, $Info_{meta}(T_2) = 0$
$Gain_{meta}(T) = Info(T) - [6/10 \times Info_{meta}(T_1) + 4/10 \times Info_{meta}(T_2)]$
$\qquad = 0.971 - [0 + 0] = 0.971$

The information gain of the attribute *forewings* is

$T_1 = membranous$, $T_2 = sclerotized$, $T_3 = hemi\text{-}sclerotized$, $T_4 = leather$
$|T_1| = 6$, $|T_2| = 1$, $|T_3| = 1$, $|T_4| = 2$
$Freq(C_1, T_1) = 5$, $Freq(C_2, T_1) = 1$
$Info_{f. wing}(T_1) = -5/6 \times \log_2[5/6] - 1/6 \times \log_2[1/6] = 0.65$
$Freq(C_1, T_2) = 1$, $Freq(C_2, T_2) = 0$, $Info_{f. wing}(T_2) = 0$
$Freq(C_1, T_3) = 0$, $Freq(C_2, T_3) = 1$, $Info_{f.wing}(T_3) = 0$

$$Freq(C_1, T_4) = 0, Freq(C_2, T_4) = 2, Info_{\text{f. wing}}(T_4) = 0$$
$$Gain_{\text{f. wing}}(T) = Info(T) - [6/10 \times Info_{\text{f. wing}}(T_1) + 1/10 \times Info_{\text{f. wing}}(T_2)$$
$$+ 1/10 \times Info_{\text{f. wing}}(T_3) + 2/10 \times Info_{\text{f. wing}}(T_4)]$$
$$= 0.971 - [6/10 \times 0.65 + 0 + 0 + 0] = 0.581$$

The information gain of attribute *mouth* is:

$$T_1 = sponging, \quad T_2 = chewing, \quad T_3 = siphoning, \quad T_4 = piercing$$
$$|T_1| = 1, |T_2| = 5, |T_3| = 2, |T_4| = 2$$
$$Freq(C_1, T_1) = 1, Freq(C_2, T_1) = 0, Info_{\text{mouth}}(T_1) = 0$$
$$Freq(C_1, T_2) = 3, Freq(C_2, T_2) = 2,$$
$$Info_{\text{mouth}}(T_2) = -3/5 \times \log_2[3/5] - 2/5 \times \log_2[2/5] = 0.97$$
$$Freq(C_1, T_3) = 2, Freq(C_2, T_3) = 0, Info_{\text{mouth}}(T_2) = 0$$
$$Freq(C_1, T_4) = 0, Freq(C_2, T_4) = 2, Info_{\text{mouth}}(T_4) = 0$$
$$Gain_{\text{mouth}}(T) = Info(T) - [5/10 \times Info_{\text{mouth}}(T_2) + 1/10 \times Info_{\text{mouth}}(T_1)$$
$$+ 2/10 \times Info_{\text{mouth}}(T_3) + 2/10 \times Info_{\text{mouth}}(T_4)]$$
$$= 0.971 - [5/10 \times 0.97 + 0 + 0 + 0] = 0.486$$

The information gain of attribute *wing scales* is:

$$T_1 = absent, \quad T_2 = present, \quad |T_1| = 8, \quad |T_2| = 2, \quad Freq(C_1, T_1) = 4,$$
$$Freq(C_2, T_1) = 4$$
$$Info_{\text{scales}}(T_1) = -4/8 \times \log_2[4/8] - 4/8 \times \log_2[4/8] = 1$$
$$Freq(C_1, T_2) = 2, Freq(C_2, T_2) = 0, Info_{\text{scales}}(T_2) = 0$$
$$Gain_{\text{scales}}(T) = Info(T) - [8/10 \times Info_{\text{scales}}(T_1) + 2/10 \times Info_{\text{scales}}(T_2)]$$
$$= 0.971 - [0.8 + 0] = 0.171$$

The information gain of attribute *hind legs* is:

$$T_1 = walking, \quad T_2 = jumping, \quad |T_1| = 9, \quad |T_2| = 1,$$
$$Freq(C_1, T_1) = 6, Freq(C_2, T_1) = 3$$
$$Info_{\text{hind leg}}(T_1) = -3/9 \times \log_2[3/9] - 6/9 \times \log_2[6/9] = 0.918$$
$$Freq(C_1, T_2) = 0, Freq(C_2, T_2) = 1, Info_{\text{hind leg}}(T_2) = 0$$
$$Gain_{\text{hind leg}}(T) = Info(T) - [9/10 \times Info_{\text{hind leg}}(T_1) + 1/10 \times Info_{\text{hind leg}}(T_2)]$$
$$= 0.971 - [9/10 \times 0.918 + 0] = 0.144$$

The information gain of attribute *abdominal needle* is the same as attribute *wing scales*, i.e., $Gain_{\text{Abdomen needle}}(T) = 0.171$.

The largest information gain is that of attribute *metamorphosis*. Therefore, it is chosen as the root of the decision tree to be constructed. Since all the branching nodes of this test are the two classes, *endopterygota* and *exopterygota*, no further testing is needed. At this point, we can observe that the value of $Info(T)$ is the same as that of $Gain_{\text{metamorphosis}}(T)$. The final decision tree is tree 2 in Figure 3.1. Notice that in tree 1, which is created by randomly selecting the test attributes, four tests are needed to classify the insects into the right suborders. However, only one test is needed in tree 2, from which the following two knowledge rules can be derived:

> Rule 1: If metamorphosis is complete, then the suborder is Endopterygota.

> Rule 2: If metamorphosis is incomplete, then the suborder is Exopterygota.

Noise

One of the notable features of the ID3 series of algorithms that are popular in data mining is their ability to handle noisy data. A problem with the decision-tree construction method discussed above is that it requires 100% accuracy, as in the Induct algorithm. The sub-datasets at the terminal leaves of a decision tree must belong to a single class. We have already discussed the problem of over-fitting in Induct. The over-fitting problem in decision trees is even worse. The decision tree can grow exponentially, much quicker than classification rules. For a large database, the decision tree may become so complicated that the rules generated from the tree may be too trivial to be comprehensible. In Quinlan's experiment with a set of noisy datasets, the expected error rate of an over-fitted decision tree was higher than a tree created randomly. In ID3, Quinlan proposed a mechanism to stop further branching. This mechanism allows the leaves of a decision tree to have a certain degree of heterogeneity.

The mechanism is based on the chi-square test for stochastic independence. Suppose that an attribute X splits a dataset T into subsets $[T_1, T_2, \ldots, T_v]$, where T_i contains p_i and n_i instances of class P and N, respectively, and v is the number of possible values of the attribute X. If a value of attribute X is irrelevant to the class of an instance in T, the expected value p_i' of p_i should be

$$p_i' = p \times (p_i + n_i)/(p + n)$$

If n_i' is the corresponding expected value of n_i, then

$$X^2 = \sum_{i=1}^{v} [(p_i - p_i')/p_i' + (n_i - n_i')/n_i']$$

is approximately chi-square with $v - 1$ degrees of freedom. The chi-square value is used to determine the confidence with which one can reject the hypothesis that X is independent of the class of instances in T.

Suppose we need to determine if further testing on attribute X is needed. Then, the chi-square value is calculated using the value of the attribute in the formula above. If the value is lower than a pre-assigned threshold, say 95%, we cannot reject that the test on attribute X is irrelevant to the classification. Further dividing of the datasets is not needed. If the value is higher than the threshold, the test on the attribute is necessary. If no attribute is found to be relevant, then the tree should stop growing at the point of the subtree. The decision tree built this way will avoid over-fitting.

A Problem of ID3

A problem with the ID3 algorithm is that it favors attributes with more possible outcomes over attributes with fewer possible outcomes. One extreme case is that each outcome of the attribute test covers only one instance in the dataset. After the splitting of the dataset, each subset will contain only one instance of one class. Since its $Info_x(T)$ value will be zero, ID3 will favor this attribute. For prediction, however, such a decision tree is less informative. For example, in Table 3.1, a distinct *insect ID number* for each insect may be added to the insect database as an additional attribute, as shown in Table 3.6.

■ TABLE 3.6 Morphological characters and suborders of insects from Table 3.1 modified with a new column "Insect ID Number" added and all other columns omitted except "Name" and "Groups"

Name	Insect ID Number	Groups
Fly	1	Endopterygota
Wasp	2	Endopterygota
Bee	3	Endopterygota
Beetle	4	Endopterygota
Butterfly	5	Endopterygota
Moth	6	Endopterygota
True Bug	7	Exopterygota
Aphid	8	Exopterygota
Grasshopper	9	Exopterygota
Cockroach	10	Exopterygota

The information gain of the attribute *insect ID number* is calculated as follows:

$$|T_1| = 1, \quad |T_2| = 1, \quad |T_3| = 1, \quad |T_4| = 1, \quad |T_5| = 1,$$
$$|T_6| = 1, \quad |T_7| = 1, \quad |T_8| = 1, \quad |T_9| = 1, \quad |T_{10}| = 1.$$
$$Freq(C_1, T_1) = 1, Freq(C_2, T_1) = 0; Freq(C_1, T_2) = 1, Freq(C_2, T_2) = 0;$$
$$Freq(C_1, T_3) = 1, Freq(C_2, T_3) = 0; Freq(C_1, T_4) = 1, Freq(C_2, T_4) = 0;$$
$$Freq(C_1, T_5) = 1, Freq(C_2, T_5) = 0; Freq(C_1, T_6) = 1, Freq(C_2, T_6) = 0;$$
$$Freq(C_1, T_7) = 0, Freq(C_2, T_7) = 1; Freq(C_1, T_8) = 0, Freq(C_2, T_8) = 1;$$
$$Freq(C_1, T_9) = 0, Freq(C_2, T_9) = 1; Freq(C_1, T_{10}) = 0, Freq(C_2, T_{10}) = 1.$$
$$Info_{Id\_no}(T_1) = 0, Info_{Id\_no}(T_2) = 0, Info_{Id\_no}(T_3) = 0, Info_{Id\_no}(T_4)$$
$$= 0, Info_{Id\_no}(T_5) = 0, Info_{Id\_no}(T_6) = 0, Info_{Id\_no}(T_7) = 0, Info_{Id\_no}(T_8)$$
$$= 0, Info_{Id\_no}(T_9) = 0, Info_{Id\_no}(T_{10}) = 0$$
$$Info_{Id\_no}(T) = [1/10 \times Info_{Id\_no}(T_1) + 1/10 \times Info_{Id\_no}(T_2)$$
$$+ 1/10 \times Info_{Id\_no}(T_3) + 1/10 \times Info_{Id\_no}(T_4)$$
$$+ 1/10 \times Info_{Id\_no}(T_5) + 1/10 \times Info_{Id\_no}(T_6)$$
$$+ 1/10 \times Info_{Id\_no}(T_7) + 1/10 \times Info_{Id\_no}(T_8)$$
$$+ 1/10 \times Info_{Id\_no}(T_9) + 1/10 \times Info_{Id\_no}(T_{10})] = 0 \text{ bits}$$
$$Gain_{Id\_no}(T) = Info(T) - Info_{Id\_no}(T) = 0.971 - 0 = 0.971$$

The information gain of this attribute is one of the highest among the other attributes considered earlier. Therefore, it could be one of the candidates for the first test attribute selected for the decision tree. If we select this attribute as the root of the decision tree, it would have ten branches connected to the root with each sub–dataset identifying only one instance. Each rule converted from the tree will be supported by only one instance in the dataset. Therefore, it will provide very poor classification information for the purpose of classifying insects. The problem above can be compensated for by the gain ratio criterion that can be used for the selection of the attributes, which will be discussed in the next section on C4.5.

■ 3.4.2 C4.5 and C5.0

C4.5 uses the same basic strategy of ID3 with gain ratio as an added feature for the attribute selection criteria to be used when branching. Several factors are used to deal with features such as missing values, noisy data, and numeric values in generating rules from the trees. The C5.0 algorithm is an extended system based on C4.5 that shows improved performance over C4.5.

Gain Ratio Criterion

Gain ratio is a remedy for the problem of favoring attributes with more possible values when determining node branching in the tree, as mentioned in algorithm ID3. It was first proposed by Quinlan and later included in his system C4.5. It takes into account how the dataset splits on each node. First, it derives a split information value that takes into account the number and the size of children nodes and ignores any information about the classes. The larger the number of possible values of an attribute, the greater the split information is. The Split Information is expressed as follows:

$$Split\ info(x) = -\sum_{i=1}^{n} [Freq\ (T_i) \times \log_2(Freq(T_i))]$$

Here, n is the number of possible values of the attribute X and $Freq(T_i)$ is the number of instances with attribute X of value i. The gain ratio is the ratio of the information gain used in ID3 divided by the Split Information, as expressed by the following formula:

$$Gain\ ratio(X) = Gain_X(T)/Split\ info_X(T).$$

In the C4.5 system, the gain ratio is used instead of information gain when selecting the next attribute to be used to split the dataset, which corrects the problem of favoring more variant attributes. In our insect example, the split information for *insect ID number* is

$$Split\ info_{ID}(T) = -\sum_{i=1}^{n} [Freq(T_i) \times \log_2(Freq(T_i))]$$

$$= 10 \times 0.1 \times 3.3219 = 3.3219$$

and its gain ratio is

$$Gain\ ratio\ (ID) = Gain_{ID}(T)/Split\ info_{ID}(T) = 0.971/3.3219 = 0.2923$$

The split information for *metamorphosis* is

$$Split\ info_{Meta}(T) = -\sum_{i=1}^{n} [Freq\ (T_i) \times \log_2(Freq(T_i))]$$

$$= -6/10 \times \log_2(6/10) - 4/10 \times \log_2(4/10)$$

$$= -0.4422 - 0.5288 = 0.971$$

and its gain ratio is

$$Gain\ ratio(Meta) = Gain_{Meta}(T)/Split\ info_{Meta}(T) = 0.971/0.971 = 1.$$

The gain ratio of the metamorphosis attribute is much higher than that of the ID attribute. Therefore, when building a decision tree, we will select the metamorphosis attribute instead of the ID attribute as the first splitting node, even though they have the same information gain value.

Gain ratio may be over-compensated for by preferring attributes with unevenly divided sub-datasets. This may be fixed by choosing the attribute that maximizes the gain ratio, provided that the information gain for that attribute is at least as big as the average information gain of all the attributes examined.

Post-Pruning

For the over-fitting problem in ID3, Quinlan used chi-square testing as the criterion to stop tree growth. This approach to dealing with the over-fitting problem in decision trees is often referred to as "pre-pruning," in contrast to another approach called "post-pruning," which trims off over-fitted branches after a complete explorative tree is built. In C4.5, Quinlan abandoned the "pre-pruning" approach and adopted the "post-pruning" approach used in Cart [Breiman 1984], although the latter needs more computation for building parts of the tree. However, the cost is offset by the benefits due to the generation of more reliable results through a more thorough exploration of possible partitions.

The "post-pruning" starts after the complete over-fitted decision tree is created. The pruning process is carried out from the bottom and works upward to the root of the tree, and occurs when an internal node is replaced with a lower-level node (possibly a leaf node) according to the error rate estimation of the internal node and its child nodes. (If the estimated error rate of the internal node is lower than the combined weighted estimated error rate of all of its child nodes, the partitioning of the dataset into subsets at this point might cause adverse effects on the prediction using the decision tree.) Then the internal node is replaced by one of the lower-level nodes (maybe a leaf node), depending on which represents the majority of instances over the sub-dataset.

To estimate the error rate of the internal nodes, Quinlan borrowed concepts from statistics. Let's assume that each sub-dataset included in an internal node is a sample of the whole dataset population (in fact it is not). Given a confidence level, we can estimate the population (i.e., whole dataset) error rate through the observed errors from the samples (the subsets). The probability of a random variable X, with 0 mean and a confidence range of $2z$ is $\Pr[-z \leq X \leq z] = c$, where c is the confidence level and z is the standard deviation of the variable X away from the mean. The z value can be obtained from the normal distribution with any given confidence level c. For example, if the confidence $c = 90\%$, then z is 1.65 from $\Pr[-1.65 \leq X \leq 1.65] = 90\%$. The implication is that there is a 90% chance that X lies between 1.65 standard deviations above and below the mean 0. If we increase the confidence level to 99%, z becomes 2.58, i.e., X lies on a wider area of random distribution. Quinlan used the upper-tailed probability to estimate the error rate. The one-tailed probability is expressed as $\Pr[X \geq z] = (1 - c)/2$ because the random distribution is symmetric. If c is 90%, the upper-tailed probability equals 5%. In fact, the random probability distribution in most statistics applications is expressed as one-tailed. Now let's see how to apply the above statistical measure to estimate the error rate of the internal nodes.

If E is the observed number of error instances, N is the total number of instances in the sub-dataset, and f is the observed error rate (i.e., $f = E/N$), then the above one-tailed random probability is expressed as $\Pr[(f - q)/\sqrt{q(1-q)/N} > z] = e$, where f (the random variable) minus the mean q (the estimated error rate of the population) is divided by $\sqrt{q(1-q)/N}$ (the standard deviation), and e is the upper-tailed confidence level. Given the one-tailed confidence level e, we can get the error rate q value by getting the z value first and then solving the inequality in the expression above, which is then converted as shown:

$$q = (f + z^2/2N + z\sqrt{f/N - f^2/N + z^2/4N^2})/(1 + z/N)$$

Since C4.5 used $e = 25\%$ as the default one-tailed confidence level, its corresponding z becomes 0.69.

Now that we have learned how to estimate the error rate of the decision-tree nodes, let's see how the estimated error rate can be applied to pruning the decision tree. The process can be summarized as follows:

1. Calculate the error rates of an internal node and all of its next-level children.

2. Sum the weighted error rates of these children, which is the combined error estimation of the direct children.

3. Compare the estimate error of the internal node and the combined error rate of its children. If the estimated error rate of the internal node is larger than the children's combined error rate, the splitting of the decision tree at the internal node will improve its prediction. Therefore, pruning of the subtrees at this node will not be done. Otherwise, the splitting at the node will degrade the prediction based on the decision tree, and pruning of the subtree is appropriate here.

4. When pruning is appropriate, the pruning is done by replacing the internal node either by a leaf child or by any other lower-level internal node. The choice is made by identifying the child node covering the most instances. If the selected node is a leaf node, it simply replaces the parent node. If the replacing node is an internal node, the child subtree should be rearranged to include all instances covered by other children being trimmed off before the pruning. Therefore, replacing with a subtree is much more expensive than replacing with a leaf node.

Rule Set

After post-pruning is done to trim the decision trees, the knowledge rules can be read directly from the pruned tree. C4.5 uses another complicated and time-consuming procedure for deriving the rules. It converts the over-fitted decision tree into a set of rules with the following steps:

1. Over-fitted rules are generated from the decision tree. They are generated directly from the over-fitted decision tree.

2. *Optimization of single rules.*

   After the over-fitted rules are created directly from the over-fitted decision tree, C4.5 uses a try-and-test strategy to simplify conditions in the original rules without decreasing accuracy. The testing mechanism used here is the same as the confidence level testing used in the tree-pruning procedure mentioned above. First, a condition is temporarily removed from the rule. Then, the estimated upper limits of the error rates are compared. If the estimated upper limit of the error rate of a rule with the condition temporarily removed has the same or lower estimated upper limit of the error rate of the original rule without temporary removal of the condition, the deletion of the condition from the rule will not degrade the performance of the rule under a certain confidence level. Therefore, the deletion of the condition will be finalized.

Now let's consider the complexity of multiple conditions in a rule. If the number of conditions in a rule is N, there are $N!$ possible combinations of the conditions. If we carry out an exhaustive search on all possible conjunctions of the conditions to determine whether to accept or reject the temporary rule, it takes $N!$ number of tests for the single rule. For a large database, the number of possible tests will become very huge. In C4.5, Quinlan used a "greedy" approach to delete the conditions, which produces reasonably accurate rules and is much faster than the exhaustive search. This approach deletes one condition at a time until no more conditions need to be removed. First, we calculate and list the estimated upper-limit error rates after deleting each condition from the original rule. Rules with estimated upper-limit error rates lower than the original rule will be accepted as new rules. If more than one condition qualifies, select the one with the lowest estimated upper-limit error rate. Since the deletion of the condition from the original rule may change the instance coverage, the default estimated upper-limit error rate of the new rule needs to be recalculated. From the discussion above, we can see that the maximal number of tests in greedy search is the same as in exhaustive deletion. Under this circumstance, all conditions are trimmed off. Since the conditions deleted are usually less than the total number of conditions in the rule, the greedy approach will speed up the process of single-rule optimization.

The possible adverse effect of rule optimization is that the rules produced from a decision tree may no longer be mutually inclusive or exclusive or both. This means that some instances may not be covered by any rule, while other instances may be covered by two or more rules. In C4.5, the former situation is resolved by adding a default rule to deal with the instances not covered by any rule. The conflict in the second situation is resolved by ranking the rules according to their priorities, and the rule with the highest priority is taken as the target rule.

3. *Optimization of rule set*

   In the previous two steps, we discussed ways to optimize individual rules. C4.5 further implemented a mechanism to optimize an entire rule set to improve the performance of the rule set as a whole. C4.5 first optimizes the rules in a rule subset, each denoting a class, by using the Minimum Description Length (MDL) principle [Rissanen 1983a & 1983b]. Then, these subsets are ranked according to their priorities. If two conflicting rules share the same conditions but predict different classes, then they are distributed in separate rule subsets with different priority values. The rule in the rule subset with a higher priority will be used to identify the instances. The sequence of the rules within the same subset of the class is irrelevant. Lastly, the default rule is set for the instances not covered by any of the rules in the rule set.

Similar to upper-limit error estimation in individual rule formation, the MDL is applied in C4.5 as the criterion to optimize the rule subset for each class. The principle is that both a sender and a receiver have identical copies of training instances, but the sender's copy also specifies the class of each instance while the receiver's copy lacks any class information. The sender must communicate this missing information to the receiver by transmitting the classification theory together with exceptions to the theory. The sender may choose the complexity of the theory he sends, for example, a relatively simple theory with a substantial number of exceptions, or a more complete theory with fewer exceptions. The MDL principle states that the best theory derivable from the training data minimizes the number of bits required to encode the total message consisting of the theory together with its exceptions.

In our classification applications, the information that is derived through the theory (the set of rules for one class) and exceptions (misidentified instances) is the identification of the instances belonging to each target class. The purpose of MDL testing is to find the best subset of rules for a class from a number of possible combinations of the rules, which minimizes the encoding of the theory and the exceptions. The process is a bit complicated and the computation is time-consuming.

- The process first encodes each rule by calculating its associated information bits based on all conditions of the rule, which are then subtracted by the ordering credit of the conditions, since the relative sequence of the conditions is irrelevant to the conclusion of the rule. The value of the ordering information is $\log_2(k!)$ if there are k conditions on the rule.
- The theory information is the sum of the information bits of all rules in the subset, subtracted by the ordering information of the individual rules,

which is $\log_2(R!)$ if the total number of rules in the subset is R, since the ordering of the rules in the same class is irrelevant, as stated previously.

- The exceptions are encoded by summing the false-positive information bits and the false-negative information bits. The false-positive instances are the instances misidentified as belonging to different classes. The false-negative instances are those that are incorrectly excluded from their classes. If the rule covers r out of n training instances, with fp false-positive instances and fn false-negative instances, the information bits of the exceptions are

$$\log_2\binom{r}{fp} + \log_2\binom{n-r}{fn}$$

The information of the whole rule subset is the sum of the theory bits and the exceptions. This value measures the performance of the rule subset. The smaller the value, the better the performance of the rule subset. The purpose of optimization is to exclude from the subset certain rules that adversely affect the MDL value of the rule subset. The question is how to find the rule subset with the lowest MDL value from all possible combinations of the rules for the class. If the size of the rule set is small, we can do an exhaustive search on all possible combinations of the rules and find the subset with the lowest MDL value. C4.5 also adopted a simulated annealing method to find a near-best rule subset in a very large rule set. This method is more computationally effective and can produce more satisfactory results. The detailed description of the method is given in [Press 1988].

After the best rule subset is found for each class, the next step of the rule set optimization is to rank the rule subsets. If a rule with a higher priority in a rule subset positively identifies a false instance, then the rule that may give a correct answer in the subset with low priority may never get a chance to be checked. Therefore, the rule subset with a lower false-positive error rate should be ranked with a higher priority.

To those instances for which there is no corresponding rule, a default class should be given. It is reasonable to set the class that appears most frequently in the training database as the default class. Although the rule-set optimization process in C4.5 is rather lengthy and complicated, it is necessary to reduce errors of prediction, especially if the dataset contains a lot of noisy data.

In the following, we are going to apply the techniques in the C4.5 algorithm to build a decision tree, post–prune the tree, and then induce knowledge rules from the contact lens database (Table 3.2). The final decision tree is shown in Figure 3.6. At the root, there are 3 classes and 24 instances in total. The information gain and gain ratio of the attributes available at this level are calculated as shown below:

Three Classes: $C_1 = none$, $C_2 = soft$, $C_3 = hard$
Total number of instances: $|T| = 24$
Frequencies of each class: $Freq(C_1, T) = 15$, $Freq(C_2, T) = 5$, $Freq(C_3, T) = 4$
Information bits of the node: $Info(T) = -[15/24] \times \log_2[15/24]$
$$- [5/24] \times \log_2[5/24]$$
$$- [4/24] \times \log_2[4/24] = 1.326 \text{ bits}$$

Attribute: *Age*

$T_1 = young$, $|T_1| = 8$, $T_2 = pre\text{-}presbyopic$, $|T_2| = 8$,
$T_3 = presbyopic$, $|T_3| = 8$
$Freq(C_1, T_1) = 4, Freq(C_2, T_1) = 2, Freq(C_3, T_1) = 2$
$Info_{age}(T_1) = -4/8 \times \log_2[4/8] - 2/8 \times \log_2[2/8] - 2/8 \times \log_2[2/8]$
$\qquad = 1.5$
$Freq(C_1, T_2) = 5, Freq(C_2, T_2) = 2, Freq(C_3, T_2) = 1$
$Info_{age}(T_2) = -5/8 \times \log_2[5/8] - 2/8 \times \log_2[2/8] - 1/8 \times \log_2[1/8]$
$\qquad = 1.299$
$Freq(C_1, T_3) = 6, Freq(C_2, T_3) = 1, Freq(C_3, T_3) = 1$
$Info_{age}(T_3) = -6/8 \times \log_2[6/8] - 1/8 \times \log_2[1/8] - 1/8 \times \log_2[1/8]$
$\qquad = 1.061$
$Gain_{age}(T) = Info(T) - [8/24 \times Info_{age}(T_1) + 8/24 \times Info_{age}(T_2) + 8/24$
$\qquad \times Info_{age}(T_3)] = 1.326 - 1.2633 = 0.0627$
$Gain\ Ratio = 0.0627/1.2633 = 0.0496$

Attribute: *Spectacle Prescription*

$T_1 = myope$, $|T_1| = 12$, $T_2 = hypermetrope$, $|T_2| = 12$
$Freq(C_1, T_1) = 7$, $Freq(C_2, T_1) = 2$, $Freq(C_3, T_1) = 3$
$Info_{pres}(T_1) = -7/12 \times \log_2[7/12] - 2/12 \times \log_2[2/12] - 3/12 \times \log_2[3/12]$
$\qquad = 1.384$

$Freq(C_1, T_2) = 8, Freq(C_2, T_2) = 3, Freq(C_3, T_2) = 1$

$Info_{pres}(T_2) = -8/12 \times \log_2[8/12] - 3/12 \times \log_2[3/12] - 1/12 \times \log_2[1/12]$
$\qquad = 1.189$

$$Gain_{pres}(T) = Info(T) - [12/24 \times Info_{pres}(T_1) + 12/24 \times Info_{pres}(T_2)]$$
$$= 1.326 - 1.287 = 0.039$$
$$Gain\ Ratio = 0.039/1.287 = 0.0303$$

Attribute: *Astigmatism*

$$T_1 = yes,\quad |T_1| = 12,\qquad T_2 = no,\quad |T_2| = 12$$
$$Freq(C_1, T_1) = 8, Freq(C_2, T_1) = 0, Freq(C_3, T_1) = 4$$
$$Info_{ast}(T_1) = -8/12 \times \log_2[8/12] - 4/12 \times \log_2[4/12] - 0 = 0.918$$

$$Freq(C_1, T_2) = 7, Freq(C_2, T_2) = 5, Freq(C_3, T_2) = 0$$

$$Info_{ast}(T_2) = -7/12 \times \log_2[7/12] - 5/12 \times \log_2[5/12] - 0 = 0.098$$

$$Gain_{ast}(T) = Info(T) - [12/24 \times Info_{ast}(T_1) + 12/24 \times Info_{ast}(T_2)]$$
$$= 1.326 - 0.949 = 0.377$$
$$Gain\ Ratio = 0.377/0.949 = 0.397$$

Attribute: *Tear Production Rate*

$$T_1 = reduced,\quad |T_1| = 12,\qquad T_2 = normal,\ |T_2| = 12$$
$$Freq(C_1, T_1) = 12, Freq(C_2, T_1) = 0, Freq(C_3, T_1) = 0$$
$$Info_{tear}(T_1) = 0$$
$$Freq(C_1, T_2) = 3, Freq(C_2, T_2) = 5, Freq(C_3, T_2) = 4$$
$$Info_{tear}(T_2) = -3/12 \times \log_2[3/12] - 5/12 \times \log_2[5/12]$$
$$-4/12 \times \log_2[4/12] = 1.555$$

$$Gain_{tear}(T) = Info(T) - [12/24 \times Info_{tear}(T_1) + 12/24 \times Info_{tear}(T_2)]$$
$$= 1.326 - 0.778 = 0.548$$
$$Gain\ Ratio = 0.548/0.778 = 0.704$$

Since the attribute *tear production rate* has the highest information gain ratio of 0.413, we select this attribute for the first test to partition the dataset. As was illustrated in Figure 3.6, the left branch has 12 *none* classified into only one class, so it requires no further splitting. The right branch contains three instances of *none*, five instances of *soft*, and four instances of *hard* classes:

$$C_1 = none,\qquad C_2 = soft,\qquad C_3 = hard,\quad |T| = 12$$
$$Freq(C_1, T) = 3, Freq(C_2, T) = 5, Freq(C_3, T) = 4$$
$$Info(T) = -[3/12] \times \log_2[3/12] - [5/12] \times \log_2[5/12]$$
$$-[4/12] \times \log_2[4/12] = 1.555\ bits$$

Attribute: *Age*

$T_1 = young, \quad |T_1| = 4, \qquad T_2 = pre\text{-}presbyopic, \quad |T_2| = 4,$
$T_3 = presbyopic, \quad |T_3| = 4$
$Freq(C_1, T_1) = 0, Freq(C_2, T_1) = 2, Freq(C_3, T_1) = 2$
$Info_{age}(T_1) = -0 - 2/4 \times \log_2[2/4] - 2/4 \times \log_2[2/4] = 1$
$Freq(C_1, T_2) = 1, Freq(C_2, T_2) = 2, Freq(C_3, T_2) = 1$

$Info_{age}(T_2) = -1/4 \times \log_2[1/4] - 2/4 \times \log_2[2/4] - 1/4 \times \log_2[1/4] = 1.5$

$Freq(C_1, T_3) = 2, Freq(C_2, T_3) = 1, Freq(C_3, T_3) = 1$

$Info_{age}(T_3) = -2/4 \times \log_2[2/4] - 1/4 \times \log_2[1/4] - 1/4 \times \log_2[1/4] = 1.5$

$Gain_{age}(T) = Info(T) - [4/12 \times Info_{age}(T_1) + 4/12 \times Info_{age}(T_2) + 4/12$
$\times Info_{age}(T_3)] = 1.555 - 1.333 = 0.222$
$Gain\ Ratio = 0.222/1.333 = 0.167$

Attribute: *Spectacle Prescription*

$T_1 = myope, \quad |T_1| = 6, \qquad T_2 = hypermetrope, \quad |T_2| = 6$
$Freq(C_1, T_1) = 1, Freq(C_2, T_1) = 2, Freq(C_3, T_1) = 3$
$Info_{pres}(T_1) = -1/6 \times \log_2[1/6] - 2/6 \times \log_2[2/6] - 3/6 \times \log_2[3/6] = 1.459$

$Freq(C_1, T_2) = 2, Freq(C_2, T_2) = 3, Freq(C_3, T_2) = 1$

$Info_{pres}(T_2) = -2/6 \times \log_2[2/6] - 3/6 \times \log_2[3/6] - 1/6 \times \log_2[1/6]$
$= 1.459$

$Gain_{pres}(T) = Info(T) - [6/12 \times Info_{pres}(T_1) + 6/12 \times Info_{pres}(T_2)]$
$= 1.555 - 1.459 = 0.096$
$Gain\ Ratio = 0.096/1.459 = 0.066$

Attribute: *Astigmatism*

$T_1 = yes, \quad |T_1| = 6, \qquad T_2 = no, \quad |T_2| = 6$
$Freq(C_1, T_1) = 2, Freq(C_2, T_1) = 0, Freq(C_3, T_1) = 4$
$Info_{ast}(T_1) = -2/6 \times \log_2[2/6] - 0 - 4/6 \times \log_2[4/6] = 0.918$
$Freq(C_1, T_2) = 1, Freq(C_2, T_2) = 5, Freq(C_3, T_2) = 0$
$Info_{ast}(T_2) = -1/6 \times \log_2[1/6] - 5/6 \times \log_2[5/6] - 0 = 0.650$
$Gain_{ast}(T) = Info(T) - [6/12 \times Info_{ast}(T_1) + 6/12 \times Info_{ast}(T_2)] = 1.555 - 0.784$
$= 0.771$
$Gain\ Ratio = 0.771/0.784 = 0.983$

Since *astigmatism* has the highest gain ratio, it is selected as the next test to split the right branch into two subsets: *yes* and *no* branches. Let's examine the *no* branch first.

$$C_1 = soft, \quad |C_1| = 5, \quad C_2 = none, \quad |C_2| = 1, \quad |T| = 6$$
$$Info(T) = -[5/6] \times \log_2[5/6] - [1/6] \times \log_2[1/6] = 0.650 \text{ bits}$$

Attribute: *Age*

$$T_1 = young, \quad |T_1| = 2, \quad T_2 = pre\text{-}presbyopic, \quad |T_2| = 2,$$
$$T_3 = presbyopic, \quad |T_3| = 2$$
$$Freq(C_1, T_1) = 2, Freq(C_2, T_1) = 0, Info_{age}(T_1) = -2/2 \times \log_2[2/2] - 0 = 0$$
$$Freq(C_1, T_2) = 2, Freq(C_2, T_2) = 0, Info_{age}(T_2) = -2/2 \times \log_2[2/2] - 0 = 0$$
$$Freq(C_1, T_3) = 1, Freq(C_2, T_3) = 1$$
$$Info_{age}(T_3) = -1/2 \times \log_2[1/2] - 1/2 \times \log_2[1/2] = 1$$
$$Gain_{age}(T) = Info(T) - [2/6 \times Info_{age}(T_1) + 2/6 \times Info_{age}(T_2) + 2/6 \times Info_{age}(T_3)]$$
$$= 0.650 - 0.333 = 0.317$$
$$Gain \ Ratio = 0.317/0.333 = 0.952$$

Attribute: *Spectacle Prescription*

$$T_1 = myope, \quad |T_1| = 3, \quad T_2 = hypermetrope, \quad |T_2| = 3,$$
$$Freq(C_1, T_1) = 2, \quad Freq(C_2, T_1) = 1$$
$$Info_{pres}(T_1) = -2/3 \times \log_2[2/3] - 1/3 \times \log_2[1/3] = 0.918$$
$$Freq(C_1, T_2) = 3, Freq(C_2, T_2) = 0, Info_{pres}(T_2) = -3/3 \times \log_2[3/3] - 0 = 0$$
$$Gain_{pres}(T) = Info(T) - [3/6 \times Info_{pres}(T_1) + 3/6 \times Info_{pres}(T_2)]$$
$$= 0.650 - 0.500 = 0.150$$
$$Gain \ Ratio = 0.15/0.5 = 0.3$$

In this branch, the attribute *age* has the highest information gain ratio. This branch is divided into three subsets: *young, pre-presbyopic*, and *presbyopic*. The two branches *young* and *pre-presbyopic* are the leaf nodes, each with two instances of *soft*. The branch *presbyopic* has one instance of *soft* and one instance of *none*, which can be further partitioned by the attribute *prescription* to reach the leaf nodes.

Let's go back to the right branch of the *astigmatism* attribute, which is the *yes* branch as shown in Figure 3.6:

$$|T| = 6, \quad C_1 = hard, \quad |C_1| = 4, \quad C_2 = none, \quad |C_2| = 2,$$
$$Info(T) = -[4/6] \times \log_2[4/6] - [2/6] \times \log_2[2/6] = 0.918 \text{ bits}$$

Attribute: *Age*

$T_1 = young$, $|T_1| = 2$, $T_2 = pre\text{-}presbyopic$, $|T_2| = 2$,
$T_3 = presbyopic$, $|T_3| = 2$,
$Freq(C_1, T_1) = 2$, $Freq(C_2, T_1) = 0$, $Info_{age}(T_1) = -2/2 \times \log_2[2/2] - 0 = 0$
$Freq(C_1, T_2) = 1$, $Freq(C_2, T_2) = 1$
$Info_{age}(T_2) = -1/2 \times \log_2[1/2] - 1/2 \times \log_2[1/2] = 1$
$Freq(C_1, T_3) = 1$, $Freq(C_2, T_3) = 1$
$Info_{age}(T_3) = -1/2 \times \log_2[1/2] - 1/2 \times \log_2[1/2] = 1$
$Gain_{age}(T) = Info(T) - [2/6 \times Info_{age}(T_1) + 2/6 \times Info_{age}(T_2) + 2/6 \times Info_{age}(T_3)]$
$\qquad\qquad = 0.918 - 0.667 = 0.251$
$Gain\ Ratio = 0.251/0.667 = 0.376$

Attribute: *Spectacle Prescription*

$T_1 = myope$, $|T_1| = 3$, $T_2 = hypermetrope$, $|T_2| = 3$
$Freq(C_1, T_1) = 3$, $Freq(C_2, T_1) = 0$, $Info_{pres}(T_1) = -2/3 \times \log_2[2/3] - 0 = 0$
$Freq(C_1, T_2) = 1$, $Freq(C_2, T_2) = 2$
$Info_{pres}(T_2) = -1/3 \times \log_2[1/3] - 2/3 \times \log_2[2/3] = 0.918$
$Gain_{pres}(T) = Info(T) - [3/6 \times Info_{pres}(T_1) + 3/6 \times Info_{pres}(T_2)]$
$\qquad\qquad = 0.918 - 0.459 = 0.359$
$Gain\ Ratio = 0.359/0.459 = 0.782$

The attribute *prescription* is selected as the test to split the subset into two children along the branches *myope* and *hypermetrope*. The first branch includes only three instances of class *hard*. The second branch includes two instances of *none* and one instance of *hard* and is further split by the attribute *age*. The final decision tree is shown in Figure 3.6.

The decision tree in Figure 3.6 is a complete (perfect) tree. It may be over-fitted, though. There are nine leaf nodes on the tree, so nine rules could be derived from the tree. Notice that the number of rules generated by this method is much greater than the Induct algorithm we used earlier. Thus, the post-pruning technique is used to trim the tree. After that, a new set of rules is generated from the trimmed tree. We use the one-tailed probability of 25% as the confidence level. Its corresponding Z value is 0.69. The process will start from the lowest-level internal node on the right side of the tree (*prescription*). The error rates of the two leaf nodes are calculated as follows:

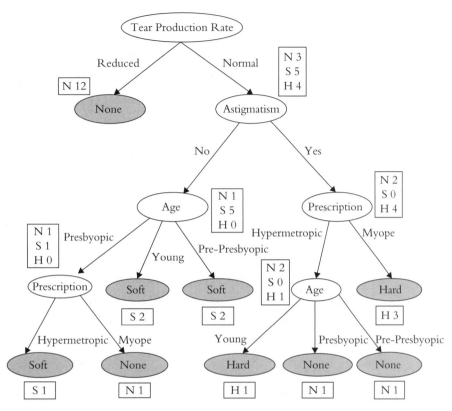

■ FIGURE 3.6
Decision tree
generated from
contact lens
dataset

1. Non–shaded circles are the internal nodes representing test attributes.
2. Shaded circles are the leaf nodes representing classes.
3. Branches represent the test values.
4. Letters and digits in squares represent the number of instances per class for each node, such as N for *none*, S for *soft*, and H for *hard* lens.

Soft:

$$f = 0, \quad z = 0.69 \text{ when } c = 25\%, N = 1,$$

$$q = (f + z^2/2N + z\sqrt{f/N - f^2/N + z^2/4N^2})/(1 + z^2/N)$$
$$= z^2/(N + z^2) = (0.69 \times 0.69)/(1 + 0.69 \times 0.69) = 0.322$$

None:

$$f = 0, \quad z = 0.69 \text{ when } c = 25\%, \quad N = 1,$$

$$q = (f + z^2/2N + z\sqrt{f/N - f^2/N + z^2/4N^2})/(1 + z^2/N)$$
$$= z^2/(N + z^2) = (0.69 \times 0.69)/(1 + 0.69 \times 0.69) = 0.322$$

The weighted average of the two children is $q = 1/2 \times 0.322 + 1/2 \times 0.322 = 0.322$. The estimated error rate of the internal node "prescription" itself is

$$f = 1/2 = 0.5, \quad N = 2,$$
$$q = (f + z^2/2N + z\sqrt{f/N - f^2/N + z^2/4N^2})/(1 + z^2/N)$$
$$= (0.5 + 0.69^2/(2 \times 2) + 0.69 \times \sqrt{f/N - f^2/N + z^2/4N^2})/(1 + 0.69^2/2)$$
$$= (0.5 + 0.119 + 0.2714)/1.24 = 0.719$$

Because the children's average error rate 0.322 is lower than the parent's 0.719, we keep the parent node. Let's move one level upward to the *age* node:

$$N = 6, \quad f = 1/6 = 0.167, \quad q = (0.167 + 0.0396 + 0.112)/1.079 = 0.295.$$

The estimated error rates of its two other children, *young* and *pre-presbyopic*, are calculated as follows:

Young:

$$N = 2, \quad f = 0, \quad q = z^2/(N + z^2) = 0.476/(2 + 0.476) = 0.192$$

Pre-presbyopic:

$$N = 2, \quad f = 0, \quad q = z^2/(N + z^2) = 0.476/(2 + 0.476) = 0.192$$

The weighted average error rate of the three children is $Q = (2/6) \times 0.192 + (2/6) \times 0.192 + (2/6) \times 0.719 = 0.368$. Because the error rate of the children (0.368) is larger than the error rate of the internal node *age* (0.295), we replace the internal node *age* with the leaf node *soft*, which is the dominant class in the subset. The replaced node has the error rate $q = 0.295$. After trimming off the nodes, the decision tree is as shown in Figure 3.7.

We now examine the right lowest-level internal node to move upwards one node along the path. The internal node *age* becomes the lowest-level internal node, as shown in Figure 3.7.

$$N = 3, \quad f = 1/3 = 0.333, \quad q = (0.333 + 0.079 + 0.204)/1.159 = 0.532$$

The error rates of its children node are as follows:

Young: $\qquad N = 1, \quad f = 0, \quad q = z^2/(N + z^2) = 0.476/(1 + 0.476)$
$$= 0.322$$

■ **FIGURE 3.7**
Decision tree
trimmed from
Figure 3.6

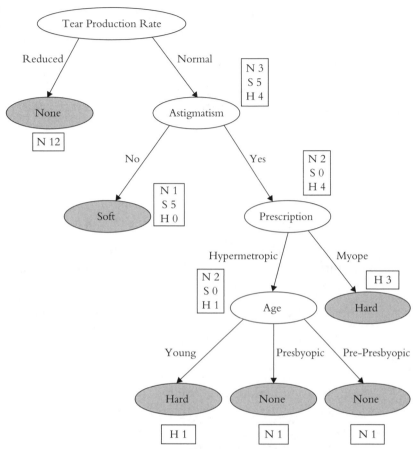

Pre-Presbyopic: $N = 1$, $f = 0$, $q = z^2/(N + z^2) = 0.476/(1 + 0.476)$
$= 0.322$

Presbyopic: $N = 1$, $f = 0$, $q = z^2/(N + z^2) = 0.476/(1 + 0.476)$
$= 0.322$

The weighted average is $q = (1/3) \times 0.322 + (1/3) \times 0.322 + (1/3) \times 0.322$
$= 0.322$. Since the internal error rate of the node *age* is bigger than those of its
children, we keep the node *age*. Now the next node to examine is the internal
node *prescription*:

$$N = 6, \quad f = 2/6 = 0.667, \quad q = (f + z^2/2N + z\sqrt{f/N - f^2/N + z^2/4N^2})/$$
$$(1 + z^2/N) = (0.333 + 0.040 + 0.139)/1.079 = 0.474$$

The right child leaf node *hard* has the following error rate:

$$N = 3, \qquad f = 0, \qquad q = z^2/(N + z^2) = 0.476/(3 + 0.476) = 0.137$$

Since the left child leaf node *age* has an error rate of 0.322, the weighted children's average error rate is $q = 3/6 \times 0.322 + 3/6 \times 0.137 = 0.230$, which is less than the internal node *prescription's* error rate 0.474. Therefore, we keep the internal node.

Now let's examine the internal node *astigmatism*:

$$f = 5/12, \qquad N = 12, \qquad q = (0.417 + 0.020 + 0.100)/1.040 = 0.516$$

The weighted error rate of the children *prescription* and *age* is

$$q = 6/12 \times 0.295 + 6/12 \times 0.474 = 0.385$$

Since the children's average error rate is less than the parent's, we keep the internal node *astigmatism*. Now the remaining node to examine is the root of the tree. The estimated error rate of the root is

$$N = 24, \qquad f = 9, \qquad q = (0.375 + 0.010 + 0.069)/1.020 = 0.445$$

The estimated error rate of child *none* is

$$N = 12, \qquad f = 0, \qquad q = z^2/(N + z^2) = 0.476/(12 + 0.476) = 0.038$$

The average estimated error rate of the children of the root is

$$q = 12/24 \times 0.038 + 12/24 \times 0.516 = 0.277$$

This is less than the parent's estimated rate. Therefore, we keep the root node.

In the post-pruning process above, we used the one-tailed confidence level $c = 0.25$ to prune the over-fit branches. The left internal node *age* is replaced by the leaf node *soft*. Other structures of the tree remain the same. The pruned tree has six leaf nodes from which new rules can be derived. Reading directly from the final pruned decision tree, six rules are generated as follows:

1. If *tear production rate* is *reduced*, then the *recommended contact lens* is *none*.
2. If *tear production rate* is *normal* and *astigmatism* is *no*, then the *recommended contact lens* is *soft*.
3. If *tear production rate* is *normal* and *astigmatism* is *yes* and *spectacle prescription* is *myope*, then the *recommended contact lens* is *hard*.

4. If *tear production rate* is *normal* and *astigmatism* is *yes* and *spectacle prescription* is *hypermetropic* and *age* is *presbyopic*, then the *recommended contact lens* is *none*.

5. If *tear production rate* is *normal* and *astigmatism* is *yes* and *spectacle prescription* is *hypermetropic* and *age* is *young*, then the *recommended contact lens* is *hard*.

6. If *tear production rate* is *normal* and *astigmatism* is *yes* and *spectacle prescription* is *hypermetropic* and *age* is *pre-presbyopic*, then the *recommended contact lens* is *none*.

When we compare the rules generated before and after post-pruning, we can see that the number of rules drops from nine to six, at the expense of the accuracy dropping from 100% to $23/24 = 95.8\%$. When comparing these rules with those generated by the "separate and conquer" approach of the Induct algorithm, we see that the number of rules is the same in both lists, although the rules in the two lists are not identical.

■ 3.5 PARTIAL DECISION TREE

The partial decision tree approach in classification learning is a mixture of the two previous approaches, "divide and conquer" and "separate and conquer." It uses a "separate and conquer" strategy, i.e., it builds a rule, removes the instances it covers, and recursively creates rules for the remaining instances until none are left. However, the method of creating a rule is different from that of the original "separate and conquer" approach. It uses a "partial decision tree" to induce individual rules, adopted from the "divide and conquer" method. A partial decision tree is built from the remaining dataset. Rules are directly generated out of the partial tree starting from the deepest leaf node in conjunction with all the nodes along the path towards the root. The partial tree is then discarded.

The approach has the efficiency of the "separate and conquer" approach because it excludes the instances used in producing the partial tree from the dataset, preventing those instances from participating in further rule induction. The accuracy of the algorithm is guaranteed by the partial tree induction process as in the "divide and conquer" approach. It may seem to be inefficient to build a different partial tree for each rule and discard it. However, the advantage of avoiding a lengthy and complicated rule-set optimization

■ **FIGURE 3.8**
Algorithm for
building a partial
decision tree

```
expand-subset (S) {
    (1) choose a test T and use it to split a dataset
            into sub-datasets
    (2) sort the subsets into ascending order according
            to the information values
    (3) while [there is a subset X that has not yet been
                    expanded AND all subsets expanded so far
                    are leaves]
                expand-subset (X);
    (4) if (all the subsets expanded are leaves AND prun-
            ing is not necessary)
                    undo expansion into subset and make node a
                    leaf;
} /* the end of expand-subset(s) */
```

process—necessary in both the "separate and conquer" and "divide and conquer" approaches—far outweighs this expense. A partial tree is far less complicated than a full tree. The "separating" mechanism makes the partial tree even simpler for less general partial trees.

The key feature of the partial decision-tree approach is building a partial tree instead of a fully explored decision tree. A partial decision tree is a regular decision tree except that it contains branches with undefined subtrees—nodes that are not leaves. The process of creating a partial decision tree is summarized in Figure 3.8.

It first selects an attribute to test and splits the dataset into subsets, as in the regular decision-tree method. The information gain value is used as the criterion to choose the attribute to test, as in C4.5. Then the subsets are expanded in order of ascending number of bits of information. The reason for this is that a subset with a low number of bits of information is more likely to result in a smaller subtree and therefore to produce a more general rule. The nodes with a higher number of bits of information may never get expanded further for the partial tree. The process of expanding the nodes proceeds recursively until all the children of the lowest-level internal node are leaves. Then, the pruning procedure starts from the internal node. It checks to see if it is better to replace the node with a single leaf. The pruning procedure continues backtracking, going through every internal node and its children that have been expanded.

After the pruning, the algorithm checks the children of lowest-level internal nodes to see if they are all leaves, since pruning causes shrinking into subtrees and may cause a higher-level unexpanded node to become a lowest-level node. If there is at least one unexpanded node, the expanding and pruning process will proceed from the unexpanded internal node with the next highest number of bits of information.

The procedure of expanding and pruning partial decision trees is illustrated in Figure 3.9. In the figure, the ellipses represent the internal nodes, the shaded color is for unexpanded nodes, and the unshaded color is for expanded nodes. The rectangle represents a leaf node. The numbers separated by a dot in the nodes indicate the level number and the sibling number of the level. The following explains the steps in the scenario of the figure in detail:

A. Select an attribute A to split dataset S into three subsets 2.1, 2.2, and 2.3 using the same method as in C4.5 algorithm.

B. Among the sibling nodes, node 2.2 has the lowest number of bits of information. Choose this node to expand (to split further) in the same way as in step A. Two subsets are created, nodes 3.1 and 3.2.

C. The subset 3.1 has fewer bits of information than the subset 3.2 and is further split into node 4.1 and a leaf node.

D. Between the two children of node 3.1, one node is a leaf node and the other non-leaf node 4.1 is expanded into two other leaf nodes.

E. The process of expanding stops at node 4.1 because both children are leaves. Next, the process of pruning starts at node 4.1 and goes upward. Suppose node 4.1 needs to be pruned and is, in fact, replaced by a leaf node. This results in step E of Figure 3.9.

F. The pruning process goes upward until a higher-level node with no unexpanded children is found. In our example, the highest-level node is node 2.2. At this point, nodes 3.1 and 2.2 are replaced by leaf nodes, as shown in step G of Figure 3.9.

G. The lowest level of the partial decision tree is now level 2. Among the sibling nodes of this level, only one is a leaf node. Therefore, further expanding is needed.

■ **FIGURE 3.9**
Expanding and
pruning of a partial
decision tree
Ellipse: internal
nodes (shaded
ellipse: unex-
panded nodes;
unshaded ellipse:
expanded nodes)
Rectangles: leaf
nodes.

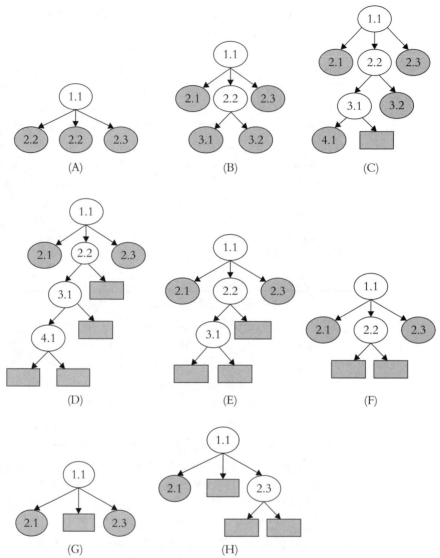

H. Node 2.3 is expanded because it has fewer bits of information than node 2.1. Both children of node 2.3 are leaves. This triggers the pruning check again. If the pruning is not needed and node 2.3 is the highest-level node with no unexpanded children, the pruning stops here and this subtree is saved. At this point, we check to see if node expansion is necessary. Since the lowest-level nodes are all leaves, no more expansion is needed. This tree (step H in Figure 3.9) is the final partial decision tree we get. A single rule can be derived by following the tree down to a lowest-level leaf.

This method is simple and surprisingly produces rule sets that compare favorably to those produced by C4.5 and C5.0 and are more accurate than those produced by RIPPER [Frank 1998]. Hence, the partial decision-tree approach outperforms (in accuracy) the RIPPER "separate and conquer" type system. The experiment also shows that the partial decision-tree approach greatly outperforms C4.5 in speed when the dataset is less noisy because perfect data prevents the algorithm from pruning partial trees. As the degree of noise increases, the speed gain of the partial-tree approach decreases. The overall time complexity of the partial-tree approach is $O(a \times n \log n)$, where a is the number of attributes and n is the number of instances in the dataset. The complexity of RIPPER is $O(a \times n \log^2 n)$.

Next, we use the contact lens database in Table 3.2 to illustrate how the partial decision-tree approach is applied to induce knowledge rules. The following steps illustrate the procedure of deriving the knowledge rules from the database:

1. At the root of the tree, we select the attribute *tear production rate*, which has the largest information gain ratio, as was shown in Figure 3.6.
2. Next, we determine which child is to be expanded. Since the left node *none* is a leaf node, there is no need to expand. The right child *astigmatism* needs to be expanded and split into two branches, *no* and *yes*.
3. Since both branches are internal nodes, we expand the *no* branch, which has bit of information 0.65, which is less than the *yes* branch, 0.918.
4. The *no* branch leads to the attribute *age*, which has the largest information gain ratio and is split into three children.
5. Among the three children, the branch *presbyopic* leads to an internal node and needs to be expanded.
6. The branch *presbyopic* is split into two leaves through the attribute *prescription*. The expanding process stops here. Next, we start the post-pruning on the partial tree, going upward from the bottom.
7. Using the same technique as in C4.5, the internal node *age* is replaced with a leaf node *soft*.

8. Now, the node *astigmatism* becomes the lowest-level internal node. Its right branch is still not a leaf node and needs to be expanded.

9. The branch *astigmatism is yes* is split into two branches *hypermetropic* and *myopic* by the attribute *prescription*. The branch *hypermetropic* leads to the attribute *age* and splits into three leaf nodes.

10. The expanding procedure stops at this point and the post-pruning starts again toward the root of the partial tree.

11. No internal node is replaced in this round of post-pruning. The final partial tree is shown in Figure 3.10.

12. Six rules are generated from the partial tree.

13. The instances covered by the partial tree are excluded from the dataset. Since the partial tree covered all the instances of the dataset, no more partial trees need to be created.

Our example demonstrates that when the dataset doesn't contain any noisy data, the partial tree created by using the partial decision-tree approach is in fact the same as the decision tree created by the C4.5 algorithm.

■ FIGURE 3.10
Partial decision tree derived from contact lens dataset

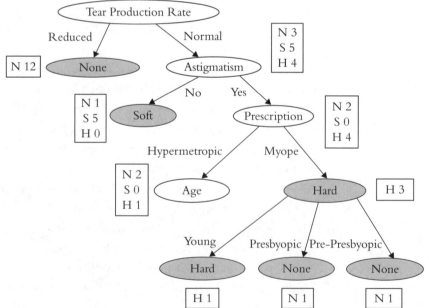

■ 3.6 CHAPTER SUMMARY

In this chapter, several algorithms for classification methods in data mining were presented. A general introduction to classification and its role in data-mining applications was also given. Every approach to classification learning has its advantages and disadvantages. The beauty of the "separate and conquer" strategy is its simplicity, while the advantage of the "divide and conquer" approach is its accuracy. The partial decision-tree approach combines the benefits of both methods.

The Prism, Induct, REP, IREP, and RIPPER algorithms, have been used to elaborate the separate-and-conquer approach. As for the divide-and-conquer approach, methods such as ID3, C4.5, and C5.0 have been used to illustrate methods and applications using practical examples. The partial decision-tree approach in classification learning, a mixture of the "divide and conquer" and "separate and conquer" approaches, was discussed in depth with examples. The partial decision-tree approach uses a "separate and conquer" strategy to build a rule, removes the instances it covers, and recursively creates rules for the remaining instances until none are left. On the other hand, it is also used to induce individual rules, adopted from the "divide and conquer" method.

■ 3.7 EXERCISES

1. Table 3.7 contains data on the effects of dietary fiber. Twelve female subjects were fed a controlled diet. Before each meal they ate crackers containing either bran fiber, gum fiber, a combination of both, or no fiber (control). Their caloric intake was monitored. Subjects reported any gastric or other problems. The table contains the following attributes:

   • Cracker: Type of fiber in the cracker
   • Diet: One of four diets (type of cracker)
   • Subject: Identification for each of the 12 subjects
   • Digested: Digested calories (difference between caloric intake and calories passed through system)
   • Bloat: Degree of bloating and flatulence reported by the subjects

   a. Use the Prism approach to generate decision rules from Table 3.7. Choose "bloat" as the class variable.

■ TABLE 3.7 High-fiber diet plan

Cracker	Diet	Subject	Digested	Bloat
Control	1	3	1772.84	None
Bran	4	3	1752.63	Low
Combo	3	9	2121.97	Med
Gum	2	4	2558.61	High
Gum	2	1	2026.91	Med
Bran	4	1	2047.42	Low
Combo	3	1	2254.75	Low
Control	1	1	2353.21	Med
Combo	3	2	2153.36	None
Gum	2	2	2331.19	None
Bran	4	2	2547.77	None
Control	1	2	2591.12	None
Gum	2	3	2012.36	Low
Combo	3	3	1956.18	Low
Combo	3	4	2025.97	None
Bran	4	4	1669.12	None
Control	1	4	2452.73	None
Bran	4	5	2207.37	Low
Gum	2	5	1944.48	Med
Control	1	5	1927.68	Low
Combo	3	5	2190.1	High
Control	1	6	1635.28	None
Combo	3	6	1693.35	Low
Bran	4	6	1707.34	Low
Gum	2	6	1871.95	High
Gum	2	7	2245.03	None
Combo	3	7	2436.79	Low
Control	1	7	2667.14	Low
Bran	4	7	2766.86	None
Bran	4	8	2279.82	None

■ TABLE 3.7 High-fiber diet plan (*continued*)

Cracker	Diet	Subject	Digested	Bloat
Combo	3	8	1844.77	High
Gum	2	8	2002.73	High
Control	1	8	2220.22	Med
Control	1	9	1888.29	Low
Gum	2	9	1804.27	High
Bran	4	9	2293.27	Med
Bran	4	10	2357.4	None
Control	1	10	2359.9	None
Combo	3	10	2292.46	Low
Gum	2	10	2433.46	High
Gum	2	11	1681.86	Low
Control	1	11	1902.75	None
Bran	4	11	2003.16	None
Combo	3	11	2137.12	Med
Combo	3	12	2203.07	Med
Control	1	12	2125.39	Low
Gum	2	12	2166.77	Med
Bran	4	12	2287.52	None

   b. List all possible decision rules that can be generated from Table 3.7 by following the Induct approach.

   c. Use the IREP algorithm presented in this chapter to generate decision rules for the high-fiber diet plan database in Table 3.7.

2. Table 3.8 contains data that were collected on the genus of flea beetle *Chaetocnema*, which contains three species: *concinna* (Con), *heikertingeri* (Hei), and *heptapotamica* (Hep). Measurements were made on the width and angle of the aedeagus of each beetle. The table contains the following attributes:

- Width: The maximal width of the aedeagus in the forepart (in microns)
- Angle: The front angle of the aedeagus (1 unit = 7.5 degrees)
- Species: The species of flea beetle from the genus *Chaetocnema*

■ **TABLE 3.8 Flea beetles**

Width	Angle	Species	Width	Angle	Species
150	15	Con	137	9	Hep
147	13	Con	141	11	Hep
144	14	Con	138	9	Hep
144	16	Con	143	9	Hep
153	13	Con	142	11	Hep
140	15	Con	144	10	Hep
151	14	Con	138	10	Hep
143	14	Con	140	10	Hep
144	14	Con	130	9	Hep
142	15	Con	137	11	Hep
141	13	Con	137	10	Hep
150	15	Con	136	9	Hep
148	13	Con	140	10	Hep
154	15	Con	128	14	Hei
147	14	Con	129	14	Hei
137	14	Con	124	13	Hei
134	15	Con	129	14	Hei
157	14	Con	145	8	Hep
149	13	Con	140	11	Hep
147	13	Con	140	11	Hep
148	14	Con	131	10	Hep
120	14	Hei	139	11	Hep

The goal of the original study was to form a classification rule to distinguish the three species. Answer the following questions:

a. Use the ID3 strategy to generate decision rules from Table 3.8.

b. Generate classification rules from the table using C4.5 strategies.

c. Apply the partial decision-tree approach to generate all possible classification rules.

d. Compare and contrast all classification rules generated in (a), (b), and (c).

■ **TABLE 3.8 Flea beetles (*continued*)**

Width	Angle	Species	Width	Angle	Species
123	16	Hei	139	10	Hep
130	14	Hei	136	12	Hep
131	16	Hei	129	11	Hep
116	16	Hei	140	10	Hep
122	15	Hei	129	14	Hei
127	15	Hei	130	13	Hei
132	16	Hei	129	13	Hei
125	14	Hei	122	12	Hei
119	13	Hei	129	15	Hei
122	13	Hei	124	15	Hei
120	15	Hei	120	13	Hei
119	14	Hei	119	16	Hei
123	15	Hei	119	14	Hei
125	15	Hei	133	13	Hei
125	14	Hei	121	15	Hei

3. Table 3.9 contains data about 40 sampled elementary school students in terms of the following nine attributes:

- Gender: Boy or girl
- Race: White or other
- Region: Rural or urban
- School: Dooley or East
- Grades: Rank of making good grades (1 = most important, 4 = least important)
- Sports: Rank of being good at sports (1 = most important, 4 = least important)
- Looks: Rank of being handsome/pretty (1 = most important, 4 = least important)
- Money: Rank of having lots of money (1 = most important, 4 = least important)
- Goal: Student's choice of personal goals (make good grades, be popular, be good at sports)

Assuming that the goal of the study is to generate classification rules to determine the role of the personal factors that affect students' perception about educational objectives, answer the following questions:

a. Use the ID3 strategy to generate decision rules from Table 3.9.

b. Generate classification rules from the table using C4.5 strategies.

c. Apply the partial decision-tree approach to generate all possible classification rules.

d. Compare and contrast all the classification rules generated in (a), (b), and (c) in terms of accuracy.

▓ TABLE 3.9 Educational objectives of elementary school kids

Gender	Race	Region	School	Goal	Grades	Sports	Looks	Money
Boy	White	Rural	Dooley	Grades	4	1	2	3
Boy	Other	Rural	Dooley	Popular	4	3	2	1
Boy	White	Rural	Dooley	Sports	3	1	2	4
Boy	White	Rural	Dooley	Grades	1	2	3	4
Boy	White	Rural	Dooley	Sports	4	1	2	3
Boy	White	Rural	Dooley	Popular	4	2	1	3
Boy	White	Rural	Dooley	Sports	4	2	1	3
Boy	White	Rural	Dooley	Grades	4	3	1	2
Boy	White	Rural	Dooley	Sports	3	1	4	2
Boy	White	Rural	Dooley	Popular	4	2	1	3
Boy	White	Rural	Dooley	Sports	3	1	4	2
Girl	Other	Urban	East	Grades	1	2	3	4
Girl	White	Urban	East	Popular	4	3	1	2
Girl	White	Urban	East	Grades	1	3	2	4
Girl	Other	Urban	East	Sports	4	1	2	3
Girl	White	Urban	East	Grades	2	1	3	4
Girl	Other	Urban	East	Grades	2	4	1	3
Girl	White	Urban	East	Grades	3	2	1	4
Girl	White	Urban	East	Grades	3	2	1	4
Girl	White	Urban	East	Grades	1	2	3	4
Girl	White	Urban	East	Popular	2	1	3	4

■ TABLE 3.9 Educational objectives of elementary school kids (*continued*)

Gender	Race	Region	School	Goal	Grades	Sports	Looks	Money
Girl	White	Urban	East	Sports	1	3	2	4
Girl	White	Urban	East	Grades	1	2	3	4
Girl	White	Urban	East	Grades	1	2	3	4
Girl	White	Urban	East	Grades	4	3	1	2
Girl	White	Urban	East	Grades	1	2	4	3
Boy	White	Urban	East	Grades	3	1	2	4
Boy	White	Urban	East	Popular	1	3	2	4
Boy	White	Urban	East	Grades	3	1	4	2
Boy	White	Urban	East	Sports	1	2	4	3
Boy	White	Urban	East	Grades	3	1	2	4
Boy	White	Urban	East	Sports	2	1	4	3
Boy	White	Urban	East	Sports	2	3	1	4
Boy	White	Urban	East	Grades	2	1	4	3
Boy	Other	Urban	East	Grades	4	1	3	2
Boy	White	Urban	East	Grades	2	1	4	3
Boy	White	Urban	East	Grades	2	1	3	4
Girl	White	Urban	East	Grades	4	2	1	3
Girl	White	Urban	East	Grades	1	2	3	4
Girl	White	Urban	East	Grades	2	1	4	3

4. Table 3.10 contains the data from a statement by Texaco, Inc. to the Air and Water Pollution Subcommittee of the Senate Public Works Committee on June 26, 1973. Mr. John McKinley, President of Texaco, cited an automobile filter developed by Associated Octel Company as effective in reducing pollution. However, questions had been raised about the effects of filters on vehicle performance, fuel consumption, exhaust gas back pressure, and silencing. For the last question, he referred to the data shown in Table 3.10 as evidence that the silencing properties of the Octel filter were at least equal to those of standard silencers. The table contains the data of 36 cases with the following four attributes:

- Noise: Noise level reading (in decibels)
- Size: Vehicle size (1 = small, 2 = medium, 3 = large)

■ **TABLE 3.10 Auto pollution filter noise**

Noise	Size	Type	Side	Noise	Size	Type	Side
810	1	1	1	770	3	1	2
820	1	1	1	820	1	2	1
820	1	1	1	820	1	2	1
840	2	1	1	820	1	2	1
840	2	1	1	820	2	2	1
845	2	1	1	820	2	2	1
785	3	1	1	825	2	2	1
790	3	1	1	775	3	2	1
785	3	1	1	775	3	2	1
835	1	1	2	775	3	2	1
835	1	1	2	825	1	2	2
835	1	1	2	825	1	2	2
845	2	1	2	825	1	2	2
855	2	1	2	815	2	2	2
850	2	1	2	825	2	2	2
760	3	1	2	760	3	1	2
825	2	2	2	760	3	2	2
770	3	2	2	765	3	2	2

- Type: Filter type (1 = standard silencer, 2 = Octel filter)
- Side: Filter location (1 = right side, 2 = left side of car)

Answer the following questions to justify and support the claims made by Texaco by generating the appropriate classification rules:

a. Use the Prism approach to generate decision rules from Table 3.10. Choose "Noise" as the class variable.

b. List all possible decision rules that can be generated from Table 3.10 by following the Induct approach.

c. Apply the IREP algorithm presented in the chapter to the auto pollution filter noise database in Table 3.10 to generate the decision rules.

■ 3.8 SELECTED BIBLIOGRAPHIC NOTES

General ideas on classification rules and decision trees described in Section 3.2 are from [Baralis 2004], [Charu 2002], and [Deshpande 2002]. Various application of classification methods are described in [Charu 2004], [Diamantini 2000], [Islam 2004], [Lesh 1999], [Lutu 2002], and [Zaki 2003]. [Frank 1999b] and [Meretakis 2000] deal with classification on text databases, whereas [Shintani 1998] and [Yu 2003] present the efficient application of classification on large datasets using hierarchical properties.

The detailed descriptions of the ID3 algorithm in Section 3.4.1 were mainly taken from [Quinlan 1979], [Quinlan 1983], and [Quinlan 1986]. The contact lens example, which was originally taken from the world of ophthalmic optics, was adopted from [Cendrowska 1987]. The Prism algorithm in Section 3.3.1, a rule induction method based on ID3, was summarized from [Cendrowska 1987], whereas the Induct algorithm, which is an extension of Prism used to deal with noisy data, was described in Section 3.3.2 using methods provided in [Gaines 1995].

[Pagallo 1990], [Brunk 1991], [Richards 1998], and [Cohen 1995] discuss the errors resulting from favoring over-fitted rules in Induct. [Furnkranz 1994] and [Cohen 1995] propose REP, IREP, and RIPPER to correct this problem. Furthermore, [Cohen 1995] claims that RIPPER produces rules that are more accurate than REP and IREP and competitive with those of C4.5. The detailed discussion in Section 3.3.3 was taken from these references.

C4.5 uses the same basic strategy as ID3 with gain ratio as an added feature for the attribute selection criteria, whereas C5.0 is an extended version of C4.5 that shows improved performance. The description given in Section 3.4.2 for C4.5 and C5.0 was taken from [Quinlan 1993] and [Quinlan 1997]. [Mingers 1989] deals with the problem of overcompensating for gain ratio by preferring attributes with unevenly divided sub-datasets. The solution to this overcompensation problem was proposed in [Frank 1998] and [Frank 1999a]. The post-pruning method adopted by Quinlan for C4.5 was used in Cart and can be found in [Breiman 1984]. The MDL (Minimum Description Length) heuristic used in C4.5 to optimize the rules in a rule subset was described in [Rissanen 1983a] and [Rissanen 1983b]. C4.5 also adopted a simulated annealing method to find the near-best rule subset in a very large rule set, which is more computationally effective and can produce more satisfactory results. A detailed description of this method can be found in [Press 1988].

The partial decision-tree approach described in Section 3.5 was primarily based on the approach proposed in [Frank 1998]. [Skomorokhov 2000] dealt with classification trees in APL, whereas [Buja 2001] focused on tree-based regression and classification. [Sattler 2001], [Ankerst 1999], and [Ding 2002] discuss the decision-tree classification method, whereas [Stern 2004] deals with a classification tree analysis. Application of the data classification method to fraud detection is found in [Phua 2004] and [Bonchi 1999].

■ 3.9 CHAPTER BIBLIOGRAPHY

[Ankerst 1999] Mihael Ankerst, Christian Elsen, Martin Ester, and Hans-Peter Kriegel: "Visual classification: an interactive approach to decision tree construction," *Proceedings of the Fifth ACM SIGKDD International Conference on Knowledge Discovery and Data Mining*, August 1999.

[Baralis 2004] Elena Baralis, Silvia Chiusano, and Paolo Garza: "Data mining (DM): On support thresholds in associative classification," *Proceedings of the 2004 ACM Symposium on Applied Computing*, March 2004.

[Bonchi 1999] F. Bonchi, F. Giannotti, G. Mainetto, and D. Pedreschi: "A Classification-based Methodology for Planning Audit Strategies in Fraud Detection," *Proceedings of the 5th ACM SIGKDD International Conference on Knowledge Discovery and Data Mining*, 1999.

[Breiman 1984] L. Breiman, J. H. Friedman, R. A. Olshen, and C. J. Stone: *Classification and Regression Trees*. Belmont, CA: Wadsworth International Group, 1984.

[Brunk 1991] Clifford Brunk, and Michael Pazzani: "Noise-tolerant relational concept learning algorithms," *Proceedings of the Eighth International Workshop on Machine Learning*, Ithaca, New York Morgan Kaufmann, 1991.

[Buja 2001] Andreas Buja and Yung-Seop Lee: "Data mining criteria for tree-based regression and classification," *Proceedings of the Seventh ACM SIGKDD International Conference on Knowledge Discovery and Data Mining*, August 2001.

[Cendrowska 1987] Jadzia Cendrowska: "PRISM: An Algorithm for Inducing Modular Rules," *International Journal of Human–Computer Studies*, 27(4), 349–370, Academic Press, 1987.

[Charu 2002] Charu C. Aggarwal: "Sequences and strings: On effective classification of strings with wavelets," *Proceedings of the Eighth ACM SIGKDD International Conference on Knowledge Discovery and Data Mining*, July 2002.

[Charu 2004] Charu C. Aggarwal, Jiawei Han, Jianyong Wang, and Philip S. Yu. "On demand classification of data streams," *Proceedings of the 2004 ACM SIGKDD International Conference on Knowledge Discovery and Data Mining*, August 2004.

[Cohen 1995] W. Cohen: "Fast effective rule induction," *Proceedings of the 12th International Conference on Machine Learning,* 115–123, Morgan Kaufmann, 1995.

[Deshpande 2002] Mukund Deshpande and George Karypis: "Classification: Using conjunction of attribute values for classification," *Proceedings of the Eleventh International Conference on Information and Knowledge Management,* November 2002.

[Diamantini 2000] Claudia Diamantini and Maurizio Panti: "An efficient and scalable data compression approach to classification," *ACM SIGKDD Explorations Newsletter,* 2(2), August 2004.

[Ding 2002] Qiang Ding, Qin Ding, and William Perrizo: "Database and digital library technologies: Decision tree classification of spatial data streams using Peano Count Trees," *Proceedings of the 2002 ACM Symposium on Applied Computing,* March 2002.

[Frank 1998] Eibe Frank and Ian H. Witten: "Generating Accurate Rule Sets Without Global Optimization," *15th International Conference on Machine Learning,* 144–151, Morgan Kaufmann, 1998.

[Frank 1999a] Eibe Frank and Ian H. Witten: "Making Better Use of Global Discretization," *16th International Conference on Machine Learning,* 115–123, Morgan Kaufmann, 1999.

[Frank 1999b] Eibe Frank, Gordon W. Paynter, Ian H. Witten: "Domain-Specific Keyphrase Extraction," *Proceedings of the 16th International Joint Conference on Articial Intelligence (IJCAI99),* Stockholm, 1999.

[Furnkranz 1994] J. Furnkranz and G. Widmer: "Incremental Reduced Error Pruning (IREP)," in W. Cohen and H. Hirsh (eds.), *Proceedings of the 11th International Conference on Machine Learning (ML-94),* 70–77, Morgan Kaufmann, 1994.

[Gaines 1995] B. R. Gaines and P. Compton: "Induction of Ripple-Down Rules Applied to Modeling Large Databases," *Journal of Intelligent Information Systems,* 5, 211–228, Kluwer, 1995.

[Islam 2004] Md. Zahidul Islam and Ljiljana Brankovic: "A framework for privacy preserving classification in data mining," *Proceedings of the Second Workshop on Australasian Information Security, Data Mining and Web Intelligence, and Software Internationalization,* Volume 32, January 2004.

[Lesh 1999] Neal Lesh, Mohammed J. Zaki, and Mitsunori Ogihara: "Mining features for sequence classification," *Proceedings of the Fifth ACM SIGKDD International Conference on Knowledge Discovery and Data Mining,* August 1999.

[Lutu 2002] Patricia E. N. Lutu: "Data Mining: An integrated approach for scaling up classification and prediction algorithms for data mining," *Proceedings of the 2002 Annual Research Conference of the South African Institute of Computer Scientists and Information Technologists on Enablement through Technology,* September 2002.

[Meretakis 2000] Dimitris Meretakis, Dimitris Fragoudis, Hongjun Lu, and Spiros Likothanassis: "Scalable association-based text classification," *Proceedings of the Ninth International Conference on Information and Knowledge Management*, November 2000.

[Mingers 1989] J. Mingers: "An Empirical Comparison of Pruning Methods for Decision Tree Induction." *Machine Learning*, 4(2):227–243, November 1989.

[Pagallo 1990] G. Pagallo and D. Haussler: "Boolean Feature Discovery in Empirical Learning," *Machine Learning*, Vol. 5, No. 1, 71–99, 1990.

[Phua 2004] Clifton Phua, Damminda Alahakoon, and Vincent Lee: "Minority report in fraud detection: Classification of skewed data," *ACM SIGKDD Explorations Newsletter*, 6(1), June 2004.

[Press 1988] W. H. Press, B. P. Flannery, S. A. Teukolsky, and W. T. Vetterling: *Numerical Recipes in C: The Art of Scientific Computing*, Cambridge University Press, Cambridge, MA, 1988.

[Quinlan 1979] J. R. Quinlan: "Discovering Rules by Induction from Large Collections of Examples," in D. Mitchie (ed.), *Expert Systems in The Microelectronic Age*, pp. 168–201, 1979.

[Quinlan 1983] J. R. Quinlan: "Learning Efficient Classification Procedures and Their Application to Chess Endgames," in R. Michalski, J. Carbonell, and T. Mitchell (eds.), *Machine Learning: An Artificial Intelligence Approach*, Vol. 1, pp. 463–482, Morgan Kaufmann, 1983.

[Quinlan 1986] J. R. Quinlan: "Induction of Decision Trees," *Machine Learning*, Vol. 1, No. 1, pp. 81–106, Kluwer, 1986.

[Quinlan 1993] J. R. Quinlan: *C4.5: Programs for Machine Learning*, Morgan Kaufmann, 1993.

[Quinlan 1997] J. R. Quinlan: "Learning Logical Definitions from Relations," *Machine Learning*, Vol. 5, pp. 239–266, 1997.

[Richards 1998] D. Richards and P. Compton: "Taking Up the Situated Cognition Challenge with Ripple Down Rules," *International Journal of Human–Computer Studies*, Vol. 49, No. 6, pp. 895–926, 1998.

[Rissanen 1983a] J. Rissanen: "A Universal Prior for Integers and Estimation by Minimum Description Length," *Annals of Statistics*, Vol. 11, No. 2, pp. 416–431, 1983.

[Rissanen 1983b] J. Rissanen: "A Universal Data Compression System," *IEEE Transactions on Information Theory*, Vol. 29, No. 5, pp. 656–664, 1983.

[Sattler 2001] Kai-Uwe. Sattler and O. Dunemann: "SQL Database Primitives for Decision Tree Classifiers," *Proceedings of the 10th International Conference on Information and Knowledge Management*, 2001.

[Shintani 1998] T. Shintani and M. Kitsuregawa: "Parallel Mining Algorithms for Generalized Association Rules with Classification Hierarchy," *Proceedings of the 1998 ACM SIGMOD International Conference on Management of Data*, 1998.

[Skomorokhov 2000] A. Skomorokhov and V. Kutinsky: "Classification Trees in APL: Implementation and Application," *Proceedings of the 2001 Conference on APL: An Arrays Odyssey*, Vol. 31, No. 2, 2000.

[Stern 2004] S. E. Stern, S. Gregor, M. A. Martin, S. Goode, and J. Rolfe: "A Classification Tree Analysis of Broadband Adoption in Australian Households," *Proceedings of the 6th International Conference on Electronic Commerce*, 2004.

[Yu 2003] H. Yu, J. Yang, and J. Han: "Classifying Large Datasets Using SVMs with Hierarchical Clusters," *Proceedings of the 9th ACM SIGKDD International Conference on Knowledge Discovery and Data Mining*, 2003.

[Zaki 2003] M. J. Zaki and C. C. Aggarwal: "XRules: An Effective Structural Classifier for XML Data," *Proceedings of the 9th ACM SIGKDD International Conference on Knowledge Discovery and Data Mining*, 2003.

CHAPTER 4

Statistics for Data Mining

■ 4.1 INTRODUCTION

Statistics is a useful tool in data mining and can be used to analyze or make inferences about data in order to discover useful information and to draw statistical conclusions about a dataset in a database. Figure 4.1 illustrates statistical query processing. The population is a collection of objects about which we try to discover new facts and information. Its member may be known or unknown. If the population is unknown, then a sample dataset has to be used to derive facts or trends about the population. On the other hand, if the population is known, the entire population may be stored in the database and used for statistical processing. If the population is known but very large, a sample dataset may also be used for further processing.

Without a database, statisticians perform statistical processing to make inferences about a population from the data directly. But when the dataset is stored in a database, it can usually be handled in a more efficient manner using the Structured Query Language. In traditional database query processing, we usually retrieve data using traditional SQL-like queries with built-in functions or operators to find the information of interest. When combining database queries with statistical processing, statisticians face two major problems. One problem is that the structure or format of the data or variables retrieved does not match the statistical variables or functions. The other problem is that the built-in functions provided by the database system may not support the statistical calculations that need to be performed.

■ **FIGURE 4.1**
Statistical query
processing

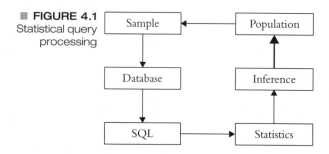

There are many statistical software packages available today, so we will not focus on how to write codes or build our own statistical function libraries. We will assume that there are some basic built-in statistical functions in the system you are using. Hence, we may call these functions when querying the database. Therefore, query processing will be performed as a two-step process. The first step involves statistical processing, and the second step involves traditional query processing. The transition from the first to the second process may involve calling functions in software external to the database to provide the statistical variables or functions needed in the traditional queries. This fact is illustrated in Figure 4.2. In this chapter, we will discuss several approaches to statistical analysis, interpretation, and implementation with examples using the data in a house sales database.

A statistic is a function implemented on a sample database, from which information on the parameter(s) or the model of interest can be derived and used for inference purposes. Usually, two hypotheses are set. The null hypothesis expresses the claim of interest, which we hope to be true. The other

■ **FIGURE 4.2**
Statistical vs.
traditional query
processing

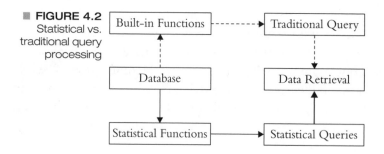

is the alternative hypothesis, which is the opposite of the null hypothesis. Statistical inference allows us to either accept or reject the null hypothesis. Based on the observed value, how possible the statistic is beyond this value under the null hypothesis (also called the p-value) is determined. Following statistical logic, when the possibility is fairly large (usually more than 0.05), the null hypothesis is not rejected. However, when the possibility is very small (usually less than 0.05), this event does not seem to occur under the null hypothesis, and the conclusion is that the null hypothesis is wrong, and the alternative hypothesis is accepted.

Under the normal assumption, two standard deviations are usually set to determine the confidence interval, which is about 0.95. When the observed value falls within the confidence interval, the null hypothesis is accepted. Otherwise, the null hypothesis is rejected, and the alternative hypothesis is preferred. In later sections, we will refer to this statistical principle to derive a logical interpretation of the data from the database being considered.

■ 4.2 HOUSE SALES DATA

The house sales dataset contains 66 observations, which are listed in Section 4.8. It describes house resale prices and property tax assessment in Albuquerque, New Mexico, which were recorded randomly during the period from February 15 to April 30, 1993. There are seven attributes of interest, as listed below:

1. Selling price (hundreds of dollars)
2. Area: square feet of living space
3. Age: age of house (years)
4. Number of features: dishwasher, refrigerator, microwave, disposal, washer, intercom, skylight, compactor, dryer, handicap access, cable TV
5. Northeast section location: yes (1), no (0)
6. Custom-built: yes (1), no (0)
7. Corner location: yes (1), no (0)
8. Tax (dollars)

Our interest lies in finding the relationships among these variables and in establishing linear regression to generate information from the database through statistical analyses. Such information can be useful for strategic decision-making. The variables are the attributes of the database, and the house number used as the index is selected as the primary key.

■ 4.3 CONDITIONAL PROBABILITY

Conditional probability is one of the basic concepts in probability theory. It generally refers to the interdependence between events. Let A and B be two events. The conditional probability of event A occurring given the occurrence of event B is represented as the probability that events A and B simultaneously occur divided by the probability of event B occurring. This is expressed as follows:

$$P(A \mid B) = \frac{P(AB)}{P(B)} \qquad (4.1)$$

where $P(A)$ and $P(B)$ are the probabilities of occurrence of the two events A and B, respectively. Similarly, we can define the conditional probability of B given A.

The conditional probability $P(A \mid B)$ measures the dependence of A on B. It ranges from 0 to 1. When $P(A \mid B)$ equals $P(A)$, event A is not constrained by event B, or we also say that event A is independent of event B. When $P(A) < P(A \mid B) < 1$, event A is more likely to occur than event B. This is called the positive dependence of A on B. On the other hand, when $0 < P(A \mid B) < P(A)$, event A is more likely to occur than event B is to not occur, or event A is not more likely to occur than event B. This is called the negative dependency of A on B. There are two special types of events: null events and sure events. Both events may be independent or dependent on each other. Note here that the conditional probability of event A given event B and the conditional probability of event B given event A may be much different, although both are measures of their interdependence.

Now let us consider the following question posed against the house sales dataset: How likely is it for a corner-located house to be located on the northeast side? There is no simple SQL query that supports the expression "how likely." In these cases, we have to rely on the conditional probability concept to analyze the relationship between the relevant variables from the house sales data: *northeast* location and *corner* location. In other words, we need to find the conditional probability of *northeast* and *corner* location given the *corner* location. Following formula (4.1), we calculate the joint frequency of occurrence of *northeast* and *corner* location divided by the frequency of occurrence of *corner* location. To find the frequencies of these two attributes, the following query can be processed. Query 1 is a natural-language style query, whereas SQL 1 is a SQL-style query:

(Query 1)
How many houses in the RmSale table are located on northeast side and corner locations?

(SQL 1)
Select count(*) from table RmSale where northeast = yes and corner = yes.

Executing the query SQL 1 will retrieve the value 9.

The frequencies of occurrence of the two variables, *northeast* and *corner* locations, are summarized in Table 4.1. The associated conditional probabilities (or strictly speaking, estimates of these conditional probabilities) can be calculated based on the formula (4.1), and they are given in Table 4.2, in which rows represent the event and columns represent the condition. Therefore, the conditional probability of *northeast* location given the *corner* location is obtained by replacing the probability in the numerator with 9/66 (the probability of both *corner* and *northeast* locations) and the probability in the denominator replaced with 15/66 (the probability of *corner* location). Thus, the conditional probability would be 9/15 = 0.6, as shown in the first non-empty cell of Table 4.2.

Table 4.2 shows that the conditional probabilities and the unconditional probabilities are very close, and we can conclude that the two attributes have a weak correlation. Or we can say that *northeast* location and *corner* location are independent (i.e., not related).

To implement the conditional probability calculations, we note that Table 4.1 is not part of the database and that the required operations are not on the

▓ **TABLE 4.1 Frequencies of northeast and corner locations**

	Northeast location, yes	Northeast location, no	Sum
Corner location, yes	9	6	15
Corner location, no	32	19	51
Sum	41	25	66

■ TABLE 4.2 Conditional probabilities of northeast and corner locations

	Northeast Yes	Northeast No	Corner Yes	Corner No	No Condition
Northeast Yes			0.6	0.6274	0.6212
Northeast No			0.4	0.3725	0.3788
Corner Yes	0.2195	0.24			0.2273
Corner No	0.7805	0.76			0.7727

table attributes themselves. To convert Table 4.1 to Table 4.2, we use the queries against the house sales dataset associated to each cell of Table 4.1. For example, the first valid cell of the conditional probability is the result of the following natural-language query or its equivalent SQL statement:

(Query 2)
Find the count of northeast and corner locations from the table RmSale divided by the count of corner location.

(SQL 2)
Select count(*) from RmSale where northeast = yes and corner = yes / count(*) from RmSale where corner = yes.

This query can be interpreted as the one asking for the likelihood of a corner location house to be on the northeast side. The first non-empty cell value in Table 4.2 is 0.6, which means that if the house is on the corner, there is about a 60% likelihood that this house is located on the northeast. We can adjust the attributes and conditions of the query to find the probabilities for the other cells in Table 4.2 in a similar manner.

■ 4.4 EQUALITY TESTS

In this section, we introduce a method that can be used to test the statistical equality of two feature-based groups in a database. For example, we may wish to compare the effectiveness of two kinds of mechanical systems, the gas mileage of two types of automobiles, house prices of corner-located houses and non-corner-located houses, and so on in order to decide whether the distinction makes a statistically significant difference. We usually show the equality of two populations by comparing the means of two distributions. In other words, we want to show whether or not, on average, the data values of one population differ from those of the other population. The null hypothesis should be $H_0: \bar{x} = \bar{y}$, against the alternative hypothesis $H_1: \bar{x} > \bar{y}$, where $\bar{x}$ and $\bar{y}$ are the means of the data distributions of two populations. To test the equality of the means of two populations, either normal distribution or student t-distribution is used in statistics. In what follows, we use the independent normal distribution for this purpose.

Let two samples be $(x_1, x_2, \ldots, x_n)$ and $(y_1, y_2, \ldots, y_m)$. Then we use the fact that under the null hypothesis $H_0: \bar{x} = \bar{y}$ (or $\bar{x} - \bar{y} = 0$), the random variable Z below is $N(0, 1)$

$$Z = \frac{\bar{x} - \bar{y}}{\sqrt{w_1 + w_2}} \qquad (4.2)$$

where

$$v = \frac{(w_1 + w_2)^2}{w_1^2 / (n-1) + w_2^2 / (m-1)} \qquad (4.3)$$

is the degree of freedom and

$$w_1 = \frac{s_1^2}{n} \qquad \text{and} \qquad w_2 = \frac{s_2^2}{m} \qquad (4.4)$$

If a sample realization of Z is much larger than zero, we reject the null hypothesis and understand that the average data values of the two populations are significantly different, i.e., $\bar{x} > \bar{y}$.

Now let's go back to the house sales data. If our interest is to test whether sale prices are the same for non–custom-built and custom-built houses, the following queries could be established:

(Query 3)
Find the price of custom-built houses from table RmSale.
Find the price of non–custom built-houses from table RmSale.
or

(SQL 3)
Select price from RmSale where custom=yes.
Select price from RmSale where custom=no.

■ **FIGURE 4.3**
Price comparison
for custom-built
and non–custom-
built houses

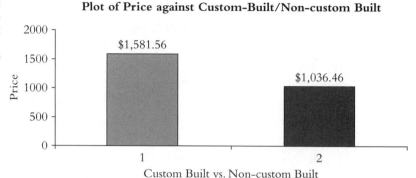

SQL 3 will retrieve data and create two tables, where one table contains the price list for the custom-built houses and the other table contains the list of prices for the non–custom-built houses. A built-in function embedded in a statistical package can be used to find the value of Z. Here, the null hypothesis is that house prices are the same regardless of the custom-built status, and the alternative hypothesis is that house prices vary depending on the custom-built status. Following the normal distribution method and formulae (4.2), (4.3), and (4.4), it follows that $n = 16$, $m = 50$, $s_1 = 482.84$, $s_2 = 268.41$, $w_1 = 14570.73$, $w_2 = 1440.87$, $Z = 4.31$, and $v = 18.06$. Hence, we reject the null hypothesis with significance level $\alpha = 0.025$ since Z is much greater than 1.96. We conclude that prices for custom-built houses are much higher than those for non–custom-built houses. Figure 4.3 also shows the averaged higher price for the custom-built houses.

Query 4 below formalizes a natural-language query for comparing the equality of house prices based on the custom-built status. SQL 4 is the SQL-style query equivalent to Query 4.

(Query 4)
Is the price of a house with custom-built features different than the price of a house without custom-built features in the table RmSale regardless of other features?

(SQL 4)
Select Z(*) from RmSale where select price from RmSale is custom=yes and select price from RmSale is custom=no.

SQL 4 retrieves the Z value 4.31, which means that the data values do not support the null hypothesis with a probability of only 97.5%. Since the value is much less than 1.96, we reject the null hypothesis that there is no difference in sale prices between custom-built and non–custom-built houses. We have sufficient evidence to conclude that the null hypothesis is wrong, and we are in favor of the alternative hypothesis. Therefore, the prices for the custom-built houses and the prices for the non–custom-built house are not considered the same statistically.

To appreciate the further application of the equality comparison method, let us consider the following query. In this query, we are going to test whether the prices are the same for corner and non-corner locations. Two hypotheses can be set as before. Query 5 establishes two lists of house prices based on the corner-location feature:

(Query 5)
Find the prices of houses with corner location from table RmSale.
Find the prices of houses with no corner location from table RmSale.

(SQL 5)
Select price from RmSale where corner=yes.
Select price from RmSale where corner=no.

Query 6 retrieves the Z value to determine the acceptance of the null hypothesis. Since there are 15 corner-located houses and 51 non–corner-located houses, $n = 51$ and $m = 15$. Following the normal distribution method and formulae (4.2), (4.3), and (4.4), it follows that $s_1 = 432.16$, $s_2 = 255.91$, $w_1 = 3661.92$, $w_2 = 4365.97$, and $Z = 2$. Hence, we may not reject the null hypothesis with significance level $\alpha = 0.025$ since Z is not much greater than 1.96. Since Z is very close to 1.96, we conclude that the prices of corner-located houses are not significantly different than those of non–corner-located houses.

Query 6 formalizes a natural-language query for comparing the equality of house prices based on corner location status. SQL 6 is the SQL-style query equivalent to Query 6:

(Query 6)
Is the price of a house with a corner location different than the price of a house with no corner location in the table RmSale regardless of other features?

(SQL 6)
Select Z(*) from RmSale where select price from RmSale is corner = yes and select price from RmSale is corner = no.

SQL 6 retrieves the Z value 2.0, which means that the data values do not strongly reject the null hypothesis with a probability of 97.5%. Since the value is not much more than 1.96, we do not reject the null hypothesis that there is no difference in sale prices between corner-located and non–corner-located houses. We do not have sufficient evidence to conclude that the null hypothesis is wrong, and we are not in favor of the alternative hypothesis. Therefore, the prices for the corner-located houses and the prices for the non–corner-located houses are not considered different.

■ 4.5   CORRELATION COEFFICIENT

In this section, we introduce the correlation coefficient, which measures the relationship between two random variables X and Y. Their correlation coefficient ρ is defined as

$$\rho(X,Y) = \frac{E[(X-E_X) \times (Y-E_Y)]}{\sqrt{\text{Var}(X) \times \text{Var}(Y)}} \tag{4.5}$$

where E_X and E_Y are the expected values of variables X and Y and $\text{Var}(X)$ and $\text{Var}(Y)$ are the variances of X and Y. Note that ρ is always between 1 and −1 as expressed in equation (4.6).

$$|\rho(X,Y)| \leq 1 \tag{4.6}$$

The correlation coefficient describes the relationship between two random variables X and Y. The interpretation of the coefficient is one of the following:

1. When $\rho = 0$, the variables are not related. In particular, assuming the variables are normally distributed, X and Y are independent random variables.
2. When $\rho > 0$, as the probability of one variable increases so does the probability of the other variable. Conversely, if the probability of one variable decreases, then the probability of the other variable also decreases.
3. When $\rho < 0$, the probability of one variable decreases while the probability of the other variable increases, and vice versa.

Table 4.3 summarizes the correlation coefficient and the relationship between those two variables. The strongest relationship measured by the correlation coefficient is the linear relation.

■ **TABLE 4.3 Correlation coefficient**

Corr ρ	Relationship
1	Positively linear relation
0	Not related
−1	Negatively linear relation
0 < and < 1	Positively related
−1 < and < 0	Negatively related

The plot of one variable against the other variable roughly displays the pattern of the relationship between two variables. A straight-line pattern indicates a strong relation with the correlation coefficient close to one either positively or negatively. When $\rho = 1$, all discrete points having positive probability must lie on the conditional mean line, and vice versa. Plot 4.1 shows the linear relationship between price and area, whereas Plot 4.2 shows the nonlinear relationship between age and area.

Now, we consider the sample correlation coefficient, which is useful for estimating the correlation coefficient. Let the observed dataset be

$$(x_1, y_1), (x_2, y_2), \cdots, (x_n, y_n) \tag{4.7}$$

Then the sample correlation coefficient γ is defined as

$$\gamma_{xy} = \frac{\sigma_{xy}}{\sigma_x \sigma_y} \tag{4.8}$$

where

$$\sigma_{xy} = \frac{1}{n} \sum_{i=1}^{n} (x_i - \bar{x})(y_i - \bar{y}) \tag{4.9}$$

$$\sigma_x^2 = \frac{1}{n} \sum_{i=1}^{n} (x_i - \bar{x})^2 \tag{4.10}$$

$$\sigma_y^2 = \frac{1}{n} \sum_{i=1}^{n} (y_i - \bar{y})^2 \tag{4.11}$$

$$\bar{x} = \frac{1}{n} \sum_{i=1}^{n} x_i \quad \text{and} \quad \bar{y} = \frac{1}{n} \sum_{i=1}^{n} y_i \tag{4.12}$$

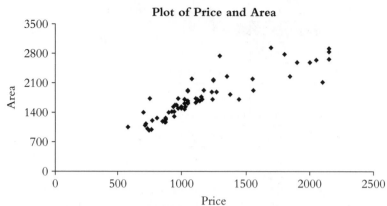

It can easily be proved that γ_{xy} is an asymptotically unbiased estimator of ρ and satisfies

$$|\gamma_{xy}| \le 1 \qquad (4.13)$$

To help with the interpretation of the distribution of the sample correlation coefficient from formula (4.8), a transformation is developed to make its distribution popular and easy to understand. Two types of transformation can be performed according to formulas (4.14) and (4.15).

The statistical significance of the sample correlation coefficient for the testing $H_0: \rho = 0$ versus $H_a: \rho \ne 0$ can be assessed by using a t-statistic, which is defined by

$$t = \gamma_{XY} \times \frac{\sqrt{n-2}}{\sqrt{1-\gamma_{XY}^2}} \qquad (4.14)$$

with degree of freedom $\nu = n - 2$. To test the nonzero value of the coefficient of correlation, $H_0: \rho = c$ versus $H_a: \rho \ne c$, where $|c| < 1$, the statistic could be

$$z_{xy} = (n-3)^{1/2} (\tanh^{-1} \gamma_{XY} - \tanh^{-1} c) \qquad (4.15)$$

which is called the z value, and $\tanh(r)$ is the inverse hyperbolic-tangent function defined by

$$\tanh^{-1}(\gamma) = \frac{1}{2} \ln \frac{1+\gamma}{1-\gamma}. \qquad (4.16)$$

■ PLOT 4.2
Relationship
between age
and area

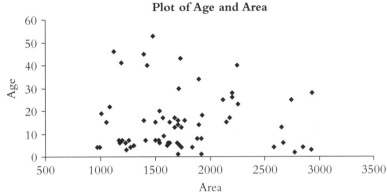

The statistic z_{xy} is approximately distributed as a standard, normal, random variable under the null hypothesis.

Let's consider an example using the house sales data. The correlation coefficients and z values after the transformation following the above formula are given in Tables 4.4 and 4.5. Note that database queries may use any set of attributes whose relationships need to be found.

From Table 4.4, *price* and *custom, price* and *tax, area* and *custom, area* and *tax* show strong positive correlations, whereas *age* and *price, age* and *feature, age* and *tax* show weak negative correlations. In addition, we can easily see that *corner* and *northeast, corner* and *custom, corner* and *area* are almost independent, i.e., not related. Statistically speaking, from Table 4.5, all the absolute z values less than 1.96 indicate no correlation of the two variables with 95%

■ TABLE 4.4 Correlation coefficients for the house sales data

	Price	Area	Age	Feature	Northeast	Custom	Corner	Tax
Price	1.0000	0.8839	−0.1667	0.2102	0.2892	0.5821	−0.1876	0.8775
Area	0.8839	1.0000	−0.0377	0.2319	0.3625	0.4919	−0.0785	0.8752
Age	−0.1667	−0.0377	1.0000	−0.1721	0.2164	0.0085	0.1627	−0.2918
Feature	0.2102	0.2319	−0.1721	1.0000	0.2547	0.1866	−0.2111	0.1302
Northeast	0.2892	0.3625	0.2164	0.2547	1.0000	0.1502	−0.0237	0.3024
Custom	0.5821	0.4919	0.0085	0.1866	0.1502	1.0000	−0.0537	0.4370
Corner	−0.1876	−0.0785	0.1627	−0.2111	−0.0237	−0.0537	1.0000	−0.1532
Tax	0.8775	0.8752	−0.2918	0.1302	0.3024	0.4370	−0.1532	1.0000

■ **TABLE 4.5** *Z* values of correlation coefficient

	Price	Area	Age	Feature	Northeast	Custom	Corner	Tax
Price	∞	11.061	−1.335	1.694	2.363	5.283	−1.507	10.834
Area	11.061	∞	−0.299	1.875	3.015	4.274	−0.624	10.756
Age	−1.335	−0.299	∞	−1.380	1.745	0.068	1.303	−2.386
Feature	1.694	1.875	−1.380	∞	2.068	1.499	−1.701	1.039
Northeast	2.363	3.015	1.745	2.068	∞	1.201	−0.188	2.478
Custom	5.283	4.274	0.068	1.499	1.201	∞	−0.427	3.719
Corner	−1.507	−0.624	1.303	−1.701	−0.188	−0.427	∞	−1.225
Tax	10.834	10.756	−2.386	1.039	2.478	3.719	−1.225	∞

confidence. For example, *custom* and *northeast* ($z = 1.20$) and *corner* and *age* ($z = 1.30$) indicate no correlation between the two variables being considered. The custom-built houses have no relation with *northeast* location, and the *corner* location has no relation with the age factor of the houses.

To use the correlation coefficients and perform calculations in the database, we implement the following SQL statement:

(Query 7)
What is the relationship between attribute_1 and attribute_2 in the table?

(SQL 7)?
Select corr(*) from table where attribute_1 and attribute_2.

The query shows the value of the correlation coefficient based on the two groups of observations *attribute_1* and *attribute_2*, where the two groups should have the same size population. Thus, in the example above, the correlation coefficient of the two attributes, *northeast* and *corner*, can be found with the following queries:

(Query 8)
Is there any relationship between the northeast and the corner locations from table RmSale?

(SQL 8)
Select corr(*) from RmSale where attribute_1=northeast and attribute_2=corner.

The coefficient value −0.0237 is retrieved from Table 4.4, and the relation is considered very weak. The corresponding z values after transformation can be found with the following queries:

(Query 9)
Does the function transformation $(n-3)^{1/2} \tanh^{-1}$ on the measurement of relationship for the northeast and corner location from the table RmSale indicate any correlation?

(SQL 9)
Select $(n-3)^{1/2} \tanh^{-1}(corr(*))$ from RmSale where northeast and corner.

The z value −0.188 is retrieved from Table 4.5. Since its absolute value is much less than 1.96, it indicates no correlation between *northeast* and *corner* location with 95% confidence. Therefore, we conclude that *northeast* and *corner* locations are not related.

■ 4.6 CONTINGENCY TABLE AND THE χ^2 TEST

The χ^2 test and contingency table are two other approaches that can be used to measure the dependency relationship among multiple attributes in a database. Although they can be used to test the independence among two or more attributes, for simplicity we only consider the case of two attributes in the example that follows. Three tables will be created to illustrate the process of determining the dependence or independence among the multiple categorical attributes. They represent observed frequencies, expected frequencies, and cell contributions among the attributes, respectively. Now, let's assume that the domain of two variables is divided into $r \times s$ disjoint subdomains, in which the frequency corresponding to each pair of values from both categories fills the corresponding cell. Table 4.6 shows the observed frequencies, and Table 4.7 shows the expected frequencies.

In both Table 4.6 and Table 4.7, we consider two categorical attributes, A and B. The attribute A has r subdomains and B has s subdomains. Here n_{ij} is the observed frequency of $A_i B_j$, which corresponds to row A_i, the ith values of A, and column B_j, the jth values of B. N_i and N_j are the marginal frequencies, and N is the total frequency. So we have

■ **TABLE 4.6 Observed frequencies**

	B_1	B_2	$B_.$	B_s	Total
Variable A_1	n_{11}	n_{12}	......	n_{1s}	$N_{1.}$
A_2	n_{21}	n_{22}	......	n_{2s}	$N_{2.}$
$A_.$	......	......	......	......	......
A_r	n_{r1}	n_{r2}	......	n_{rs}	$N_{r.}$
Total	$N_{.1}$	$N_{.2}$	......	$N_{.s}$	N

■ **TABLE 4.7 Expected frequencies**

	B_1	B_2	$B_.$	B_s	Total
Variable A_1	e_{11}	e_{12}	......	e_{1s}	$E_{1.}$
A_2	e_{21}	e_{22}	......	e_{2s}	$E_{2.}$
$A_.$	......	......	......	......	......
A_r	e_{r1}	e_{r2}	......	e_{rs}	$E_{r.}$
Total	$E_{.1}$	$E_{.2}$	......	$E_{.s}$	E

$$N_{i.} = \sum_{j=1}^{s} n_{ij}, \qquad N_{.j} = \sum_{i=1}^{r} n_{ij} \tag{4.17}$$

and

$$N = \sum_{i=1}^{r} N_{i.} = \sum_{j=1}^{s} N_{.j} \tag{4.18}$$

The expected frequencies are based on all the observed frequencies, and their corresponding marginal and total frequencies calculated as follows are given in Table 4.7.

$$e_{ij} = \frac{N_{i.} \times N_{.j}}{N} \tag{4.19}$$

$$E_{i.} = \sum_{j=1}^{s} e_{ij}, \qquad E_{.j} = \sum_{i=1}^{r} e_{ij} \tag{4.20}$$

$$E = \sum_{i=1}^{r} E_{i.} = \sum_{j=1}^{s} E_{.j} \tag{4.21}$$

■ **TABLE 4.8 Cell contributions**

	B_1	B_2	$B_.$	B_s	**Total**
Variable A_1	c_{11}	c_{12}	......	c_{1s}	$C_{1.}$
A_2	c_{21}	c_{22}	......	c_{2s}	$C_{2.}$
$A_.$	......	......	......	......	......
A_r	c_{r1}	c_{r2}	......	c_{rs}	$C_{r.}$
Total	$C_{.1}$	$C_{.2}$	......	$C_{.s}$	Q_ν

From the previous formulae, it can easily be proved that

$$E_{i.} = N_{i.}, \quad E_{.j} = N_{.j}, \quad \text{and } E = N \tag{4.22}$$

Next, we can construct a cell contributions table (Table 4.8) from the expected frequencies and the observed frequencies. Each value in the cells, calculated by formulae (4.23) and (4.24), contributes to the χ^2 statistics. A large cell value indicates that the corresponding cell has a greater contribution to the χ^2 statistics. That means the hypotheses of independence of the two variables will most likely be rejected.

$$c_{ij} = \frac{(n_{ij} - e_{ij})^2}{e_{ij}} \tag{4.23}$$

$$C_{i.} = \sum_{j=1}^{s} c_{ij}, \qquad C_{.j} = \sum_{i=1}^{r} c_{ij} \tag{4.24}$$

$$Q_{(r-1)(s-1)} = \sum_{i=1}^{r}\sum_{j=1}^{s} c_{ij} = \sum_{i=1}^{r} C_{i.} = \sum_{j=1}^{s} C_{.j} \tag{4.25}$$

$$\nu = (r-1)(s-1) \tag{4.26}$$

According to the χ^2 test, Q_ν in formula (4.25) has an approximate χ^2 distribution with ν degrees of freedom. If the computed Q_ν gets too large, i.e., exceeds $\chi^2[\alpha; \nu]$, we reject the hypothesis H_0 that the two attributes are independent.

To illustrate the application of the χ^2 test in the context of a contingency table, we will use the house sales data again. Let us assume that our goal is to analyze the relationship between the two variables *price* and *feature* from the house sales data. The testing hypotheses would be that the two attributes are

■ TABLE 4.9 Observed frequencies

	Feature 1	Feature 2	Feature 3	Feature 4	Feature 5	Feature 6	Feature >6	Sum
Price 1000 or less	2	3	6	12	1	3	0	27
Price 1000–2000	0	1	7	19	4	2	1	34
Price 2000 or above	1	0	1	0	1	2	0	5
Sum	3	4	14	31	6	7	1	66

independent (i.e., not related) for the null hypothesis and they are dependent (i.e., related) for the alternative hypothesis.

As before, simple database queries can be used to retrieve the relevant data and to calculate the observed frequencies as shown in Table 4.9. Table 4.10 is constructed by following formulae (4.19) through (4.21) and shows the expected frequencies of the two attributes.

Both Table 4.9 and Table 4.10 are used to construct Table 4.11 following formulae (4.23) through (4.25). Each cell in Table 4.11 shows a contribution to the χ^2 statistics. In this case the value of Q_v is 17.15, which is not greater than $\chi^2[0.05; 12] = 21.03$. This indicates that the two variables *price* and *feature* are not dependent (i.e., not related), which is the same conclusion reached in the previous section.

■ TABLE 4.10 Expected frequencies

	Feature 1	Feature 2	Feature 3	Feature 4	Feature 5	Feature 6	Feature >6	Sum
Price 1000 or less	1.2273	1.6364	5.7273	12.6818	2.4545	2.8636	0.4091	27.00
Price 1000–2000	1.5455	2.0606	7.2121	15.9697	3.0909	3.6061	0.5152	34.00
Price 2000 or above	0.2273	0.3030	1.0606	2.3485	0.4545	0.5303	0.0758	5.000
Sum	3.0000	4.0000	14.000	31.000	6.0000	7.0000	1.0000	66.00

■ **TABLE 4.11 Cell contributions**

	Feature 1	Feature 2	Feature 3	Feature 4	Feature 5	Feature 6	Feature >6	Sum
Price 1000 or less	0.4865	1.1364	0.0130	0.0367	0.8620	0.0065	0.4091	2.9501
Price 1000–2000	1.5455	0.5459	0.0062	0.5750	0.2674	0.7153	0.4563	4.1116
Price 2000 or above	2.6273	0.3030	0.0035	2.3485	0.6545	4.0732	0.0758	10.086
Sum	4.6593	1.9853	0.0227	2.9602	1.7839	4.7950	0.9412	17.147

To implement the χ^2 test and its calculations, a number of SQL queries must be used. The queries must deal with the three tables: the observed frequency, the expected frequency, and the cell contribution. Most statistical packages will provide a function that performs the χ^2 test, which normally requires two arguments, the observed frequency and the expected frequency over the same experiment size. To match the parameter passing for the function, we can establish the observed frequency table as the first parameter and the expected frequency table as the second parameter, and we can drop the cell contribution table. The χ^2 statistic can be directly obtained without recording the cell contributions. For the frequency table, we can use the count function, which retrieves the frequency. A group of count(*) calls are required to retrieve an array of multiple counts, and we may rewrite it as *(count(*) from table where attribute_1, count(*) from table where attribute_2, ..., count(*) from table where attribute_n)*. Further considerations should be taken for the array output. For the multiplication, we can define SQL statements similar to those for division in the previous section. Query 10 is used to select the two attributes:

(Query 10)
Choose attribute_1 and attribute_2 from the table.

(SQL 10)
Select attribute_1 × attribute_2 from the table where attribute_1 and attribute_2.

Then, for the combination of multiplication and division, we define a new SQL statement as follows:

(Query 11)
Find attribute_1 times attribute_2 divided by attribute_3 from the table.

(SQL 11)
Select attribute_1 × attribute_2 / attribute_3 from the table.

These queries compute the value of the expected frequency based on three groups of data: *attribute_1*, *attribute_2*, and *attribute_3*, where their size must be the same. Finally, we define the χ^2-based query as follows, which involves two subqueries, one for the observed variable and the other for the expected variable:

(Query 12)
Are attribute_1 and attribute_2 independent in the table?

(SQL 12)
Select chi-square(*) from the table where variable is observed and variable is expected.

From the previous example dealing with price and feature attributes, we can use the following χ^2-based query to perform the analysis of the relationship between the two attributes:

(Query 13)
Are the two attributes price and feature independent in the table RmSale?

(SQL 13)
Select chi-square(*) from RmSale where (select count(*) from RmSale where price and feature for each subdomain) and ((select count(*) from RmSale where price) × (select count(*) from RmSale where feature)/(select count(*) from RmSale)).

As we recall, SQL 13 retrieves the Q_ν value of 17.15, which is not greater than $\chi^2[0.05; 12] = 21.03$. Therefore, we do not reject the null hypothesis, and we conclude that price and feature are independent attributes.

As another example, we can establish the contingency table to analyze the relationship between two variables, price and tax, from the house sales data. The three tables showing the observed frequencies, the expected frequencies, and the cell contributions are shown in Tables 4.12, 4.13, and 4.14. Following the χ^2 test, the Q_ν value of 49.66 is obtained from Table 4.14.

■ **TABLE 4.12 Observed frequencies**

Tax↓ Price→	1000 or less	1000–1500	1500–2000	2000 or more	Sum
500 or less	5	0	0	0	5
500–1000	22	21	1	0	44
1000–1500	0	6	3	3	12
1500 or more	0	0	3	2	5
Sum	27	27	7	5	66

This value is greater than $\chi^2[0.05; 9] = 16.92$, which results in the rejection of the null hypothesis and indicates that price and tax are not independent (i.e., they are closely related).

(Query 14)
Are the two attributes price and tax independent in the table RmSale?

(SQL 14)
Select chi-square(*) from RmSale where (select count(*) from RmSale where price and tax for each subdomain) and (select count(*) from RmSale where price) × (select count(*) from RmSale where tax) / (select count(*) from RmSale)).

Query 14 implements the χ^2-based query to retrieve the Q_v value of 49.66 from the last cell of Table 4.14 to reject the null hypothesis and conclude that price and tax are related attributes. SQL 14 contains two main subqueries. The query "*select count(*) from RmSale where price and tax for each subdomain*" retrieves the observed frequencies in Table 4.12. The other query consists of three subqueries: "*(select count(*) from RmSale where price) * (select*

■ **TABLE 4.13 Expected frequencies**

Tax↓ Price→	1000 or less	1000–1500	1500–2000	2000 or more	Sum
500 or less	2.0455	2.0455	0.5303	0.3788	5
500–1000	18.0000	18.0000	4.6667	3.3333	44
1000–1500	4.9091	4.9091	1.2727	0.9091	12
1500 or more	2.0455	2.0455	0.5303	0.3788	5
Sum	27	27	7	5	66

■ **TABLE 4.14 Cell contributions**

Tax↓ Price→	1000 or less	1000–1500	1500–2000	2000 or more	Sum
500 or less	4.2677	2.0455	0.5303	0.3788	7.2222
500–1000	0.8889	0.5000	2.8810	3.3333	7.6032
1000–1500	4.9091	0.2424	2.3442	4.8091	12.3048
1500 or more	2.0455	2.0455	11.5017	6.9388	22.5314
Sum	12.1111	4.8333	17.2571	15.4600	49.6616

count(*) from RmSale where tax)/(select count(*) from RmSale," which retrieve the expected frequencies in Table 4.13. Finally, the χ^2-based query retrieves the total cell contribution of 49.66 from Table 4.14. The functions and operators used, such as count(*), multiplication, and division retrieve arrays, and $\chi^2(*)$ retrieves the cumulative cell contributions.

■ **4.7 LINEAR REGRESSION**

The linear regression approach is used to fit a linear relationship between one variable, called the dependent variable, and one or more other variables, called the independent variable(s). Regression analysis is concerned with developing approximating models dealing with such variables. It is assumed that the dependent variable, Y, and the independent variables, X_i, satisfy the following linear equation:

$$Y = \beta_0 + \beta_1 \times X_1 + \beta_2 \times X_2 + \cdots + \beta_n \times X_n \qquad (4.27)$$

where $\beta_0, \beta_1, \ldots, \beta_n$ are the coefficients (parameters) in the linear relationship. Unfortunately, in many cases, the relationship among variables is not linear. But we can try to fit a line among the variables by slightly modifying the above formula by adding a random term as shown in equation (4.28).

$$Y = \beta_0 + \beta_1 \times X_1 + \beta_2 \times X_2 + \cdots + \beta_n \times X_n + \varepsilon \qquad (4.28)$$

where ε is a random error that creates the scatter around the linear relationship. If it is successful, then the linear relationship will be approximately true. Plot 4.3 displays a scatter plot of price against tax. It clearly shows the positive linear relation between the two attributes, and the line is quite well fit among the dots. The main advantages of linear regression are these:

1. It is a very useful and widely employed tool of data analysis.
2. It leads to simple, yet often powerful descriptions of the main features of the relationships among variables.

Two important questions we face when formulating a linear regression are these:

1. How do we find the coefficients $\beta_0, \beta_1, \ldots, \beta_n$?
2. How good is the fit?

Many approaches have been developed to find the coefficients, $\beta_0, \beta_1, \ldots, \beta_n$. These parameters are ordinarily unknown and must be estimated from sample data. So the objective is to find the estimates of the coefficients such that the fitted line constructed with the estimates is "close to" the observation points. One popular measure considers the squares of each deviation of an observed point and the corresponding estimated point and adds these squared deviations. This is called the least-squares method, which can be formulated as follows. The observed data listed in Table 4.15 are used in the formulation of equations (4.29) and (4.30).

We assume that

$$y_i = \beta_0 + \beta_1 \times x_{i1} + \beta_2 \times x_{i2} + \cdots + \beta_n \times x_{in} + \varepsilon_i \qquad (4.29)$$

is true for $i = 1, 2, \ldots, m$, where ε_i is identically, independently, and normally distributed. In other words, ε_i is an independent random variable, normally distributed $N(0, \alpha^2)$. Let

$$L = \sum \left(y_i - \beta_0 - \beta_1 \times x_{i1} - \beta_2 \times x_{i2} - \cdots - \beta_n \times x_{in} \right)^2 \qquad (4.30)$$

which is the summation of the distances between the predicted values and the observed dependent values. Since our goal is to minimize L, we take the

▧ **TABLE 4.15 Dataset for linear regression**

	X_1	X_2	......	X_n	Y
1	x_{11}	x_{12}	......	x_{1n}	y_1
2	x_{21}	x_{22}	......	x_{2n}	y_2
3	x_{31}	x_{32}	......	x_{3n}	y_3
......	......	......	......	......	......
m	x_{m1}	x_{m2}	......	x_{mn}	y_m

partial derivative and equate it to zero. We can derive the following formulae for $\beta_0, \beta_1, \ldots, \beta_n$, in the form of a matrix equation:

$$\mathbf{b} = (\mathbf{\Phi}^T \times \mathbf{\Phi})^{-1} \, \mathbf{\Phi}^T \times \mathbf{Y} \tag{4.31}$$

where

$$\mathbf{b} = (\beta_0, \beta_1, \ldots, \beta_n)^T \tag{4.32}$$

$$\mathbf{Y} = (y_1, y_2, \ldots, y_m)^T$$

and

$$\mathbf{\Phi} = (x_{ij}), \qquad x_{0j} = 1 \tag{4.33}$$

$i = 0, 1, 2, \ldots, n$ and $j = 1, 2, \ldots, m$. The linear equation can be written in matrix form as follows:

$$\mathbf{Y} = \mathbf{\Phi} \times \mathbf{b} + \varepsilon. \tag{4.34}$$

The numerical calculation for the coefficients is rather tedious. Since computer programs for least-squares estimation are generally available, we do not discuss the numerical solution. We expect that you can use the locally available computer software.

Now, to simplify the calculation so that it can be performed manually, we suppose the case of only one independent variable. Let the linear relation be

$$y_i = \beta_0 + \beta_1 \times x_i + \varepsilon_i \tag{4.35}$$

■ PLOT 4.3
Relationship between price and tax

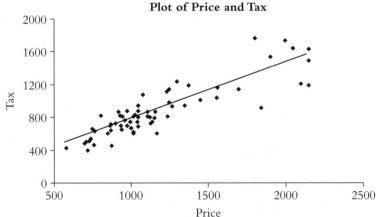

Plot of Price and Tax

where $x_1, x_2, \ldots, x_m$, and $y_1, y_2, \ldots, y_m$ are the observed data. Then, by following the same procedure, we get

$$b_1 = \frac{S_{xy}}{S_{xx}} \tag{4.36}$$

and

$$b_0 = \overline{y} - b_1 \times \overline{x} \tag{4.37}$$

where

$$S_{xy} = \frac{1}{m-1} \times \sum_{i=1}^{m} (y_i - \overline{y})(x_i - \overline{x}) \tag{4.38}$$

and

$$S_{xx} = \frac{1}{m-1} \times \sum_{i=1}^{m} (x_i - \overline{x})^2 \tag{4.39}$$

Here, b_1 is called the slope, and b_0 is called the intercept. Once we have the intercept and slopes, the straight line can be drawn easily. But the question is, "Does the line fit the data?" It depends. Since the data are random, the slopes and the intercept we have calculated are actually just the estimators of true ones. Therefore, the line is also random.

To test the accuracy of the fitted line, an analysis of variance (ANOVA) table is used in which the decomposition of the total sum of squares is usually summarized. The ANOVA table for the multiple linear regression model is shown in Table 4.16, where n is the number of independent variables and m is the number of observations. We define the following sets of sum of squares used in the ANOVA table, where TSS is the total sum of squares, SSR is the sum of squares due to regression, and SSE is the sum of squares due to error or the error sum of squares.

$$TSS = \sum_{i=1}^{m} (y_i - \overline{y})^2 = \sum_{i=1}^{m} y_i^2 - \left(\sum_{i=1}^{m} y_i \right)^2 \bigg/ m \tag{4.40}$$

$$SSE = \sum_{i=1}^{m} (y_i - \hat{y}_i)^2 = TSS - SSR \tag{4.41}$$

$$SSR = \sum_{i=1}^{m} (\hat{y}_i - \overline{y})^2 = \sum_{i=1}^{m} \hat{y}_i^2 - \left(\sum_{i=1}^{m} y_i \right)^2 \bigg/ m \tag{4.42}$$

where $\hat{y}_i$ is the predicted Y (i.e., fitted value) by $x_{i1}, x_{i2}, \ldots, x_{im}$.

■ **TABLE 4.16 ANOVA table**

Source of variation	Degree of freedom	Sum of squares	Mean squares	F-statistics
Regression	N	SSR	$MSR = SSR/n$	$F = MSR/MSE$
Error	$m - n - 1$	SSE	$MSE = SSE/(m - n - 1)$	
Total	$m - 1$	TSS		

The first column in Table 4.16 shows the sources of variation. The second column contains the degrees of freedom for the various sums of squares that are given above. The degrees of freedom are the number of independent components that are necessary to calculate a sum of squares. The third column gives the corresponding sums of squares; the total sum of squares is partitioned into a SSR and a SSE. The fourth column in the ANOVA table is called the mean-square column. It contains the ratios of the various sums of squares and their degrees of freedom. $MSR = SSR/n$ is the mean square due to regression, and $MSE = SSE/(m - n - 1)$ is the mean square due to error (or the mean square error). MSE is an unbiased estimate of σ^2.

Finally, the fifth column provides the F-ratio, MSR/MSE, used to test the null hypothesis H_0: $\beta_1 = \beta_2 = \cdots = \beta_n = 0$ against the alternative H_1 that not all $\beta_j = 0$. The null hypothesis means the regression line is fit, whereas the alternative hypothesis means the line is not fit. Virtually all standard regression programs print the ANOVA table as part of their output. Hence, the appropriate test statistic is the F-ratio from the ANOVA table, $F = MSR/MSE$. Since it can be shown that SSE and SSR are independent, $F = MSR/MSE$ follows an F-distribution with n and $m - n - 1$ degrees of freedom. If H_1 is true, then the F-ratio will tend to be much larger than what can be expected under H_0. This leads to the following decision rule: Calculate $F = MSR/MSE$ from the ANOVA table and if $F \geq F(\alpha; n, m - n - 1)$, accept H_1 at significance level α; otherwise, do not reject H_0. Alternatively, many computer programs calculate the p value $= P[F(n, m - n - 1) \geq F]$, where F is the calculated F. If this p value is small (less than or equal to the significance level α), it is very unlikely that we have found such a large F-ratio by chance alone; thus, we accept H_1.

One useful measure of the adequacy of the fitted model is the coefficient of determination, $R^2 = SSR/TSS = 1 - SSE/TSS$, which lies between 0 and 1. It expresses the regression sum of squares as a percentage of the TSS. A high R^2 value indicates that the regression model with n independent attributes explains a large portion of the variability among the observations y_1, y_2, ..., y_m. Hence, when the value of R^2 is close to 1, the predicted dependent variable is closer to the observed dependent variable and the fitting is better. Since this R^2 value by itself does not tell us which of the n variables are the most important ones, care should be taken when using the R^2 to interpret the fitting of the regression line. Also note that the F-ratio and R^2 are related through the very simple equation $F = R^2/1 - R^2(m-n-1/n)$. Although there are many other methods to measure the goodness of the fit, they are beyond the scope of this book.

Now we consider the house sales data again. Assume that our goal is to try to build the linear regression model for *tax* based on *area, age, feature, northeast*, and *corner*. There are many computer programs that perform the functions of linear regression and not only find the regression coefficients and R^2, but also establish the ANOVA table. Formula (4.43) is the linear regression equation, and Table 4.17 is the ANOVA table.

$$tax = 195 + 0.52 \times area - 7.36 \times age - 40.17 \times feature \qquad (4.43)$$
$$+ 61.6 \times northeast + 27.06 \times custom - 51.35 \times corner$$

$$R^2 = 0.86 \qquad (4.44)$$

In Table 4.17, the F-value is 60.18, which is far greater than $F(0.05; 6, 59) = 2.249$, so we do not reject the null hypothesis. Our conclusion is that the regressor attributes (*area, age, feature, northeast, custom*, and *corner*) have a significant impact on the tax of the houses. Also, the $R^2 = 0.86$ value in (44)

■ TABLE 4.17 ANOVA table

Source of variation	Degree of freedom	Sum of squares	Mean squares	F-statistics
Regression	6	5594856	932476	60.18
Error	59	914132	15494	
Total	65			

■ **TABLE 4.18   ANOVA table**

Source of variation	Degree of freedom	Sum of squares	Mean squares	F-statistics
Regression	5	2612765	522553	42.77
Error	44	537638	12219	
Total	49			

is fairly large (i.e., close to 1), which supports our conclusion that the line fitting is quite good.

Some attributes or variables can be dropped or partially selected to build the regression model of different interests. For example, assume that we want to establish the regression model for *tax* on the attributes *area, age, feature, northeast*, and *corner* with no *custom* built-in feature. The regression model is given as follows, and the corresponding ANOVA table is given in Table 4.18. In this case, the F-value of 42.77 is far greater than F (0.05; 5, 44) = 2.43, so we do not reject the null hypothesis and conclude that the regressor values (*area, feature, northeast*, and *corner*) have a significant impact on the tax calculation of the houses. Also, the high value of R^2 (0.83) close to 1 strongly supports the conclusion that the line fitting is pretty accurate. The F-value and R^2 on both examples indicate the significance and goodness of the fitting of the model.

$$tax = 135 + 0.4938 \times area - 6.566 \times age - 16.7 \times feature \qquad (4.45)$$
$$+ 57.29 \times northeast - 25.57 \times corner$$

$$R^2 = 0.83 \qquad (4.46)$$

The sequence of the queries needed to solve the regression model problem would be as follows:

(Query 15)
Choose tax, area, age, northeast, custom, and corner from table RmSale.

(SQL 15)
Select tax, area, age, northeast, custom, and corner from table RmSale.

These queries retrieve the dependent and independent variables. Also, for the linear regression model for *tax* on the attributes *area, age, feature, northeast,* and *corner,* with no *custom* built-in, use the following query statements to retrieve the independent and dependent attributes:

(Query 16)
Choose tax, area, age, feature, northeast, and corner with no custom built-in from table RmSale.

(SQL 16)
Select tax, area, age, feature, northeast, and corner from RmSale where custom = no.

The query statements for the regression model can be given as follows:

(Query 17)
Build the linear regression model for dependent variable attribute_1 and independent variables attribute_2, attribute_3, … from the table.

(SQL 17)
*Create table **reg_anova** as select attribute_1, **reg** attribute_2, attribute_3… from the table.*

In the above, *attribute_1* is the dependent variable and the attributes after **reg** are the independent variables. The **reg_anova** table displays the regression coefficients, R^2, and the ANOVA table obtained from the database table.

Thus, the earlier regression example can be implemented by the following:

(Query 18)
Build the linear regression model for dependent variable tax and independent variables area, age, feature, northeast, custom, and corner from table RmSale.

(SQL 18)
*Create table **reg_anova** as select tax, **reg** area, age, feature, northeast, custom, corner from table RmSale.*

These queries will retrieve the regression equation (4.43), R^2(4.44), and the ANOVA table as shown in Table 4.17. Hence, we conclude that the line is a good fit for the data. Other retrieved metadata is not of interest to us and is ignored here. For the other example, of a regression model for *tax* on the attributes *area, age, feature, northeast,* and *corner* with no *custom* built-in feature, we may use the following queries:

(Query 19)
Build the linear regression model for dependent variable tax and independent variables area, age, feature, northeast, and corner from table RmSale with no custom built-in observations.

(SQL 19)
*Create table **reg_anova** as select tax, **reg** area, age, feature, northeast, corner from table RmSale where custom = no.*

As a result of the analysis, the query retrieves the regression equation (4.45), R^2 (4.46), and the ANOVA table as shown in Table 4.18. The new function **reg** and **reg_anova** are not built-in and should be defined by the user who may combine any of the statistical built-in functions available in commercial software.

■ 4.8 HOUSE SALES DATABASE REVISITED

Throughout the chapter, we used the house sales database (Table 4.19) for the purpose of data analysis. The table consists of nine columns. The first column is the house ID column used as the primary key of the table. The second column (*price*) shows the house prices in hundreds. The third and fourth columns (*area* and *age*) represent the square footage and the age of the houses in years. The *feature* column (the fifth attribute) indicates the number of features (out of 11) furnished in each house. The *northeast, custom,* and *corner* columns (the sixth through the eighth) are Boolean attributes that indicate whether the house is located in the northeast side, whether the house is custom-built, and whether the house is located on a corner. The last attribute (*tax*) shows the amount of tax in dollars paid for each house. The table contains a total of 66 entries.

■ TABLE 4.19 House sales data

House ID	Price	Area	Age	Feature	Northeast	Custom	Corner	Tax
1	$2,050.00	2650	13	1	1	1	0	$1,639.00
2	$2,150.00	2664	6	5	1	1	0	$1,193.00
3	$2,150.00	2921	3	6	1	1	0	$1,635.00
4	$1,999.00	2580	4	4	1	1	0	$1,732.00
5	$1,900.00	2580	4	4	1	0	0	$1,534.00
6	$1,800.00	2774	2	4	1	0	0	$1,765.00
7	$1,560.00	1920	1	5	1	1	0	$1,161.00
8	$1,449.00	1710	1	3	1	1	0	$1,010.00
9	$1,375.00	1837	4	5	1	0	0	$1,191.00
10	$1,270.00	1880	8	6	1	0	0	$930.00
11	$1,250.00	2150	15	3	1	0	0	$984.00
12	$1,235.00	1894	14	5	1	1	0	$1,112.00
13	$1,170.00	1928	18	8	1	1	0	$600.00
14	$1,155.00	1767	16	4	1	0	0	$794.00
15	$1,110.00	1630	15	3	1	0	1	$867.00
16	$1,139.00	1680	17	4	1	0	1	$750.00
17	$995.00	1500	15	4	1	0	0	$743.00
18	$900.00	1400	16	2	1	0	1	$731.00
19	$960.00	1573	17	6	1	0	0	$768.00
20	$1,695.00	2931	28	3	1	0	1	$1,142.00
21	$1,553.00	2200	28	4	1	0	0	$1,035.00
22	$1,020.00	1478	53	3	1	0	1	$626.00
23	$1,020.00	1713	30	4	1	0	1	$600.00
24	$850.00	1190	41	1	1	0	0	$600.00
25	$720.00	1121	46	4	1	0	0	$398.00
26	$749.00	1733	43	6	1	0	0	$656.00
27	$2,150.00	2848	4	6	1	1	0	$1,487.00
28	$1,350.00	2253	23	4	1	1	0	$939.00
29	$1,299.00	2743	25	5	1	1	1	$1,232.00
30	$1,250.00	2180	17	4	1	0	1	$1,141.00
31	$1,239.00	1706	14	4	1	0	0	$810.00
32	$1,125.00	1710	16	4	1	1	0	$800.00
33	$1,080.00	2200	26	4	1	0	0	$1,076.00

■ **TABLE 4.19 House sales data (*continued*)**

House ID	Price	Area	Age	Feature	Northeast	Custom	Corner	Tax
34	$1,050.00	1680	13	4	1	0	0	$875.00
35	$1,049.00	1900	34	3	1	0	0	$690.00
36	$934.00	1543	20	3	1	0	0	$820.00
37	$875.00	1173	6	4	1	0	0	$456.00
38	$805.00	1258	7	4	1	0	1	$821.00
39	$759.00	997	4	4	1	0	0	$461.00
40	$729.00	1007	19	6	1	0	0	$513.00
41	$710.00	1083	22	4	1	0	0	$504.00
42	$975.00	1500	7	3	0	1	1	$700.00
43	$939.00	1428	40	2	0	0	0	$701.00
44	$2,100.00	2116	25	3	0	1	0	$1,209.00
45	$580.00	1051	15	2	0	0	0	$426.00
46	$1,844.00	2250	40	6	0	1	0	$915.00
47	$699.00	1400	45	1	0	1	1	$481.00
48	$1,160.00	1720	5	4	0	0	0	$867.00
49	$1,109.00	1740	4	3	0	0	0	$816.00
50	$1,129.00	1700	6	4	0	0	0	$725.00
51	$1,050.00	1620	6	4	0	0	0	$800.00
52	$1,045.00	1630	6	4	0	0	0	$750.00
53	$1,050.00	1920	8	4	0	0	0	$944.00
54	$1,020.00	1606	5	4	0	0	0	$811.00
55	$1,000.00	1535	7	5	0	0	1	$668.00
56	$1,030.00	1540	6	2	0	0	1	$826.00
57	$975.00	1739	13	3	0	0	0	$880.00
58	$940.00	1305	5	3	0	0	0	$647.00
59	$920.00	1415	7	4	0	0	0	$866.00
60	$945.00	1580	9	3	0	0	0	$810.00
61	$874.00	1236	3	4	0	0	0	$707.00
62	$872.00	1229	6	3	0	0	0	$721.00
63	$870.00	1273	4	4	0	0	0	$638.00
64	$869.00	1165	7	4	0	0	0	$694.00
65	$766.00	1200	7	4	0	0	1	$634.00
66	$739.00	970	4	4	0	0	1	$541.00

■ 4.9 CHAPTER SUMMARY

In this chapter we focused on certain statistical methods used as tools for data mining. Statistical tools are very useful for finding relationships among attributes of a database through the quantitative analysis of the data. House sales data was used for analysis. The meaning of the statistical analysis results themselves are not that significant to us since our purpose was to illustrate the methods and implementation tools used to build a bridge between database and statistics.

Five statistical methods were illustrated with examples applied to the house sales database: conditional probability, equality tests, correlation coefficient, contingency table and χ^2 test, and linear regression. Since statistical tests may need only part of the information from a raw database, the table structures or formats may not be suitable for implementing statistical analysis. The raw database may need to be modified or processed before it is provided to automatic programs for further processing. SQL queries as well as other built-in statistical functions can also be used for statistical analysis of data in a database. Often, separate computer programs must be written to handle query implementation and data interpretation when the built-in functions and SQL queries are not sufficient to complete the analysis of the data. In most cases, summary and test statistics are not database tables. They are used for the converting data into a form of knowledge and information that can be used for strategic decision making.

■ 4.10 EXERCISES

The following exercises are based on the house sales data given in Table 4.19. Answer all of the questions below using this data.

1. Based on the table RmSale, answer the following query. What is the likelihood of a northeast location house to be on a corner? Use the following three equivalent queries to derive the answer:

   a. *Find the conditional probability of corner location given by the northeast section.*

   b. *Find the count of northeast and corner locations from table RmSale over the count of locations.*

   c. *Select count(*) from RmSale where northeast = yes and corner = yes / count(*) from RmSale where northeast = yes.*

2. Based on the table RmSale, answer the following query. What is the likelihood of a northeast-location house to be custom-built? Use the following three equivalent queries to derive the answer:

   a. *Find the conditional probability of a house with custom built-in given by northeast location.*

   b. *Find the count of houses with custom built-in and northeast locations from table RmSale over the count of northeast location.*

   c. *Select count(*) from RmSale where custom = yes and northeast = yes / count(*) from RmSale where northeast = yes.*

3. Determine whether the house tax for northeast location is the same as that of all other locations. Use the following queries to derive the answer:

   a. *Is the house tax with northeast location different than the house tax with no northeast location in the table RmSale regardless of other features?*

   b. *Select Z(*) from RmSale where select tax from RmSale where northeast = yes and select tax from RmSale where northeast = no.*

4. Determine whether the house price of northeast *and* corner location is different than all other locations. Use the following queries to derive the answer:

   a. *Is the house price with northeast and corner location different from the house price with no location restriction in the table RmSale without changing other features?*

   b. *Select Z(*) from RmSale where select price from RmSale where northeast = yes and corner = yes and select price from RmSale.*

5. Find and test the relationship between the house price with custom built-in and the house tax with custom built-in. Use the following queries to derive the answer:

   a. *What is the relationship between price and tax with custom built-in in table RmSale?*

   b. *Select corr(*) from RmSale where select price from RmSale where custom = yes and select tax from RmSale where custom = yes.*

   c. *Do function transformation $(n-3)^{1/2} \tanh^{-1}$ on the measurement of the relationship for price and tax with custom built-in from table RmSale.*

   d. *Select $(n-3)^{1/2} \tanh^{-1}(corr(*))$ from RmSale where select price from RmSale where custom = yes and select tax from RmSale where custom = yes.*

6. Find and test the relationship between house price with no custom built-in and house tax with no custom built-in. Use the following queries to derive the answer:

   a. *What is the relationship between price and tax without custom built-in in table RmSale?*

   b. *Select corr(*) from RmSale where select price from RmSale where custom = no and select tax from RmSale where custom = no.*

   c. *Do function transformation $(n - 3)^{1/2} \tanh^{-1}$ on the measurement of the relationship for price and tax without custom built-in in table RmSale.*

   d. *Select $(n - 3)^{1/2} \tanh^{-1}(corr(*))$ from RmSale where select price from RmSale where custom = no and select tax from RmSale where custom = no.*

7. Determine if house price and age are related. Use the following queries to derive the answer:

   a. *Are price and age independent in table RmSale?*

   b. *Select chi-square(*) from RmSale where (select count(*) from RmSale where price and age for each subdomain) and ((select count(*) from RmSale where price) * (select count(*) from RmSale where age)/(select count(*) from RmSale)).*

8. Determine if house area and corner location are related. Use the following queries to derive the answer:

   a. *Are house area and feature with corner location independent in table RmSale?*

   b. *Select chi-square(*) from RmSale where (select count(*) from RmSale where select area from RmSale where corner = yes and select feature from RmSale where corner = yes for each subdomain) and ((select count(*) from RmSale where select area from RmSale where corner = yes) × (select count(*) from RmSale where select feature from RmSale where corner = yes) / (select count(*) from RmSale where corner = yes)).*

9. Build the regression models for house price based on area, age, and features with corner location and analyze them. Use the following queries to derive the answer:

   a. *Build the linear regression model for dependent variable price and independent variables area, age, feature from table RmSale with corner location observations.*

   b. *Create a table **reg_anova** as select price, **reg** area, age, feature from RmSale where corner = yes.*

10. Build the regression model for house price based on area, feature, north-east, and corner location with age older than 10 years and analyze. Use the following queries to derive the answer:

   a. *Build the linear regression model for dependent variable price and independent variables area, feature, northeast, and corner from table RmSale with age older than 10 years.*

   b. *Create table **reg_anova** as select price, **reg** area, feature, northeast, corner from RmSale where age > 10.*

■ 4.11   SELECTED BIBLIOGRAPHIC NOTES

[Agarwal 2002], [Glymour 1997], [Hosking 1997], [Hand 1999], [Mani 1999], and [Palmerini 2004] discuss the role of statistics in data mining in general. The use of covariance and correlation estimates for data mining was dealt with by [Alqallaf 2002]. [Aumann 1999] demonstrate the usefulness of statistical theory for quantitative association rules, whereas the role of statistics in information technology was elaborated on by [Dudewicz 1999]. [Hou 1996] and [Hou 1999] demonstrated a framework for statistical data mining with summary tables and statistical relationships.

Other areas where statistical data mining has been applied include gene expression and DNA sequencing, pattern recognition, prediction and policy making, and spatial data mining [Curran 2003], [Jain 2000], [Zellner 2002], and [Wang 1997]. [Eliassi–Rad 2002] demonstrates how large-scale simulation data can be dealt with by statistical modeling. Furthermore, [Nie 2001] shows the effectiveness of statistical data mining for web data. Pattern discovery in post-marketing drug safety was studied by [Fram 2003], whereas Bayesian analysis of massive datasets was introduced by [Ridgeway 2002].

[Lambert 1996] and [Nie 2001] address the issue of on-line and web-based data mining using statistics, whereas [Morishita 2000] and [Nie 1999] deal with the application of statistical methods for efficiency in data management and integration.

■ 4.12   CHAPTER BIBLIOGRAPHY

[Agarwal 2002] D. K. Agarwal: "Statistical Methods II: Shrinkage Estimator Generalizations of Proximal Support Vector Machines," *Proceedings of the 8th ACM SIG-KDD International Conference on Knowledge Discovery and Data Mining*, 2002.

[Alqallaf 2002] F. A. Alqallaf, K. P. Konis, R. D. Martin, and R. H. Zamar: "Statistical Methods I: Scalable Robust Covariance and Correlation Estimates for Data Mining," *Proceedings of the 8th ACM SIGKDD International Conference on Knowledge Discovery and Data Mining*, 2002.

[Aumann 1999] Y. Aumann and Yehuda Lindell: "A Statistical Theory for Quantitative Association Rules," *Proceedings of the 5th ACM SIGKDD International Conference on Knowledge Discovery and Data Mining*, 1999.

[Curran 2003] M. D. Curran, H. Liu, F. Long, and N. Ge: "Statistical Methods for Joint Data Mining of Gene Expression and DNA Sequence Database," *ACM SIGKDD Explorations*, Vol. 5, No. 2, 2003.

[Dudewicz 1999] E. J. Dudewicz and Z. A. Karian: "The Role of Statistics in IS/IT: Practical Gains from Mined Data," *Information Systems Frontiers*, Vol. 1, No. 3, 1999.

[Eliassi–Rad 2002] T. Eliassi–Rad, T. Critchlow, and G. Abdulla: "Statistical Modeling of Large-scale Simulation Data," *Proceedings of the 8th ACM SIGKDD International Conference on Knowledge Discovery and Data Mining*, 2002.

[Fram 2003] D. M. Fram, J. S. Almenoff, and W. DuMouchel: "Empirical Bayesian Data Mining for Discovering Patterns in Post-marketing Drug Safety," *Proceedings of the 9th ACM SIGKDD International Conference on Knowledge Discovery and Data Mining*, 2003.

[Glymour 1997] C. Glymour, D. Madigan, D. Pregibon, and P. Smyth: "Statistical Themes and Lessons for Data Mining," *Data Mining and Knowledge Discovery*, Vol, 1, No. 1, 1997.

[Hand 1999] D. J. Hand: "Statistics and Data Mining: Intersecting Disciplines," *ACM SIGKDD Explorations*, Vol. 1, No. 1, 1999.

[Hosking 1997] J. Hosking, E. Pednault, and M. Sudan: "A Statistical Perspective on Data Mining," *Future Generation Computer Systems*, 1997.

[Hou 1996] W. C. Hou: "Extraction and Applications of Statistical Relationships in Relational Databases," *IEEE Transactions on Knowledge and Data Engineering*, Vol. 8, No. 6, pp. 939–945, 1996.

[Hou 1999] W. C. Hou: "A Framework for Statistical Data Mining with Summary Tables," *The 11th International Conference on Scientific and Statistical Database Management*, 1999.

[Jain 2000] A. K. Jain, R. Duin, and J. Mao: "Statistical Pattern Recognition: A Review," *IEEE Transactions on Pattern Analysis and Machine Intelligence*, Vol. 22, No. 1, pp. 4–38, 2000.

[Lambert 1996] N. Lambert: "Online Statistical Techniques Not for Patent Searchers Only, Part 1: Patent Indexing, Patent Citations," *Database*, Vol. 19, No. 1, pp. 74–78.

[Mani 1999] D. R. Mani, J. Drew, A. Betz, and P. Datta: "Statistics and Data Mining Techniques for Lifetime Value Modeling," *Proceedings of the 5th ACM SIGKDD International Conference on Knowledge Discovery and Data Mining*, 1999.

[Morishita 2000] S. Morishita and J. Sese: "Transversing Itemset Lattices with Statistical Metric Pruning," *Proceedings of the 19th ACM SIGMOD-SIGACT-SIGART Symposium on Principles of Database Systems*, 2000.

[Nie 1999] Z. Nie, S. Kambhampati, and U. Nambiar: "Effectively Mining and Using Coverage and Overlap Statistics for Data Integration," *VLDB Conference*, 1999.

[Nie 2001] Z. Nie, S. Kambhampati, U. Nambiar, and S. Vaddi: "Web Data Mining: Mining Source Coverage Statistics for Data Integration," *Proceedings of the 3rd International Workshop on Web Information and Data Management*, 2001.

[Palmerini 2004] P. Palmerini, S. Orlando, and R. Perego: "Data Mining (DM): Statistical Properties of Transactional Databases," *Proceedings of the 2004 ACM Symposium on Applied Computing*, 2004.

[Ridgeway 2002] G. Ridgeway and D. Madigan: "Statistical Methods: Bayesian Analysis of Massive Datasets via Particle Filters," *Proceedings of the 8th ACM SIGKDD International Conference on Knowledge Discovery and Data Mining*, 2002.

[Wang 1997] W. Wang, J. Yang, and R. Muntz: "STING: A Statistical Information Grid Approach to Spatial Data Mining," *Proceedings of the 23rd VLDB Conference*, Athens, Greece, Vol. 1, pp. 186–195, 1997.

[Zellner 2002] A. Zellner: "Econometric and Statistical Data Mining, Prediction and Policy-Making," *Studies in Nonlinear Dynamics and Econometrics*, Vol. 6, No. 2, pp. 1–16, 2002.

CHAPTER 5

Rough Sets and Bayes' Theories

■ 5.1 INTRODUCTION

In the last decade, we have experienced explosive growth in the efforts made to collect data and retrieve information from it. At the same time, there has been a growing need for techniques and tools to intelligently and automatically analyze the data for extraction of useful knowledge from databases. These databases play a very crucial role in the knowledge discovery process. Knowledge Discovery in Databases (KDD) is a process of searching for relationships and global patterns that implicitly exist in large databases with vast amounts of data. This is a process of extracting previously unknown and potentially useful information. KDD often involves knowledge acquisition through both structured and unstructured interviews with domain experts and requires access to data within a database. While KDD refers to the overall process of discovering useful knowledge from data, data mining refers to the steps of applying various algorithms to different applications to extract patterns from the data. KDD assesses the significance of the findings resulting from the extraction process. On the other hand, data mining without proper domain knowledge interpretation and validation may lead to the "discovery" of spurious and invalid patterns.

The two main areas of data mining are prediction and interpretation. For prediction, the available datasets are analyzed to predict the future value of unknown variables. In some cases, domain knowledge may not be readily available, and some assumptions about the incomplete data may be required. The interpretation, on the other hand, is about finding interesting and meaningful patterns in the data and presenting the findings to end users in a meaningful way. Both prediction and interpretation enable decision-making processes to be more effective.

Data mining and knowledge discovery have become increasingly important topics in database development. In many applications, the size of the database grows rapidly as transactions continue to occur on a day-by-day basis. Databases with huge amounts of data can be analytically exploited to discover concepts, patterns, and relationships. But real-life databases often contain data that is imprecise, incomplete, and noisy, which makes it difficult for many data-mining techniques to extract knowledge from the data. Therefore, there is a strong need for knowledge discovery techniques that can identify patterns under noisy conditions.

To deal with uncertain or inaccurate data for knowledge extraction, Bayes' theory and rough sets are the two methods widely used for data analysis. Bayesian analysis is based on probability theory. Hence, the interpretation of data analysis is based on the computation of conditional probabilities. Rough-set theory, on the other hand, employs rigorous mathematical techniques for discovering regularities in data and is particularly useful for dealing with ambiguous and inconsistent data. Unlike other methods, such as the fuzzy-set theory and various forms of neural-network methods, rough-set analysis requires no external parameters and uses only the information present in the obtained data. These two techniques have been successfully applied to medical data analysis, decision making in business, industrial design, voice recognition, image processing, and process modeling and identification.

For applications with a great deal of invalid data, it is often difficult to know exactly which features are relevant, important, and useful for the given tasks. Furthermore, certain attributes in the dataset may be undesirable, irrelevant, or unimportant. Some tuples may even contain redundant information. The number of attributes found in data form practical applications is often more than 20, and the number of tuples is often more than several hundred thousand or even more. Since the size of a database and its attributes grows rapidly, effective data analysis techniques are needed to simplify the knowledge-extraction process.

In this chapter, Bayes' and rough-set theories are introduced as effective methods for analyzing large amounts of data to discover knowledge about the database. The application of Bayes' and rough-set approaches to several groups of data samples in different fields is discussed, and the process of automated discovery of rules from databases is described. In rough-set analysis, important and useful information is generated through the removal and separation of redundant tuples and irrelevant attributes.

We will begin by defining some of the main concepts of rough sets and Bayes' in the next few sections. These theories are then applied to the following four application areas to discover useful information:

1. Customer purchase data (Using Bayes' theory)
2. Fitting contact lenses (Using rough-set theory)
3. Welding procedures (Using rough-set theory)
4. Car data (Using Bayes' and rough-set theories)

In the above examples, the datasets are composed of condition and decision parts. In the condition part, each object is described in terms of condition attributes, and the decision part specifies generated results that can be used for effective decision making. Normally, it is not easy to determine what portion of data is important and practical and what relationship exists between the condition attributes and the decision attributes, due to data size and the large number of attributes. Through the examples, rough sets and Bayes' are compared to show the effectiveness of each technique in different application domains.

■ 5.2 BAYES' THEOREM

The Bayesian approach is based on probability theory. This approach uses a mathematically and statistically sound method to handle uncertainty. The fundamental notion of Bayesian statistics is the same as conditional probability. It has successfully been applied to several fields of Artificial Intelligence (AI). By assuming a random distribution of events, it is possible to calculate even more complex probabilities from previously known results. This approach provides a means of incorporating new data with known probability information. It is a useful method for combining experimental, judgmental, or survey-type data.

Using Bayes' theorem, we try to estimate or find the probability of a hypothesis A when we have a certain evidence B. To calculate this, we need to know the following two probabilistic measures:

1. The probability that we will obtain evidence B, given that hypothesis A is true.
2. The probabilities of A and B in the absence of any specific evidence. These probabilities are called prior probabilities.

Bayes' theorem then states that

$$P(A \mid B) = \frac{P(B \mid A) \times P(A)}{P(B)} = \frac{P(A \cap B)}{P(B)}$$

$P(A)$ is the prior probability that hypothesis A is true.
$P(B)$ is the prior probability that evidence B is true.
$P(A \mid B)$ is the probability that hypothesis A is true given evidence B.
$P(B \mid A)$ is the probability of evidence B given that hypothesis A is true.

The notation $P(A \mid B)$ can be read as "the probability of A given that all we know is B." This simple equation underlies all modern AI systems for probabilistic inference. Yet its usefulness depends on the assumption that attributes are independent. It can be used to handle changes in a database without recalculating everything, i.e., with less time and less memory.

■ 5.3 ROUGH SETS

■ 5.3.1 Data Analysis and Representation

An information system can be considered a relational database that consists of columns labeled by attributes. Each object in column p and row x is labeled with the value $p(x)$. The information system S is a quadruple $S = \{U, A, V, F\}$. $U = \{x_1, x_2, \ldots, x_n\}$ is the finite set of objects in the database, where n is the number of objects. A is the finite set of attributes $\{a_1, a_2, \ldots, a_m\}$, where m represents the number of distinct attributes. The attributes in A are further classified into the set of disjoint condition attributes, C, and decision attributes, D. Therefore, $A = C \cup D$ and $C \cap D = \varnothing$. $V_a = U_{a \in A}$, where V_a is a domain of an attribute a. $F: U \times A \rightarrow V$ is an information function such that $F(x_i, a) \in V_a$ for every $a \in A$ and $x_i \in U$.

Let $B \subset A$ and $x_i, x_j \in U$ $(0 \leq i \leq n, 0 \leq j \leq n)$. A binary relation $R(B)$, also called an indiscernibility relation, is defined as $R(B) = \{(x_i, x_j) \in U \times U$: for every $a \in B, a(x_i) = a(x_j)\}$. We say that the two objects x_i and x_j are indiscernible by the set of attributes B in S if $a(x_i) = a(x_j)$ for every attribute $a \in B$. For example, consider the following relation R shown in Table 5.1, where $A = \{a_1, a_2, a_3, a_4\}$, $B = \{a_1, a_3\}$, and $a_i \in \{0, 1, 2\}$.

In this relation, the objects X_1 and X_3 are indiscernible by B. Since $R(B)$ is an equivalence relation on U for every $B \subset A$, we see that $R(B) = \{(X_1, X_3), (X_2, X_6)\}$ from the relation above. Therefore, naturally we can define two

■ TABLE 5.1 A sample relation with six objects

	a_1	a_2	a_3	a_4
X_1	0	0	1	1
X_2	1	2	1	2
X_3	0	2	1	0
X_4	1	0	0	1
X_5	0	3	3	1
X_6	1	2	1	2

natural equivalence relations, $R(C)$ and $R(D)$ on U, for an information system S (recall that the attributes in A are classified into the condition attributes C and the decision attributes D). A concept Y is an equivalence class of the relation $R(D)$. Based on the group of condition attributes C, an object x_i specifies the equivalence class $[x_i]_C$ of the relation $R(C)$, which satisfies the following:

$$[x_i]_C = \{x_j \in U \mid \forall\ a \in C, F(x_j, a) = F(x_i, a)\}$$

We say that $x_i \in U$ definitely belongs to a concept Y if $[x_i]_C \subseteq Y$ and that $x_i \in U$ possibly belongs to the concept Y if $[x_i]_C \cap Y \neq \emptyset$.

For example, consider the relation shown in Table 5.2, where $C = \{$ GRE, GPA, major, recommendation$\}$ and $D = \{$ admitted, conditional, rejected$\}$. Notice that $[John]_R = \{$ John, Tom, Joan $\}$.

■ TABLE 5.2 An admission relation

	GRE	GPA	Major	Recommendation	Admitted	Conditional	Rejected
John	>1500	>3.5	CS	Good	Y	–	–
Bob	<1000	>3.0	CS	Good	–	Y	–
Mary	<1000	<2.5	EE	Poor	–	–	Y
Tom	>1500	>3.5	CS	Good	Y	–	–
Rosa	<1000	>3.0	CS	Good	–	Y	–
Becky	<1000	<2.5	MS	Good	–	–	Y
Joan	>1500	>3.5	CS	Good	Y	–	–
Sam	<1000	>3.0	CS	Good	Y	–	–
Tony	>1500	>3.5	EE	Poor	Y	–	–

From the relation above, three different concepts can be derived from the three equivalence classes of relation $R(D)$. They are $D_1 = \{$John, Tom, Joan, Sam, Tony$\} \equiv \{$the set of admitted students$\}$, $D_2 = \{$Bob, Rosa$\} \equiv \{$the set of conditionally admitted students$\}$, and $D_3 = \{$Mary, Becky$\} \equiv \{$the set of rejected students$\}$. Therefore, we can say that (1) Tom definitely belongs to the concept D_1, (2) Bob possibly belongs to the concepts D_1 and D_2, and (3) Bob does not belong to the concept D_3. Now, we can define conditional probabilities as

$$P(Y \,|\, [x_i]_C) = \frac{P(Y \cap [x_i]_C)}{P([x_i]_C)} = \frac{|Y \cap [x_i]_C|}{|[x_i]_C|}$$

where $P(Y|\,[x_i]_C)$ is the probability of the occurrence of event Y conditioned on event $[X]_C$, i.e., $P(Y|[X]_C) = 1$ if and only if $[X]_C \subseteq Y$; $P(Y|[X]_C) > 0$ if and only if $[X]_C \cap Y \neq \varnothing$, and $P(Y|[X]_C) = 0$ if and only if $[X]_C \cap Y = \varnothing$. The following is the simplified conditional probability of the conditional probability of an equivalence class, where $i = 1, 2, \ldots, n$.

$$P(Y|X_i) = P(Y\,|[x_i]_C) = \frac{|Y \cap [x_i]_C|}{|[x_i]_C|} = \frac{|Y \cap X_i|}{|X_i|}$$

Here, X is an object or a group of objects that has the same condition attributes, and Y is a group of objects that has the same values in the decision attributes.

Let us now consider the given information system $S = \{U, A, V, F\}$, the equivalence relation $R(C)$ (the indiscernibility relation) on U, and an ordered pair $AS = \langle U, C \rangle$, which is called an approximation space based on the condition attributes C. The equivalence classes of the relation $R(C)$ are called elementary sets in AS because they represent the smallest sets of objects that are distinguishable in terms of the attributes and their values. Let $Y \subseteq U$ be a subset of objects representing a concept, and $R\times(C) = \{X_1, X_2, \ldots, X_n\} = \{[x_1]_C, [x_2]_C, \ldots, [x_n]_C\}$ be the collection of equivalence classes induced by the relation $R(C)$. The lower and upper approximations of set Y are defined by the following formulae in the standard rough set model:

$$\underline{R(C)}(Y) = \bigcup_{P(Y|X_i)=1} \{X_i \in R\times(C)\}$$

and

$$\overline{R(C)}(Y) = \bigcup_{P(Y|X_i)>0} \{X_i \in R\times(C)\}$$

■ **FIGURE 5.1**
Domain
representation

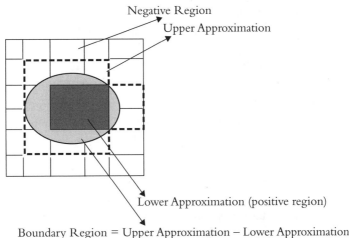

Boundary Region = Upper Approximation − Lower Approximation

The domain representation of the lower and upper approximation is shown in Figure 5.1. They can be called either a strong or weak membership, respectively, since X is a certain subset of U. We say either "X surely belongs to AS" or "X possibly belongs to AS." For illustration purposes, we apply β-probabilistic approximation for classification.

A β-approximation space AS_p is a triple $<U, R(C), P>$, where P is a probability measure and β is a real number in the range (0.5, 1]. The β-approximation space AS_p can be divided into the following regions:

β-positive region of the set Y: $POS_C(Y) = U_{P(Y|Xi)\geq\beta}\{X_i \in R \times (C)\}$

β-negative region of the set Y: $NEG_C(Y) = U_{P(Y|Xi)<\beta}\{X_i \in R \times (C)\}$

The β-positive region of the group Y corresponds to all elementary groups of U that can be classified into the concept Y with conditional probability $P(Y \mid X_i)$ greater than or equal to the parameter β. Similarly, the negative region of group Y corresponds to all elementary groups of U that can be classified into group $\neg Y$.

An object x_i is classified as belonging to concept Y if $x_i \in POS_C(Y)$, or it is classified as belonging to $\neg Y$, the complement of concept Y if $x_i \in NEG_C(Y)$. Since we want to decide whether x_i is in concept Y on the basis of the set of equivalence classes in AS_p rather than on the basis of group Y, we apply $POS_C(Y)$ and $NEG_C(Y)$ instead of group Y. If $x_i \in U$ is in $POS_C(Y)$, we conclude that it belongs to concept Y with the conditional probability $P(Y|X_i)$ greater than or equal to the parameter β.

■ 5.3.2 Reduction of Condition Attributes and Generation of Decision Rules

Reducing condition attributes and generating decision rules based on them are the two fundamental concepts of rough set. *Reduct*, a reduced condition attribute set, is produced as a result of reducing condition attributes and is the essential part of an information system that can discern all objects discernible by the original information system. Some condition attributes that cannot provide any additional information about the objects in U are often included in the information system. Removing these attributes can reduce the complexity and cost of analysis and decision making for a large amount of data. We use the *reduct* concept in rough sets to describe the process of condition attribute reduction. Let $S = \{U, A, V, F\}$ be an information system, $A = C \cup D$, and $B \subset C$. We can obtain an attribute value system $T = <U, C \cup \{d\}, V, F>$, where $a \in B$ is an dispensable attribute in C with respect to $\{d\}$ if $POS_{C-\{a\}}(Y) = POS_C(Y)$. B is an independent set with respect to $\{d\}$. A *reduct* of the attribute set C is a maximal independent subset with respect to $\{d\}$. Consider a condition attribute $a \in C$. If the β-positive region $POS_{C-\{a\}}(Y)$ of set Y is the same as $POS_C(Y)$, then attribute a is marked redundant and is removed from the set of condition attributes, C. Otherwise, a relative *reduct* of the set of condition variables will be defined as a maximal independent subset of condition variables. The computational procedure for finding a *reduct* is straightforward as follows:

1. Remove the marked attribute from the set C.
2. Check to see if the dependency predicate is satisfied for each condition attribute.
3. Mark the attribute *redundant* if the predicate is valid and permanently remove it from the set of condition attributes.
4. Repeat steps 1–3 until all condition attributes in C are tested.

The final collection of condition attributes includes only the non-redundant attributes and preserves the dependency with the set of decision attributes D. The remaining set of condition attributes is the *reduct*. The dispensable attributes in C are the attributes that can be removed from C

without affecting the ability to predict decision D with the estimated probability. After eliminating the dispensable attributes, there will not be any redundant objects in C.

Once the *reduct* is obtained, we can consider probabilistic decision rules. Rule generation is a crucial task in any information system. Let $R \times (RED) = \{X_1, X_2, \ldots, X_n\}$ be the collection of equivalence classes of relation $R(RED)$, where RED is the *reduct*, that is, the reduced set of condition attributes in C. Moreover, let $R \times (D) = \{Y, \neg Y\}$ be the partition induced by the decision attributes. Every equivalence class X_i of equivalence relation $R(RED)$ is associated with a unique combination of the values of the attributes in RED. This combination of values is called the description of equivalence class $X_i \in R \times (RED)$. Thus, we can express the description of X_i by the following formula, where $\wedge$ denotes the conjunction operator and x_i is an object in the equivalence class X_i:

$$Des(X_i) = \bigwedge_{a \in RED} (a = F(x_i, a))$$

Similarly, we can express the descriptions of Y and $\neg Y$ as $Des(Y) = (D = F(x_i, D))$ and $Des(\neg Y) = (D \neq F(x_i, D))$, where D is the decision attribute set and $x_i \in Y$.

The relationships between the partition $R \times (RED)$ and the partition $R \times (D)$ are described in the form of decision rules by the following formulae, where $X_i \in R \times (RED)$ and c_i is the uncertainty factor: $Des(X_i) \rightarrow {}^{Ci}Des(Y)$ if $P(Y|X_i) \geq \beta$ and $Des(X_i) \rightarrow {}^{Ci}Des(\neg Y)$ if $P(Y|X_i) < \beta$. This means that x_i belongs to Y with uncertainty c_i if $P(Y|X_i) \geq \beta$, and it belongs to the complementary concept $\neg Y$ if $P(Y|X_i) < \beta$. A decision rule obtained by dropping the maximum possible numbers is called the maximally general rule, which can be found by using the decision matrix technique.

Let X_i^+ denote the equivalence classes of relation $R \times (RED)$ such that $X_i^+ \subseteq POS_{RED}(Y)$ and X_j^- denote the equivalence classes of relation $R \times (RED)$ such that $X_j^- \subseteq NEG_{RED}(Y)$, where $i = 1, 2, \ldots, m$ and $j = 1, 2, \ldots, n$. Then $M_{ij} = \{(a, F(X_i^+, a)): a \in RED, F(X_i^+, a) \neq F(X_j^-, a)\}$ is a decision matrix, where a is a condition attribute in RED. M_{ij} contains all attribute value pairs that are not identical between equivalence class X_i^+ and equivalence class X_j^-. Using the *reduct* and the decision matrix for rules, we can find maximally general rules.

■ 5.4   APPLICATIONS BASED ON BAYES' AND ROUGH SETS

■ 5.4.1   Customer Tendency Analysis Using Bayes' Theory

Consider a store manager who wants to derive a purchase pattern of coffee and sugar buyers. He wants to find out how likely a person buying coffee will also buy sugar. The store manager knows that generally 50% of people buying sugar also buy coffee. The prior probability of a customer buying sugar is 1/200 and prior probability of a customer buying coffee is 1/50. Therefore, we can obtain the following by using Bayes' theorem:

$$P(Coffee \,|\, Sugar) = 50\% = 0.5$$

$$P(Coffee) = 1/50$$

$$P(Sugar \,|\, Coffee) = \frac{P(Coffee \,|\, Sugar) \times P(Sugar)}{P(Coffee)} = \frac{0.5 \times (1/200)}{(1/50)} = 0.125$$

$$P(Sugar) = 1/200$$

This implies that only one out of eight customers (0.125) buying coffee will also buy sugar. We could also state this fact in rule form as follows:

$$\text{CustomerBuy}(Coffee) \rightarrow^{0.125} \text{CustomerBuy}(Sugar)$$

With an appropriate threshold value for probability, data entered into the database will affect the classification of data according to the query, "How likely is a customer buying coffee to also buy sugar." The usefulness of this method depends on the assumption that attributes being considered are independent. One disadvantage of this method is that it may be difficult to determine prior distribution, whereas the advantage is its simplicity and accuracy in calculating probabilities.

■ 5.4.2   Contact Lens Prescription Using Rough Set Theory

In this example, we use rough set theory to analyze a group of objects in a database that contains contact lens information. In this case, we assume the following three classes of decision attributes (D):

1. The patient should use hard contact lenses.
2. The patient should use soft contact lenses.
3. The patient should not use contact lenses.

There are four condition attributes that can be considered for deriving each of the decision classes given above. The values that these condition attributes may take are given below:

a_1: Age of the patient: (1) young,   (2) pre-presbyopic,   (3) presbyopic
a_2: Spectacle prescription: (1) myope,   (2) hypermetrope
a_3: Astigmatic: (1) no,   (2) yes
a_4: Tear production rate: (1) reduced, (2) normal

Our main purpose is to find the decision rules holding in this database. To derive the decision rules, first we need to know which condition attributes are most closely related to three of these decision attributes and determine the optimal relationships among them. Table 5.3 shows a database that contains a sample contact lens dataset showing the relationships between the condition attributes and the decision attributes.

Upon analysis of this table, we generate the following equivalence classes with respect to relation $R(D)$:

$$Y_1 = \{ Obj_1, Obj_4, Obj_8, Obj_{10} \}$$
$$Y_2 = \{ Obj_2, Obj_3, Obj_7, Obj_{11} \}$$
$$Y_3 = \{ Obj_5, Obj_6, Obj_9, Obj_{12} \}$$

■ TABLE 5.3 Contact lens table

	a_1	a_2	a_3	a_4	D
Obj_1	1	1	2	2	1
Obj_2	1	1	1	2	2
Obj_3	1	2	1	2	2
Obj_4	1	2	2	2	1
Obj_5	2	1	1	1	3
Obj_6	3	2	1	1	3
Obj_7	2	1	1	1	2
Obj_8	2	1	2	2	1
Obj_9	2	1	2	1	3
Obj_{10}	2	1	1	1	1
Obj_{11}	2	1	1	2	2
Obj_{12}	3	2	2	1	3

The equivalence classes obtained with respect to relation $R(C)$ are

$$X_1 = [Obj_1]_R, X_2 = [Obj_2]_R, \ X_3 = [Obj_3]_R, X_4 = [Obj_4]_R$$
$$X_5 = [Obj_5] = [Obj_7] = [Obj_{10}] = \{Obj_5, Obj_7, Obj_{10}\}, X_6 = [Obj_6]_R$$
$$X_7 = [Obj_8]_R, X_8 = [Obj_9]_R, \ X_9 = [Obj_{11}]_R, \ X_{10} = [Obj_{12}]_R$$

In this example, class X_5 contains three elements, Obj_5, Obj_7, and Obj_{10}, which are indiscernible with respect to the set of condition attributes, C. Next, we can obtain the probability of occurrence of event Y conditioned on event $[X]_c$ according to the following conditional probability formula:

$$P(Y\,|[x_i]_c) = \frac{P(Y \cap [x_i]_c)}{P([x_i]_c)} = \frac{|Y \cap [x_i]_c|}{|[x_i]_c|}$$

The conditional probabilities of each equivalence class are

$P(Y_1 \mid X_1) = 1$	$P(Y_2 \mid X_1) = 0$	$P(Y_3 \mid X_1) = 0$
$P(Y_1 \mid X_2) = 0$	$P(Y_2 \mid X_2) = 1$	$P(Y_3 \mid X_2) = 0$
$P(Y_1 \mid X_3) = 0$	$P(Y_2 \mid X_3) = 1$	$P(Y_3 \mid X_3) = 0$
$P(Y_1 \mid X_4) = 1$	$P(Y_2 \mid X_4) = 0$	$P(Y_3 \mid X_4) = 0$
$P(Y_1 \mid X_5) = 0.333$	$P(Y_2 \mid X_5) = 0.333$	$P(Y_3 \mid X_5) = 0.333$
$P(Y_1 \mid X_6) = 0$	$P(Y_2 \mid X_6) = 0$	$P(Y_3 \mid X_6) = 1$
$P(Y_1 \mid X_7) = 1$	$P(Y_2 \mid X_7) = 0$	$P(Y_3 \mid X_7) = 0$
$P(Y_1 \mid X_8) = 0$	$P(Y_2 \mid X_8) = 0$	$P(Y_3 \mid X_8) = 1$
$P(Y_1 \mid X_9) = 0$	$P(Y_2 \mid X_9) = 1$	$P(Y_3 \mid X_9) = 0$
$P(Y_1 \mid X_{10}) = 0$	$P(Y_2 \mid X_{10}) = 0$	$P(Y_3 \mid X_{10}) = 1$

The lower and upper approximations of set Y are defined by

$$\underline{R(C)}(Y) = \bigcup_{P(Y|X_i)=1} \{X_i \in R \times (C)\}$$

$$\overline{R(C)}(Y) = \bigcup_{P(Y|X_i)>0} \{X_i \in R \times (C)\}$$

The lower approximation of set Y_1 is X_1, X_4, X_7.
The upper approximation of set Y_1 is X_1, X_4, X_7, X_5.

■ **TABLE 5.4 Reduced table with respect to Y_1**

	C		Y_1
	a_3	a_4	
X_1	2	2	1
X_4	2	2	1
X_7	2	2	1
X_5	1	1	1, 2, 3

The lower approximation of set Y_2 is	X_2, X_3, X_9.
The upper approximation of set Y_2 is	X_2, X_3, X_9, X_5.
The lower approximation of set Y_3 is	X_6, X_8, X_{10}.
The upper approximation of set Y_3 is	X_6, X_8, X_{10}, X_5.

With the approximation parameter β set to 1 based on the theory, if the β-positive region $POS_{C-\{a\}}(Y)$ of set Y is the same as $POS_C(Y)$, then attribute a is treated as redundant and can be removed from the set of condition attributes C. Next, we can get the reduced information concerning $\{a_3, a_4\}$ as follows. The following are the reduced upper approximation tables (Tables 5.4, 5.5, and 5.6) on the three decision classes Y_1, Y_2, and Y_3:

The description of these equivalence classes is

$$Des(X1,4,7) = (a_3 = 2) \wedge (a_4 = 2)$$
$$Des(X2,3,9) = (a_3 = 1) \wedge (a_4 = 2)$$
$$Des(X6) \quad = (a_3 = 1) \wedge (a_4 = 1)$$
$$Des(X8,10) = (a_3 = 2) \wedge (a_4 = 1)$$

■ **TABLE 5.5 Reduced table with respect to Y_2**

	C		Y_2
	a_3	a_4	
X_2	1	2	2
X_3	1	2	2
X_9	1	2	2
X_5	1	1	1, 2, 3

■ **TABLE 5.6 Reduced table with respect to Y_3**

	C		Y_3
	a_3	a_4	
X_6	1	1	3
X_8	2	1	3
X_{10}	2	1	3
X_5	1	1	1, 2, 3

Next, we can obtain the decision rules with respect to Y_1, Y_2, and Y_3:

$$r_1^+: (a_3 = 2) \wedge (a_4 = 2) \to {}^1(D = 1)$$

$$r_1^-: (a_3 = 1) \wedge (a_4 = 1) \to {}^{0.333}(D = 1)$$

$$r_2^+: (a_3 = 1) \wedge (a_4 = 2) \to {}^1(D = 2)$$

$$r_2^-: (a_3 = 1) \wedge (a_4 = 1) \to {}^{0.333}(D = 2)$$

$$r_3^+: (a_3 = 1,2) \wedge (a_4 = 1) \to {}^1(D = 3)$$

$$r_3^-: (a_3 = 1) \wedge (a_4 = 1) \to {}^{0.333}(D = 3)$$

By comparing these decision rules with the descriptions above, we get the following decision rules:

Rule 1: When a patient is astigmatic ($a_3 = 2$) and his/her tear production rate is normal ($a_4 = 2$), the patient should use hard contact lenses.

Rule 2: When a patient is not astigmatic ($a_3 = 1$) and his/her tear production rate is normal ($a_4 = 2$), the patient should use soft contact lenses.

Rule 3: When a patient's tear production rate is reduced, then she/he should not use contact lenses.

For the first two rules, we can draw a rule that is more concise and simple by combining them and factoring out any common part. Since both rules have a common part (normal tear production rate ($a_4 = 2$)), we can extract only the factors that are different . We now have the following two rules:

Rule 1: When a patient is astigmatic, then he/she should use hard contact lenses.

Rule 2: When a patient is not astigmatic, then he/she should use soft contact lenses.

■ 5.4.3 Welding Procedure Using Rough-Set Theory

To obtain higher-quality welding products, welding procedures emphasize control of parameters such as welding voltage, welding current, wire speed rate, welding travel speed, room temperature, and work plate. Constraints of the factors involved in the welding procedure are often vague and can cause conflict. It is difficult for engineers to decide which factors are more important than others when generating optimal schedules and designs. In this section, we use a rough-set model to help engineers identify the important factors. The dataset used in this section contains real-world data collected from a practical production environment. Here are some of the condition and decision factors involved in a welding procedure.

Condition attributes:

a_1: Welding voltage   (V)
a_2: Wire speed rate   (ipm)
a_3: Welding travel speed (ipm)
a_4: Room temperature   (°F)
a_5: Work plate   (mm)
a_6: Weld length   (m)
a_7: Welding current   (A)

Decision attributes:

D: Welding product quality
1: Best case
2: May have some welding defects
3: Worst case

Table 5.7 shows the welding parameters for different cases in terms of these seven condition attributes. The values for these condition attributes can be simplified for manipulation as shown below. The simplified table is given in Table 5.8.

For a_7:

1: Welding current < 200 (amps)
2: Welding current = 200–250 (amps)
3: Welding current > 250 (amps)

■ **TABLE 5.7 Welding parameters**

Objects	a_1 (V)	a_2 (ipm)	a_3 (ipm)	a_4 (°F)	a_5 (mm)	a_6 (m)	a_7 (A)	D
Obj_1	27.0	190	20	60	18	Middle	220	1
Obj_2	71.0	190	20	60	25	Middle	270	3
Obj_3	28.1	140	25	40	30	Short	225	1
Obj_4	26.5	190	20	60	18	Middle	240	1
Obj_5	70.0	190	20	60	25	Middle	255	2
Obj_6	29.0	190	20	60	25	Middle	170	3
Obj_7	70.0	190	20	60	25	Middle	300	3
Obj_8	42.0	150	25	65	18	Middle	150	2

For a_1:

  5: Welding voltage = 20–25 (volts)
  6: Welding voltage = 25–30 (volts)
  9: Welding voltage = 40–45 (volts)
14: Welding voltage = 65–70 (volts)
15: Welding voltage = 70–75 (volts)

For a_6:

5: Weld length (middle) = 5 (m)
2: Weld length (short) = 2 (m)

    Figure 5.2 illustrates the overlapping of welding-parameter cycles reflecting the data in Table 5.7. In this example, we will consider the normalized data given in Table 5.8. Although any set of attributes can be used for describing the objects in the dataset, a predetermined set of given attributes might be insufficient for characterizing an object uniquely. Any two objects are indistinguishable from each other whenever they have the same attribute values. In a given information system $<U, A, V, F>$, where the objects x_i and x_j are the members of U, if x_i and x_j have the same attribute values for both condition attributes and decision attributes, we say that x_i and x_j are indiscernible with respect to the set of attributes in $C \cup D$. For example, in Table 5.8, the two objects Obj_1 and Obj_4 are indiscernible with respect to the set of attributes $C \cup D$. If x_i and x_j have the same attribute values for condition attributes, we say that x_i and x_j are indiscernible with respect to the set of condition attributes C. From Table 5.8, we see that the three objects Obj_2, Obj_5, and Obj_7 are

■ **FIGURE 5.2**
Overlapping
welding–parame-
ter cycles

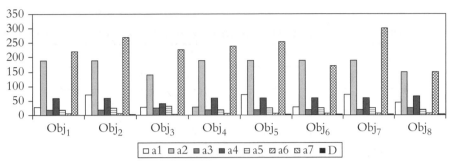

indiscernible with respect to the set of attributes C, whereas Obj_2 and Obj_7 are indiscernible with respect to the set of attributes $C \cup D$.

Let us consider the equivalence classes on relations $R(D)$ and $R(C)$. The equivalence classes on relation $R(D)$ are:

$$Y_1 = \{Obj_1, Obj_3, Obj_4\}$$
$$Y_2 = \{Obj_5, Obj_8\}$$
$$Y_3 = \{Obj_2, Obj_6, Obj_7\}$$

On the other hand, the equivalence classes on relation $R(C)$ are

$$X_1 = [Obj_1]_R = [Obj_4]_R = \{Obj_1, Obj_4\}$$
$$X_2 = [Obj_2]_R = [Obj_5]_R = [Obj_7]_R = \{Obj_2, Obj_5, Obj_7\}$$
$$X_3 = [Obj_3]_R = \{Obj_3\}$$
$$X_4 = [Obj_6]_R = \{Obj_6\}$$
$$X_5 = [Obj_8]_R = \{Obj_8\}$$

■ **TABLE 5.8 Welding parameters simplified from Table 5.7**

Objects	a_1 (V)	a_2 (ipm)	a_3 (ipm)	a_4 (°F)	a_5 (mm)	a_6 (m)	a_7 (A)	D
Obj_1	6	190	20	60	18	5	2	1
Obj_2	15	190	20	60	25	5	3	3
Obj_3	6	140	25	40	30	2	2	1
Obj_4	6	190	20	60	18	5	2	1
Obj_5	15	190	20	60	25	5	3	2
Obj_6	6	190	20	60	25	5	1	3
Obj_7	15	190	20	60	25	5	3	3
Obj_8	9	150	25	65	18	5	1	2

■ TABLE 5.9 Indiscernible objects with respect to C ∪ D

Objects	a_1 (V)	a_2 (ipm)	a_3 (ipm)	a_4 (°F)	a_5 (mm)	a_6 (m)	a_7 (A)	D
$Obj_1, Obj_4 (X_1)$	6	190	20	60	18	5	2	1
$Obj_2, Obj_7 (X_2)$	15	190	20	60	25	5	3	3
$Obj_3 (X_3)$	6	140	25	40	30	2	2	1
$Obj_5 (X_4)$	15	190	20	60	25	5	3	2
$Obj_6 (X_5)$	6	190	20	60	25	5	1	3
$Obj_8 (X_6)$	9	150	25	65	18	5	1	2

After joining the indiscernible objects in $C \cup D$, the Table 5.9 is obtained. Table 5.9 contains six indiscernible objects with respect to $C \cup D$.

Recall that the conditional probability of an equivalence class is obtained by the following formula:

$$P(Y | X_i) = P(Y | [x_i]_R) = \frac{|Y \cap [x_i]_R|}{|[x_i]_R|} = \frac{|Y \cap X_i|}{|X_i|}$$

Therefore, the conditional probabilities of each equivalence class in Table 5.9 are obtained as follows:

For the best case $(D = 1)$:

$$P(Y_1 | X_1) = \frac{|Y_1 \cap X_1|}{|X_1|} = \frac{Obj_1, Obj_3, Obj_4 \cap Obj_1, Obj_4}{Obj_1, Obj_4} = 1$$

$$P(Y_1 | X_2) = \frac{|Y_1 \cap X_2|}{|X_2|} = \frac{Obj_1, Obj_3, Obj_4 \cap Obj_2, Obj_5, Obj_7}{Obj_2, Obj_5, Obj_7} = 0$$

$$P(Y_1 | X_3) = \frac{|Y_1 \cap X_3|}{|X_3|} = \frac{Obj_1, Obj_3, Obj_4 \cap Obj_3}{Obj_3} = 1$$

$$P(Y_1 | X_4) = \frac{|Y_1 \cap X_4|}{|X_4|} = \frac{Obj_1, Obj_3, Obj_4 \cap Obj_6}{Obj_6} = 0$$

$$P(Y_1 | X_5) = \frac{|Y_1 \cap X_5|}{|X_5|} = \frac{Obj_1, Obj_3, Obj_4 \cap Obj_8}{Obj_8} = 0$$

For the worst case ($D = 3$):

$$P(Y_3 | X_1) = \frac{|Y_3 \cap X_1|}{|X_1|} = \frac{Obj_2, Obj_6, Obj_7 \cap Obj_1, Obj_4}{Obj_1, Obj_4} = 0$$

$$P(Y_3 | X_2) = \frac{|Y_3 \cap X_2|}{|X_2|} = \frac{Obj_2, Obj_6, Obj_7 \cap Obj_2, Obj_5, Obj_7}{Obj_2, Obj_5, Obj_7} = \frac{2}{3} = 0.667$$

$$P(Y_3 | X_3) = \frac{|Y_3 \cap X_3|}{|X_3|} = \frac{Obj_2, Obj_6, Obj_7 \cap Obj_3}{Obj_3} = 0$$

$$P(Y_3 | X_4) = \frac{|Y_3 \cap X_4|}{|X_4|} = \frac{Obj_2, Obj_6, Obj_7 \cap Obj_6}{Obj_6} = 1$$

$$P(Y_3 | X_5) = \frac{|Y_3 \cap X_5|}{|X_5|} = \frac{Obj_2, Obj_6, Obj_7 \cap Obj_8}{Obj_8} = 0$$

According to the lower and upper approximations of the set Y defined by

$$\overline{R(C)}(Y) = \bigcup_{P(Y|X_i)>0} \{X_i \in R \times (C)\}$$

and

$$\underline{R(C)}(Y) = \bigcup_{P(Y|X_i)=1} \{X_i \in R \times (C)\}$$

we can reduce unimportant condition attributes and build a decision matrix. Reducing the number of attributes from a table with a large number of cases will make the generated rules more meaningful and easier to interpret and use. Recall that we have already obtained the probabilities of each set X_i with respect to the decision attribute set Y as follows:

The lower approximation of set Y_1 is X_1, X_3.
The upper approximation of set Y_1 is X_1, X_3.
The lower approximation of set Y_3 is X_4.
The upper approximation of set Y_3 is X_2, X_4.

Recall now that the β region is defined as follows:

β-positive region of set Y: $POS_C(Y) = U_{P(Y|X_i) \geq \beta} \{X_i \in R \times (C)\}$
β-negative region of set Y: $NEG_C(Y) = U_{P(Y|X_i) < \beta} \{X_i \in R \times (C)\}$

■ **TABLE 5.10 Reduct table with respect to Y_1 after reduction from Table 5.9**

Objects	a_1 (V)	a_7 (A)	Y_1	No. of objects in Y_1	No. of objects in $\neg Y_1$
Obj_1, Obj_4, Obj_3	6	2	1	3	0
Obj_2, Obj_5, Obj_7	15	3	0	0	3
Obj_6	6	1	0	0	1
Obj_8	9	1	0	0	1

Let us set the approximation parameter β to 0.6. The objects with value 1 or any value greater than or equal to 0.667 for attribute Y_1 belong to the β-positive region of set Y_1. On the other hand, the objects with value 0 for attribute Y_1 belong to the β-negative region of set Y_1. When generating the decision rules, some condition values in the information system may be unnecessary. We can remove as many unnecessary condition attributes as possible without losing any essential information that can be retrieved from the table. Thus, we can obtain the *reduct* table shown in Table 5.10.

Table 5.10 shows a reduced information system based on the set of two attributes $\{a_1, a_7\}$ with respect to concept Y_1. The objects with value 1 for attribute Y_1 belong to the β-positive region of set Y_1, whereas the objects with value 0 for attribute Y_1 belong to the β-negative region of set Y_1. Table 5.11 shows the Y_3 counterpart of Table 5.10.

Let RED denote the *reduct* of $\{a_1, a_7\}$. $R\times(RED)$, the collection of the equivalence classes of the relation $R(RED)$, is obtained as follows:

$$R\times(RED) = \{X_1, X_2, X_3, X_4\}$$
$$= \{\{Obj_1, Obj_3, Obj_4\}, \{Obj_2, Obj_5, Obj_7\}, \{Obj_6\}, \{Obj_8\}\}$$

■ **TABLE 5.11 Reduct table with respect to Y_3 after reduction from Table 5.9**

Objects	a_1 (V)	a_7 (A)	Y_3	No. of objects in Y_3	No. of objects in $\neg Y_3$
Obj_1, Obj_4, Obj_3	6	2	0	0	3
Obj_2, Obj_5, Obj_7	15	3	1	2	1
Obj_6	6	1	1	1	0
Obj_8	9	1	0	0	1

The descriptions of the equivalence classes are

$$Des(X_1) = (a_1 = 6) \wedge (a_7 = 2)$$
$$Des(X_2) = (a_1 = 15) \wedge (a_7 = 3)$$
$$Des(X_3) = (a_1 = 14) \wedge (a_7 = 1)$$
$$Des(X_4) = (a_1 = 9) \wedge (a_7 = 1)$$

The descriptions of Y_1 and $\neg Y_1$ are

$$Des(Y_1) = 1$$
$$Des(\neg Y_1) \neq 1$$

The conditional probabilities we can obtain are

$$P(Y_1 \mid X_1) = 1$$
$$P(Y_1 \mid X_2) = 0$$
$$P(Y_1 \mid X_3) = 0$$
$$P(Y_1 \mid X_4) = 0$$

Thus, the decision rules with respect to concept Y_1 can be generated as follows:

$$R_1^+ : (a_1 = 6) \quad \wedge (a_7 = 2) \quad \rightarrow {}^1(Y_1 = 1)$$
$$R_1^- : (a_1 = 15) \wedge (a_7 = 3) \quad \rightarrow {}^1(Y_1 \neq 1)$$
$$R_2^- : (a_1 = 6) \quad \wedge (a_7 = 1) \quad \rightarrow {}^1(Y_1 \neq 1)$$
$$R_3^- : (a_1 = 9) \quad \wedge (a_7 = 1) \quad \rightarrow {}^1(Y_1 \neq 1)$$

Finally, the equivalence classes of relation $R(RED)$ are given as follows:

$$X_1^+ = X_1 = \{Obj_1, Obj_4, Obj_3\}$$
$$X_1^- = X_2 = \{Obj_2, Obj_5, Obj_7\}$$
$$X_2^+ = X_4 = \{Obj_6\}$$
$$X_2^- = X_5 = \{Obj_8\}$$

Table 5.12 shows the decision matrix $\mathbf{M}_{ij}$ where $1 \leq i \leq 2$ and $1 \leq j \leq 3$. From this table, we see that the maximally general rules for equivalence class $X_i^+ (i = 1, 2)$ are

$$R_1 : \quad (a_7 = 2) \qquad\qquad \rightarrow {}^1 (D = 1)$$
$$R_2 : \quad (a_1 = 6) \wedge (a_7 = 2) \quad \rightarrow {}^1 (D = 1)$$

■ **TABLE 5.12 The decision matrix for the decision rules with respect to set Y_1**

	X_1^-	X_2^-	X_3^-
X_1^+	$(a_1,6), (a_7,2)$	$(a_7,2)$	$(a_1,6), (a_7,2)$
X_2^+	$(a_1,6), (a_7,2)$	$(a_7,2)$	$(a_1,6), (a_7,2)$

Here, the symbol ∧ denotes the conjunction operator.

The final set of all maximally general rules for this information system S can be stated as follows:

> *When we apply rough-set theory to the welding current region 200–250 A($a_7 = 2$), or the welding voltage 25–30 V ($a_1 = 6$) matches with the welding current 200–250 A($a_7 = 2$), then the higher-quality welding product will be obtained.*

We can easily see the result in Figure 5.3.

■ 5.4.4 Classification of Automobiles Using Both Bayes' and Rough Set Theory

In this example, we consider a dataset representing a collection of cars as shown in Table 5.13. The table consists of six columns showing the relationships among the size of the car, its type, power, weight, compressibility, and mileage. This dataset will be used to find the relationships among these attributes expressed in the form of rules so that their patterns can be generalized.

Table 5.13 can be simplified with the following value replacements:

$$
\begin{aligned}
High &= 1 \\
Medium &= 0 \\
Light &= 5 \\
Compact &= C \\
Subcompact &= S
\end{aligned}
$$

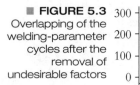

■ **FIGURE 5.3** Overlapping of the welding-parameter cycles after the removal of undesirable factors

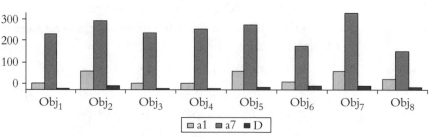

■ **TABLE 5.13 The automobiles dataset**

Object	Size	Door	Compress	Power	Weight	Mileage
e_1	Subcompact	4	High	High	Light	High
e_2	Compact	2	High	High	Medium	High
e_3	Compact	4	High	Medium	Light	Medium
e_4	Subcompact	2	Medium	High	Medium	High
e_5	Compact	4	High	Medium	Light	Medium
e_6	Subcompact	2	High	Medium	Medium	High
e_7	Subcompact	2	High	High	Medium	High
e_8	Compact	2	Medium	High	Medium	Medium
e_9	Compact	4	Medium	Medium	Light	High
e_{10}	Compact	2	Medium	High	Medium	Medium
e_{11}	Subcompact	2	High	Medium	Medium	High
e_{12}	Compact	2	High	High	Medium	Medium
e_{13}	Subcompact	4	High	High	Light	High
e_{14}	Compact	4	High	Medium	Light	Medium
e_{15}	Compact	2	Medium	High	Medium	Medium

Table 5.14 represents the simplified automobiles dataset. The representation shows each of the attributes assigned to different values representing different characteristics of the attributes. For additional simplification, we adopt the following notational changes:

1. *Size* (S)
2. *Door* (D)
3. *Compress* (C)
4. *Power* (P)
5. *Weight* (W)
6. *Mileage* (M)

This problem is approached here using two different methods, Bayes' theory and rough-set theory, respectively.

■ TABLE 5.14 The simplified automobiles dataset

Object	Size	Door	Compress	Power	Weight	Mileage
e_1	S	4	1	1	5	1
e_2	C	2	1	1	0	1
e_3	C	4	1	0	5	0
e_4	S	2	0	1	0	1
e_5	C	4	1	0	5	0
e_6	S	2	1	0	0	1
e_7	S	2	1	1	0	1
e_8	C	2	0	1	0	0
e_9	C	4	0	0	5	1
e_{10}	C	2	0	1	0	0
e_{11}	S	2	1	0	0	1
e_{12}	C	2	1	1	0	0
e_{13}	S	4	1	1	5	1
e_{14}	C	4	1	0	5	0
e_{15}	C	2	0	1	0	0

Method 1: Using Bayes' theorem

First, the threshold value β for probability is set to 0.5. Next, the conditional probabilities of the attributes related to the cars are calculated to generate the rules associated with them. From Table 5.14, the following list of rules is generated:

1. The relationship of a car's high compressibility with mileage:

$$P[M(high)\,|\,C(high)] = \frac{P[C(high)\,|\,M(high)] \times P[M(high)]}{P[C(high)]}$$

$$= \frac{(6/8) \times (8/15)}{(10/15)} = 0.60 \; (> \beta).$$

RULE 1: Cars with high compressibility will also have high mileage (with 60% probability).

2. The relationship of a car's weight with mileage:

$$P[M(high)|W(light)] = \frac{P[W(light)|M(high)] \times P[M(high)]}{P[W(light)]}$$

$$= \frac{(3/8) \times (8/15)}{(6/15)} = 0.50 \ (= \beta).$$

RULE 2: Lightweight cars will have high mileage (with 50% probability).

3. The relationship of a car's power with mileage:

$$P[M(high)|P(high)] = \frac{P[P(high)|M(high)] \times P[M(high)]}{P[P(high)]}$$

$$= \frac{(5/8) \times (8/15)}{(9/15)} = 0.56 \ (> \beta).$$

RULE 3: Cars with high power will also have high mileage (with 56% probability).

4. The relationship of a car's size with mileage:

$$P[M(high)|S(subcompact)] = \frac{P[S(subcompact)|M(high)] \times P[M(high)]}{P[S(subcompact)]}$$

$$= \frac{(6/8) \times (8/15)}{(6/15)} = 1 \ (> \beta)$$

$$P[M(high)|S(compact)] = \frac{P[S(compact)|M(high)] \times P[M(high)]}{P[S(compact)]}$$

$$= \frac{(2/8) \times (8/15)}{(9/15)} = 0.22 \ (< \beta)$$

RULE 4: Cars of subcompact size will _definitely_ have high mileage.

Method 2: Using rough-set theory

Recall that the attribute set includes six elements, {*size, door, compress, power, weight, mileage*}. All attributes are considered to be conditional attributes except *mileage*, which is chosen as the decision attribute. There are two possible concepts that can be generated for the mileage attribute: "Either the mileage is *high* or *medium*." Let us consider the dataset shown in Table 5.11 and Table 5.12. The concepts in this dataset and the equivalence classes on relations $R(D)$ and $R(C)$ are given as follows:

For relation $R(D)$:

$Y_{(M=high)}$: The decision attribute "mileage is high."
$Y_{(M=medium)}$: The decision attribute "mileage is medium."

Set $Y_1 = Y_{(M=high)}$ and $Y_2 = Y_{(M=medium)}$.
    Then we get $Y_1 = \{e_1, e_2, e_4, e_6, e_7, e_9, e_{11}, e_{13}\}$ and $Y_2 = \{e_3, e_5, e_8, e_{10}, e_{12}, e_{14}, e_{15}\}$.

For relation $R(C)$ (the condition attributes):

$$X_1 = \{e_1, e_{13}\}$$
$$X_2 = \{e_4\}$$
$$X_3 = \{e_6, e_{11}\}$$
$$X_4 = \{e_9\}$$
$$X_5 = \{e_3, e_5, e_{14}\}$$
$$X_6 = \{e_8, e_{10}, e_{15}\}$$
$$X_7 = \{e_2, e_{12}\}$$
$$X_8 = \{e_7\}$$

According to the following conditional probability formula,

$$P(Y|X_i) = P(Y|[x_i]_R) = \frac{|Y \cap [x_i]_R|}{|[x_i]_R|} = \frac{|Y \cap X_i|}{|X_i|}$$

we get the conditional probabilities for each equivalence class as follows:

$$P(Y_1|X_1) = \frac{|Y_1 \cap X_1|}{|X_1|} = \frac{e_1, e_2, e_4, e_6, e_7, e_9, e_{11}, e_{13} \cap e_1, e_{13}}{e_1, e_{13}} = 1$$

$$P(Y_1|X_2) = \frac{|Y_1 \cap X_2|}{|X_2|} = \frac{e_1, e_2, e_4, e_6, e_7, e_9, e_{11}, e_{13} \cap e_4}{e_4} = 1$$

$$P(Y_1 \mid X_3) = \frac{|Y_1 \cap X_3|}{|X_3|} = \frac{e_1, e_2, e_4, e_6, e_7, e_9, e_{11}, e_{13} \cap e_6, e_{11}}{e_6, e_{11}} = 1$$

$$P(Y_1 \mid X_4) = \frac{|Y_1 \cap X_1|}{|X_4|} = \frac{e_1, e_2, e_4, e_6, e_7, e_9, e_{11}, e_{13} \cap e_9}{e_9} = 1$$

$$P(Y_1 \mid X_5) = \frac{|Y_1 \cap X_5|}{|X_5|} = \frac{e_1, e_2, e_4, e_6, e_7, e_9, e_{11}, e_{13} \cap e_3, e_5, e_{14}}{e_3, e_5, e_{14}} = 0$$

$$P(Y_1 \mid X_6) = \frac{|Y_1 \cap X_6|}{|X_6|} = \frac{e_1, e_2, e_4, e_6, e_7, e_9, e_{11}, e_{13} \cap e_8, e_{10}, e_{15}}{e_8, e_{10}, e_{15}} = 0$$

$$P(Y_1 \mid X_7) = \frac{|Y_1 \cap X_7|}{|X_7|} = \frac{e_1, e_2, e_4, e_6, e_7, e_9, e_{11}, e_{13} \cap e_2, e_{12}}{e_2, e_{12}} = 0.5$$

$$P(Y_1 \mid X_8) = \frac{|Y_1 \cap X_8|}{|X_8|} = \frac{e_1, e_2, e_4, e_6, e_7, e_9, e_{11}, e_{13} \cap e_7}{e_7} = 1$$

According to the upper and lower approximation of set Y defined by

$$\overline{R(C)}(Y) = \bigcup_{P(Y|X_i)>0} \{X_i \in R \times (C)\}$$

and

$$\underline{R(C)}(Y) = \bigcup_{P(Y|X_i)=1} \{X_i \in R \times (C)\},$$

we get the following lower and upper approximation for set Y_1:

The lower approximation for Y_1: X_1, X_2, X_3, X_4, X_8.
The upper approximation for Y_1: $X_1, X_2, X_3, X_4, X_7, X_8$.

The above definition is in the boundary region of a standard rough-set model. This limitation can be rectified by using β-approximation space. In this case, we can choose 0.5 as the value for the approximation parameter as shown below:

β-positive region of set Y:

$$POS_C(Y) = U_{P(Y|X_i) \geq 0.5} \{X_i \in R \times (C)\} = \{X_1, X_2, X_3, X_4, X_7, X_8\}.$$

β-negative region of set Y:

$$NEG_C(Y) = U_{P(Y|X_i)<0.5} \{X_i \in R \times (C)\} = \{X_5, X_6\}.$$

The objects with value 1 or any value greater than or equal to 0.5 for attribute Y_1 belong to the β-positive region of set Y_1; the objects with value 0 or any value less than 0.5 for attribute Y_1 belong to the β-negative region of set Y_1. Based on the fact above, unnecessary condition attributes can be reduced by building a decision matrix.

Reduction of Condition Attributes

Reduction of the number of attributes in a database with a large number of objects will simplify the process of decision-rule generation. The interpretation of the generated rules will also be much easier. In addition, the generated rules will be more meaningful. The attribute-reduction process can be performed by following the steps described below:

1. First, compute the conditional probability as discussed earlier.
2. The probability of each equivalence class X_i, $P(Y_i|X_i)$, is tested by temporarily removing one condition attribute at a time from set C.
3. If the probability is still in a positive region (no change), the attribute is marked as redundant, and it can be removed from the set of condition attributes C (because it does not affect the probability of the set after it is removed).
4. The redundant attribute is deleted permanently from the set of condition attributes C.
5. Steps 1–4 are repeated until all the condition attributes in C have been tested. The final collection of condition attributes constitutes the nonredundant attributes set and preserves the dependency with respect to decision Y_i.

After reducing the unnecessary condition attributes as described, the *reduct* table can be obtained as shown in Table 5.15.

Generation of Decision Rules

RED is the *reduct*, that is, a reduced set of condition attributes C. The collection $R \times (RED)$ of equivalence classes of relation $R(RED)$ is given as follows:

■ TABLE 5.15 Reduct table with respect to Y_1 reduced from Table 5.14

Object	Size	Compress	Power	Weight	Mileage
e_1, e_{13}	S	1	1	5	1
e_4	S	0	1	0	1
e_6, e_{11}	S	1	0	0	1
e_9	C	0	0	5	1
e_3, e_5, e_{14}	C	1	0	5	0
e_8, e_{10}, e_{15}	C	0	1	0	0
e_2, e_{12}	C	1	1	0	1
e_7	S	1	1	0	1

$$R \times (RED) = \{X_1, X_2, X_3, X_4, X_5, X_6, X_7, X_8\}$$
$$= \{\{e_1, e_{13}\}, \{e_4\}, \{e_6, e_{11}\}\{e_9\}, \{e_3, e_5, e_{14}\}, \{e_8, e_{10}, e_{15}\},$$
$$\{e_2, e_{12}\}, \{e_7\}\}$$

The descriptions of the equivalence classes are

$$Des(X_1) = (Size = S) \wedge (Compress = 1) \wedge (Power = 1) \wedge (Weight = 5)$$
$$Des(X_2) = (Size = S) \wedge (Compress = 0) \wedge (Power = 1) \wedge (Weight = 0)$$
$$Des(X_3) = (Size = S) \wedge (Compress = 1) \wedge (Power = 0) \wedge (Weight = 0)$$
$$Des(X_4) = (Size = C) \wedge (Compress = 0) \wedge (Power = 0) \wedge (Weight = 5)$$
$$Des(X_5) = (Size = C) \wedge (Compress = 1) \wedge (Power = 0) \wedge (Weight = 5)$$
$$Des(X_6) = (Size = C) \wedge (Compress = 0) \wedge (Power = 1) \wedge (Weight = 0)$$
$$Des(X_7) = (Size = C) \wedge (Compress = 1) \wedge (Power = 1) \wedge (Weight = 0)$$
$$Des(X_8) = (Size = S) \wedge (Compress = 1) \wedge (Power = 1) \wedge (Weight = 0)$$

The descriptions of $Y_{(M = high)}$ and $\neg Y_{(M = high)}$ are $Des(Y_{high}) \rightarrow \beta \geq 0.5$ and $Des(\neg Y_{high}) \rightarrow \beta < 0.5$.

Recall that the conditional probabilities are

$$P(Y_1 \mid X_1) = 1$$
$$P(Y_1 \mid X_2) = 1$$
$$P(Y_1 \mid X_3) = 1$$
$$P(Y_1 \mid X_4) = 1$$
$$P(Y_1 \mid X_5) = 0$$

$$P(Y_1 \mid X_6) = 0$$
$$P(Y_1 \mid X_7) = 0.5$$
$$P(Y_1 \mid X_8) = 1$$

The decision rules with respect to concept $Y_{(M = high)}$ are given below:

R_1^+: $(Size = S) \wedge (Compress = 1) \wedge (Power = 1) \wedge (Weight = 5) \rightarrow {}^1(Y_{M=high})$

R_2^+: $(Size = S) \wedge (Compress = 0) \wedge (Power = 1) \wedge (Weight = 0) \rightarrow {}^1(Y_{M=high})$

R_3^+: $(Size = S) \wedge (Compress = 1) \wedge (Power = 0) \wedge (Weight = 0) \rightarrow {}^1(Y_{M=high})$

R_4^+: $(Size = C) \wedge (Compress = 0) \wedge (Power = 0) \wedge (Weight = 5) \rightarrow {}^1(Y_{M=high})$

R_5^+: $(Size = C) \wedge (Compress = 1) \wedge (Power = 1) \wedge (Weight = 0) \rightarrow {}^{0.5}(Y_{M=high})$

R_6^+: $(Size = S) \wedge (Compress = 1) \wedge (Power = 1) \wedge (Weight = 0) \rightarrow {}^1(Y_{M=high})$

R_1^-: $(Size = C) \wedge (Compress = 1) \wedge (Power = 0) \wedge (Weight = 5) \rightarrow {}^0(Y_{M \neq high})$

R_2^-: $(Size = C) \wedge (Compress = 0) \wedge (Power = 1) \wedge (Weight = 0) \rightarrow {}^0(Y_{M \neq high})$

Construction of a Decision Matrix

Table 5.16 shows the decision matrix $\mathbf{M}_{ij}$, $1 \leq i \leq 6$ and $1 \leq j \leq 2$, which is generated from Table 5.14. A set of decision rules can be generated for a given equivalence class X_i^+ by treating each element as a Boolean expression and constructing the following Boolean function:

$$B_i = \bigwedge_j (\bigvee \mathbf{M}_{ij}),$$

where $\wedge$ and $\vee$ are the usual conjunction and disjunction operators. First, we note that the equivalence classes of relation $R(RED)$ can be generated as follows:

$$X_1^+ = X_1 = \{e_1, e_{13}\}$$
$$X_2^+ = X_2 = \{e_4\}$$
$$X_3^+ = X_3 = \{e_6, e_{11}\}$$
$$X_4^+ = X_4 = \{e_9\}$$
$$X_5^+ = X_7 = \{e_2, e_{12}\}$$
$$X_6^+ = X_8 = \{e_7\}$$
$$X_1^- = X_5 = \{e_3, e_5, e_{14}\}$$
$$X_2^- = X_6 = \{e_8, e_{10}, e_{15}\}$$

■ **TABLE 5.16 Decision matrix generated from Table 5.14**

	X_1^-	X_2^-
X_1^+	(Size, S), (Power, 1)	(Size, S), (Compress, 1), (Weight, 5)
X_2^+	(Size, S), (Compress, 0), (Power, 1), (Weight, 0)	(Size, S)
X_3^+	(Size, S), (Weight, 0)	(Size, S), (Compress, 1), (Power, 0)
X_4^+	(Compress, 0)	(Power, 0), (Weight, 5)
X_5^+	(Power, 1), (Weight, 0)	(Compress, 1)
X_6^+	(Size, S), (Power, 1), (Weight, 0)	(Size, S), (Compress, 1)

Then, we can obtain the Boolean functions for each X_i^+ ($i = 1, 2, 3, 4, 5, 6$) as follows:

$B_1 = [(Size = S) \vee (Power = 1)] \wedge [(Size = S) \vee (Compress = 1) \vee (Weight = 5)]$
$\quad = (Size = S)$

$B_2 = [(Size = S) \vee (Compress = 0) \vee (Power = 1) \vee (Weight = 0)] \wedge (Size = S)$
$\quad = (Size = S)$

$B_3 = [(Size = S) \vee (Weight = 0)] \wedge [(Size = S) \vee (Compress = 1) \vee (Power = 0)]$
$\quad = (Size = S)$

$B_4 = (Compress = 0) \wedge [(Power = 0) \vee (Weight = 5)]$

$B_5 = [(Power = 1) \vee (Weight = 0)] \wedge (Compress = 1)$

$B_6 = [(Size = S) \vee (Power = 1) \vee (Weight = 0)] \wedge [(Size = S) \vee (Compress = 1)]$
$\quad = (Size = S)$

Therefore, the maximally general rules for each equivalence class X_i^+ are generated as follows:

$$X_1^+: (Size = S) \rightarrow {}^1(Y_{M=high})$$
$$X_2^+: (Size = S) \rightarrow {}^1(Y_{M=high})$$
$$X_3^+: (Size = S) \rightarrow {}^1(Y_{M=high})$$
$$X_4^+: (Compress = 0) \wedge [(Power = 0) \vee (Weight = 5)] \rightarrow {}^1(Y_{M=high})$$
$$X_5^+: [(Power = 1) \vee (Weight = 0)] \wedge (Compress = 1) \rightarrow {}^{0.5}(Y_{M=high})$$
$$X_6^+: (Size = S) \rightarrow {}^1(Y_{M=high})$$

Finally, the rules generated yield the following interpretations:

1. Cars with subcompact size will definitely have high mileage.
2. Cars with low compressibility AND low power OR light weight will have high mileage.
3. Cars with high compressibility AND high power OR medium weight are likely to have high mileage.

■ 5.5 CHAPTER SUMMARY

The rough-sets approach and the Bayesian approach are two different methods for classification used to predict the future values of certain attributes of a dataset. Both methods employ conditional probability as a method for generating rules. Rules are identified and generated by selecting different sets for attribute-value pairs. Thus, the main difference between these two methods lies in their methodologies.

Rough sets offer another powerful method for knowledge discovery that can be useful for solving classification problems. No assumptions about the structure of the attributes are required for classification. The knowledge derived from an information system is often expressed by simple decision rules composed of some logical operators. Decision rules can be generated from a decision matrix. They reflect a simplified summary of complex database systems. The rules generated by the rough classifiers are based on the most important attribute set selected for analysis purposes. Redundant attributes are automatically removed from the attribute set being considered through an attribute-trimming process. The generated rules can be evaluated with estimated decision probabilities. Overall, the rough-sets method provides an option to find the set of maximally general rules from the information system being considered. The rough-sets method has been proven to be especially effective for databases with incomplete information.

The Bayesian approach, on the other hand, employs calculation of conditional probability as the crucial step in generating rules. The probability calculation becomes more complicated as the number of attributes considered increases. One problem with Bayes' method is that it is often difficult to determine the threshold values for the probabilities. In addition, the set of generated rules may not be exhaustive as they are dependent on human judgment. This method is very useful, however, in representing the overall context of simple systems with very few attributes.

In this chapter, general theories for rough-set and Bayes' methods were presented. These theories were illustrated and applied to a number of practical applications including an automobiles dataset, a contact lens dataset, and a welding parameters dataset. Through the application of these methods, a number of useful decision rules were generated from each dataset. These rules can be used for classification purposes in each domain. The validity of the generated rules can be checked by comparing the rules generated by both the Bayesian approach and the rough-set approach. The chapter concludes with a bibliography that contains a list of related material on both concepts.

■ 5.6 EXERCISES

1. Consider the cheddar cheese taste database table shown in Table 5.17. As cheese ages, various chemical processes take place that determine the taste of the final product. The table contains concentrations of various chemicals in 30 samples of mature cheddar cheese, and a subjective measure of taste for each sample. The variables *Acetic* and H_2S are the natural logarithm of the concentration of acetic acid and hydrogen sulfide, respectively. The variable *Lactic* has not been transformed. The table contains the following attributes:

   - *Case*: Sample number
   - *Taste*: Subjective taste test score, obtained by combining the scores of several tasters
   - *Acetic*: Natural log of concentration of acetic acid
   - *H2S*: Natural log of concentration of hydrogen sulfide
   - *Lactic*: Concentration of lactic acid
      a. Apply the rough set approach to generate classification rules by selecting *Taste* as the decision attribute. Perform table simplification, if necessary, with appropriate value replacement.
      b. Use Bayes' theorem to generate as many as probabilistic rules as possible. Choose various threshold values for probability to adjust confidence.

■ **TABLE 5.17 Cheddar cheese taste**

Case	Taste	Acetic	H_2S	Lactic
1	12.3	4.543	3.135	0.86
2	20.9	5.159	5.043	1.53
3	39	5.366	5.438	1.57
4	47.9	5.759	7.496	1.81
5	5.6	4.663	3.807	0.99
6	25.9	5.697	7.601	1.09
7	37.3	5.892	8.726	1.29
8	21.9	6.078	7.966	1.78
9	18.1	4.898	3.85	1.29
10	21	5.242	4.174	1.58
11	34.9	5.74	6.142	1.68
12	57.2	6.446	7.908	1.9
13	0.7	4.477	2.996	1.06
14	25.9	5.236	4.942	1.3
15	54.9	6.151	6.752	1.52
16	40.9	6.365	9.588	1.74
17	15.9	4.787	3.912	1.16
18	6.4	5.412	4.7	1.49
19	18	5.247	6.174	1.63
20	38.9	5.438	9.064	1.99
21	14	4.564	4.949	1.15
22	15.2	5.298	5.22	1.33
23	32	5.455	9.242	1.44
24	56.7	5.855	10.199	2.01
25	16.8	5.366	3.664	1.31
26	11.6	6.043	3.219	1.46
27	26.5	6.458	6.962	1.72
28	0.7	5.328	3.912	1.25
29	13.4	5.802	6.685	1.08
30	5.5	6.176	4.787	1.25

2. Table 5.18 shows a high-fiber diet plan data table that reflects the effects of dietary fiber. Twelve female subjects were fed a controlled diet. Before each meal they ate crackers containing either bran fiber, gum fiber, a combination of both, or no fiber (control). Their caloric intake was monitored. Subjects reported any gastric or other problems. The table contains the following attributes:

- *Cracker*: Type of fiber in the cracker
- *Diet*: One of four diets (type of cracker)
- *Subject*: An identification for each of the 12 subjects
- *Bloat*: Degree of bloating and flatulence reported by the subjects
- *Digested*: Difference between caloric intake and calories passed through system

■ TABLE 5.18 High-fiber diet plan

Cracker	Diet	Subject	Digested	Bloat
Control	1	3	1772.84	None
Bran	4	3	1752.63	Low
Combo	3	9	2121.97	Med
Gum	2	4	2558.61	High
Gum	2	1	2026.91	Med
Bran	4	1	2047.42	Low
Combo	3	1	2254.75	Low
Control	1	1	2353.21	Med
Combo	3	2	2153.36	None
Gum	2	2	2331.19	None
Bran	4	2	2547.77	None
Control	1	2	2591.12	None
Gum	2	3	2012.36	Low
Combo	3	3	1956.18	Low
Combo	3	4	2025.97	None
Bran	4	4	1669.12	None
Control	1	4	2452.73	None
Bran	4	5	2207.37	Low

(continued)

■ **TABLE 5.18 High fiber diet plan (*continued*)**

Cracker	Diet	Subject	Digested	Bloat
Gum	2	5	1944.48	Med
Control	1	5	1927.68	Low
Combo	3	5	2190.1	High
Control	1	6	1635.28	None
Combo	3	6	1693.35	Low
Bran	4	6	1707.34	Low
Gum	2	6	1871.95	High
Gum	2	7	2245.03	None
Combo	3	7	2436.79	Low
Control	1	7	2667.14	Low
Bran	4	7	2766.86	None
Bran	4	8	2279.82	None
Combo	3	8	1844.77	High
Gum	2	8	2002.73	High
Control	1	8	2220.22	Med
Control	1	9	1888.29	Low
Gum	2	9	1804.27	High
Bran	4	9	2293.27	Med
Bran	4	10	2357.4	None
Control	1	10	2359.9	None
Combo	3	10	2292.46	Low
Gum	2	10	2433.46	High
Gum	2	11	1681.86	Low
Control	1	11	1902.75	None
Bran	4	11	2003.16	None
Combo	3	11	2137.12	Med
Combo	3	12	2203.07	Med
Control	1	12	2125.39	Low
Gum	2	12	2166.77	Med
Bran	4	12	2287.52	None

a. Apply the rough-set approach to generate as many classification rules as possible by selecting *Bloat* as the decision attribute. Perform table simplification, if necessary, with appropriate value replacement.

b. Use Bayes' theorem to generate probabilistic rules. Choose various threshold values for probability to adjust confidence. Use *Bloat* as the selected decision attribute.

3. Table 5.19 is a table that contains a dataset on ice cream consumption. Ice cream consumption was measured over 30 four-week periods from March 18, 1951 to July 11, 1953. The purpose of the study was to

■ TABLE 5.19 Ice cream consumption

Date	IC	Price	Income	Temp	Lag-temp	Year
1	0.386	0.270	78	41	56	0
2	0.374	0.282	79	56	63	0
3	0.393	0.277	81	63	68	0
4	0.425	0.280	80	68	69	0
5	0.406	0.272	76	69	65	0
6	0.344	0.262	78	65	61	0
7	0.327	0.275	82	61	47	0
8	0.288	0.267	79	47	32	0
9	0.269	0.265	76	32	24	0
10	0.256	0.277	79	24	28	0
11	0.286	0.282	82	28	26	1
12	0.298	0.270	85	26	32	1
13	0.329	0.272	86	32	40	1
14	0.318	0.287	83	40	55	1
15	0.381	0.277	84	55	63	1
16	0.381	0.287	82	63	72	1
17	0.470	0.280	80	72	72	1
18	0.443	0.277	78	72	67	1
19	0.386	0.277	84	67	60	1
20	0.342	0.277	86	60	44	1

(continued)

■ **TABLE 5.19 Ice cream consumption (*continued*)**

Date	IC	Price	Income	Temp	Lag-temp	Year
21	0.319	0.292	85	44	40	1
22	0.307	0.287	87	40	32	1
23	0.284	0.277	94	32	27	1
24	0.326	0.285	92	27	28	2
25	0.309	0.282	95	28	33	2
26	0.359	0.265	96	33	41	2
27	0.376	0.265	94	41	52	2
28	0.416	0.265	96	52	64	2
29	0.437	0.268	91	64	71	2
30	0.548	0.260	90	71	72	2

determine whether ice cream consumption depends on the variables *price, income*, or *temperature*. The variables *Lag-temp* and *Year* have been added to the original data. The table contains the following attributes:

- *Date*: Time period (1–30) of the study (from 3/18/51 to 7/11/53)
- *IC*: Ice cream consumption in pints per capita
- *Price*: Price of ice cream per pint in dollars
- *Income*: Weekly family income in dollars
- *Temp*: Mean temperature in degrees F
- *Lag-temp*: Temp variable lagged by one time period
- *Year*: Year within the study (0 = 1951, 1 = 1952, 2 = 1953)

    a. Follow the rough-set approach to generate as many classification rules as possible. Select *IC* as the decision attribute and all others as the condition attributes. Perform table simplification, if needed, with appropriate value replacement.

    b. Apply Bayes' theorem to generate any probabilistic rules. Use 0.2, 0.3, 0.5, and 0.7 as possible threshold values (β) for probability to adjust confidence. Select *IC* as the decision attribute.

4. Table 5.20 shows a pottery table that contains a dataset of 26 samples of Romano-British pottery found at four different kiln sites in Wales, Gwent, and the New Forest. The sites are Llanederyn (L), Caldicot (C), Island Thorns (I), and Ashley Rails (A). The other variables are the

■ **TABLE 5.20 Pottery table**

Al	Fe	Mg	Ca	Na	Site
14.4	7.00	4.30	0.15	0.51	L
13.8	7.08	3.43	0.12	0.17	L
14.6	7.09	3.88	0.13	0.20	L
11.5	6.37	5.64	0.16	0.14	L
13.8	7.06	5.34	0.20	0.20	L
10.9	6.26	3.47	0.17	0.22	L
10.1	4.26	4.26	0.20	0.18	L
11.6	5.78	5.91	0.18	0.16	L
11.1	5.49	4.52	0.29	0.30	L
13.4	6.92	7.23	0.28	0.20	L
12.4	6.13	5.69	0.22	0.54	L
13.1	6.64	5.51	0.31	0.24	L
12.7	6.69	4.45	0.20	0.22	L
12.5	6.44	3.94	0.22	0.23	L
11.8	5.44	3.94	0.30	0.04	C
11.6	5.39	3.77	0.29	0.06	C
18.3	1.28	0.67	0.03	0.03	I
15.8	2.39	0.63	0.01	0.04	I
18.0	1.50	0.67	0.01	0.06	I
18.0	1.88	0.68	0.01	0.04	I
20.8	1.51	0.72	0.07	0.10	I
17.7	1.12	0.56	0.06	0.06	A
18.3	1.14	0.67	0.06	0.05	A
16.7	0.92	0.53	0.01	0.05	A
14.8	2.74	0.67	0.03	0.05	A
19.1	1.64	0.60	0.10	0.03	A

percentage of oxides of various metals measured by atomic absorption spectrophotometry. The data were collected to see whether different sites contained pottery of different chemical compositions. The table contains the following attributes:

- *Al*: Percentage of aluminum oxide in sample
- *Fe*: Percentage of iron oxide in sample
- *Mg*: Percentage of magnesium oxide in sample
- *Ca*: Percentage of calcium oxide in sample
- *Na*: Percentage of sodium oxide in sample
- *Site*: Site where pottery sample was collected

   a. Use the rough-set approach to generate any classification rules if possible. Perform table simplification, if needed, with appropriate value replacement. Using the generated rules, determine whether different sites contain pottery of different chemical compositions.

   b. Apply Bayes' theorem to generate any probabilistic rules. Use different threshold values (β) for probability to adjust confidence. Choose the *Site* attribute as the selected decision attribute.

   c. Compare and contrast Bayes' method with the rough-set approach in terms of rule generation and table simplification. Discuss any difficulties that you may have encountered in applying either of the approaches to generate decision rules.

■ 5.7   SELECTED BIBLIOGRAPHIC NOTES

A general introduction to rough-set theory and knowledge discovery is given in [Arciszewski 1993], [Bell 1998], [Siromoney 2000], [Ziarko 1993], [Miyamoto 1998], [Ziarko 1999], [Pawlak 1995a], and [Pawlak 1995b]. [An 1997] shows how to use the rough-set theory to predict water-supply consumption. Generating knowledge rules from databases following the rough-set approach is described in [Hu 1996], [Tsumoto 1999], [Hu 1997], [Tsumoto 1999], [Tsumoto 1996], [Ziarko 1999], and [Beynon 2000]. Variable-precision rough sets and rough classifiers were studied by [Katzberg 1993] and [Lenarcik 1993].

The role of dependencies and relations of databases in rough sets were reported by [Missaoui 1993], [Hu 1995], and [Slowinski 1992]. Axiomatic rough-set theory was described by [Lin 1993], whereas similarity based on rough approximation was described by [Slowinski 2000]. [Cattaneo 1997] introduced generalized rough sets. The extension of rough sets for data mining is described by [Lingras 1998]. Rough sets used for feature selection and classification was reported by [Bao 2001], [Deogun 1998], [Lingras 2001], and [Zhong 2001].

Information retrieval is another area where rough-set theory was applied for data mining. [Miyamoto 1998], [Ramanna 2002], and [Possas 2002] proposed various methods for information retrieval based on rough sets. [Hirano 2001] introduced a knowledge-oriented clustering technique based on rough sets, whereas [Ruhe 1994] showed how data analysis based on rough sets could be performed in Goal-Oriented Software Measurement. [Lin 1994] showed how rough sets could be applied to detect anomalies in databases. Web-based application using rough sets was given in [Chiang 2000].

■ 5.8 CHAPTER BIBLIOGRAPHY

[An 1997] A. An, C. Chan, N. Shan, N. Cercone, and W. Ziarko: "Applying Knowledge Discovery to Predict Water-Supply Consumption," *IEEE Expert*, pp. 72–78, 1997.

[Arciszewski 1993], T. Arciszewski, W. Ziarko, and T. L. Khan: "Learning Conceptual Design Rules: A Rough Sets Approach," *Proceedings of the International Workshop on Rough Sets*, Banff, Alberta, Canada, 1993.

[Bao 2001] Y. Bao, X. Du, and N. Ishii: "Improving Performance of the K–Nearest Neighbor Classification by Tolerant Rough Sets," CODAS, pp. 183–188, 2001.

[Bell 1998] D. A. Bell and J. W. Guan: "Computational methods for rough classification and discovery," *Journal of the American Society for Information Science,* Vol. 49, pp. 403-414, 1998.

[Beynon 2000] M. J. Beynon, B. Curry, and P. H. Morgan: "Classification and Rule Induction Using Rough Set Theory," *Expert Systems*, Vol. 17, No. 3, pp. 136–148, 2000.

[Cattaneo 1997] G. Cattaneo: "Generalized Rough Sets (Preclusivity Fuzzy–Intuitionistic (BZ) Lattices)," *Studia Logica*, Vol. 58, No. 1, pp. 47–77, 1997.

[Chiang 2000] I. J. Chiang and T. Y. Lin: "Using Rough Sets to Build-up Web-Based One to One Customer Services," *Proceedings of the Annual International Computer Software and Applications Conference (COMPSAC)*, HsingChu, Taiwan, 2000.

[Deogun 1998] J. Deogun, S. Choubey, V. Raghavan, and H. Sever: "Feature Selection and Effective Classifiers," *Journal of ASIS*, Vol. 49, No. 5, pp. 403–414, 1998.

[Hirano 2001] Shoji Hirano and Shusaku Tsumoto. "A Knowledge-Oriented Clustering Technique Based on Rough Sets," *COMPSAC*, pp. 632–637, 2001.

[Hu 1995] X. Hu and N. Cerone: "Rough Set Similarity-based Learning from Databases," *Proceedings of the First International Conference on Knowledge Discovery*, 1995.

[Hu 1996] X. Hu and N. Cercone: "Mining Knowledge Rules from Databases: A Rough Set Approach," *Proceedings of the 12th International Conference on Data Engineering*, pp. 96–105, 1996.

[Hu 1997] X. Hu and N. Cercone: "Learning Maximal Generalized Decision Rules via Discretization, Generalization, and Rough Set Feature Selection," *ICTAI*, pp. 548, 1997.

[Katzberg 1993] J. Katzberg and W. Ziarko: "Variable Precision Rough Sets with Asymmetric Bounds," *Proceedings of the International Workshop on Rough Sets and Knowledge Discovery*, pp. 167–177, 1993.

[Lenarcik 1993] A. Lenarcik and Z. Piasta: "Rough Classifiers," *Proceedings of the International Workshop on Rough Sets and Knowledge Discovery*, pp. 298–316, 1993.

[Lin 1993] T. Y. Lin and Qing Lui: "Rough Approximate Operators: Axiomatic Rough Set Theory," *Proceedings of the International Workshop on Rough Sets and Knowledge Discovery: Rough Sets, Fuzzy Sets and Knowledge Discovery*, pp. 256–260, 1993.

[Lin 1994] T.Y. Lin. "Anomaly Detection: A Soft Computing Approach," *Proceedings of the 1994 Workshop on New Security Paradigms*, pp. 44–53, 1994.

[Lingras 1998] P. J. Lingras and Y.Y. Yao: "Data Mining Using Extensions of Rough Set Model," *Journal of the American Society for Information Science*, Vol. 49, No. 5, pp. 415–422, 1998.

[Lingras 2001] P. Lingras: "Unsupervised Rough Set Classification Using Gas," *Journal of Intelligent Information Systems*, Vol. 16, No. 3, pp. 215–228, 2001.

[Missaoui 1993] R. Missaoui and R. Godin: "Search for Concepts and Dependencies in Databases," *Proceedings of the International Workshop on Rough Sets and Knowledge Discovery: Rough Sets, Fuzzy Sets and Knowledge Discovery*, pp. 16–23, 1993.

[Miyamoto 1998] S. Miyamoto: "Application of rough sets to information retrieval," *Journal of the American Society for Information Science*, Vol. 49, No. 3, pp. 195–205, 1998.

[Pawlak 1995a] Z. Pawlak, J. W. Grzymala–Busse, R. Slowinski, and W. Ziarko: "Rough Sets," *Communications of the ACM*, Vol. 38, No. 11, pp. 88–95, 1995.

[Pawlak 1995b] Z. Pawlak: "Rough Sets," *ACM Conference on Computer Science*, pp. 262–264, 1995.

[Possas 2002] B. Possas, N. Ziviani, W. Meira, Jr., and B. Ribeiro–Neto: "Set-Based Model: A New Approach for Information Retrieval," *Proceedings of the 25th Annual International ACM SIGIR Conference on Research and Development in Information Retrieval*, Tampere, Finland, pp. 230–237, 2002.

[Ramanna 2002] S. Ramanna, J. F. Peters, and T. Ahn: "Software Quality Knowledge Discovery: A Rough Set Approach," *COMPSAC*, pp. 1140–1145, 2002.

[Ruhe 1994] G. Ruhe and F. Gesellschaft: "Rough Set Based Data Analysis in Goal Oriented Software Measurement," *The 3rd International Software Metrics Symposium (METRICS) From Measurement to Empirical Results*, 1994.

[Siromoney 2000] A. Siromoney and K. Inoue: "Consistency and Completeness in Rough Sets," *Journal of Intelligent Information Systems*, Vol. 15, pp. 207–220, 2000.

[Slowinski 1992] R. Slowinski: "Rough Sets with Strict and Weak Indiscernibility Relations," *IEEE International Conference on Fuzzy Systems*, pp. 695–702, 1992.

[Slowinski 2000] R. Slowinski and D. Vanderpooten: "A Generalized Definition of Rough Approximations Based on Similarity," *IEEE Transactions on Knowledge and Data Engineering*, Vol. 12, No. 2, pp. 331–336, 2000.

[Tsumoto 1996] S. Tsumoto and H. Tanaka: "Automated Discovery of Medical Expert System Rules from Clinical Databases Based on Rough Sets," *KDD*, pp. 63–69, 1996.

[Tsumoto 1999] S. Tsumoto: "Discovery of Rules for Medical Expert Systems-Rough Set Approach," *Proceedings of the Third International Conference on Computational Intelligence and Multimedia Applications (ICCIM)*, New Delhi, India, pp. 212–216, 1999.

[Zhong 2001] N. Zhong, J. Dong, and S. Ohsuga: "Using Rough Sets with Heuristics for Feature Selection," *Journal of Intelligent Information Systems (JIIS)*, Vol. 16, pp. 199–214, 2001.

[Ziarko 1993] W. Ziarko: "Rough Sets and Knowledge Discovery: An Overview," *Proceedings of the International Workshop on Rough Sets and Knowledge Discovery: Rough Sets, Fuzzy Sets and Knowledge Discovery*, pp. 11–15, 1993.

[Ziarko 1996] W. Ziarko and N. Shan: "A Rough Set Based Method for Computing All Minimal Deterministic Rules in Attribute-Value Systems," *Computational Intelligence*, Vol. 12, No. 2, pp. 223–234, 1996.

[Ziarko 1999] W. Ziarko: "Discovery Through Rough Set Theory," *Communications of the ACM*, Vol. 42, No. 11, pp. 54–57, 1999.

CHAPTER 6

Neural Networks

■ 6.1 INTRODUCTION

A neural network is a massively parallel and distributed processor that has a natural ability to store experiential knowledge and make use of it for effective decision making in many applications. The neural network acquires knowledge through a series of learning processes, and a connection of synaptic weights is used to store the acquired knowledge. Neural networks generally give a lower classification error rate and greater robustness to noise than decision trees, but they require longer time to create.

Neural networks consist of numerous, simple processing units called *neurons*. A neural network is a trainable system that can estimate input–output functions using the neurons. We can program or train neural networks to store, recognize, and associatively retrieve patterns or database entries and to generate estimated functions for sample data.

Neural networks can learn new associations, patterns, and functional dependencies. In all cases, the learning results in changes, which may or may not be accurate. The learning changes the network's memory either by updating its status or by adding new facts. Since neural networks do not use a mathematical model of how a system's output depends on its input, they behave as model-free estimators. Therefore, neural network architecture and dynamics can be applied to a wide variety of problems. This chapter describes ways to improve the quality of the results of database operations by applying neural network techniques.

■ 6.2 NEURAL COMPUTING AND DATABASES

Most traditional database management systems store data in the form of structured records. When a query is submitted, the database system searches for and retrieves records that match the user's criteria. Artificial neural networks offer an attractive approach for realizing intelligent query processing in large databases, especially for data retrieval and knowledge extraction based on partial matches. The employment of Artificial Intelligence (AI) techniques allows database systems to capture meaningful and interesting patterns and rules and to widen their applicability. AI technology can be used for a wide variety of applications, such as recognition of spoken and written texts, diagnosis of medical problems, stock market prediction, and satellite-image classification.

All traditional data analysis techniques make predictions about the future from past data based on a sequence of generated rules. Knowledge is obtained from a database in the form of these rules, which are used to make predictions about the future and perform classifications and contain empirical knowledge. Neural networks are different. They do not need to identify empirical rules in order to make predictions. Instead, a neural network is generated by examining a database and identifying and mapping all significant patterns and relationships that exist between different attributes. The net then uses a particular pattern to generate a predictable outcome.

The neural net tries to identify a particular mix of attributes that reveals a particular pattern. This process is repeated with a lot of training data, consequently making changes to the weights for more accurate pattern matches. The model is normally built without the need for interactive human participation because the neural network can automatically identify these patterns.

The patterns that exist among the attributes in a database can be identified, and the influence of each attribute can be quantified. Neural networks simply concentrate on identifying these patterns without human guidance, whereas in traditional systems the database and any predictions based on it can only be described through the rules that exist behind them.

In the following paragraph, we provide a brief description of the process of a neural network for generating results that are used for prediction. The neural network structure is first built with three different kinds of nodes. These nodes are classified by where they get input, what they do with the input, and where they send the output, as follows:

Input Nodes: Nodes that accept input patterns.

Hidden Nodes: Nodes that accept data from the input nodes, perform further computation on them, and then send the results to output nodes.

Output Nodes: Nodes that accept data from hidden nodes and give the output to a user or user interface, or compare the output with the target patterns.

In addition, three different types of datasets are classified and used to support the pattern-generation process of neural networks.

Training set: The training set is used for training and teaching the network to recognize patterns. The training process is done by adjusting the weights according to the input patterns.

Validation set: A set of examples is used to tune the parameters of a classifier by choosing the number of hidden nodes or hidden layers in a neural network. This set is called a validation set.

Test set: A test set is used to test the performance of a neural network. This set consists of a set of examples used only to assess the performance of a fully specified classifier.

Since our goal is to build a network with the best performance on new data, the simplest approach to comparing different networks is to evaluate an error function using the data that is different from the data used for training. Various networks are trained through the process of minimizing an appropriate error function defined with respect to the training set. The performance of the networks applied to an independent validation set is compared based on evaluating the error function. The network giving the smallest error rate when tested with the validation set is selected. Finally, the performance of the selected network is confirmed by measuring its performance on the test set.

Figure 6.1 shows the roles and relationships of the training set, the validation set, and the test set. First, the validation set is used in the untrained neural network to determine the number of hidden layers and the number of hidden nodes. Next, the training set is used to train the neural network. After training, results can be generated in response to provided test sets. In the next section the different learning models used for classification are briefly described.

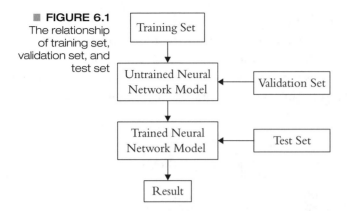

■ FIGURE 6.1
The relationship
of training set,
validation set, and
test set

■ 6.3   NETWORK CLASSIFICATION

There are several neural-network learning models that support the process of knowledge discovery from a database. These models can be distinguished as supervised learning or unsupervised learning. An unsupervised learning process requires no examples of desired output. In this model, rules can be produced from the relationships among the attributes. Supervised learning requires that examples of desired output be specified, from which rules are generated. If the value of an output node does not match the desired output, the weights are adjusted to obtain the desired goal. This section gives a brief description of these learning models.

■ 6.3.1   Unsupervised Learning Models

Unsupervised learning does not involve target values. In fact, in most unsupervised learning models, the targets are the same as the inputs. The objective is to categorize or discover features or regularities in the training data. In other words, unsupervised learning usually performs the same task as an auto–associative network, compressing the information from the inputs. Success of the unsupervised learning process normally depends on using a network model that encompasses a task-independent criterion of the quality of representation the network is required to learn. The weights are optimized with respect to this criterion, and the goal is to train the network to perform the prediction tasks.

Unsupervised competitive learning is used in a wide variety of fields under various names, the most common of which is called "cluster analysis." The name is derived from the fact that it adaptively classifies patterns into clusters.

In these competitive learning systems the "winning" neuron in a neuronal competition for activation is induced by randomly sampled input patterns.

Hebbian learning is the most common variety of unsupervised learning. Hebbian learning minimizes the same error function used in an auto-associative network with a linear hidden layer, is trained by the least squares method, and is therefore a form of dimensionality reduction.

There are two types of unsupervised learning models based on how an error signal is propagated or used by the net for learning. They are feedback nets and feedforward-only nets.

Feedback Nets

These nets allow the output to be fed back to the input. The following is a list of neural network models that fall into this category:

- Additive Grossberg (AG)
- Shunting Grossberg (SG)
- Binary Adaptive Resonance Theory (ART1)
- Analog Adaptive Resonance Theory (ART2, ART2a)
- Discrete Hopfield (DH)
- Continuous Hopfield (CH)
- Discrete Bidirectional Associative Memory (BAM)
- Temporal Associative Memory (TAM)
- Adaptive Bidirectional Associative Memory (ABAM)
- Kohonen Self-Organizing Map/Topology-Preserving Map (SOM/TPM)
- Competitive Learning

Feedforward-only Nets

Contrary to feedback nets, feedforward-only nets do not allow any feedback from the output to the input. Generally, all neurons in a layer are connected to all neurons in the adjacent layers through unidirectional links. These links are represented by synaptic weights that act as signal multipliers on the corresponding links (interconnections). In this model, link connections within a layer or from higher to lower layers are not permitted. The following is a list of neural network models that fall into this category:

- Learning Matrix (LM)
- Driver-Reinforcement Learning (DR)

- Linear Associative Memory (LAM)
- Optimal Linear Associative Memory (OLAM)
- Sparse Distributed Associative Memory (SDM)
- Fuzzy Associative Memory (FAM)
- Counterpropogation Network (CPN)

■ 6.3.2 Supervised Learning Models

In contrast to the unsupervised learning model, the supervised learning process requires that target values be provided. From a training dataset the input vector will generate the rules according to the desired output by adjusting the weights. The weights are used for evaluating the input test data. The desired output will be provided to the net, and then the weights are adjusted to fit the model to the desired goal. If the desired goal is not met, the learning process will continue to iterate.

The network receives a global reward/penalty signal. Weights are changed to develop an input/output behavior that maximizes the probability of receiving a reward and minimizes the probability of receiving a penalty. So the weights are increased for properly performed actions and decreased for poorly performed actions. There are two types of supervised learning models based on how an error signal is used to make the net learn. They are feedback nets and feedforward-only nets.

Feedback Nets

In these nets the output is percolated toward the input, and the weights are manipulated on the way back. This learning system can reduce the time of learning by actively adjusting the weights until it learns input patterns. The following is a list of neural network models that falls into this category:

- Brain-State-in-a-Box (BSB)
- Fuzzy Cognitive Map (FCM)
- Boltzmann Machine (BM)
- Mean Field Annealing (MFT)
- Recurrent Cascade Correlation (RCC)
- Backpropagation Through Time (BPTT)
- Real-Time Recurrent Learning (RTRL)
- Recurrent Extended Kalman Filter (EKF)

Feedforward-only Nets

Supervised feedforward models are the most tractable and the most applied neural network models. In these types of nets, if the user does not get the desired output, then instead of propagating the error signal back to the input, the process is iterated using the connected nodes. The following is a list of neural network models that fall into this category:

- Perceptron
- Adaline, Madaline
- Backpropagation (BP)
- Cauchy Machine (CM)
- Adaptive Heuristic Critic (AHC)
- Time Delay Neural Network (TDNN)
- Associative Reward Penalty (ARP)
- Avalanche Matched Filter (AMF)
- Backpercolation (Perc)
- Artmap
- Adaptive Logic Network (ALN)
- Cascade Correlation (CasCor)
- Extended Kalman Filter (EKF)
- Learning Vector Quantization (LVQ)
- Probabilistic Neural Network (PNN)
- General Regression Neural Network (GRNN)

■ 6.4 PARAMETERS OF THE LEARNING PROCESS

Learning is an essential process in neural network implementation. As mentioned in the previous sections, learning is a complicated process that involves a number of parameters. These parameters are used to determine the structure of a network (which affects the learning process in the network). In the following paragraphs, a brief description of these parameters is given.

■ 6.4.1 Number of Hidden Layers

In most neural-network models, the number of hidden layers is either manually decided at the beginning or is determined automatically by the training dataset. For multiple-layer perceptrons with continuous, non-linear hidden-layer activation functions, there is one hidden layer with an arbitrarily large number of units. However, there is no unified theory yet as to how many hidden units are needed to approximate any given function. Unfortunately, using two hidden layers increases the problem of local minima, and it is important to use random initializations or other methods for global optimization. Local minima arising with two hidden layers can have extreme spikes even when the number of weights is much smaller than the number of training cases.

■ 6.4.2 Number of Hidden Nodes

There is no way of determining good network architecture just from the number of inputs and outputs. This mainly depends on the number of training cases, the amount of noise, and the complexity of the function the network is trying to learn. An intelligent choice for the number of hidden units depends on whether you are using early stopping or some other form of regularization. Otherwise, you must simply try several networks with different numbers of hidden units, estimate the generalization error for each model, and choose the one with the least estimated generalization error.

■ 6.4.3 Early Stopping

In some neural-network models, the learning time may be very long because it involves training and validation. To reduce this learning time, a method called "early stopping" can be used. Neural-network practitioners often use networks with the same number of parameters as training cases. The method for early stopping is briefly described as follows:

1. Divide the available data into training and validation sets.
   This can decrease the complexity of the data and promote the convergence of the neural network.
2. Use a large number of hidden nodes.
   The greater the number of nodes there are, the easier it is to distinguish among the generated rules and the more useful the rules are. But this also increases calculation time.
3. Use very small random initial values.
   Usually, an initial value between −0.1 and 0.1 can be used. These initial values are used to prevent all nodes from reaching the same state.
4. Use a slow learning rate.
   Decreasing the learning rate helps to avoid oscillation of the result.

FIGURE 6.2
The learning process with less oscillation

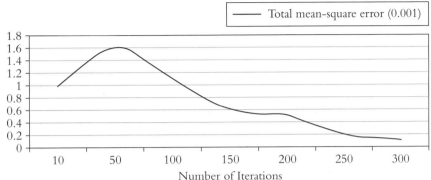

5. Compute the validation error rate periodically during training.
6. Stop training when the validation error rate "starts to go up."

■ 6.4.4 Convergence Curve (Back-Propagation Neural Network)

How can we determine when the iteration process should be stopped? The total mean-square error for the network can be used to determine this because it measures the oscillation rate for convergence. Comparing Figure 6.2 with Figure 6.3, we find that there are more oscillations in Figure 6.3. Since oscillation hinders the convergence process of the network, the process shown in Figure 6.2 is a better learning process than the process shown in Figure 6.3.

FIGURE 6.3
The learning process with more oscillation

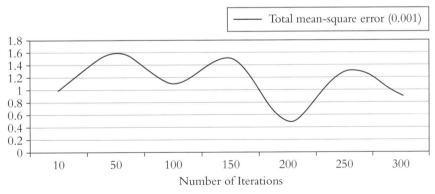

■ 6.5 NETWORK STRUCTURES

There are several network structures that can be followed to describe a network model. Two main categories of network structures are feed-forward and feedback architectures. In a feed-forward neural network, the signal propagates forward from nodes in a layer to the next nodes without any feedback, as shown in Figure 6.4. The nodes of the next layer use the values produced by the previous layer as their input values. On the other hand, the feedback network model allows the signals to come back to the previous nodes as shown in Figure 6.5. Many feedback neural networks can learn simultaneously new patterns and can recall old patterns.

■ **FIGURE 6.4**
Feed-forward
architecture

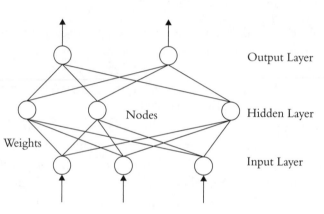

■ **FIGURE 6.5**
Feedback
architecture

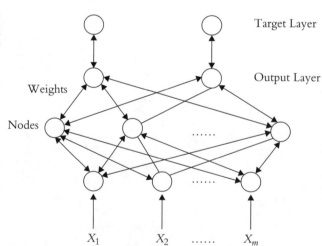

■ **FIGURE 6.6**
One node

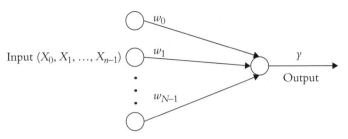

■ 6.5.1 Neural Net and Traditional Classifiers

Computational elements or nodes in a neural network form a weighted sum of N inputs and pass it through a nonlinear function y, as shown in Figure 6.6. In practice, signal values are usually either binary or bipolar. Binary signal functions take on any values in the unit interval $[0, 1]$. On the other hand, bipolar signals are signed values that take on any values in the bipolar interval $[-1, 0]$. Both binary and bipolar signals can be transformed into each other by simple scaling and translation methods. The details of the parameters used in Figure 6.6 are given as follows:

w_i: weight between the ith and $(i-1)$-th nodes
x_i: the input value at the ith unit
θ: threshold value

$$y = f\left(\sum_{i=0}^{N-1} w_i x_i - \theta\right)$$

For example, suppose your input data is $(1, 2, 3)$, the initial connection weights are $(0.1, -0.1, 0.05)$, and the threshold is $\theta = 0.2$. Then we have

$$y = f(0.1 \times 1 + (-0.1) \times 2 + 0.05 \times 3 - 0.2)$$

■ 6.6 KNOWLEDGE DISCOVERY IN DATABASES

Neural networks use a set of relevant variables and represent their relationships in the problem domain to formulate a problem-solving model. Problem-solving knowledge is extracted, used, and dynamically updated in response to a specific problem-solving task. Because of the dynamic update property in neural networks, they must provide a way to deal with the dynamics of a database. When user queries are submitted to retrieve specific information from a database, the neural network performs the analysis of search criteria as the first step in information retrieval from the database. The process of knowledge discovery in databases using a neural-network model starts by constructing an initial neural network. The initial neural network is constructed to form and represent the initial set of goals. These goals are expanded in the database exploration process so that the knowledge discovery process is conducted in a more content-controllable manner. Once an initial network containing some background knowledge and the probabilities is obtained from the database, the network is propagated and refined for convergence of the model. Finally, the user is presented with the result through a user-friendly interface. The overall description of knowledge discovery process using a neural network is shown in Figure 6.7.

■ 6.6.1 Normalization

Learning input nodes can accept any value. If the input values are significantly different from each other, the smaller values will not be significant in the learning process. The variables with dramatic value changes will control the whole learning process. To avoid this situation, a mapping function may be applied to the training data for preprocessing. In the following sections a few mapping methods are briefly described. Any one of these mapping methods can be used for the purpose of normalization.

Maximum–Minimum Mapping

In the maximum–minimum mapping process, the output values are restricted to the interval $[D_{min}, D_{max}]$. The formula used to produce the output values is given below with a description of the parameters used in the formula.

$$X_{new} = \frac{X_{old} - X_{min}}{X_{max} - X_{min}}(D_{max} - D_{min}) + D_{min}$$

X_{max}: The maximum input value
X_{min}: The minimum input value
X_{old}: The input data. These values are retrieved from a database or training dataset.
D_{max}: Maximum value of the desired output interval
D_{min}: Minimum value of the desired output interval
X_{new}: The output value. These values will be put in the input layer units.

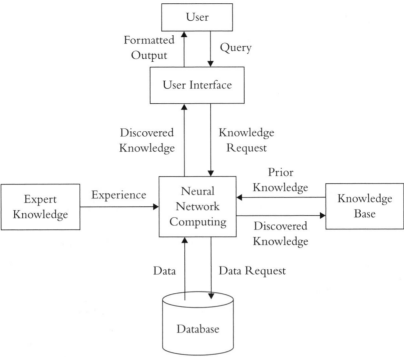

For example, let us assume that the input sample is $(2, 3, 4, 5)$. If you want to restrict the output values to the interval $[0, 1]$, the above formula can be used for normalization. From the formula, we get $X_1 = (2 - 2)/(5 - 2) \times (1 - 0) + 0 = 0$, $X_2 = (3 - 2)/(5 - 2) \times (1 - 0) + 0 = 0.3333$, and so on. Hence, the list of sample values is converted to the list of normalized values $(0, 0.3333, 0.6667, 1)$.

Probabilistic Mapping

In the probabilistic mapping process, the output values are restricted to the interval $[D_{min}, D_{max}]$ by the following formula in which k is a constant used to control the mapping process. The probabilistic mapping is very similar to the maximum–minimum mapping in that both restrict the output values to $[D_{min}, D_{max}]$, but differs from it in the formula used for normalization. The probabilistic mapping formula is

$$X_{new} = \left(\frac{1}{2}\right)^{\dfrac{X_{old} - (\mu - k \times \sigma)}{k \times \sigma}} (D_{max} - D_{min}) + D_{min}$$

■ **FIGURE 6.8**
Coarse coding

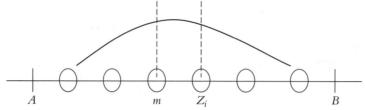

μ: The mean of the input dataset
σ: The standard deviation of the input dataset
X_{old}:   An input data item. These values are retrieved from a database or train-
      ing dataset.
X_{new}: An output value. These values will be put in the input layer units.

Coarse Coding

The output values produced from coarse coding are separated into several small intervals of input values, as shown in Figure 6.8.

$$O_i(m) = \exp\left\{\frac{-(m - Z_i)^2}{\sigma^2}\right\}$$

$O_i(m)$: The ith unit value of the output. These values will be fed back to the
      input layer.
m: Input data item
Z_i: The ith unit value. It is obtained from $[A, B]$ divided by n.
σ: Smoothing factor. This value depends on the complexity of the train-
      ing data. This value can be adjusted.

For the analysis of data in a database, data-mining tools are used to look for patterns and trends to be used for prediction without any knowledge about the meaning of the data. The unsupervised learning model in neural networks provides another way to generate association rules from a group of data, which can be used for predicting future instances.

In the process of learning in neural networks, a pruning method is used to remove redundant links and units without increasing the classification error rate of the network. The benefit of network pruning is reduction of training time and recall time. A small number of units and links left in the network after the pruning process enables us to extract more concise and comprehensible rules than the ones generated from the unpruned networks.

■ 6.7 BACKPROPAGATION NEURAL NETWORK (BPNN) MODEL

The backpropagation training algorithm is an iterative gradient algorithm designed to minimize the mean-square error between the actual output of a multilayer feed-forward perceptron and the desired output [Lippmann 1987]. Since a BPNN learns classification rules by going through many passes over the training data vector, the learning time of a neural network using back-propagation is usually long [Lu 1996].

Standard backpropagation can be used for an incremental training dataset in which the weights are updated after processing each case, but it does not converge to a stationary point in the error function. To obtain convergence, the learning rate must be slowly reduced. Generally, the BPNN model has the following characteristics:

Application: It is a very suitable model that can be applied to pattern classification, adaptive control, noise filtering, data compression, and expert systems.

Strength: A BPNN gives good performance and easily handles complex pattern recognition.

Weakness: The learning speed is slow and may become trapped at local minima.

■ 6.7.1 Network Architecture

The network architecture of BPNN consists of three layers: the input layer, the output layer, and the hidden layer. These layers are connected to accept and process input data. The final output from the network is produced from the nodes of the output layers. A brief description of these layers is given below. Figure 6.9 shows the architecture of the network.

1. **Input layer:** The input layer represents the input variables, which use the linear transformation function, i.e., $f(x) = x$.

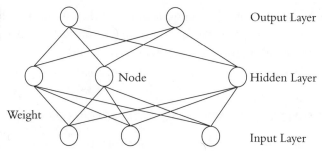

2. **Hidden layer:** The hidden layer represents the interaction among the input nodes, which use a nonlinear transformation function that is a sigmoid function.

3. **Output layer:** The output layer represents the output variables. The number of the output nodes is determined by the problem.

The nonlinear transformation function (sigmoid function) that is used by the hidden nodes to perform the transformation process is $f(x) = 1/(1+e^{-x})$. The variable x in the formula represents the input value on each node. After the network architecture is determined and constructed using these transformation functions, the learning and recall process described in the following section can be applied to the network to generate the output dataset.

■ **6.7.2 Algorithm**
Learning Process

1. Set the parameter of the network.
2. Set the uniform random numbers for W_{xh}, W_{hy}, θ_h, and θ_y.
3. Obtain an input training vector X and the desired output vector T.
4. Calculate the output vector Y as follows:

$$net[h] = \sum_i W[i][h] \times X[i] - \theta[h]$$

a. Calculate the output vector H in the hidden layer.

b. Calculate the output vector Y.

$$net[j] = \sum_h W[h][j] \times H[h] - \theta[j]$$

$$Y[j] = f(net[j]) = \frac{1}{1 + e^{-net[j]}}$$

5. Calculate the value δ.

$$\delta_j = Y_j (1 - Y_j)(T_j - Y_j)$$

a. Calculate the value δ_j in the output layer.

b. Calculate the value δ_h.

$$\delta_h = H_h (1 - H_h) \sum_j W_{hj} \delta_j$$

6. Adjust the weight.

a. At the output layer: $\Delta W y_{hj} = \eta \delta_j H_h$, $\Delta \theta y_j = -\eta \delta_j$.

b. At the hidden layer: $\Delta W x_{ih} = \eta \delta_h X_i$, $\Delta \theta h_h = -\eta \delta_h$.

7. Update W and θ.

a. At the output layer: $W y_{hj} = W y_{hj} + \Delta W y_{hj}$, $\theta y_j = \theta y_j + \Delta \theta y_j$.

b. At the hidden layer: $W h_{ih} = W x_{ih} + \Delta W x_{hj}$, $\theta h_h = \theta h_h + \Delta \theta h_h$.

8. Repeat steps 3–7 until the network converges.

Recall Process

1. Set the network parameter.
2. Read in the weights W_{xh} and W_{hy} and the vectors θ_h and θ_y.
3. Read in the test vector X.
4. Calculate the output vector Y as follows:

$$net[h] = \sum_i W[i][h] \times X[i] - \theta[h]$$

a. Calculate the output vector H in the hidden layer.

b. Calculate the output vector Y.

$$net[j] = \sum_h W[h][j] \times H[h] - \theta[j]$$

$$Y[j] = f(net[j]) = \frac{1}{1 + e^{-net[j]}}$$

Training data	(Attribute 1) X_1	(Attribute 2) X_2	Desired output
1	−1	−1	0
2	−1	1	1
3	1	−1	1
4	1	1	0

■ FIGURE 6.10 Initial network architecture with five nodes

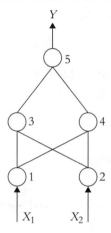

In the next two examples that follow, the learning and recall processes of BPNN are applied to demonstrate the transformation process of the network to produce the output data.

■ 6.7.3 Example I

In this example, the data classification problem is presented with a description of how to use the attribute data in the learning process. The table in Figure 6.10 consists of four columns with four entries, which constitute the training dataset. The first column is used for the purpose of identifying data items, while the last column contains the corresponding desired outputs with a value of either 0 or 1.

The initial weights and thresholds are $W_{13} = 1$, $W_{23} = -1$, $W_{14} = -1$, $W_{24} = 1$, $W_{35} = 1$, $W_{45} = 1$, $\theta_3 = 1$, $\theta_4 = 1$, and $\theta_5 = 1$. If we set the learning rate to $\eta = 10$, then the initial learning dataset becomes $x_1 = -1$, $x_2 = -1$, $T = 0$. Next, we proceed with the learning process by calculating the outputs from different layers.

1. Calculate the outputs of the hidden layer:

$$net_3 = W_{13} \times x_1 + W_{23} \times x_2 - \theta_3 = (1)(-1) + (-1)(-1) - 1 = -1$$
$$H_1 = 1/[1 + \exp(-net_3)] = 1/[1 + \exp(1)] = 0.269$$
$$net_4 = W_{14} \times x_1 + W_{24} \times x_2 - \theta_4 = (-1)(-1) + (1)(-1) - 1 = -1$$
$$H_2 = 1/[1 + \exp(-net_4)] = 1/[1 + \exp(1)] = 0.269$$

2. Calculate the outputs of the output layer:

$$net_5 = W_{35} \times H_1 + W_{45} \times H_2 - \theta_5 = (1)(0.269) + (1)(0.269) - 1 = -0.462$$

$$Y = 1/[1 + \exp(-net_5)] = 1/[1 + \exp(0.462)] = 0.386$$

$$\delta_5 = Y(1 - Y)(T - Y) = 0.386\,(1 - 0.386)(0 - 0.386) = -0.0915$$

$$\delta_3 = H_1(1 - H_1) \times \Sigma W_{3j}\delta_j - 0.269(1 - 0.269)[(1)(-0.0915)] = -0.0180$$

$$\delta_4 = H_2(1 - H_2) \times \Sigma W_{4j}\delta_j = 0.269(1 - 0.269)[(1)(-0.0915)] = -0.0180$$

3. Calculate the Δw of the output layer:

$$\Delta W_{35} = \eta\delta_5 H_1 = (10)(-0.0915)(0.269) = -0.246$$

$$\Delta W_{45} = \eta\delta_5 H_2 = (10)(-0.0915)(0.269) = -0.246$$

$$\Delta\theta_5 = -\eta\delta_5 = -(10)(-0.0915) = 0.915$$

4. Calculate the Δw of the hidden layer:

$$\Delta W_{13} = \eta\delta_3 x_1 = (10)(-0.0180)(-1) = 0.180$$

$$\Delta W_{23} = \eta\delta_3 x_2 = (10)(-0.0180)(-1) = 0.180$$

$$\Delta\theta_3 = -\eta\delta_3 = -(10)(-0.0180) = 0.180$$

$$\Delta W_{14} = \eta\delta_4 x_1 = (10)(-0.0180)(-1) = 0.180$$

$$\Delta W_{24} = \eta\delta_4 x_2 = (10)(-0.0180)(-1) = 0.180$$

$$\Delta\theta_4 = -\eta\delta_4 = -(10)(-0.0180) = 0.180$$

Repeat steps 1–4 until the network converges.

■ 6.7.4 Example II (Retrieval of Data Using the BPNN Model)

In this example, we illustrate how to retrieve information from a database using the BPNN model. For this purpose, a table with eight input nodes and ten training samples is used as shown in Table 6.1. The initial network is first built and trained as was done in the previous example. Next, a testing sample is used to test the BPNN model constructed with the training sample. In the following, the learning process is performed to construct the initial BPNN architecture.

In the learning process, the following vectors are used to train the BPNN:

X_1 = Number of times pregnant

X_2 = Plasma glucose concentration for 2 hours in an oral glucose tolerance test

X_3 = Diastolic blood pressure (mm Hg)

X_4 = Triceps skin fold thickness (mm)

X_5 = 2-hour serum insulin (mu U/ml)

X_6 = Body mass index (weight in kg/(height in m)^2)

X_7 = Diabetes pedigree function

X_8 = Age (years)

Class = − or + (The class + is interpreted as "result positive for diabetes")

Before we continue, any column(s) containing textual values such as + and − need to be converted into columns of numerical values. For example, since the Class column contains one of the two values + or −, it can be converted into two columns C_1 and C_2 in which the values 1 or 0 represent the existence (or not) of diabetes. In this case ($C_1 = 0$, $C_2 = 1$) represents the non-existence of diabetes and ($C_1 = 1$, $C_2 = 0$) represents the existence of diabetes. Table 6.2 is the result of converting Table 6.1, which will be used to train BPNN.

■ TABLE 6.1 An original table with textual class information

	X_1	X_2	X_3	X_4	X_5	X_6	X_7	X_8	Class
Sample 1	1	85	66	29	0	26.6	0.351	31	−
Sample 2	6	148	72	35	0	33.6	0.627	50	+
Sample 3	8	183	64	0	0	23.3	0.672	32	+
Sample 4	1	89	66	23	94	28.1	0.167	21	−
Sample 5	0	137	40	35	168	43.1	2.288	33	+
Sample 6	5	116	74	0	0	25.6	0.201	30	−
Sample 7	3	78	50	32	88	31.0	0.248	26	+
Sample 8	10	115	0	0	0	35.3	0.134	29	−
Sample 9	2	197	70	45	543	30.5	0.158	53	+
Sample 10	8	125	96	0	0	0.0	0.232	54	+

■ TABLE 6.2 Training sample ready for BPNN

	X_1	X_2	X_3	X_4	X_5	X_6	X_7	X_8	C_1	C_2
Sample 1	1	85	66	29	0	26.6	0.351	31	0	1
Sample 2	6	148	72	35	0	33.6	0.627	50	1	0
Sample 3	8	183	64	0	0	23.3	0.672	32	1	0
Sample 4	1	89	66	23	94	28.1	0.167	21	0	1
Sample 5	0	137	40	35	168	43.1	2.288	33	1	0
Sample 6	5	116	74	0	0	25.6	0.201	30	0	1
Sample 7	3	78	50	32	88	31.0	0.248	26	1	0
Sample 8	10	115	0	0	0	35.3	0.134	29	0	1
Sample 9	2	197	70	45	543	30.5	0.158	53	1	0
Sample 10	8	125	96	0	0	0.0	0.232	54	1	0

The BPNN structure constructed with the training sample above is shown in Figure 6.11. The architecture shown contains eight nodes in the input layer. Each of the nodes in the input layer corresponds to attributes X_1 to X_8 since the number of nodes in the input layer depends on how many attributes there are in the database. Similarly, the number of nodes in the output layer is two, which corresponds to C_1 and C_2, respectively, since

■ FIGURE 6.11
BPNN architecture

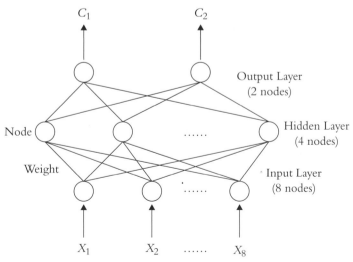

the number of classes determines the number of nodes in the output layer. Finally, the number of nodes in the hidden layer is four, which is determined by the size of the training sample and the number of output nodes.

In the recall process the values of attributes X_1 through X_8 of the test samples are fed into the nodes of the input layer to run the BPNN model. Through this process, the model will generate an answer corresponding to a test sample to determine which class each sample belongs to. The following two examples show the test case for different classes, one for the positive result and the other for the negative result for diabetes.

Testing Examples

CASE 1:

We use the following testing example to show how the BPNN works correctly:

$$7 \; 107 \; 74 \; 0 \; 0 \; 29.6 \; 0.254 \; 31 \; (X_1, X_2, \ldots, X_8) \Rightarrow +$$

After getting this testing example as input to the BPNN, the sigmoid function is used to calculate the values for C_1 and C_2. As a result, we get the value of C_1 almost equal to 1 and the value of C_2 nearly equal to 0. Thus, we can come to the conclusion that the testing example shows positive for diabetes mellitus.

CASE 2:

In the next case, consider the following testing sample as another input to the BPNN:

$$1 \; 103 \; 30 \; 38 \; 83 \; 43.3 \; 0.183 \; 33 \; (X_1, X_2, \ldots, X_8) \Rightarrow -$$

After following the same procedure to calculate C_1 and C_2, we obtain the value of C_1 nearly equal to 0 and the value of C_2 almost equal to 1. Thus, the conclusion is that this testing example shows negative for diabetes mellitus.

■ 6.8 BIDIRECTIONAL ASSOCIATIVE MEMORY (BAM) MODEL

In the BAM model, every training vector takes values in the unit interval $[-1, 1]$. At the same time, the vector is divided into two parts: front and rear. According to the BAM rule, the network can remember the relationships from the front part to the rear part. As the testing vector is entered into the nets, the model can associate it with the most similar vector that was used to

■ FIGURE 6.12
The BAM model

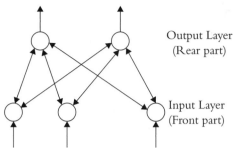

Output Layer
(Rear part)

Input Layer
(Front part)

train the net. This model is especially suitable for applications in databases and signal processing. The strength of the BAM dynamical system is that it can quickly recall the original uncorrupted pattern, while the weakness of it is its poor internal capacity to hold information required to perform reasoning.

■ 6.8.1   Network Architecture

In the BAM model there are only two layers, the input layer and the output layer, as can be seen from Figure 6.12. Input nodes are used to store the input data, while the output nodes are for storing the computed values. Since the purpose of the architecture is to associate the output nodes with the input nodes, a number of iterations are performed to create the relationship between the front layer and the rear layer as implied by the figure. In the next section, brief descriptions of the learning and recall algorithms for the BAM model are given.

■ 6.8.2   Algorithm
Learning Process

1. Set the network parameter.
2. Calculate the weight matrix $\mathbf{W}$ using the following formula:

$$\mathbf{W}_{ij} = \sum_p X_i^p \times Y_j^p$$

x_i: The input value for the front part
y_j: The input value for the rear part
p: Learning data at the pth element
$\mathbf{W}_{ij}$:   Weight matrix

Recall Process

1. Read in weight matrix $\mathbf{W}$.

2. Input a test vector X.

3. Calculate the output vector Y using the following formula:

$$net_j = \sum_j \mathbf{W}_{ij} \times X_i$$

$Y_j = 1$ if $net_j > 0$
$Y_j = Y_j$ if $net_j = 0$
$Y_j = -1$ if $net_j < 0$

4. Calculate the vector X at the input layer as follows:

$$net_i = \sum_j \mathbf{W}_{ij} \times Y_j$$

$X_j = 1$ if $net_j > 0$
$X_j = X_j$ if $net_j = 0$
$X_j = -1$ if $net_j < 0$

5. Repeat steps 3 and 4 until the network converges to learn a rule.

■ 6.8.3 Example with Four Training Vectors

In this example, we are given a table with four training vectors in which 1 means good and −1 means bad in the learning process as shown in Table 6.3. The first six columns (except the first column, which is used only for identification purpose) show nodes for the front layer with the following meaning: S (score), RP (rate of presence), RC (response in class), P (project), H (homework), L (leadership), and DO (desired output of rear part).

■ TABLE 6.3 A training example with four vectors

	S	RP	RC	P	H	L	DO			
No. 1	1	−1	1	−1	1	−1	1	−1	1	−1
No. 2	−1	1	−1	1	−1	1	−1	1	−1	1
No. 3	1	1	1	1	1	1	−1	−1	−1	−1
No. 4	−1	−1	−1	−1	−1	−1	1	1	1	1

The front part: $(1, -1, 1, -1, 1, -1)$ $\rightarrow$ the rear part: $(1, -1, 1, -1)$

            $(-1, 1, -1, 1, -1, 1)$ $\rightarrow$ $(-1, 1, -1, 1)$

            $(1, 1, 1, 1, 1, 1)$ $\rightarrow$ $(-1, -1, -1, -1)$

            $(-1, -1, -1, -1, -1, -1) \rightarrow$ $(1, 1, 1, 1)$

Then, $\mathbf{W}_{ij}$ becomes

$$
\begin{bmatrix}
0 & -4 & 0 & -4 & 0 & -4 \\
-4 & 0 & -4 & 0 & -4 & 0 \\
0 & 0 & -4 & 0 & -4 & 0 \\
-4 & 0 & -4 & 0 & -4 & 0
\end{bmatrix}
$$

For the recall process, assume the testing vector $X = (1, 1, 1, -1, 1, -1)$. At the first iteration, we get the following:

$$
\begin{bmatrix} Y_1 \\ Y_2 \\ Y_3 \\ Y_4 \end{bmatrix} = f \left(\begin{bmatrix}
0 & -4 & 0 & -4 & 0 & -4 \\
-4 & 0 & -4 & 0 & -4 & 0 \\
0 & 0 & -4 & 0 & -4 & 0 \\
-4 & 0 & -4 & 0 & -4 & 0
\end{bmatrix} \times \begin{bmatrix} 1 \\ 1 \\ 1 \\ -1 \\ 1 \\ -1 \end{bmatrix} \right) = f \left(\begin{bmatrix} 4 \\ -12 \\ 4 \\ -12 \end{bmatrix} \right) = \begin{bmatrix} 1 \\ -1 \\ 1 \\ -1 \end{bmatrix}
$$

$$
\begin{bmatrix} X_1 \\ X_2 \\ X_3 \\ X_4 \\ X_5 \\ X_6 \end{bmatrix} = f \left(\begin{bmatrix} 1 & -1 & 1 & -1 \end{bmatrix} \times \begin{bmatrix}
0 & -4 & 0 & -4 & 0 & -4 \\
-4 & 0 & -4 & 0 & -4 & 0 \\
0 & 0 & -4 & 0 & -4 & 0 \\
-4 & 0 & -4 & 0 & -4 & 0
\end{bmatrix} \right) = f \left(\begin{bmatrix} 8 \\ -8 \\ 8 \\ -8 \\ 8 \\ -8 \end{bmatrix} \right) = \begin{bmatrix} 1 \\ -1 \\ 1 \\ -1 \\ 1 \\ -1 \end{bmatrix}
$$

Next, we continue the process for the second iteration as follows:

$$
\begin{bmatrix} Y_1 \\ Y_2 \\ Y_3 \\ Y_4 \end{bmatrix} = f \left(\begin{bmatrix} 0 & -4 & 0 & -4 & 0 & -4 \\ -4 & 0 & -4 & 0 & -4 & 0 \\ 0 & 0 & -4 & 0 & -4 & 0 \\ -4 & 0 & -4 & 0 & -4 & 0 \end{bmatrix} \times \begin{bmatrix} 1 \\ 1 \\ 1 \\ -1 \\ 1 \\ -1 \end{bmatrix} \right) = f \left(\begin{bmatrix} 4 \\ -12 \\ 4 \\ -12 \end{bmatrix} \right) = \begin{bmatrix} 1 \\ -1 \\ 1 \\ -1 \end{bmatrix}
$$

$$
\begin{bmatrix} X_1 \\ X_2 \\ X_3 \\ X_4 \\ X_5 \\ X_6 \end{bmatrix} = f \left(\begin{bmatrix} 1 & -1 & 1 & -1 \end{bmatrix} \times \begin{bmatrix} 0 & -4 & 0 & -4 & 0 & -4 \\ -4 & 0 & -4 & 0 & -4 & 0 \\ 0 & 0 & -4 & 0 & -4 & 0 \\ -4 & 0 & -4 & 0 & -4 & 0 \end{bmatrix} \times \begin{bmatrix} 1 \\ 1 \\ 1 \\ -1 \\ 1 \\ -1 \end{bmatrix} \right) = f \left(\begin{bmatrix} 8 \\ -8 \\ 8 \\ -8 \\ 8 \\ -8 \end{bmatrix} \right) = \begin{bmatrix} 1 \\ -1 \\ 1 \\ -1 \\ 1 \\ -1 \end{bmatrix}
$$

At this point, we see that the network converges since there are no state changes. Since the result is the same as the first training vector $(1, -1, 1, -1, 1, -1)$, the desired output becomes $(1, -1, 1, -1)$, which can be either defined or interpreted as an average student.

■ 6.9 LEARNING VECTOR QUANTIZATION (LVQ) MODEL

A multilayered Learning Vector Quantization (LVQ) model is trained by the data coming from the input training pair. In this model, the learning vector quantization is applied to represent the relevant variables and their relationships in a problem domain, and the network is updated according to the extracted knowledge of the network. The LVQ network acts as a learning model because it saves a lot of learning time and provides a way to deal with the dynamics of a database. Figure 6.13 shows the steps of the LVQ learning process.

The process of knowledge discovery followed by this model starts with the construction of an initial LVQ network. The initial LVQ network is used to form and represent the initial set of goals.

FIGURE 6.13
The flowchart of
the system

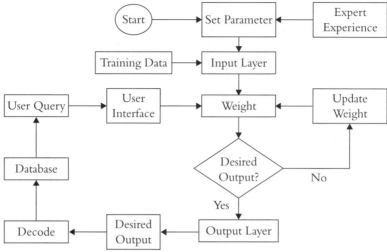

▪ 6.9.1 Network Architecture

The knowledge discovery process starts by putting the training data into the input layer. An example of training data may be a relation containing data such as the relationships of blood pressure and the chances of having a heart attack. According to domain expert knowledge, the initial set of rules are formed to be provided to the model, and then the weights are adjusted

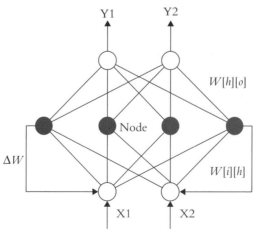
FIGURE 6.14
LVQ network
architecture

via the LVQ network. If the output is not the desired one, then the process is iterated using the connected nodes. Finally, the obtained knowledge is stored in the form of connected weights. Meanwhile, users form queries of a specific problem via the friendly interface, and then get the desired answer from the database system.

The process of knowledge discovery, defined in the above model, starts with the construction of an initial LVQ network. An initial LVQ network is constructed to form and represent the initial set of goals. These goals are expanded in the database exploration process so that knowledge discovery will be conducted in a more content-controllable manner. Given the initial LVQ network structure, which contains some background knowledge, the probabilities obtained from the database are propagated in the network and then used to refine the LVQ network.

■ 6.9.2 Algorithm
Learning Process

1. Set the parameter.
2. Set the weight $W[i][h]$ between the input layer and the hidden layer. Use a uniform random number. Let say, for example, that Ng is a random number generator.
3. Set the weight $W[h][y]$ between the hidden layer and the output layer.
4. If $Ng \times (j-1) \leq h \leq Ng \times j$, then $W[h][j] = 1$ else $W[h][j] = 0$.
5. Input: A training vector X and a desired output vector T.
6. Calculate the output vector Y.
7. Calculate ΔW:

If the output is the desired output,

$$\text{then } \Delta W[i][h] = \eta_1 (X[i] - W[i][h^*])$$
$$\text{else } \Delta W[i][h] = -\eta_2 (X[i] - W[i][h^*])$$

Update W: $W[i][h] = W[i][h] + \Delta W[i][h]$.
Iterate steps 4 through 7.

In the learning process above, the parameters η_1 and η_2 and the learning rate must initially be set. Usually they are set between 0 and 1. Then, the initial weights are set as random numbers between −1 and 1. Next, set the connecting weights as 0 or 1 between the hidden layer and the output layer. These values are called *training pairs*. In the learning process, if the training pair and the hidden nodes are close enough, then set the weight between the inner node and the input layer as 1, otherwise choose 0. In the hidden layer and the output layer, the computed values are forced to be the same as the desired values by changing the weights. The process described above is iterated as many times as needed until the desired output is obtained.

Recall Process

1. Set the parameter.
2. Read in $W[i][h]$ and $W[h][y]$.
3. Input the test data X.
4. Calculate the output Y.
5. Calculate the output H in the hidden layer.

$$net[h] = \sum_i (x[i] - W[i][h])^2$$
$$net[h^*] = \min \ net[h]$$
If $h = h^*$, then $H[h] = 1$ else $H[h] = 0$

6. Calculate the output Y.

If $net[j] > 0$, then $Y[j] = 1$ else $Y[j] = 0$

■ 6.9.3 Example

In the example shown below, we consider a medical diagnosis domain where medical knowledge for diagnostic suggestion needs to be retrieved from medical doctors. The retrieved medical expert's knowledge needs to be embedded into the diagnostic system. The knowledge base of the diagnostic system is believed to contain official medical knowledge including thousands of cases, which is more than an experienced doctor can handle.

In the training process, let us assume that about 700 training data were given to the network and that the desired output is measured in score. The desired output is then used to analyze the conditions for a healthy body. The network will adjust the weights to fit the desired output. After learning, the patient's record is then put into the model to get the suggestions faster. Tables 6.4 and 6.5 show a part of the testing dataset as an example.

■ **TABLE 6.4 Training dataset with patient's health conditions**

Patient's ID	Total cholesterol/ HDL ratio	Triglycerides (mg %)	Glucose (mg %)	Body fat %	Systolic (mm Hg)	Diastolic (mm Hg)	Score
1	2.7	46.1	82	5.2	101.6	61	8
2	2.8	45.4	83	5.0	100.3	62	7
3	3.1	80.2	90	10.1	121.2	78	5
4	6.9	230.7	116	28.1	142.7	95	2
5	3.2	81.1	89	9.6	119.2	75	5
6	3.7	83	92	10.3	119.4	76	5

■ **TABLE 6.5 Training dataset with patient's health profile**

Patient's ID	Age	Weight	Smoking history (years)	Smoking amount (packs/day)	Nutrition habit
1	45	185	0–5	0–1	Egg, beef
2	50	190	0–5	0–1	Vegetable
3	47	180	0–5	2–3	Fish, beef, candy
4	55	175	6–10	2–3	Chicken, beef
5	30	179	0–5	0–1	Fish, beef, fowl
6	38	230	6–10	2–3	Fried foods, beef

In Table 6.6, several important factors are shown that affect the diagnostics of the doctors. This table shows two extreme cases: one good condition and one poor condition of the patients. These values can be obtained from patients' records or may be entered by users when seeking advice. Some personal habits (as shown in Table 6.7) are also considered because they can affect the results. But they are believed to have less influence than the factors

■ **TABLE 6.6 Blood test results**

Patient's ID	Total cholesterol/ HDL ratio	Triglycerides (mg %)	Glucose (mg %)	Body fat %	Systolic (mm Hg)	Diastolic (mm Hg)
1	2.6	45	80.5	5.3	100	62
2	6.9	240.7	115.5	29.1	145.7	96

■ **TABLE 6.7 Personal information**

Patient's ID	Age	Weight	Smoking history (years)	Smoking amount (packs/day)	Nutrition habit
1	32	175	0–5	0–1	Fish, beef, fowl
2	35	240	6–10	1–2	Fried foods, beef

■ **TABLE 6.8 Weekly eating and exercise suggestion**

Patient's ID	Fitness category	Jogging (hours)	Swimming (hours)	Bicycling (hours)	Sleeping time (hours/day)	Food
1	Excellent	2–3	3–4	3–4	>7	Reduce oily food, eat fresh meal
2	Poor	5.5–6	6–7.5	7–7.5	>8	Reduce oily food, eat fresh meal, more vegetable, reexam each 6 months

in Table 6.6. The diagnostic suggestions are shown in Table 6.8. Given the data in the input layer in Tables 6.6 and 6.7, the results shown in Table 6.8 can be obtained following the learning process of the LVQ model.

■ 6.10 PROBABILISTIC NEURAL NETWORK (PNN) MODEL

A Probabilistic Neural Network (PNN) model computes and uses nonlinear decision boundaries that approach the optimal function of Bayes' theory. The decision boundaries can be modified using new training data. Provision is also made for estimating the probability and reliability of a classification as well as making decisions [Specht 1990].

Application: The PNN model is a very suitable tool for application into databases and signal processing.

Strengths: The strengths of the PNN model are as follows:

1. *High computation capability*—Becuase it takes a lot of time to deal with huge databases and figure out which category a new pattern belongs to, applying this type of artificial neural network model can save

time and effort, not to mention improve the accuracy of the computation results.

2. *Learning*—The PNN dynamical system can quickly learn the data from the learning data source. The decision boundaries can be modified in real time using new data as they become available, and they can be implemented using artificial hardware "neurons" that operate entirely in a parallel processing manner.

3. *Fault tolerance*—Unlike a computer part that may be damaged when a computer operation malfunctions, in an artificial neural network slight damage to the connections will not result in a serious problem, but will just decrease functionality slightly. This is partly due to the fact that in an artificial neural network the information is stored in distributed memory. If the input information is incomplete or has noise, the artificial neural network can still perform proper processing.

Weaknesses: The weaknesses of the PNN model are as follows:

1. *Needs a large memory space*—In the PNN model, the information is stored in a matrix. If the number of training examples is very large and every example has a lot of attributes, then the matrix will become very large.

2. *Slower recall process*—The computation speed of the recall process can be slow due to processing of the large matrices.

■ 6.10.1 Network Architecture

Donald Specht proposed the first PNN model in his article "Probabilistic Neural Networks" [Specht 1990]. He outlined how the algorithm developed by Bayes and Parzen could be broken up into many simple processes, each of which could be run independently and in parallel. The outline of the architecture of the original PNN is shown in Figure 6.15.

In the example shown in the figure, there are six training-vector samples that are divided into three population classes. The first layer is the input layer, and in this case there is one input layer. This means that there is only one input to be classified. The second layer is called the pattern layer. In this layer, there is one neuron for each training vector sample. The third layer, called the summation layer, shows that there is one neuron for each population class.

FIGURE 6.15
The architecture of
the PNN model

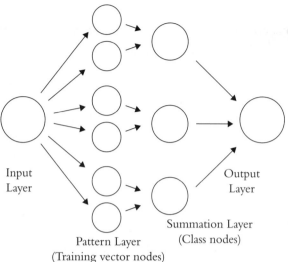

Finally, the fourth layer, the output layer, is nothing more than a threshold discriminator. The threshold discriminator helps to decide which of the summation units gives the maximum output.

The network starts the execution with the input vectors going into all of the neurons in the pattern layer. The pattern layers calculate the distance between the input vector and the training vector (this is why there is one neuron for each training vector). After calculating the distance, the value is applied to an activation function. The activation function is the bell-curve window found in the discussion of Parzen's work referenced above. The result of the function is fed to the summation neuron on the third layer, which adds all the results in a particular class together and then feeds them to the output layer in which the largest value is chosen. In this manner the population with which the input vector most closely resembles is selected as the output.

In the supervised learning network, the learning process is described as follows:

1. Use random numbers to initialize the original network weights.
2. Place the input vectors of the training samples into the input layer of the network, and then compute the deductive output vectors through the recall process.

3. Modify the network weights based on the difference of the deductive output vectors and the target output vectors of the training sample.
4. Repeat steps 2 and 3 until convergence is achieved.

PNN belongs to the supervised learning network. However, the difference between the PNN and other neural network models is in the learning process. In the PNN, the weights are determined directly by the input and output vectors of the training samples. Therefore, the basic concepts of PNN can be summarized as follows:

1. Assume that there are k possible classifications: $C_1, C_2, C_3, \ldots, C_k$.
2. The classification rule is determined by the following M-dimensional vector:

$$X = (X_1, X_2, X_3, \ldots, X_m)$$

3. The probability of classifying the input vector into each class is determined by the function f, which is described in detail in the following discussion:

$$f_1(X), f_2(X), f_3(X), \ldots, f_k(X)$$

Since the PNN is based on Gaussian distribution, it uses the following mathematical formula:

$$f_k(X) = \frac{1}{(2\pi)^{m/2}\,\sigma^m}\,\frac{1}{N_k}\sum_{j=1}^{N_k}\exp\left(-\frac{|X - X_{kj}|}{2\sigma^2}\right)$$

where

$$|X - X_{kj}| = \sum_i (X_i - X_{kji})^2$$

X = input vectors $(X_1, \ldots, X_m)$
N_k = total number of training patterns for category k
j = pattern number
m = dimensionality of measurement space
σ = smoothing parameter
X_{kj} = jth training pattern from category k

Since in PNN we only care about the relative probability between each category, the constant part in the above formula can be omitted. Consequently, the formula that we can use to code the learning program can be obtained as shown below by removing the constant portion from the formula above. In the next section, we will see the algorithm used for the learning and recalling processes illustrated with an example.

$$f_k(X) = \left(\frac{1}{N_k}\right) \sum_{j=1}^{N_k} \exp\left(-\frac{|X - X_{kj}|}{2\sigma^2}\right)$$

■ 6.10.2 Algorithm
Learning Process

1. Set the network parameter (smoothing parameter).
2. Input the input vector X of the training sample and the target output vector T.
3. Set the matrix **W**.

   a. The matrix **W_xh** is between the input layer and the hidden layer.

   $$\mathbf{W\_xh}_{ih} = X_i^h$$

   X_i^h is the value of one of the input vectors in one of the training samples.

   b. The matrix **W_hy** is between the hidden layer and the output layer.

   $$\mathbf{W\_hy}_{hj} = 1 \text{ if } T_j^h = 1$$
   $$\mathbf{W\_hy}_{hj} = 0 \text{ if } T_j^h = 0$$

   T_j^h is the value of one of the output vectors in one of the training samples.

Recalling Process

1. Set the network parameter (smoothing parameter).
2. Read in the matrices **W_xh** and **W_hy**.
3. Input the input vector X of one of the testing samples.
4. Compute the deductive output vector Y.

   a. Compute the output vector H of the hidden layer.

   $$net_h = \sum(X_i - \mathbf{W\_xh}_{ih})^2$$
   $$H_h = \exp(-net_h/2\sigma^2)$$

b. Compute the deductive output vector Y.

$$N_j = \sum \mathbf{W\_hy}_{hj}$$
$$net_j = 1/N_j \sum \mathbf{W\_hy}_{hj} \times H_h$$

If $net_j = \max net_k$, then $Y_j = 1$ else $Y_j = 0$

■ 6.10.3 Example

In this example, we consider a database with medical information related to diabetes. The medical information contained in the database classifies patients into two groups: one for the normal condition and the other for the diabetes-positive condition. Eight medical conditions related to diabetes are represented in the table to show how they affect the diagnosis of diabetes.

Figure 6.16 shows the flowchart for the PNN model used to handle the diagnosis of diabetes. Training data from the database is fed into the PNN model together with testing samples from the patients. Through the PNN's learning process, a decision is made on the diagnosis of the disease. In the following, detailed parameters required for following the learning and recall processes are described.

FIGURE 6.16
The flowchart of
the PNN model

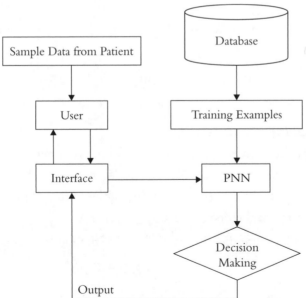

1. Assume that the task required is to determine the two classifications:

   C_1: represents the normal group (diabetes negative)
   C_2: represents the DM group (diabetes positive)

2. The classification rule is determined by the vectors with eight elements:

$$X = (X_1, X_2, X_3, \ldots, X_8)$$

   This means that the dimensionality of the measurement space is eight. In other words, the following eight attributes are used to determine or predict whether or not a patient has diabetes mellitus.

   X_1 = Number of times pregnant
   X_2 = Plasma glucose concentration for 2 hours in an oral glucose tolerance test
   X_3 = Diastolic blood pressure (mm Hg)
   X_4 = Triceps skin fold thickness (mm)
   X_5 = 2-hour serum insulin (mu U/ml)
   X_6 = Body mass index (weight in kg/(height in m)^2)
   X_7 = Diabetes pedigree function
   X_8 = Age (years)

3. So, the probability of belonging to each class for a specific input vector is given by $f_A(X)$ and $f_B(X)$. Figure 6.17 draws the relationship between the probabilistic density functions and the input data. Based on these

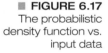

FIGURE 6.17
The probabilistic density function vs. input data

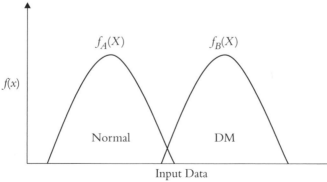

functions the learning and recalling processes are performed as described in the following.

$$f_A(X) = \left(\frac{1}{N_A}\right) \sum_{j=1}^{N_A} \exp\left(-\frac{|X - X_{Aj}|}{2\sigma^2}\right)$$

$$f_B(X) = \left(\frac{1}{N_B}\right) \sum_{j=1}^{N_B} \exp\left(-\frac{|X - X_{Bj}|}{2\sigma^2}\right)$$

Learning Process

1. Set the smoothing parameter value to 0.5.
2. Input the input vector X of the training sample and the target output vector T.

Table 6.9 is used to train our PNN model by which each record is classified as either + or −. The class + is interpreted as "tested positive for diabetes," while the class − is interpreted as "tested negative for diabetes."

Since the computation required for figuring out probability uses numeric values, the columns of non-numerical values must be transformed to numerical values. In this case, since the "class" column contains two values, we could create two columns, C_1 and C_2, and use ($C_1 = 0$, $C_2 = 1$) to

■ TABLE 6.9 A sample training dataset for the PNN model

	X_1	X_2	X_3	X_4	X_5	X_6	X_7	X_8	Class
Sample 1	1	85	66	29	0	26.6	0.351	31	−
Sample 2	6	148	72	35	0	33.6	0.627	50	+
Sample 3	8	183	64	0	0	23.3	0.672	32	+
Sample 4	1	89	66	23	94	28.1	0.167	21	−
Sample 5	0	137	40	35	168	43.1	2.288	33	+
Sample 6	5	116	74	0	0	25.6	0.201	30	−
Sample 7	3	78	50	32	88	31.0	0.248	26	+
Sample 8	10	115	0	0	0	35.3	0.134	29	−
Sample 9	2	197	70	45	543	30.5	0.158	53	+
Sample 10	8	125	96	0	0	0.0	0.232	54	+

■ **TABLE 6.10 Textual class data converted to numeric data**

	X_1	X_2	X_3	X_4	X_5	X_6	X_7	X_8	C_1	C_2
Sample 1	1	85	66	29	0	26.6	0.351	31	0	1
Sample 2	6	148	72	35	0	33.6	0.627	50	1	0
Sample 3	8	183	64	0	0	23.3	0.672	32	1	0
Sample 4	1	89	66	23	94	28.1	0.167	21	0	1
Sample 5	0	137	40	35	168	43.1	2.288	33	1	0
Sample 6	5	116	74	0	0	25.6	0.201	30	0	1
Sample 7	3	78	50	32	88	31.0	0.248	26	1	0
Sample 8	10	115	0	0	0	35.3	0.134	29	0	1
Sample 9	2	197	70	45	543	30.5	0.158	53	1	0
Sample 10	8	125	96	0	0	0.0	0.232	54	1	0

represent DM negative and ($C_1 = 1$, $C_2 = 0$) to represent DM positive. The resulting table, Table 6.10, therefore, can be used to train the PNN network model.

3. Set the matrices **W_xh** and **W_hy**.

At this step, the architecture of our PNN model can be organized with the following characteristics:

The number of nodes in the *input layer* is 8: X_1 to X_8.
(The number of nodes in the input layer depends on how many attributes there are.)
The number of nodes in the *hidden layer* is 10.
(The number of nodes in the hidden layer depends on the number of training examples.)
The number of nodes in the *output layer* is 2: C_1 and C_2.
(The number of nodes in the output layer depends on how many final classes there are.)

Figure 6.18 reflects the network structure of the PNN model based on the data included in the preceding table. In the network structure, there are 80 weights (i.e., connections) between the input layer and the hidden layer, and there are 20 weights (connections) between the hidden layer and the

■ **FIGURE 6.18**
The structure of
input, hidden, and
output layers

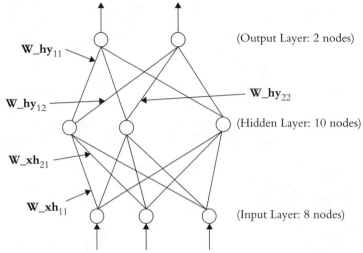

output layer. For example, when Sample 1 is passed to the PNN, the following is obtained:

$$\mathbf{W\_xh}_{11} = 1, \mathbf{W\_xh}_{21} = 85, \mathbf{W\_xh}_{31} = 66, \mathbf{W\_xh}_{41} = 29, \mathbf{W\_xh}_{51} = 0,$$
$$\mathbf{W\_xh}_{61} = 26.6, \mathbf{W\_xh}_{71} = 0.351, \mathbf{W\_xh}_{81} = 31, \mathbf{W\_hy}_{11} = 0, \mathbf{W\_hy}_{12} = 1$$

After all 10 training examples are provided to the PNN, the matrix between the input layer and the hidden layer and the matrix between the hidden layer and the output layer can all be determined accordingly. At this point the testing samples can be used as input to test the network.

Recall Process

In the recalling process, the values of X_1 to X_8 of the testing sample are fed into the input layer to run the PNN model. The output from the network will show which class the sample can be classified into. Consider the following examples to see how the PNN model responds to two different testing samples.

Testing Examples

1. The first example uses the following data as input to the network:

$$7 \ 107 \ 74 \ 0 \ 0 \ 29.6 \ 0.254 \ 31 \ (X_1, X_2, ..., X_8) \Rightarrow +$$

Then we get the following sequence of values to use for recalling:

$net_h = \Sigma(X_i - \mathbf{W\_xh}_{ih})^2$

$net_1 = 18811.224516$, $net_2 = 3288.139129$, $net_3 = 1434.009409$,
$net_4 = 5917.864724$, $net_5 = 9891.257569$, $net_6 = 31744.387156$,
$net_7 = 102.002809$, $net_8 = 10227.960036$, $net_9 = 5585.5044$,
$net_{10} = 305499.819216$

$H_h = \exp(-net_h/2\sigma^2)$

$H_1 - H_{10}$ is too small to display

Obtain the deductive output vector Y as follows:

$$N_j = \Sigma W\_hy_{hj}$$
$$N_1 = 6, N_2 = 4$$
$$net_j = 1/N_j \Sigma \mathbf{W\_hy}_{hj} \times H_h$$
$$net_1, net_2 \text{ are too small to display}$$

If $net_j = \max net_k$, **then** $Y_j = 1$ **else** $Y_j = 0$.

After providing all the test examples as inputs to the PNN for density calculation, we can get the probability of C_1 as 0.005050 and the probability of C_2 as 0. Therefore, we can conclude that the test example is positive for diabetes mellitus.

2. The second example uses the following data as input to the network:

    1 103 30 38 83 43.3 0.183 33 $(X_1, X_2, ..., X_8) \Rightarrow -$

After providing all the test examples as inputs to the PNN for density calculation, we can get the probabilities of C_1 as 0 and C_2 as 0.002688. Therefore, we can conclude that the second test example is negative for diabetes mellitus.

■ 6.10.4 Parameter Adjustment Using a Smoothing Factor

A factor that plays an important role in the learning and recalling processes of the PNN network is the smoothing factor. It controls the degree of scatter. Since the nodes in the output layer of a PNN represent the relative probability of each class, the smoothing factor controls the accuracy of recall in the PNN. Usually, the smoothing factor is between 0.1 and 1.0. In the following, we observe two extreme cases of the smoothing factor.

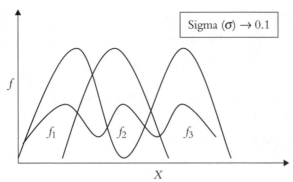

When sample data is chosen and provided as an input to the PNN model, it is treated like a point in space. The model determines the classification by calculating the probability of the point to see which probability density function the point will fall into. At this point, if the smoothing factor is chosen to be very close to 0.1, the probability density function will behave as shown in Figure 6.19. With this function, it is fairly easy to identify which probability density function a given point falls into.

As the other extreme case, if the smoothing factor is close to 1.0, it is far more difficult to classify which particular probability density function a point falls into because the probability density function will be a fusion as shown in Figure 6.20.

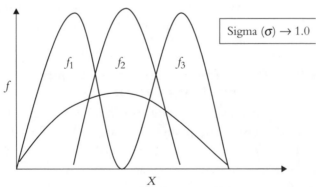

■ 6.11 CHAPTER SUMMARY

Creating computer systems embedded with "knowledge" or "intelligence" has long been a major goal of researchers in the AI community. Many interesting knowledge-based systems have been developed in the past few decades for applications such as medical diagnosis, engineering troubleshooting, and business decision making. Grounded on various AI-based learning techniques, several approaches have been followed to acquire knowledge or identify patterns directly from examples or from databases for an automatic data classification process.

Neural-network approaches, which are diverse in their origins and behaviors, have shown unique capabilities for analyzing qualitative symbolic data as well as quantitative numeric data. In connectionist learning, on the other hand, knowledge is synthesized and remembered by a network of interconnected neurons, weighted synapses, and threshold logic units. Learning algorithms can be applied to adjust connection weights so that the network can predict or classify unknown examples correctly. Learning systems rely on these algorithms to extract knowledge or identify patterns that exist in samples or databases.

In this chapter, four effective neural network models used for data classification were described with examples. Two types of learning models, supervised and unsupervised, used in data classification were briefly discussed, with a list of examples that belong to each model. Parameters used in the learning process were also discussed together with a detailed description of the network structures used in different models. The BPNN model was described in Section 6.7. Network structures and algorithms for learning and recall were given, and two examples were used to illustrate the algorithm. In Section 6.8, the BAM model was discussed and illustrated with its architecture, the learning algorithm, and an example. Two additional network models, the LVQ model and the PNN model, were also described.

This chapter contains numerous references to books and technical papers that are listed in the bibliography. Readers with further interest in neural network applications for data mining may find the additional references helpful. Finally, the list of websites provided here offers further information on neural network applications for data mining. These websites contain a wealth of information on neural network approaches in a wide range of areas.

SOME HELPFUL WEBSITES:

http://www.cs.qub.ac.uk/~F.Murtagh/data-mining.html#sect4
http://www.geocities.com/CapeCanaveral/1624/
http://www.spss.com/datamine/networks.htm
http://ulcar.uml.edu/~iag/CS/Intro-to-ANN.html
http://www.shef.ac.uk/psychology/gurney/notes/index.html
http://www.emsl.pnl.gov:2080/proj/neuron/neural/neural.journals.html
http://www.aist.go.jp/NIBH/~b0616/Lab/BSOM1/index.html
http://www.aic.nrl.navy.mil/~aha/references/rule-extraction-from-anns
http://attrasoft.com/decision/credit.html
http://fuzzy.cs.uni-magdeburg.de/papers.html
http://www.geocities.com/CapeCanaveral/1624/
http://www.nd.com/
http://www.wkap.nl/sampletoc.htm?1384-5810+1+1+1997
http://rfhs8012.fh-regensburg.de/~saj39122/jfroehl/diplom/e-1.html
http://www.oup-usa.org/acadref/nc_toc.html

■ 6.12 EXERCISES

Use Tables 6.11 and 6.12 to answer questions 1–3:

1. Train a BPNN model using the tables. Generate input data that are not included in the tables to simulate the model. Find the result for the new input data.

■ **TABLE 6.11 Training dataset**

ID	Internet shopping	Sex	Age range	Defaulted once	Defaulted twice	Defaulted more	Credit history
1	Y	M	17–21	N	N	N	Good
2	N	F	17–21	Y	Y	N	Medium
3	Y	M	22–34	N	N	N	Good
4	Y	F	22–34	Y	N	N	Medium
5	N	M	35–45	Y	Y	Y	Bad
6	N	F	35–45	N	N	N	Good
7	N	M	46–above	Y	Y	Y	Bad
8	N	F	46–above	N	N	N	Good

■ TABLE 6.12 Training dataset

ID	Years being driven	Sex	Age range	1st accident	2nd accident	3rd or more accident	Driving history
1	0–1	M	17–21	N	N	N	Good
2	5–10	F	17–21	Y	Y	N	Medium
3	5–10	M	22–34	N	N	N	Good
4	2–5	F	22–34	Y	N	N	Medium
5	2–5	M	35–45	Y	Y	Y	Bad
6	0–1	F	35–45	N	N	N	Good
7	10–more	M	46–above	Y	Y	Y	Bad
8	10–more	F	46–above	N	N	N	Good

2. Can you use the LVQ or PNN model to train for the data in the tables? Explain. If yes, train them with the same tables and simulate them with the same input as you used in question 1. Compare the results.

3. Among the models used in questions 1 and 2, which method do you prefer and why? What can you say about the results generated from these models?

4. The calcium database shown in Table 6.13 contains the results of a randomized comparative experiment to investigate the effect of calcium on blood pressure in African-American men. A treatment group of 10 men received a calcium supplement for 12 weeks, and a control group of 11 men received a placebo during the same period. All subjects had their blood pressure tested before and after the 12-week period. The table contains the following attributes:

   • *Treatment:* Whether subject received calcium or placebo
   • *Begin:* Seated systolic blood pressure before treatment
   • *End:* Seated systolic blood pressure after treatment
   • *Decrease:* Decrease in blood pressure (*Begin − End*)

   a. Train a BPNN network model using the table. Test the model with different sets of input data.

   b. Train a PNN model using the table. Test it with different sets of input data. Compare this result with the BPNN model.

■ **TABLE 6.13 Calcium table**

Treatment	Begin	End	Decrease
Calcium	107	100	7
Calcium	110	114	−4
Calcium	123	105	18
Calcium	129	112	17
Calcium	112	115	−3
Calcium	111	116	−5
Calcium	107	106	1
Calcium	112	102	10
Calcium	136	125	11
Calcium	102	104	−2
Placebo	123	124	−1
Placebo	109	97	12
Placebo	112	113	−1
Placebo	102	105	−3
Placebo	98	95	3
Placebo	114	119	−5
Placebo	119	114	5
Placebo	112	114	2
Placebo	110	121	−11
Placebo	117	118	−1
Placebo	130	133	−3

5. The fiber table shown in Table 6.14 contains the results of a study of the effects of dietary fiber on gastric problems. Twelve female subjects were fed a controlled diet. Before each meal they ate crackers containing either bran fiber, gum fiber, a combination of both, or no fiber (control). Their caloric intake was monitored. Subjects reported any gastric or other problems. The table contains the following attributes:

- *Cracker:* Type of fiber in the cracker
- *Diet:* One of four diets (type of cracker)
- *Subject:* An identification for each of the 12 subjects

■ **TABLE 6.14 Fiber table**

Cracker	Diet	Subject	Digested	Bloat
Control	1	3	1772.84	None
Bran	4	3	1752.63	Low
Combo	3	9	2121.97	Med
Gum	2	4	2558.61	High
Gum	2	1	2026.91	Med
Bran	4	1	2047.42	Low
Combo	3	1	2254.75	Low
Control	1	1	2353.21	Med
Combo	3	2	2153.36	None
Gum	2	2	2331.19	None
Bran	4	2	2547.77	None
Control	1	2	2591.12	None
Gum	2	3	2012.36	Low
Combo	3	3	1956.18	Low
Combo	3	4	2025.97	None
Bran	4	4	1669.12	None
Control	1	4	2452.73	None
Bran	4	5	2207.37	Low
Gum	2	5	1944.48	Med
Control	1	5	1927.68	Low
Combo	3	5	2190.1	High
Control	1	6	1635.28	None
Combo	3	6	1693.35	Low
Bran	4	6	1707.34	Low

- *Digested:* Digested calories. Difference between caloric intake and calories passed through system
- Bloat: Degree of bloating and flatulence reported by subjects
  a. Train a BPNN network model using the table. Test the model with different sets of input data.
  b. Train a PNN model using the table. Test it with different sets of input data. Compare this result with the BPNN model.

■ **TABLE 6.14** Fiber table (*Continued*)

Cracker	Diet	Subject	Digested	Bloat
Gum	2	6	1871.95	High
Gum	2	7	2245.03	None
Combo	3	7	2436.79	Low
Control	1	7	2667.14	Low
Bran	4	7	2766.86	None
Bran	4	8	2279.82	None
Combo	3	8	1844.77	High
Gum	2	8	2002.73	High
Control	1	8	2220.22	Med
Control	1	9	1888.29	Low
Gum	2	9	1804.27	High
Bran	4	9	2293.27	Med
Bran	4	10	2357.4	None
Control	1	10	2359.9	None
Combo	3	10	2292.46	Low
Gum	2	10	2433.46	High
Gum	2	11	1681.86	Low
Control	1	11	1902.75	None
Bran	4	11	2003.16	None
Combo	3	11	2137.12	Med
Combo	3	12	2203.07	Med
Control	1	12	2125.39	Low
Gum	2	12	2166.77	Med
Bran	4	12	2287.52	None

6. Use the stepping data table, Table 6.15, to conduct various learning and recall tasks using all the models discussed in this chapter including both the BPNN and PNN models.

This experiment was conducted by students at The Ohio State University in the fall of 1993 to explore the nature of the relationship between a person's heart rate and the frequency at which that person

■ TABLE 6.15 Stepping data table

Order	Block	Height	Frequency	RestHR	HR
16	2	0	0	60	75
18	2	0	1	63	84
19	2	1	2	69	135
21	2	1	0	69	108
25	2	0	2	69	93
17	4	1	1	96	141
20	4	1	0	87	120
22	4	0	0	90	99
23	4	1	2	93	153
27	4	0	2	87	129
24	3	1	1	72	99
26	3	0	1	69	93
28	3	1	0	78	93
29	3	0	2	72	99
30	3	1	2	78	129
1	5	0	0	87	93
2	1	1	1	87	111
3	6	1	2	81	120
4	5	0	2	75	123
5	1	0	1	81	96
6	6	1	0	84	99
7	1	1	0	84	99
8	5	1	1	90	129
9	6	0	1	75	90
10	1	0	0	78	87
11	6	0	0	84	84
12	5	0	1	90	108
13	1	0	2	78	96
14	6	1	1	84	90
15	5	1	2	90	147

stepped up and down steps of various heights. The response variable, heart rate, was measured in beats per minute. There were two different step heights: 5.75 inches (coded as 0) and 11.5 inches (coded as 1). There were three rates of stepping: 14 steps/min (coded as 0), 21 steps/min (coded as 1), and 28 steps/min (coded as 2). This resulted in six possible height/frequency combinations. Each subject performed the activity for three minutes. Subjects were kept on pace by the beat of an electric metronome. One experimenter counted the subject's pulse for 20 seconds before and after each trial. The subject always rested between trials until her or his heart rate returned to close to the beginning rate. Another experimenter kept track of the time spent stepping. Each subject was always measured and timed by the same pair of experimenters to reduce variability in the experiment. Each pair of experimenters was treated as a block. The table contains the following attributes:

- *Order:* The overall performance order of the trial
- *Block:* The subject and experimenters' block number
- *Height:* Zero if step at the low height (5.75"), 1 if at the high height (11.5")
- *Frequency:* The rate of stepping. Zero if slow (14 steps/min), 1 if medium (21 steps/min), 2 if high (28 steps/min)
- *RestHR:* The resting heart rate of the subject before the trial, in beats per minute
- *HR:* The final heart rate of the subject after the trial, in beats per minute

■ 6.13 SELECTED BIBLIOGRAPHIC NOTES

A general introduction to neural networks and data mining is given in [Eide 1996], [Klimasauskas 1989], [Costa 1996], [Lewin 2000], [Lu 1996], and [Towell 1994]. [Looney 1996] describe advances in feed-forward neural networks, whereas [Ye 1989] introduces application of the PCMN neural network for isolated word recognition. [Wang 1998] and [Liang 2002] introduced the application of neural networks to biological data mining. [Andrews 1995], [Hongchun 1996], [Hruschka 1999], [Hruschka 2000a], [Fu 1998], and [Hruschka 2000b] introduced various methods based on neural networks to extract rules from various databases.

[Boz 2002] describes a method of decision-tree extraction from trained neural networks. A network intrusion detection system based on artificial neural networks was introduced by [Wang 2004]. [Guo 2004] introduced the application of probabilistic neural networks. [Potts 1999] presented a generalized additive neural network approach for data mining, while [Maglaveras 1998] presented an adaptive backpropagation neural network for real-time ischemia. [Khan 2004] and [Brendon 2004] worked on multimedia data mining for automatic classification of speech and music using neural networks, whereas [Lin 2000] worked on temporal data mining using neural networks.

Furthermore, the application of neural networks was extended to medical and pharmaceutical areas as reported by [Tham 2003] and [Kewley 2000]. Diagnosis and control of highway surfaces using a neural system was presented by [Luchetta 1998], whereas sales data mining using a neural network was demonstrated by [Thomas 1999]. [Jelonek 1993] showed the comparison and combination of neural networks and rough sets for classification of histological pictures. [Merkl 1997] showed the effectiveness of hierarchical neural networks for the exploration of legal text, whereas [Shanmugasundaram 2002] presented the use of recurrent neural networks for strategic data mining of sales. [Chen 1997] described the application of self-organizing neural networks, whereas [Feng 1996] showed the effectiveness of neural network applications to gold mines.

■ 6.14 CHAPTER BIBLIOGRAPHY

[Andrews 1995] R. Andrews, J. Diederich, and A. Tickle: "A Survey and Critique of Techniques For Extracting Rules From Trained Artificial Neural Networks," *Knowledge Based Systems,* Vol. 8, pp. 373–389, 1995.

[Boz 2002] O. Boz: "Extracting Decision Trees from Trained Neural Networks," *Proceedings of the 8th ACM SIGKDD International Conference on Knowledge Discovery and Data Mining,* 2002.

[Brendon 2004] J. W. Brendon, D. Deng, G. L. Benwell: "A Wavelet-based Neuro-Fuzzy System for Data Mining Small Image Sets," *Proceedings of Australasian Information Security, Data Mining and Web Intelligence, and Software Internationalisation,* 2004.

[Chen 1997] L. Chen and J. Gasteiger: "Knowledge Discovery in Reaction Databases: Landscaping Organic Reactions by a Self-Organizing Neural Network," *Journal of the American Chemical Society,* Vol. 17, No. 119, pp. 4033–4042, 1997.

[Costa 1996] M. C. A. Costa: "Data Mining High Performance Computing Using Neural Networks," *Advances in Knowledge Discovery and Data Mining*, MIT Press, California, 1996.

[Eide 1996] Å. Eide, R. Johansson, Th. Lindblad, and C. S. Lindsey: "Data Mining and Neural Networks for Knowledge Discovery," *The 5th International Workshop on Software Engineering, Artificial Intelligence, and Expert Systems, for High Energy and Nuclear Physics (AIHENP)*, Lausanne, Switzerland, pp. 251–254, 1996.

[Feng 1996] X. Feng, S. Webber, and M. U. Ozbay: "Neural Network Assessment of Rockburst Risks for Deep Gold Mines in South Africa," *International Journal of Rock Mechanics and Mining*, 1996.

[Fu 1998] L. M. Fu: "A Neural Network Model for Learning Domain Rules Based on Its Activation Function Characteristics," *IEEE Transactions on Neural Networks*, Vol. 9, No. 5, pp. 787–795, 1998.

[Guo 2004] J. Guo, Y. Lin, and Z. Sun: "A Novel Method for Protein Subcellular Localization Based on Boosting and Probabilistic Neural Network," *Proceedings of the 2nd Conference on Asia-Pacific Bioinformatics*, Vol. 29, 2004.

[Hongchun 1996] Y. Hongchun, X. Fanlun, and D. Chao: "Neural Network Method for Extraction of Evaluation Rules of Soil Fertility," *IEEE Transactions on Knowledge and Data Engineering*, Vol. 8, No. 1, pp. 183–188, 1996.

[Hruschka 1999] E. R. Hruschka and N. F. Ebecken: "Rule Extraction from Neural Networks: Modified RX Algorithm," *International Joint Conference on Neural Networks*, Vol. 4, pp. 2504–2508, 1999.

[Hruschka 2000a] E. R. Hruschka and N. F. Ebecken: "Using a Clustering Genetic Algorithm for Rule Extraction from Artificial Neural Networks," *IEEE Symposium on Combinations of Evolutionary Computation and Neural Networks*, 11–13, 199–206, 2000.

[Hruschka 2000b] E. R. Hruschka and N. F. Ebecken: "Applying a Clustering Genetic Algorithm for Extracting Rules From a Supervised Neural Network," *Proceedings of the IEEE-INNS-ENNS International Joint Conference on Neural Networks (IJCNN)*, Vol. 3, pp. 24–27; 407–412, 2000.

[Jelonek 1993] J. Jelonek, K. Krawiec, R. Slowinski, J. Stefanowski, and J. Szymas: "Neural Networks and Rough Sets—Comparison and Combination for Classification of Histological Pictures," *RSKD*, pp. 426–433, 1993.

[Kewley 2000] R. Kewley, M. Embrechts, and C. Breneman: "Data Strip Mining for the Virtual Design of Pharmaceuticals with Neural Networks," *IEEE Transactions on Neural Networks*, Vol. 11, No. 3, pp. 668–679, 2000.

[Khan 2004] M. K. S. Khan, W. G. Al-Khatib, and M. Moinuddin: "Multimedia Data Mining: Automatic Classification of Speech and Music Using Neural Networks," *Proceedings of the 2nd ACM International Workshop on Multimedia Databases*, 2004.

[Klimasauskas 1989] C. C. Klimasauskas: "Neural Networks: A New Technology for Information Processing," *DATABASE*, Vol. 20, No. 1, pp. 21–23, 1989.

[Lewin 2000] D. I. Lewin: "Getting Clinical About Neural Networks," *IEEE Intelligent Systems*, 2000.

[Liang 2002] Y. Liang and A. Kelemen: "Mining Heterogeneous Gene Expression Data with Time Lagged Recurrent Neural Networks," *Proceedings of the 8th ACM SIGKDD International Conference on Knowledge Discovery and Data Mining*, 2002.

[Lin 2000] S. Lin, C. Sun, and C. Chen: "Temporal Data Mining Using Genetic Algorithm and Neural Network," *Journal of Geographical Systems*, 2000.

[Lippmann 1987] R. P. Lippmann: "An Introduction to Computing with Neural Nets," *IEEE ASSP Magazine*, Vol. 3, No. 4, PP. 4–22, April, 1987.

[Looney 1996] C. G. Looney: "Advances in Feedforward Neural Networks: Demystifying Knowledge Acquiring Black Boxes," *IEEE Transactions on Knowledge and Data Engineering*, Vol. 8, No. 2, pp. 211–226, 1996.

[Lu 1996] H. Lu, R. Setiono, and H. Liu: "Effective Data Mining Using Neural Networks," *IEEE Transactions on Knowledge and Data Engineering*, Vol. 8, No. 6, pp. 957–961, 1996.

[Luchetta 1998] A. Luchetta, S. Manetti, and F. Francini: "Forecast: A Neural System for Diagnosis and Control of Highway Surfaces," *IEEE Intelligent Systems*, Vol. 13, No. 3, pp. 20–26, 1998.

[Maglaveras 1998] N. Maglaveras, T. Stamkopoulos, C. Pappas, and M. Strintz: "An Adaptive Backpropagation Neural Network for Real-Time Ischemia Episodes Detection: Development and Performance Analysis Using the European ST–T Database," *IEEE Transactions on Biomedical Engineering*, Vol. 45, 805–813, 1998.

[Merkl 1997] D. Merkl and E. Schweighofer: "The Exploration of Legal Text Corpora with Hierarchical Neural Networks: A Guided Tour in Public International Law," *Proceedings of the 6th International Conference on Artificial Intelligence and Law*, 1997.

[Potts 1999] W. J. Potts: "Generalized Additive Neural Networks," *Proceedings of the 5th ACM SIGKDD International Conference on Knowledge Discovery and Data Mining*, 1999.

[Shanmugasundaram 2002] J. Shanmugasundaram, M. V. Nagendra Prasas, S. Vadhavkar, and A. Gupta: "Use of Recurrent Neural Networks for Strategic Data Mining of Sales," MIT Sloan Working Paper No. 4347–02; Eller College Working Paper No. 1029–05, February, 2002. Available at http://ssrn.com/abstract=300679.

[Specht 1990] Donald Specht: "Probabilistic Neural Network," *Neural Networks*, Vol. 3, No. 1, pp. 109–118, Elsevier Publishing, 1990.

[Tham 2003] C. K. Tham, C. K. Heng, and W. C. Chin: "Predicting Risk of Coronary Artery Disease from DNA Microarray-Based Genotyping Using Neural

Networks and Other Statistical Analysis Tools," *Journal of Bioinformatics and Computational Biology*, Vol. 1, No. 3, p. 2003.

[Thomas 1999] T. S. Gruca, B. R. Klemz, and E. Petersen: "Mining Sales Data Using a Neural Network Model of Market Response," *ACM SIGKDD Explorations*, Vol. 1, No. 1, 1999.

[Towell 1994] G. Towell and J. W. Shavlik: "Knowledge-Based Artificial Neural Networks," *Artificial Intelligence*, Vol. 70, No. 1–2, pp. 119–165, 1994.

[Wang 1998] J. Wang, Q. Ma, D. Shasha, and C. H. Wu: "Application of Neural Networks to Biological Data Mining: A Case Study in Protein Sequence Classification," *The PIR-International Protein Sequence Database, Nucleic Acids Research*, Vol. 26, No. 1, pp. 27–32, 1998.

[Wang 2004] J. Wang, Z. Wang, and K. Dai: "A Network Intrusion Detection System Based on Artificial Neural Networks," *Proceedings of the 3rd International Conference on Information Security*, 2004.

[Ye 1989] H. Ye, S. Wang, and F. Robert: "A PCMN Neural Network for Isolated Word Recognition," *Speech Communication*, Vol. 8, No. 4, pp. 141–153, 1989.

CHAPTER 7

Clustering

■ 7.1 INTRODUCTION

In the previous chapters, we discussed several data-mining techniques including association rules, classification, statistics, rough sets, and neural networks as methods to retrieve useful and meaningful information from a database. The basic concepts of these techniques were discussed and a number of examples were given as illustrations. In this chapter, clustering will be described as another efficient knowledge discovery method that can be used to search for interesting patterns in large collections of data. Various clustering algorithms will be illustrated by examples.

Clustering can be used for data mining to group together items in a database with similar characteristics. A *cluster* is a set of data items that share common properties and can be considered as a separate entity. Hence, a database can be viewed as consisting of multiple clusters. This has several advantages. One is that the clusters can be profiled according to specific data analysis objectives, and high-level queries can be formed to achieve goals such as "identifying critical business values" or "discovering interesting patterns from the database." More advantages will be seen as we discuss the techniques and procedures clustering for data mining, which will also be demonstrated with practical examples. Four categories of clustering algorithms and methods will be examined and compared, and their strengths and weaknesses will be discussed.

■ 7.2 DEFINITION OF CLUSTERS AND CLUSTERING

As the amount of data stored and managed in a database increases, the need to simplify the vast amount of data also increases. Clustering is defined as the process of classifying a large group of data items into smaller groups that share the same or similar properties. Due to its usefulness in classifying and simplifying data, clustering has been extensively studied and has been demonstrated as a tool for dealing with massive amounts of data. This process is called *cluster analysis* in many statistical publications (see the bibliography at the end of this chapter for complete references). Therefore, the terms clustering and cluster analysis are interchangeable.

Clustering can be used to analyze various datasets in different fields for various purposes, and many algorithms have been proposed and developed. It is very difficult to describe and evaluate all of them in one chapter, so interested readers should refer to specific books or published papers related to cluster analysis for more detailed information. The generic properties of clustering procedures are summarized and illustrated here.

A cluster is a basic unit of classification of initially unclassified data based on common properties. Understanding the various characteristics of clusters will help us understand the details of the algorithms used for cluster analysis. Unfortunately, it is somewhat difficult to explicitly say what a cluster is due to the diverse goals of clustering, and different researchers define it differently. For example, Dubes and Jain define a cluster as a number of *similar objects* collected or grouped together in [Dubes 1988]. In addition, Everitt documented various definitions of a cluster as follows [Everitt 1980]:

- A cluster is a set of entities that are *alike* or a set of entities from different clusters that are *not alike*.
- A cluster is an aggregation of points in the test space such that the distance between any two points in the cluster is *less than* the distance between any point within the cluster and any other point outside the cluster.
- A cluster is a connected region of a multidimensional space containing a relatively *high density* of points.
- A cluster is a group of contiguous elements of a statistical population.

From these definitions, we can see that whether clusters consist of entities, points, or regions, the components within a cluster are more similar in some respects to each other than to other components outside of the cluster or to entities classified into other clusters. This description covers two important points. One is *similarity*, which can be reflected with distance measures, and the other is *classification*, which suggests the objective of clustering. Therefore, clustering can be defined as a process of identifying groups of data that are similar in a certain aspect and building a classification among them.

For example, in psychiatry an objective of clustering may be to identify individuals who are likely to attempt suicide. The results of clustering in this case could become the basis for studies of the causes and treatments of common problems associated with suicidal actions. In social services, an objective of clustering may be to select groups of elderly people who can suggest how services should be economically and efficiently allocated. In market research the objective of clustering may be to identify groups of customers that with similar consumer habits.

In summary, the main objective of clustering is to identify groups of data that meet one of the following two conditions:

1. The members in a group are very similar (similarity-within criterion).
2. The groups are clearly separated from one another (separation-between criterion).

The following examples of clustering represented with scatter plots will help illustrate the concept and the challenges of clustering. The two clusters in Figure 7.1(a) are very homogeneous because no two points within a cluster are very far apart. In addition, these clusters are also clearly separated from each other. In Figure 7.1(b), the two clusters satisfy the separation-between criterion, but they do not meet the similarity-within criterion. Some points at the right boundary of the left cluster are closer to some points in the right cluster than they are to the points at the opposite side of their own cluster. Figure 7.1(c) shows a more extreme example of this case. Figure 7.1(d) indicates that the data are clustered into only one group under either criterion, whereas in Figure 7.1(e) the two clusters seem to satisfy the similarity-within criterion if some points considered as noise are excluded. Both Figure 7.1(f) and 7.1(g) show the clustered data that can satisfy either the separation-between or similarity-within criterion if points considered as noise are excluded and the rest of the points are concentrated. These clusters

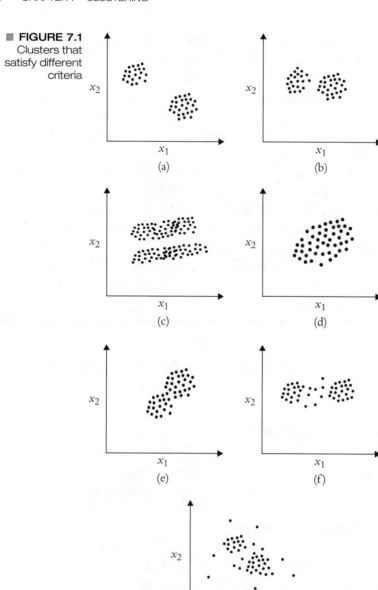

■ FIGURE 7.1
Clusters that
satisfy different
criteria

are the result of adding extra points, known as *noise*, to both Figure 7.1(a) and Figure 7.1(b), respectively.

In general, clustering is situation-specific and often exploratory. For instance, people can be grouped by gender, age, address, education, occupation, earned income per year, number of dependents, and so on. If a management team for a real estate company wants to decide how many buildings at various price levels should be constructed, potential customers may be better grouped according to earned income per year rather than age, because decision making for a home purchase is more likely to depend on annual income. As another example, for an insurance company to set appropriate driver's insurance premiums, customers should be grouped by age, number of dependents, and annual insurance claims rather than by annual income and education. This is because the number of accidents is more likely to be related to age and number of dependents than to annual income and education of a driver.

■ 7.3 CLUSTERING PROCEDURES

Because of the diversity of cluster definitions, there are a variety of clustering algorithms handling different types of clusters. However, some common aspects can be identified. A clustering process usually involves the following steps:

1. *Object Selection*: The entities to be clustered are selected in a manner such that the entities are representatives of the cluster structures that are inherent in the data.

2. *Variable Selection*: The variable that will represent the measurements of the entities must be selected. Correct selection of the variable will result in a meaningful cluster structure. The variable should contain adequate information to produce the correct clustering results.

3. *Variable Standardization*: Since variables may be measured with different systems, they may initially be incomparable. To solve this problem, the variables are usually standardized, although this step is optional. Standardizing variables will be discussed in Section 7.4.

4. *Similarity Measurement*: Similarity or dissimilarity between a pair of data items or among many items must be calculated. This will usually be the basis for a similarity matrix. Sometimes more than one attribute can be considered and analyzed. This is called *multivariate analysis*.

5. *Clustering Entities*: Based on the similarity or dissimilarity measurement, a pair of items can be compared and classified into the same group or different groups. This process is applied to all items in one data record until the items can be classified into two clusters. Recursively following this step will result in a classification with various clusters. This step is a critical part of clustering. Grouping data items into the same or different groups is dependent on the criteria used in the clustering algorithm. Obviously, different algorithms will produce different cluster structures.

6. *Cluster Refinement*: The data items that compose the clusters should be tested to see whether the items are clustered correctly. If they are not, items must be rearranged among the clusters until a final classification system is formed.

7. *Interpretation of Classification System*: Based on the objectives of the clustering and the algorithms used for the clustering, the results must be explained and justified. The results are interpreted to determine whether there is an important cluster structure in the dataset or whether the obtained cluster structure can be replicated in a second sample, for example. Comments can also be presented to evaluate the clustering.

■ 7.4 CLUSTERING CONCEPTS

After following the seven steps of the general clustering procedure, the items in the database will be ready for analysis through clustering. Before proceeding with clustering, however, we will discuss how to choose variables, how to standardize them if needed, what methods we should use to measure similarity, why we need weight and threshold values in clustering, and how to make our resultant clustering patterns meaningful and informative. Answering these questions will help us produce an optimal clustering result.

■ 7.4.1 Choosing Variables

The variables chosen for clustering must be relevant to the problem being considered. For example, if the problem is identifying which type of drivers are at high risk of insurance claims, then age, penalty points received, auto make, marital status, and zip code are all valid choices for variables because they all directly or indirectly affect the number of claims. On the other hand, the inclusion of a variable such as the height or weight of an automobile may adversely affect the outcome of the categorization because they are not relevant to the problem. Therefore, a potential investigator has many choices when deciding the strategy of the initial process. How many variables should an investigator choose to adequately categorize an object? The answer is *the fewer the better* to adequately address the problem since the inclusion of irrelevant variables drastically affects the outcome. If a single variable will bring about a straightforward clustering result, it will be easy to interpret the cluster structures. If more than one variable is selected, interpretation of the results will be less clear. If the variables selected are not tightly related, it will be extremely difficult to interpret the clustering, and the results may not be informative. To instructively interpret the results from a multivariate selection, tools such as Principal Component Analysis (PCA) and Discrimination Analysis (DA) may be needed. Information about these tools is provided in the bibliography at the end of this chapter.

Another issue with variable selection arises when objects have missing values for variables such as a *no response* choice in a survey. Should those values be estimated or should the investigator just ignore the objects with missing values? The choice is not easy because estimating the omitted values using (say) the mean of known values might inadvertently distort any potentially useful information. Furthermore, the omission of the objects with missing data might cause useful inferences to be missed, especially if just one or two out of many variables are missing on a project involving very few objects to begin with.

■ 7.4.2 Similarity and Dissimilarity Measurement

Similarity or dissimilarity refers to the likeness of two objects. A proximity measure can be used to describe similarity or dissimilarity. There are several techniques in widespread use to determine the proximity of one object in relation to another. The most intuitive of these is a distance measure. Unlike correlation or association, measures of distance are based on the magnitudes of objects, not the patterns of their variation. Since the magnitude is normally the most important grouping criterion, distance measures are most commonly used to define how far apart one object is from another.

■ TABLE 7.1 Number of claims and ages
of the insured

Name	Age	Claim
a	1	1
b	2	2
c	10	2
d	13	3
e	8	0

The Euclidean distance is defined as follows, where $D(a, b)$ is the distance between object a and b with respect to attribute i:

$$D(a, b) = \left(\sum_{i=1}^{k} (a_i - b_i)^2 \right)^{\frac{1}{2}}$$

Let's look at an example to see how similarity is measured. Table 7.1 shows the number of claims and the ages of the insured of an insurance company.

If we consider two objects, a and b, the distance between them is $D(a, b) = [(1 - 2)^2 + (1 - 2)^2]^{1/2} = 1.414$. In a similar way, the distances between all pairs of objects can be calculated, as shown in Table 7.2.

The dissimilarity measurement is the distance between the two objects being considered. The larger the measure of distance, the more dissimilar the two objects are. Some investigators prefer using similarity to describe proximity. The similarity is often defined as the complement of dissimilarity, i.e., *Similarity = 1 − Distance.*

■ TABLE 7.2 Distances between any pair of the insured

Names	a	b	c	d	e
a	0.000				
b	1.414	0.000			
c	9.055	8.000	0.000		
d	12.166	11.045	3.162	0.000	
e	7.071	6.325	2.828	5.831	0.000

■ 7.4.3 Standardization of Variables

In the example of the insured data shown in Table 7.1, we considered two variables (age and claims). These two variables are measured with different units. If we examine further, a very important problem arises. The problem is how to represent variables with different magnitudes in relation to one another on the same scale. This is a common question because different variables are often represented in different dimensions (units) as can be seen from the following examples of representational units:

1. *Counts*: How many people voted for Ronald Reagan? This unit has no scale at all.
2. *Ratio*: The number of moles of an element. This is determined by calculating a sample's mass in relation to its atomic weight.
3. *Interval Scale*: Barometric pressure. This is determined by how much a variable deviates from the standard pressure of, say, 760 torrs at sea level.
4. *Ordinal Scale*: Gross domestic product. An arbitrary scale that changes when its variables are changed.
5. *Categorical Scale*: Taxonomy. This will change with the input of different information. For example, a plant can be *evergreen* or *deciduous*.

Using our previous example, we can see how different system units will influence the similarity measurement. Suppose that the attribute *age* is represented as a month rather than year. The range of values will become much greater, and the distance between two objects will be mostly determined by *age*. The contribution of the attribute *claims* will be insignificant. For example, the recalculated distance between objects a and b will be: $D(a, b) = [(12 - 24)^2 + (1 - 2)^2]^{1/2} = (144 + 1)^{1/2} = 12.04$. A clustering result based on this kind of similarity measurement would be incorrect and uninformative.

To correct this problem, data with different units should be standardized for a uniform scale. The standardization of an attribute involves two steps: (1) calculate the difference between the value of the attribute and the mean of all samples involving the attribute, and (2) divide the difference by its standard deviation. After standardization, all objects can be considered as being measured with the same unit, and the contributions of each attribute to the similarity measurement can be balanced. As a result, we can obtain an informative and reliable clustering result. In addition to the standardization of data, we also have other ways of adjusting data to produce more informative clustering patterns—namely, weight and threshold values (sometimes called critical values).

■ 7.4.4 Weights and Threshold Values

Weight is the preference of certain attributes of a database. It is assigned by investigators and is usually defined by a value between zero and one [0–1]. A value of 1 means investigators want the highest degree of consideration for the attribute, while the zero value means the contribution of the attribute will be ignored. Using weights, investigators can value the contribution of one attribute more than others for more effective data analysis. However, weighting may make clustering results arguable because it is often difficult to set a correct weighting value.

Weights can also be represented with the inverse of variance of an attribute. However, it should *not* be applied on an equal-variance scale where the weighting is inversely proportional to the data. The following example illustrates this case. From Table 7.1, we know that the variance for age is 26.7 and is 1.3 for claim. So, the inverse of 26.7 is 0.037 and the inverse of 1.3 is 0.77. These two inverses become the weights of *age* and *claim*, respectively. If these weights are used in calculating the Euclidean distances between the two objects to make all variables have the same average contribution to the squared distances, we will have a new matrix as shown in Table 7.3. Note that the distance between a and b can be calculated by $[0.037(1 - 2)^2 + 0.77(1 - 2)^2]^{1/2} = 0.898$.

Comparing the recalculated distance from a to b with a to d, we find that there seems to be a less distinct clustering effect. Overall, the inter-cluster variance will be reduced proportionally to the intra-cluster variance. This will make the clusters less distinct. Because of this, weights should be used with caution.

■ TABLE 7.3 Distances between two insurance customers with weights

	a	*b*	*c*	*d*	*e*
a	0.000				
b	0.989	0.000			
c	1.941	1.539	0.000		
d	2.900	2.291	1.050	0.000	
e	1.607	2.100	1.800	2.803	0.000

Threshold value is a designated number specified by investigators to determine the placement of an individual object or a group of objects in a cluster. This value is used as decision criteria to determine which components of potential clusters will be examined based on their similarities. If the similarity measurement is larger than the threshold value, it is very likely that the components can be placed into the same cluster and vice versa. Because of this, the threshold value is called a critical value in some algorithms. Since threshold values are arbitrarily set by investigators, clusters resulting from the threshold value approach will be somewhat subjective. Even if it is essential for an algorithm to set a threshold value, selecting a correct threshold value is not an easy task. We will illustrate the use of threshold values in Section 7.5, where different clustering algorithms are presented.

■ 7.4.5 Association Rules

An association rule is an expression $X \Rightarrow Y$ that shows a frequently occurring pattern of information in a database, where $X = \{X_1, X_2, ..., X_n\}$ and $Y = \{Y_1, Y_2, ..., Y_m\}$ are sets of attributes. The rule represents the fact that the occurrence of pattern X implies the occurrence of pattern Y. Patterns X and Y can be either transaction data or non-transaction data. For transaction data, which is also called market basket data, X and Y represent sets of items in a market transaction. For example,

$$(\text{milk, butter}) \Rightarrow (\text{bread})$$

is an association rule that states *if customers buy milk and butter, then it is highly likely that they will also buy bread.* The rules generated from market basket data represent associations among the items purchased together by customers at the checkout counter.

For non-transaction data, however, an attribute can be classified either as categorical or non-categorical. Categorical (or nominal) attributes are those that have a finite number of values without relative ordering or meaning among themselves. Examples of categorical attributes include *name, zip code, account types, hair color, make of car, and degree.* Non-categorical attributes, also referred to as ordinal or quantitative attributes, do have an implicit ordering and meaning in relation to each other and can assume continuous values, usually within a specified range. Examples of non-categorical attributes include *salary, age, insurance premium,* and *interest rate.*

For non-transaction data, patterns X and Y are conjunctions of (attribute = value) equalities. For example, (*no.-in-household* = 4) $\wedge$ (*household-income* = \$50,000) $\Rightarrow$ (*no.-of-cars* = 2) is an association rule with respect to the non-transaction data. The rule implies that if the number of family members in a household is four and the entire household income is \$50,000, then it is highly likely that the number of cars in the family is 2.

Since the number of specific attribute values for these non-transaction data may be hundreds or even thousands, there can be an exponential number of rules to be examined. Clustering rules that are similar and adjacent can significantly reduce the overall number of association rules. Instead of having a set of (attribute = value) equalities, value ranges using inequalities such as (value1 $\leq$ attribute < value2) are used in clustered rules. For example, the following four association rules

(*no.-in-household* = 5) $\wedge$ (*household-income* = \$59,000) $\Rightarrow$ (*no.-of-cars* = 3)

(*no.-in-household* = 4) $\wedge$ (*household-income* = \$55,000) $\Rightarrow$ (*no.-of-cars* = 3)

(*no-in-household* = 5) $\wedge$ (*household-income* = \$58,000) $\Rightarrow$ (*no.-of-cars* = 3)

(*no.-in-household* = 4) $\wedge$ (*household-income* = \$58,000) $\Rightarrow$ (*no.-of-cars* = 3)

can be combined into the following clustered rule:

$$(4 \leq \textit{no.-in-household} < 6) \wedge (\$55,000 \leq \textit{household-income} < \$60,000)$$
$$\Rightarrow (\textit{no.-of-cars} = 3)$$

The rules generated from a given database should be meaningful, understandable, and useful to the user. Clustered rules are much easier to interpret, understand, and visualize than non-clustered rules when the number of generated rules is very large. In the next section, we will see how association rules are used to partition a database and make the database intelligent.

■ 7.5   CLUSTERING ALGORITHMS

Although it is well established that the similarity of objects is used for clustering, the definitions of similarity and the methods employed to obtain similarity are varied. This fact, along with the variety of definitions for clusters, has brought about many algorithms for clustering databases. For example, Everitt discussed four types of clustering algorithms: hierarchical, optimization, density-search, and clumping algorithms [Everitt 1980]. Other authors introduced k-prototype, k-mode, hypergraph and association rule algorithms. (For more information, refer to the selected bibliographic notes at the end of the chapter.) In this section, we will introduce hierarchical, partition, k-means, k-prototype, density-search, and association rule algorithms using some database examples.

■ 7.5.1 Hierarchical Algorithms

The algorithm for hierarchical clustering mainly involves transforming a proximity matrix, which records the dissimilarity measurements of all pairs of objects in a database, into a sequence of nested partitions. The sequence can be represented with a tree-like dendrogram in which each cluster is nested into an enclosing cluster. The number of nodes and leaves in the dendrogram is not determined until clustering is complete. To determine the number of nodes and leaves, investigators must set an appropriate critical value so that the resulting clusters can include a variable number of individual objects. In other words, the size of the clusters can range from a single object to all of the objects. Hierarchical algorithms can be further categorized into two kinds: agglomerative and divisive.

An agglomerative algorithm starts with a disjoint clustering, which places each of the n objects in a cluster by itself and then merges clusters based on their similarities. The merging continues until all the individual objects are grouped into a single cluster. Whenever a merger occurs, the number of clusters is reduced by one. The similarities between the new merged cluster and any of the other clusters need to be recalculated. The similarity measurement is often a Euclidean distance. The merging can be done in two situations. The first is when two individual objects or clusters are very similar. The second is when the population of a cluster is very small. In this case the cluster may be merged with the most similar one, even if the similarity is not very close.

A divisive algorithm separates an initial cluster containing all n individuals into finer groups. To decide splitting, the population of the cluster is used. If the population is too large, the splitting decision has to be carefully made. Non-symmetrical distributions and distributions with large variances along one direction are possible candidates for splitting.

The similarity measurement with the Euclidean distance can be determined by minimum, maximum, average, or centroid distance between two clusters to be merged. There are four hierarchical clustering methods corresponding to each criterion. They are called single-link, complete-link, group-average, and centroid clustering methods, respectively. The single-link and complete-link methods consider the distance between each individual object in each cluster, whereas the group-average method concerns the distances of all objects in the clusters. When two attributes are selected for clustering, the centroid method is used. The method considers the two attributes as the two values in a coordinate and measures the distance between the two objects in the coordinate. The single-link method differs from the complete-link method in that it is based on the shortest distance. In this method, after merging the two individual objects with the shortest distance, the third object with the next shortest distance is considered. The third object can either join the first two objects to form a single cluster or become a new cluster by itself so that two separate clusters are formed. After that a new object is considered again. This process continues until all individual objects are classified into a single cluster. On the other hand, the complete-link method is based on the maximum distance within a cluster. The maximum distance between any two individual objects in each cluster represents the smallest sphere that can enclose all of the objects in the cluster.

Since the distances can be represented by a graph using geometric structures, graph theory algorithms are used for hierarchical clustering. The graph theory algorithm with the single-link method begins with the Minimum Spanning Tree (MST) for $G(\infty)$, which is the proximity graph containing all $n(n-1)/2$ edges, where n is the number of vertices. Although a single-link hierarchy can be derived from the MST, the MST cannot be generated from a single-link hierarchical clustering method. For simplicity, we assume that no two edges in the MST have the same weight.

The procedure of the agglomerative hierarchical algorithms can be summarized into the following steps:

1. Sort the values of the attribute that is considered for clustering;
2. With the disjoint clustering, let each cluster contain a single object;
3. Find the distances between all pairs of objects;
4. Merge the objects or the groups based on their similarities so that the total number of clusters is decreased by one, and recalculate the distances

between any pairs of clusters according to the clustering criteria of different methods;

5. Repeat step 4 until the total number of clusters becomes one.

To illustrate how the algorithm works, we will present the four specific methods of agglomerative algorithms with three example databases.

Single-link Method

The key point of the single-link method is to use the minimum or shortest Euclidean distance as the similarity measure to merge the objects. The example database used for this method contains information about the yearly income of people with different education levels and work experience. The data is shown in Table 7.4. The following abbreviations are used for the values of major and degree: CS = Computer Science, EE = Electrical Engineering, MS = Master's Degree, and BS = Bachelor's Degree. The unit of salary is 1000 in U.S. dollars.

As mentioned in Section 7.4, before clustering we should choose the target attributes to be used as our clustering criterion. In this example, we select *salary* as the criterion. After following step 1 (sort the attribute) and step 2 (create clusters with a single object), we obtain the results shown in Table 7.5. There are eight clusters in the table named $C_1, C_2, \ldots, C_8$.

■ TABLE 7.4 Yearly income with different education levels and work experience

ID	Major	Degree	Salary (K)	Year(s)
S_1	CS	MS	48	2
S_2	EE	MS	51	2
S_3	CS	BS	38	1
S_4	CS	MS	85	4
S_5	EE	BS	41	3
S_6	CS	MS	90	5
S_7	CS	MS	48	1
S_8	CS	MS	48	3

■ TABLE 7.5 Clusters based on salary attribute

Cluster ID	Salary (K)
C_1	38
C_2	41
C_3	48
C_4	48
C_5	48
C_6	51
C_7	85
C_8	90

Using the data in Table 7.5, we calculate the distances between any pair of clusters according to Step 3. The result is the matrix presented in Table 7.6. From the table, we can see that $D(C_1, C_2) = 3$, $D(C_1, C_3) = 10$, and so on.

In step 4, we merge the clusters that have the shortest distances. Because C_3, C_4, and C_5 have the shortest distances (values are zero), they are merged together to reduce the number of clusters. The merged cluster is named C_{345}.

Because the three merged clusters have the same distances among them, we do not need to recalculate the distances concerning other clusters. Table 7.7 shows the result of step 4.

■ TABLE 7.6 Distances between any pair of clusters

	C_1	C_2	C_3	C_4	C_5	C_6	C_7	C_8
C_1	0							
C_2	3	0						
C_3	10	7	0					
C_4	10	7	0	0				
C_5	10	7	0	0	0			
C_6	13	10	3	3	3	0		
C_7	47	44	37	37	37	34	0	
C_8	52	49	42	42	42	39	5	0

▦ TABLE 7.7 Distances between clusters after merger
of C_3, C_4, and C_5

	C_1	C_2	C_{345}	C_6	C_7	C_8
C_1	0					
C_2	3	0				
C_{345}	10	7	0			
C_6	13	10	3	0		
C_7	47	44	37	34	0	
C_8	52	49	42	39	5	0

After the first merger, we still have six clusters. Because the number of clusters is not one, we should repeat step 4 until the number becomes one. It is easy to see that the shortest distances involve two pairs of clusters, (C_1, C_2) and (C_{345}, C_6). Let us work with (C_1, C_2) first. Because C_1 and C_2 have different distance values from other clusters, we face a problem. For example, $D(C_1, C_{345}) = 10$ and $D(C_2, C_{345}) = 7$. If C_1 and C_2 are merged, which distance should we choose, $D(C_1, C_{345})$ or $D(C_2, C_{345})$? In the single-link method, we select the minimum distance. Hence, $D(C_2, C_{345}) = 7$ is used for $D(C_{12}, C_{345})$ after the merger of C_1 and C_2. After recalculating the distances between all clusters, we get the new distance matrix presented in Table 7.8. At this point, we have five clusters remaining to be merged.

The merging process should continue until there is only one cluster that contains all the objects. We recommend that readers complete this example

▦ TABLE 7.8 Distances between clusters after merger
of C_1 and C_2 with the single-link method

	C_{12}	C_{345}	C_6	C_7	C_8
C_{12}	0				
C_{345}	7	0			
C_6	10	3	0		
C_7	44	37	34	0	
C_8	49	42	39	5	0

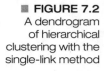

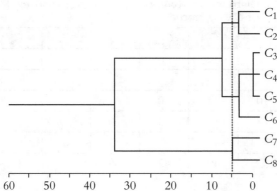

following the procedure described above. The final result represented with a tree-like dendrogram is shown in Figure 7.2.

When C_{12} and C_{3456} are merged together to form C_{123456}, the only other remaining cluster left to be merged is C_{78}. Merging it with C_{123456}, we finally have only one cluster that contains all the objects. At this point, we must apply a critical value to determine the expected number of clusters to make the result of our clustering meaningful and informative. If we set the value to be less than or equal to $5,000 (i.e., the distance ranges between two objects are smaller than or equal to $5,000), three clusters will meet this criterion: C_{12}, C_{3456}, and C_{78}. In Figure 7.2, the critical value is represented with a dotted line. The bottom of the line shows the distance scale. It is easy to locate these three clusters on the right side of the dotted line. The details of the clusters are given in Table 7.9.

If we set the critical value to be $25,000 rather than $5,000, the dotted line will move further to the left and will indicate that two clusters (C_{123456} and C_{78}) on the right meet the criteria. Thus, in the hierarchical algorithm, setting an appropriate critical value is very important because it determines the number of clusters that will result from the clustering.

The interpretation of the three clusters determined by the critical value of $5,000 is given as follows:

1. With a BS degree with either a CS or EE major and 1–3 years of working experience, the salary range is $38,000–$41,000 (from C_{12}).

■ **TABLE 7.9 The three clusters produced by the single-link method with the critical value ≤ $5,000**

Clusters	ID#	Major	Degree	Salary	Year (s)
C_{12}	S_3	CS	BS	38,000	1
	S_5	EE	BS	41,000	3
C_{3456}	S_1	CS	MS	48,000	2
	S_7	CS	MS	48,000	1
	S_8	CS	MS	48,000	3
	S_2	EE	MS	51,000	2
C_{78}	S_4	CS	MS	85,000	4
	S_6	CS	MS	90,000	5

2. With a MS degree with either a CS or EE major and 1–3 years of working experience, the salary range is $48,000–$51,000 (from C_{3456}).

3. With an MS degree with a CS major and 4–5 years of working experience, the salary range is $85,000–$90,000 (from C_{78}).

This information can be used to derive answers to queries involving *degree, major, work experience*, and *salary*. For example, a query regarding a person with an MS degree and 1–3 years of working experience can be answered from cluster C_{3456}.

Complete-link Method

Unlike the single-link method, the complete-link method applies the maximum or longest Euclidean distance as the similarity measure to merge the objects. Using the same database shown in Table 7.4 and the same attribute selection used in the single-link method, as a result of step 3 (the distances between any pair of clusters), we get a table that is identical to Table 7.6. From the table, it is easy to see that clusters C_3, C_4, and C_5 should be merged together in step 4. When merging with C_1 and C_2, the maximum distance $D(C_1, C_{345}) = 10$ is chosen as the similarity measure, and as a result we have a new matrix as shown in Table 7.10. Because there is more than one cluster in the table after merging C_1 and C_2, the merging process continues with the

■ **TABLE 7.10 Distances between clusters after the merger of C_1 and C_2 with the complete-link clustering method**

	C_{12}	C_{345}	C_6	C_7	C_8
C_{12}	0				
C_{345}	10	0			
C_6	13	3	0		
C_7	47	37	34	0	
C_8	52	42	39	5	0

remaining clusters: first merge C_{345} with C_6, then C_{12} with C_{3456}, and finally C_{123456} with C_{78}. The final result of clustering is shown in Figure 7.3.

In terms of topology, the two dendrograms produced by the complete-link method (Figure 7.3) and the single-link method (Figure 7.2) are identical. However, some distances between two clusters in the dendrograms are different. For example, in Figure 7.3, C_{12} and C_{3456} are apart by 13 and C_{123456} and C_{78} by 52, whereas in Figure 7.2, they are apart by 7 and 34, respectively. The function of the dotted line in Figure 7.3 is the same as in Figure 7.2. This suggests that we set the critical value to be \$5,000, and then we get three resultant clusters that make the clustering informative. Because the structures of the three clusters are totally identical to those produced from the single-linked method, the interpretation of them is the same as for the single-link method (Table 7.9).

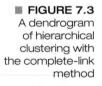

■ **FIGURE 7.3**
A dendrogram of hierarchical clustering with the complete-link method

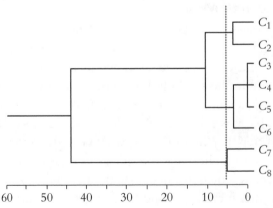

■ TABLE 7.11 Distances between clusters after merger of C_3, C_4, and C_5 with the group-average method

	C_1	C_2	C_{345}	C_6	C_7	C_8
C_1	0					
C_2	3	0				
C_{345}	10	7	0			
C_6	13	10	3	0		
C_7	47	44	37	34	0	
C_8	52	49	42	39	5	0

Group-average Method

The group-average method uses neither minimum distances nor maximum distances for clustering. Instead, it uses the average distances among a group of objects for merging objects. Using the same table used for the single-link and the complete-link methods, we will illustrate this method step by step. Because the first three steps are the same as the two previous methods, we omit them here. After step 4, we have a matrix that is identical to Table 7.11.

When merging C_1 and C_2, we face two different distances between each of the two clusters and the other remaining clusters. For example, $D(C_1, C_{345}) = 10$ and $D(C_2, C_{345}) = 7$. Since the merging criterion of the group-average method is to use the mean distance of the different distances, we obtain the mean distance of the two by $(10 + 7)/2 = 8.5$. Thus, after merging C_1 and C_2 and calculating the average distances, we get a new matrix as shown in Table 7.12.

■ TABLE 7.12 Distances between clusters after merger of C_1 and C_2 with the group-average method

Name	C_{12}	C_{345}	C_6	C_7	C_8
C_{12}	0				
C_{345}	8.5	0			
C_6	11.5	3	0		
C_7	45.5	37	34	0	
C_8	50.5	42	39	5	0

■ **TABLE 7.13** Distances between clusters after merger of C_{345} and C_6 with the group-average method

Name	C_{12}	C_{3456}	C_7	C_8
C_{12}	0			
C_{3456}	10	0		
C_7	45.5	35.5	0	
C_8	50.5	40.5	5	0

Since there is more than one cluster, we continue to merge the remaining clusters. The next clusters to be merged are C_{345} and C_6. A new matrix is generated in Table 7.13 as the result of merging them. From Table 7.13, it is easy to see that the next clusters to be merged are C_7 and C_8. Continuing to merge the remaining clusters until there is only one cluster left, we get the final result shown in Figure 7.3.

The topology of the dendrogram produced by the group-average method is totally identical to those generated from the single-link and the complete-link methods, suggesting that the three methods can produce the same clustering patterns. The dotted line in Figure 7.3 indicates that when the critical value is set to be smaller than or equal to $5,000, three clusters will remain in the final cluster set (C_{12}, C_{3456}, and C_{78}). The three clusters have been explained in previous sections (see Table 7.9).

Centroid Method

The three methods described in the previous sections considered a single attribute as the clustering criteria. When two attributes are selected for clustering a database, however, a new method called the centroid method is used. In this method, the data items are considered objects being distributed on a two-dimensional plane on which the two attributes work as the coordinate values.

To illustrate how this method works, we will use an insurance database, given in Table 7.14(a), as an example. Two attributes, *age* and *number of claims*, are selected for clustering, and *age* is sorted in ascending order. After sorting, each object is named as a cluster C_i to be merged, as presented in Table 7.14(b). For the convenience of our discussion, other attributes are omitted

■ **TABLE 7.14(a) Database of an insurance company**

Age	No. of claims	Sex	Occupation	Marital status
35	2	Female	Salesman	Married
18	5	Female	Student	Single
41	1	Male	Lawyer	Married
22	4	Male	Student	Single
56	2	Male	Professor	Married
27	3	Female	Student	Single
38	3	Male	Engineer	Married
43	1	Male	Accountant	Married

■ **TABLE 7.14(b) Database of an insurance company after sorting age and omitting other attributes**

Cluster No.	Age	No. of claims
C_1	18	5
C_2	22	4
C_3	27	3
C_4	35	2
C_5	38	3
C_6	41	1
C_7	43	1
C_8	56	2

in Table 7.14(b). The data of the insured is plotted in Figure 7.4 with the number of claims against ages.

Following steps 1 and 2 of the hierarchical clustering, we can calculate the distances between any pair of objects to obtain the result presented in Table 7.15. For example, the distance between C_1 and C_2 is $D(C_1, C_2) = [(18 - 22)^2 + (5 - 4)^2]^{1/2} = 4.12$. From this table, it is easy to see that clusters C_6 and C_7 have the smallest distance, so they should be merged first in step 3.

Merging C_6 with C_7 requires recalculation of the distances between the new cluster C_{67} and other clusters. The new matrix after recalculation is shown in Table 7.16.

■ **FIGURE 7.4**
Number of claims
plotted against
ages

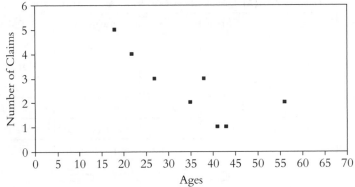

■ **TABLE 7.15 Distances between any pair of clusters using the centroid method**

	C_1	C_2	C_3	C_4	C_5	C_6	C_7	C_8
C_1	0.00							
C_2	4.12	0.00						
C_3	5.39	5.10	0.00					
C_4	17.26	13.15	8.06	0.00				
C_5	20.10	10.03	11.00	3.16	0.00			
C_6	23.35	19.24	14.14	2.65	3.61	0.00		
C_7	25.32	21.21	16.12	8.06	5.39	2.00	0.00	
C_8	38.12	34.06	29.02	21.00	18.03	15.03	13.04	0.00

■ **TABLE 7.16 Distances between any pair of clusters after merging C_6 and C_7 using the centroid method**

	C_1	C_2	C_3	C_4	C_5	C_{67}	C_8
C_1	0.00						
C_2	4.12	0.00					
C_3	5.39	5.10	0.00				
C_4	17.26	13.15	8.06	0.00			
C_5	20.10	10.03	11.00	3.16	0.00		
C_{67}	24.33	20.22	15.13	7.07	4.47	0.00	
C_8	38.12	34.06	29.02	21.00	18.03	14.04	0.00

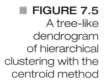

FIGURE 7.5
A tree-like dendrogram of hierarchical clustering with the centroid method

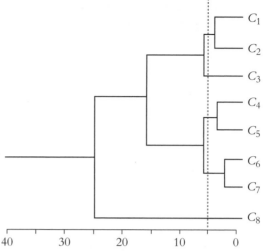

As in the previous methods, we should continue to merge the clusters that have the smallest distances until all clusters are grouped into one cluster. From Table 7.16, we can easily see that the clusters to be merged are C_4 and C_5. We omit the intermediate matrices and only show the final result in Figure 7.5. If we set the critical value to be less than or equal to 5 as indicated with the dotted line in the figure, we have five clusters. The explanation of the five clusters is presented in Table 7.17. Cluster C_{12} includes people who

TABLE 7.17 The five clusters produced from the centroid method with critical value = 5

Clusters	Age	No. of claims	Sex	Occupation	Marital status
C_{12}	18	5	Female	Student	Single
	22	4	Male	Student	Single
C_3	27	3	Female	Student	Single
C_{45}	35	2	Female	Salesman	Married
	38	3	Male	Engineer	Married
C_{67}	41	1	Male	Lawyer	Married
	43	1	Male	Accountant	Married
C_8	56	2	Male	Professor	Married

are students, not married, and are between the ages of 18 and 22. People in this group have the highest number of claims. Cluster C_{67} includes people who are married and around 41 to 43 years of age. They have the lowest number of claims.

■ 7.5.2 Graph Theory Algorithm with the Single-link Method

A graph theory algorithm uses a graph to represent the distances among objects. In this section, a graph theory algorithm with the single-link method is described. The data that will be used for illustration is given in Table 7.18, which contains information about people with different majors, different annual salaries, and different locations. As with the single-link method, first we select *salary* as the attribute for the clustering criterion and sort it in ascending order. After step 1, we have eight initial clusters to process. In step 2, we need to calculate the distances between any pair of objects and find the MST. Table 7.19 shows the distances among the eight clusters and Figure 7.6 represents the distances. The MST is shown in Figure 7.7. The length of the line connecting two points represents the distance between them.

In step 3, we merge the two points that represent two objects to reduce the number of individual clusters. Because C_6 and C_7 have the smallest distance, they should be merged first; then C_1 and C_2 are selected as the next two clusters to be merged. We continue to merge the clusters until all

■ TABLE 7.18 Yearly incomes with different majors and locations

Cluster	ID	Major	Location	Salary (K)
C_1	S_7	CS	Garland	28
C_2	S_4	CS	Garland	30
C_3	S_3	CS	Richardson	38
C_4	S_5	EE	Richardson	41
C_5	S_1	CS	Plano	48
C_6	S_8	EE	Dallas	53
C_7	S_6	CS	Dallas	54
C_8	S_2	EE	Forth Worth	58

TABLE 7.19 Distances between any pair of individual clusters

	C_1	C_2	C_3	C_4	C_5	C_6	C_7	C_8
C_1	0							
C_2	2	0						
C_3	10	8	0					
C_4	13	11	3	0				
C_5	20	18	10	7	0			
C_6	25	23	15	12	5	0		
C_7	26	24	16	13	6	1	0	
C_8	30	28	20	17	10	5	4	0

FIGURE 7.6
Distances between
any pair of objects
represented in a
graph

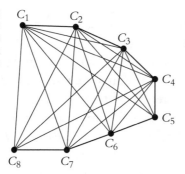

FIGURE 7.7
The MST obtained
from Table 7.19

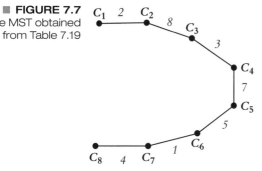

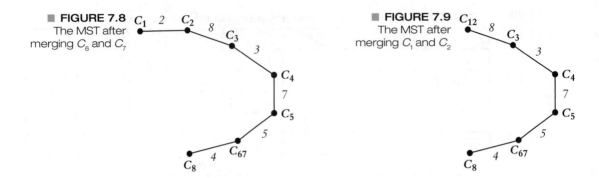

■ **FIGURE 7.8**
The MST after
merging C_6 and C_7

■ **FIGURE 7.9**
The MST after
merging C_1 and C_2

individual clusters are merged into one cluster, $C_{12345678}$. For simplicity we do not show every MST. Only the first two MSTs (after merging C_6 with C_7 and then C_1 with C_2) are shown in Figures 7.8 and 7.9. We recommend that readers finish the other MSTs.

When all individual clusters become a single cluster, $C_{12345678}$, the final clustering result can be represented in the dendrogram shown in Figure 7.10. If we set the critical value to be smaller than or equal to $5,000, we have four clusters (C_{12}, C_{34}, C_5, and C_{678}). The dotted line in Figure 7.10 represents the critical value. The branches are cut by the dotted line to identify the four clusters. Cluster C_{12} represents people who have a major in computer science and live in Garland. People in this group earn the smallest salary. The people classified in cluster C_{678} live in Dallas or Fort Worth and have the highest annual salary. A detailed explanation is given in Table 7.20.

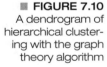

■ **FIGURE 7.10**
A dendrogram of
hierarchical cluster-
ing with the graph
theory algorithm

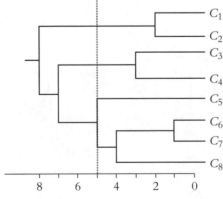

▨ TABLE 7.20 The four clusters produced from the graph theory algorithm with critical value ≤ $5,000

Clusters	ID	Major	Location	Salary (K)
C_{12}	S_7	CS	Garland	28
	S_4	CS	Garland	30
C_{34}	S_3	CS	Richardson	38
	S_5	EE	Richardson	41
C_5	S_1	CS	Plano	48
C_{678}	S_8	EE	Dallas	53
	S_6	CS	Dallas	54
	S_2	EE	Forth Worth	58

■ 7.5.3 Partition Algorithms: *K*-means Algorithm

In the previous sections, hierarchical clustering algorithms were discussed and illustrated with various examples. In hierarchical clustering algorithms, data items are categorized into a nested sequence of groups and the results are represented in a dendrogram. While the hierarchical clustering algorithms try to obtain clusters from a tree-like dendrogram by using a critical value against similarities, non-hierarchical clustering algorithms, also known as partition algorithms or optimization algorithms, try to find partitions (resulting clusters) that minimize either intra-cluster distances or inter-cluster distances through various algorithms, including *k*-means. Unlike hierarchical algorithms, partition algorithms allow reallocation of objects in the final stage of clustering. An investigator decides the number of final clusters at the beginning; then the poorly initialized clusters can be corrected and reallocated based on optimality criteria. In order to find the best possible clustering solution, all possible partitions need to be examined. This means that computation time will skyrocket. Another problem is the definitions of the optimality criteria. Because different investigators use different criteria, a variety of methods have been proposed. These methods, however, do not guarantee finding an optimum solution. While hierarchical algorithms are mainly used in soft science because they are inherently easier to use with ordinal values, partition algorithms are mainly applied to engineering problems because of their use of continuous-value vectors.

To demonstrate how partition algorithms work, we will use a k-means algorithm that is classified as a partition algorithm used to cluster multiple objects in a database. The algorithm will be described and illustrated with examples. The k-means algorithm can process large databases quickly and can produce optimal clusters within a short time. The algorithm is guided by a cost function that is defined as follows:

$$E = \sum_{l=1}^{k} \sum_{i=1}^{n} y_{il} d(X_i, Q_i),$$

where n is the number of objects in a dataset X, Q_l is the mean of cluster l, y_{il} is an element of a partition matrix $Y_{n \times k}$, and d is a similarity measure often defined as the squared Euclidean distance. The objective of clustering with this algorithm is to minimize the cost function.

The k-means algorithm involves four basic operations. We will consider a simple table, shown in Table 7.21, that contains data about schools in a small town to illustrate how the four operations are performed. The table shows five schools with the number of students and teachers, the results of TAS (Texas Academic Scores) exams, and the existence of a PTA (Parents and Teachers Association). As we have discussed before, clustering can be performed based on either one attribute or on multiple attributes. To simplify the process of computation, a single attribute, *students*, is chosen, which represents the size of the school.

The first operation begins by selecting the initial k-means for the k clusters. Unlike hierarchical algorithms, k-means requires users to define the number of clusters to construct at the beginning. Let's arbitrarily define $k = 2$ by placing objects A and B into one cluster and the remaining objects into the other. Then the means of each cluster can be calculated on the student attribute.

■ **TABLE 7.21 Students and teachers of five schools in a town**

School Name	Teachers	Students	TAS	PTA
A	50	500	95	Y
B	120	1000	98	Y
C	50	800	90	N
D	10	300	75	N
E	20	600	80	N

The mean of cluster 1 (A, B) is 750, and the mean of cluster 2 (C, D, E) is 566.67.

Second, calculate the dissimilarity between an object and the means of the k clusters. The dissimilarity is represented as a squared Euclidean distance. For example, the dissimilarities of object A from cluster 1 and cluster 2 are the following:

$$d(A, Cluster1) = \sqrt{(500-750)^2} = 250$$

$$d(A, Cluster2) = \sqrt{(500-566.67)^2} = 66.67$$

Third, allocate the object to the cluster whose mean is nearest to the object, that is, allocate the object to the cluster from which the distance of the object is smallest. Object A should be placed in cluster 2 rather than cluster 1 since it is closer to cluster 2. Hence, we rearrange object A from cluster 1 to cluster 2 so that the two clusters now are (B) and (A, C, D, E).

Fourth, recalculate the means of the clusters to and from which the objects are reallocated so that the intra-cluster dissimilarity is minimized. After removing School A, cluster 1 has a mean of 1000 and cluster 2 has a mean of 550.

Then repeat operations 2 through 4 for the remaining objects until no further reallocation occurs. At that point, the cost function is minimized. We now consider School B. Obviously, it is not necessary to reallocate School B because its distance with cluster 1 is zero. Table 7.22 lists successive calculations and reallocations for the remaining schools.

In the table, it is shown that after School C is reallocated from cluster 2 to cluster 1, no further reallocation occurs. Afterward the algorithm

■ TABLE 7.22 Calculations and reallocations for remaining schools

Sch	D(clus 1)	D(clus 2)	Cluster 1	Means	Cluster 2	Means
C	200	250	(B, C)	900	(A, D, E)	466.67
D	600	166.67	(B, C)	900	(A, D, E)	466.67
E	300	133.33	(B, C)	900	(A, D, E)	466.67
A	400	33.33	(B, C)	900	(A, D, E)	466.67
B	100	533.33	(B, C)	900	(A, D, E)	466.67
C	100	333.33	(B, C)	900	(A, D, E)	466.67

converges, and the five schools are finally classified into the two clusters (B, C) and (A, D, E). The table is divided into two parts: one representing larger schools (i.e., schools with a larger number of students) and the other representing smaller schools. It should be pointed out that if other attributes such as teachers and TAS were considered together with students, the pattern of clusters might be different.

From the example above we can see that the k-means algorithm can reach optimal clusters fairly quickly, which makes it very suitable for processing large databases. However, the shortcomings of the algorithm are the determination of k clusters at the beginning and the limitation of processing categorical attributes.

■ 7.5.4 Density-Search Algorithms

The density-search algorithm is based on the idea that the objects to be clustered can be depicted as points in a matrix. An acceptable cluster is an area with high density of objects and is separated from other clusters by areas of low density. The goal of this algorithm is to search for the sparse spaces, the regions with low density, and separate them from the high–density regions. The clusters produced from this algorithm are considered natural clusters. However, finding the sparse regions is the key problem in this algorithm, and many investigators have proposed various methods to solve it. The method adopted by most uses distance similarity measures that are defined and used in the hierarchical algorithms. Because of this, there is no significant difference between hierarchical and density-search algorithms.

Because this technique uses the similarity measure between any two points to determine the density of a region and because the definitions of similarity measure vary, many algorithms are proposed. In this section we introduce the Taxmap algorithm of Carmichael and Sneath as an example of a density-search algorithm (see [Everitt 1980] for more information). The similarity measure in the Taxmap algorithm is defined by the following:

$$S_{ij} = \sum_{k=1}^{p} S_{ijk} \Big/ \sum_{k=1}^{p} W_{ijk}$$

In the equation, W_{ijk} is the weight of comparison of two individual objects i and j for attribute k, and S_{ijk} is the comparison score of i and j for attribute k. The value of W_{ijk} is set to 1 if the two individual objects are comparable for attribute k; otherwise, it is set to zero. For categorical attributes, if the values of attribute k are the same for i and j, then S_{ijk} is set to 1; otherwise, S_{ijk} is set to zero. When dealing with numerical attributes, S_{ijk} can be calculated by the following formula, where X_{ik} is the value of object i on attribute k and R_k is the range of values of attribute k:

$$S_{ijk} = 1 - \frac{|X_{ik} - X_{jk}|}{R_k}$$

To search for the sparse regions that should be separated from the high-density regions, the algorithm must first define how far apart two points can be in order to be considered to be in a sparse region. This means that a threshold value must be used as a measure to determine the addition of a point to a cluster. The algorithm involves the following steps:

1. Calculate the similarities between any two points based on the selected attributes. This will produce a matrix.
2. Form an initial cluster with the two points that have the nearest similarity measure.
3. Identify a point that has the nearest similarity measure with the points that are already in the cluster. Add the point to the cluster.
4. Adjust the similarity measure of the cluster by averaging and determine the discontinuity.
5. Determine whether the point should be placed into the cluster against a threshold value. If it is not allowed to be in the cluster, a new cluster should be initialized.
6. Repeat steps 3–5 until all points are examined and classified into the clusters.

The school database in Table 7.21 is chosen to illustrate how the density-search algorithm produces the clusters. As with the k-means algorithm, we only consider one attribute, the number of students, to simplify the implementation. After step 1, a similarity matrix given in Table 7.23 is produced.

In step 2, we form an initial cluster with Schools A and E because they show the nearest similarity measure (0.857) of all the comparisons. During step 3, we find three identical similarity measures (0.714) that are the second nearest to 0.857. They are the measures between Schools B and C, A

■ TABLE 7.23 Similarity measures among the five schools in a town

School	A	B	C	D	E
A	1.000				
B	0.286	1.000			
C	0.571	0.714	1.000		
D	0.714	0.000	0.286	1.000	
E	0.857	0.429	0.714	0.571	1.000

and D, and C and E. Because both Schools A and E have been placed into the cluster, we may choose either D or C as the next school to be added to the cluster. If D is first selected, the average similarity measure among Schools A, E, and D is calculated by $S = (0.857 + 0.714 + 0.571)/3 = 0.714$. The drop in similarity is $0.857 - 0.714 = 0.143$, and consequently the measure of discontinuity is $0.714 - 0.143 = 0.571$. For step 5, the threshold value of 0.6 is selected, suggesting that the candidate point should not be added to the cluster if the measure of discontinuity is smaller than 0.6. In this case, School D is not allowed to be in the cluster so two clusters $(A\ E)$ and (D) are formed at this point.

We repeat step 3 to add a new point to the cluster. The next candidate point to be considered is School C, which has a similarity measure of 0.714 with School E. Considering School C with cluster $(A\ E)$, we obtain the average similarity measure of a candidate cluster $(A\ E\ C)$ by $S = (0.857 + 0.571 + 0.714)/3 = 0.714$. In this case the measure of discontinuity is $0.714 - 0.143 = 0.571$, which is smaller than the threshold 0.6. Hence, we do not add C to $(A\ E)$. Continuing in this manner and repeating steps 3–5, we get four clusters: $(A\ E)$, (B), (C), and (D).

It should be noted that as the value of the discontinuity measure decreases, the number of clusters formed increases. For example, we can easily see that if the discontinuity measure in the example above decreases to 0.5, then there will be only one cluster formed, $(A\ B\ C\ D\ E)$.

Compared to the k-means algorithm, the density-search technique can produce natural clusters, but it requires more computations. As the database size gets larger, it will be more difficult to find the point that has the nearest similarity measure with the points already in the clusters. The computation will be expensive. In addition, the density-search technique requires users to set the threshold values. The threshold setting may not be natural and is relatively difficult since the number of final clusters to be formed depends on this value. Thus, as a method for clustering a large database, the density-search technique may not be as efficient as the k-means algorithm.

■ 7.5.5 Association Rule Algorithms

Association rules identify frequently used patterns of information in a database that consists of non-transaction data. In this section, we study an algorithm that deals with association rules for clustering. The algorithm will perform the process of clustering on a set of association rules to identify clustered rules over interval data from a large database. The association rules generated from the database can be meaningful and useful to users and can have a significant impact on strategic decision making.

A practical use of clustering on association rules is to partition large databases with nontransaction data. For example, let us consider a credit card company that regularly increases the credit limits of existing customers. The company keeps a record of monthly or yearly transactions and places them in a database, which contains credit history and demographic information for each customer. At some point in time, the company may want to offer credit limit increases to its customers. By grouping existing customers based on their credit history into groups of *excellent*, *good*, *above average*, *average*, and *poor*, the company could generate clustered association rules on the attributes of the demographic database to classify its customers and offer appropriate credit-limit increases.

In general, clustered association rules take the following form:

$$A_1 \wedge A_2 \wedge A_3 \cdots \wedge A_n \Rightarrow G$$

where A_i's are attribute ranges such as ($50 \leq age < 60$) or ($\$40,000 \leq income < \$50,000$). The G is one of the target attribute values such as *excellent*, *good*, or *poor*.

Technically speaking, clustering of association rules is similar to clustering based on the hierarchical and density-search algorithms in that all of them apply distances between any two points to determine clusters and do not have a predetermined number of clusters. In data mining with association rules, a cluster is a set of tuples. For a particular set of attributes X, restrictions can be placed on the properties of those tuples in the clusters. We can define the cluster restricted on X as C_X. For illustration, let us consider the following six tuples again:

$(no.\text{-}in\text{-}household = 5) \wedge (household\text{-}income = \$59,000) \Rightarrow (no.\text{-}of\text{-}cars = 3)$
$(no.\text{-}in\text{-}household = 4) \wedge (household\text{-}income = \$55,000) \Rightarrow (no.\text{-}of\text{-}cars = 3)$
$(no.\text{-}in\text{-}household = 5) \wedge (household\text{-}income = \$58,000) \Rightarrow (no.\text{-}of\text{-}cars = 3)$
$(no.\text{-}in\text{-}household = 4) \wedge (household\text{-}income = \$58,000) \Rightarrow (no.\text{-}of\text{-}cars = 3)$
$(no.\text{-}in\text{-}household = 4) \wedge (household\text{-}income = \$57,000) \Rightarrow (no.\text{-}of\text{-}cars = 3)$
$(no.\text{-}in\text{-}household = 5) \wedge (household\text{-}income = \$57,000) \Rightarrow (no.\text{-}of\text{-}cars = 3)$

These six tuples can be represented by a grid structure as shown in Figure 7.11. Clearly, these six points can be combined into a group. By doing so, all six original association rules are clustered together to form the following single association rule:

$$(4 \leq no.\text{-}in\text{-}household < 6) \wedge (\$55,000 \leq household\text{-}income < \$60,000)$$
$$\Rightarrow (no.\text{-}of\text{-}cars = 3)$$

The clustering process for association rules is often made difficult by noise and outliers. Noise occurs in the data of the tuples that belong to other groups rather than the group that they are clustered into. Any tuples containing the target values not equal to 3 as the *no.-of-cars* in the previous example will be considered noise that will affect both the support and confidence of

■ **FIGURE 7.11**
Six points forming
a cluster

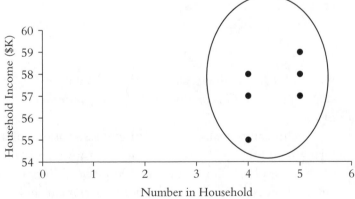

the generated clusters. On the other hand, the outliers are tuples that should belong to the same group but lie outside of the cluster for the group. A good quality measure of the clustering of association rules should reflect the density and coverage of points within a cluster. For this purpose, a distance measure using the average distance between the tuples projected on a set of attributes is used for defining and identifying clusters.

The process of clustering association rules has two phases: (1) identifying qualified clusters and (2) generating association rules from the clusters that are identified in the first phase. In the cluster identification phase, the entire database is divided into a set of clusters in which the data objects are considered very similar. The task of the next phase (after these clusters are identified) is to generate representative rules for each of these clusters. These representative rules are used to summarize the entire database and possibly to provide useful information for strategic decision making. Because the databases to be clustered are often very large, it can be difficult to find the association rules. Thus, before describing the two phases of the association rules algorithm in detail, we present ways to reduce the complexity of clustering large databases.

Pre-clustering Large Databases

As the size of a database grows, the search for an association rule pattern in the database becomes more complex. The complexity depends not only on the number of domain attributes involved but also on the number of possible values that each attribute may take. As a way to reduce the complexity of the search in a database with a large number of attribute values, the attribute values may be grouped together and managed collectively by a hierarchy. For example, Figure 7.12 shows a hierarchy of a university student database.

FIGURE 7.12
Hierarchy of
university students

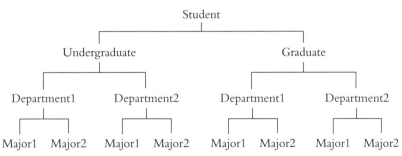

■ **TABLE 7.24 Employee relation with interval data**

Name	Salary	Sex	City
Barns John	83,000	Male	Dallas
Burns Bill	40,000	Male	Dallas
Flemming Gary	15,000	Male	Garland
Li Jinjun	41,000	Female	Richardson
Little Marie	84,200	Female	Richardson
Pina Rosa	83,500	Female	Dallas

The student–status–department–major hierarchy shown in the tree may be used to group the student classification values.

In addition, if an attribute is linearly ordered, the complexity can be further reduced by grouping the attribute values into ranges. For example, the values of the *income* attribute can be partitioned into ranges of $5,000 increments, instead of considering all possible values of the attribute. The problem of finding classical association rules involving all possible values of attributes can get very complex and even prohibitive. Although higher support and confidence thresholds can be used to reduce the number of generated rules, they may also produce very few rules, preventing interesting and meaningful information from being discovered. To illustrate this problem further, consider a relation containing interval data as shown in Table 7.24.

To group a set of values into a range we must impose some quality metrics to select a "good" interval. If the intervals are too large, the rules that exist between the intervals may be hidden. On the other hand, if the intervals are too small, there may not be enough rules to meet a minimal support threshold value. Quality metrics must be used to ensure that the selected intervals are neither too large nor too small to generate a set of rules that closely reflect the contents of the database without losing any useful information.

Using the ordinal properties of values, groups of adjacent values may be formed into intervals in an equi-depth partitioning. In the equi-depth partitioning, the depth of each partition is determined by the relative ordering of data values and the partial completeness level. For a depth value of n, the first n values in order are placed in one interval, the next n values are placed in the next interval, and so on. For example, the employee relation data in Table 7.24 can be partitioned with a depth value 2 as can be seen from the relation in Table 7.25.

■ TABLE 7.25 Employee relation partitioned
        with depth *n* = 2

Name	Salary	Sex	City
Flemming Gary	15,000	Male	Garland
Burns Bill	40,000	Male	Dallas
Li Jinjun	41,000	Female	Richardson
Barns John	83,000	Male	Dallas
Pina Rosa	83,500	Female	Dallas
Little Marie	84,200	Female	Richardson

Table 7.25 shows the tuples in the relation grouped into three partitions. Each partition consisting of two tuples is the result of equi-depth partitioning on attribute *salary* with depth 2. In this case the more meaningful partitions, however, would be those that contain close salary values. For example, considering the distance between each data value, the partition (83000, 83500, 84200) on attribute *salary* would be more meaningful than the partition (41000, 83000). It would be less likely that a rule containing the (41000, 83000) interval would be of any interest. Equi-depth partitioning, therefore, would be an appropriate technique to use only when there is no semantic meaning between the data values. When creating partitions with interval data, where there may be semantic meaning on attribute values, the distance between each attribute value has to be taken into account. The equi-depth partition in Table 7.25 may be repartitioned into another pattern as shown in Table 7.26 using the distance measure between the data points.

■ TABLE 7.26 Repartitioned employee relation
        with distance

Name	Salary	Sex	City
Flemming Gary	15,000	Male	Garland
Burns Bill	40,000	Male	Dallas
Li Jinjun	41,000	Female	Richardson
Barns John	83,000	Male	Dallas
Pina Rosa	83,500	Female	Dallas
Little Marie	84,200	Female	Richardson

■ **TABLE 7.27 Relation S**

ID	Major	Degree	Salary (K)
S_1	CS	MS	48,000
S_2	EE	MS	51,000
S_3	CS	BS	38,000
S_4	CS	MS	85,000
S_5	EE	BS	41,000
S_6	CS	MS	90,000
S_7	CS	MS	48,000
S_8	CS	MS	48,000

To alleviate the problem of separating close values with the same behavior when selecting a group of data values as an interval, we need a measure of interval quality that is based on the distance range between the data points. The semantics of interval data used in clustering a set of data values into a pattern may influence not only the choice of data grouping but also the semantic interpretation of the rules generated.

The relations S and T in Tables 7.27 and 7.28 illustrate the importance of the semantics of interval data. From both relations the following association rule can be generated:

$$(major = CS) \land (degree = MS) \Rightarrow (salary = 48,000)$$

■ **TABLE 7.28 Relation T**

ID	Major	Degree	Salary (K)
T_1	CS	MS	48,000
T_2	EE	MS	51,000
T_3	CS	BS	38,000
T_4	CS	MS	49,000
T_5	EE	BS	41,000
T_6	CS	MS	50,000
T_7	CS	MS	48,000
T_8	CS	MS	48,000

The rule has the same support and confidence factors for both relations. Five out of eight employees in both the S and T relations have a Master's degree in Computer Science with 62.5% support value. The confidence factor is 60% for both relations since three of five employees with an MS degrees in Computer Science earn $48,000. Intuitively, this rule seems to represent the relation T more precisely than S because it is more likely that a person with an MS degree in Computer Science earns about $48,000. For example, the S_6 tuple in relation S shows that a person with a MS degree in Computer Science earns $90,000, which is much more than $48,000.

Although the confidence factor indicates a certain degree of approximation in a relation, it fails to indicate appropriate approximation for data values in a relation. Therefore, the confidence factor 60% cannot be an effective measure to express a rule such as "a person with a MS degree in CS earns about $48,000." Even if both relations produce the same support factor for the generated rule based on the exact set membership, tuples T_4 and T_6 may provide additional support values to the rule although they may not as much as tuples T_1, T_7, and T_8. This means that the rule more closely reflects the contents of relation T than S. We can be more confident of the rule in relation T than in S since the possibility that a person with a MS degree in CS will earn close to $48,000 is higher in T than S.

To capture these points, a traditional association rule $X \Rightarrow Y$ can be interpreted as "all items in X closely satisfy all items in Y" so that the rule can be assigned higher support and confidence values in T than S. Therefore, for the interval data the quality measures of the interest and frequency of the rules and the strength of rule implication should consider the distance between data points.

Identifying Qualified Clusters

Identifying qualified clusters is the first phase of operations in an association rules clustering algorithm. A cluster is a set of tuples that are closely located within the given range. A cluster can be defined on a set of attributes, say X, and denoted as C_X. For example, a cluster may be a range or small interval of all closely located points on a single dimension or an area of a small grid box containing closely related data points on two dimensions. As was discussed in the previous section, the clustered area should reflect the density and coverage of points within a cluster to generate more meaningful and useful patterns. For this purpose, a distance metric such as Euclidean or Manhattan distance based on the values of the set of the attributes should be used. Hence, the definition of a cluster should include the average intra–cluster distance.

The intra–distance $d(S[X])$ on a set of attributes X of a set of tuples $S = \{t_1, t_2, t_3, \ldots, t_n\}$ is the average pair–wise distance between the tuples projected on X and can be defined by the following formula:

$$d(S[X]) = \sum_{i=1}^{n} \sum_{j=i}^{n} \text{length}(t_i[X], t_j[X])/n \times n$$

Therefore, the cluster C_X on a set of attributes X can be defined with threshold values on the size of the cluster and the intra–cluster distance within the cluster.

Cluster Definition

A cluster C_X defined on a set of attributes X is a subset of tuples that satisfies the following criteria with some density threshold d_1 and frequency threshold f_1, where $|C_X|$ is the number of tuples in the cluster and $d(C_X[X])$ is an intra–distance on a set of attributes X of the cluster C_X. The intra–distance is an average pairwise distance between tuples or data points projected on X. Functionally, d_1 is the same as the critical value used in the hierarchical and density-search algorithms because it ensures that the points in a cluster are close enough to be grouped together. The first criterion ensures that the cluster is sufficiently dense and the second criterion ensures that the cluster is supported by a sufficient number of tuples as follows.

$$d(C_X[X]) \leq d_1$$
$$|C_X| \geq f_1$$

The cluster identification process consists of three steps. The first step qualifies the density of the cluster with the density threshold value generally provided by users. On the other hand, the frequency of the cluster is determined by the frequency threshold value also given by users. The three steps are summarized below:

Step 1: Use the nearest–neighbor method used for the hierarchical clustering algorithm to group a set of data points into a cluster based on the set of selected attributes. Repeat this step until all pairs of data points are considered and checked against the density threshold d_1 provided by the user. This step checks for sufficient density of the clusters being identified.

■ TABLE 7.29 Insurance claims with age

Point	Age	Annual Insurance Claims
a	1	1
b	2	2
c	10	2
d	13	3
e	8	0

Step 2: Select the qualified clusters from the clusters identified in step 1 using the support threshold value, f_1. A cluster is considered qualified only if the number of tuples in the cluster is greater than or equal to the minimum support threshold value f_1 provided by the user. This step checks for frequency density of the clusters.

Step 3: Repeat steps 1 and 2 with the remaining attributes until no more clusters are identified from the original set of data.

The set of qualified clusters obtained as a result of the three steps is used to generate association rules. In fact, the clusters produced from the hierarchical or density-search algorithms can become the qualified clusters if they are tested following steps 2 and 3. To illustrate how the process works, let us process a simple table as given in Table 7.29 with two attributes, *age* and the *number of annual insurance claims*. The cluster identification algorithm described above will be used to group a set of data points into a cluster.

Step 1: The original database (Table 7.29) contains five tuples that can be represented as data points on a grid with X and Y axes (Figure 7.13).

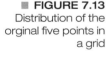

■ **FIGURE 7.13**
Distribution of the orginal five points in a grid

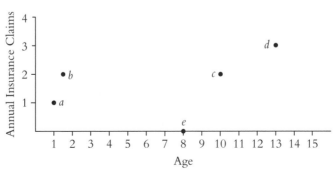

■ **TABLE 7.30 Distance matrix of the five points**

	a	b	c	d	e
a	0				
b	1	0			
c	9	8	0		
d	12	11	3	0	
e	7	6	2	5	0

Because any attribute can be used for clustering, for illustration we select the *age* attribute, and the data points are grouped based on it only. We assume the density threshold value d_1 to be 5. Step 1 of the cluster identification process can be further categorized into four substeps as follows:

1. Calculate the distance between each data point based on the X values: Based on the age values from Table 7.29, the distance between each data point is calculated and represented in a distance matrix as shown in Table 7.30. Each value in the table represents the absolute distance between one data point and another data point with respect to age. For example, the X value of data point a is 1 and that of c is 10. Therefore, the distance between the two data points is $|10 - 1| = 9$.

2. Based on the nearest-neighbor concept, determine the shortest distance between two data points. As shown in Table 7.30, the shortest distance is 1, which is the distance between points a and b. This suggests that the two points are closest to each other and should be included first in the same cluster.

3. Check if the distance obtained from substep 2 meets the distance threshold criterion against d_1 ($d(C_X[X] \leq d_1)$. In this case, since the distance between points a and b is 1, which is less than $d_1 = 5$, the two points are grouped into the same cluster. Again, this is to ensure that the cluster formed is sufficiently dense. Once a new cluster is formed, it is considered an entity in the subsequent processing of cluster identification. Therefore, points a and b form an entity. The clustering of the points a and b is shown in Figure 7.14.

4. Repeat substeps 1 through 3 until no distance between any two points is less than or equal to the density threshold distance, d_1. In this example, we now perform three iterations to complete substep 4 as follows:

■ **FIGURE 7.14**
A cluster formed
by two points
a and *b*

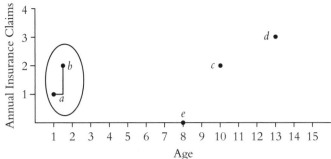

4.1. The first iteration:

After point *a* and *b* are grouped into the same cluster, they are considered one entity so the distance between each of the remaining data points and this cluster has to be recalculated. The results of the recalculation are shown in Table 7.31. To calculate the distance between two entities that are composed of more than one data point, the nearest-neighbor concept is applied, that is, the distance between a new entity and another point or entity is the shortest distance among the distances between any point in the new entity and any other points in other entities. For example, according to Table 7.30, the distance between points *a* and *c* is 9 and the distance between points *b* and *c* is 8, so the distance between entity *ab* and point *c* is 8 rather than 9. This process is repeated to calculate the distance between the newly grouped cluster and other remaining entities. By processing further, two points *e* and *c* are grouped into the same cluster and considered an entity because the distance between them is 2, that is, the shortest distance as shown in Table 7.31 and less than $d_1 = 5$.

■ **TABLE 7.31 Distance matrix of the five
points after the first iteration**

	ab	*c*	*d*	*e*
ab	0			
c	8	0		
d	11	3	0	
e	6	2	5	0

■ **FIGURE 7.15**
Two clusters
containing points
a, b, c, and *e*

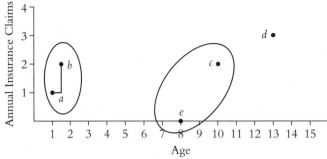

4.2. The second iteration:

The recalculated distances between entity *ab* and entity *ce* and other remaining points are shown in Table 7.32. For example, the distance between entity *ab* and point *e* is 6 and the distance between entity *ab* and point *c* is 8. The shorter one is 6 so the distance between entities *ab* and *ce* is 6 rather than 8 as shown in Table 7.32. Figure 7.15 shows two clusters formed by points *ab* and *ce*. By continuing the process, entity *ce* and point *d* are merged into the same cluster and considered a single entity because the distance between them is 3, which is the shortest one among the distances in the table and less than the distance threshold value of 5.

4.3. The third iteration:

The clusters identified thus far through the above two iterations are compared with the remaining data point, *d*. The absolute distance between cluster *ab* and data point *d* is 11, whereas the distance between cluster *ce* and data point *d* is 3. Thus, cluster *ce* and data point *d* is merged to form a new cluster *cde* as shown in Figure 7.16. The resulting two clusters are now tested to see whether they can be combined.

■ **TABLE 7.32 Distance matrix after
the second iteration**

	ab	*ce*	*d*
ab	0		
ce	6	0	
d	11	3	0

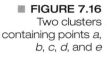

■ **FIGURE 7.16**
Two clusters
containing points *a*,
b, c, d, and *e*

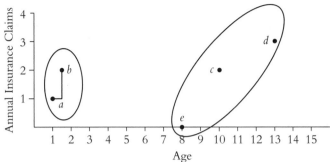

The absolute distance between the clusters is 6, larger than the density threshold value of 5 as shown in Table 7.33. So the two clusters *ab* and *cde* are not merged due to low density and are thus treated as independent clusters. Now, the cluster identification process stops because there are no more clusters or data points to be considered for combination. Clusters *ab* and *cde* are final.

Step 2: All of the clusters identified in step 1 satisfy the density criterion, which implies that these clusters are sufficiently dense. In step 2 these clusters are checked for frequency to ensure that each cluster has a sufficient number of tuples or points. The total number of tuples in the identified cluster must be greater than the frequency threshold, f_t. In our example, the frequency threshold was initially assumed to be 3. It is compared with the frequencies of the two identified clusters, 2 and 3, respectively. Therefore, the only qualified cluster is the entity, *cde*. The cluster *ab* is discarded because it contains only two tuples.

Step 3: In step 3, the processes of steps 2 and 3 are repeated for the remaining attributes of the relation being considered. In our example, attribute *Y*, the number of annual insurance claims, is the only remaining attribute to be considered. If we use the same density threshold d_1 and frequency

■ **TABLE 7.33 Distance matrix after
the third iteration**

	ab	*cde*
ab	0	
cde	6	0

■ **FIGURE 7.17**
Three clusters
generated based
on two attributes

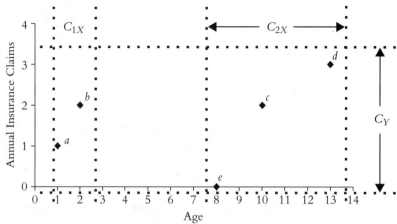

threshold f_1 as we did for attribute X, we will have only one cluster as shown in Figure 7.17. Note that we have one cluster formed on attribute Y, while we have two clusters formed on attribute X, but only one of them is qualified for processing at phase 2.

Generating Association Rules

After identifying the qualified clusters, the next task is to generate rules from each cluster. This task is done during phase 2 of the association rules clustering algorithm. Since the qualified cluster contains a set of tuples that are closely located within the given range, generating association rules from the cluster is actually generating clustered association rules based on the intra-cluster distance within the valid range of values of the attributes. Thus, we need a new tool called a Distance-based Association Rule (DAR).

Let X and Y be disjoint sets of attributes. A DAR is a rule of the form R: $C_X \rightarrow C_Y$, where C_X is a cluster on X and C_Y is a cluster on Y. The rule R holds with the degree of association D_0 if $D(C_Y | Y |, C_X | Y |) \leq D_0$. A DAR models the semantics that tuples with X values in C_X will have Y values close to C_Y.

Just as we did during phase 1, the process of finding association rules among the qualified clusters during phase 2 can also be divided into three steps as follows:

Step 1: Calculate the *centroid* of Y values of the cluster based on attribute X, denoted $C_X | Y |$. The centroid is the average value of all points in that group.

In Figure 7.17, the qualified cluster on attribute X is C_{2X}, which is composed of points c, d, and e. Only the Y values of these points are included for calculating the centroid of this cluster. Thus, $C_X|Y| = (2 + 3 + 0)/3 = 1.667$.

Step 2: Calculate the *centroid* of Y values of the cluster based on attribute Y, denoted $C_Y|Y|$. As with step 1, the centroid $C_Y|Y|$ is the average Y value of all points in that group. Because the cluster C_Y consists of all tuples, we get $C_Y|Y| = (1 + 2 + 2 + 3 + 0)/5 = 1.60$.

Step 3: Determine whether C_X is associated with C_Y or not according to the criterion $D(C_X|Y|, C_Y|Y|) \leq D_0$.

Here, D_0 is a confidence threshold provided by the user. $D(C_X|Y|, C_Y|Y|)$ is the distance between the two centroids of clusters, C_Y and C_X. If the distance between the centroids is less than or equal to the threshold, it can be concluded that the DAR $C_X \rightarrow C_Y$ holds. This DAR suggests that the interval data clustered on attribute X is closely associated with the interval data clustered on attribute Y. In our example, if we assume the confidence threshold to be 1, then the distance is $D(C_X|Y|, C_Y|Y|) = C_X|Y| - C_Y|Y| = 1.67 - 1.60 = 0.07$. Because $0.07 \leq 1$, the interval data clustered based on age closely associates with the interval data clustered based on annual insurance claim. We can express the DAR as follows:

$$(8 \leq age < 14) \rightarrow (0 \leq annual\ insurance\ claims < 3)$$

Since we have seen how the association rules clustering algorithm works, it is now easy to see that it has high potential for practical use. Not only can it simplify a large database by partitioning, it can also retrieve meaningful and useful information for strategic decision making. As a method of data mining, its potential applications include insurance planning and strategy management, customer relationship management, real estate management, and so on. For example, in an insurance company the management team may want to know how age and number of dependents of a driver are associated with annual insurance claims. If the team has this information available, it can more accurately set annual insurance premiums that vary with the age and number of dependents of drivers.

As shown in Figure 7.18, using the association rules clustering algorithm to cluster the database based on *age, dependents,* and *annual insurance claims* attributes, it is found that drivers who are 41–47 years old and have 2–5

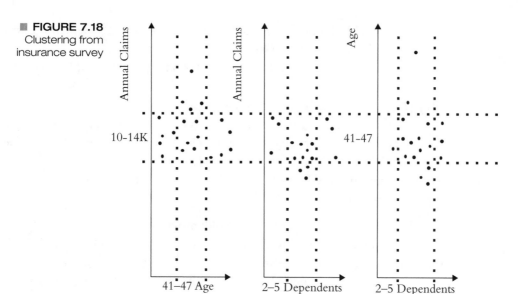

dependents are likely to have an annual insurance claim between 10K and 14K dollars as indicated by the following rule:

$$(41 \leq age \leq 47) \wedge (2 \leq dependent \leq 5) \rightarrow (10 \leq insurance\_claims \leq 14)$$

With this information, management can establish an efficient policy for setting insurance premiums that cover the annual insurance claims for this group of drivers.

Although the results produced by the association rules clustering algorithm seem to be the most meaningful and useful ones, this algorithm has some disadvantages. First, it requires a number of complex steps to identify qualified clusters and find DARs from the clusters. This process is also very computation intensive. For instance, to form a cluster, the distance between each point and every other point has to be determined and compared to the distance threshold criterion (D_0) provided by the user. In addition, to select a qualified cluster, the tuples in every cluster have to be compared to the support threshold (S_0) also determined by the user. Second, as with other algorithms, the user has to set several threshold criteria. The threshold setting itself is very difficult. For example, if the data interval determined by a threshold is too large, it may hide rules that exist between the portions of the interval. On the other hand, if the interval is too small, it may not be easy for the generated rules to have sufficient support so that only a few rules will be found.

■ 7.6 CHAPTER SUMMARY

Clustering is a very powerful and effective tool used for data mining to discover interesting patterns from large collections of data. As a method of data mining, clustering can be used for virtually any type of data. The main goals of clustering are to partition the database by grouping data items based on the similarities of the data properties and to present them as knowledge in the form of decision rules. This chapter started with an introduction to important clustering concepts, including various definitions and types of clusters, clustering procedures, variable standardization, similarity and dissimilarity measures, weights, and thresholds. To illustrate the details of some clustering procedures, a number of clustering algorithms were presented. The four different categories of algorithms presented in this chapter are hierarchical clustering algorithms, partition algorithms, density-search algorithms, and association rules clustering algorithms. To show how clustering works on a database, each algorithm was illustrated with a real example.

■ 7.7 EXERCISES

1. Compare and contrast five categories of database clustering methods described in the chapter and list the advantages and disadvantages of each.

2. Discuss how attribute selection is done by database clustering algorithms in each of the four categories. Do we need to consider all the attributes of a database? If not, what criteria should be used to determine the optimal set of attributes?

3. Discuss the relationship between threshold values and the number of clusters generated as a result of clustering. Which algorithms are affected most by threshold values?

4. What are the main differences between a hierarchical algorithm and a partition algorithm? Give an example database table that produces different results after applying each of these algorithms.

5. How do similarity and dissimilarity measures affect clustering? What is their role in determining clustering criteria? Give an example of a similarity and dissimilarity measure different from those discussed in the chapter.

6. Consider the following alcohol and tobacco consumption database table, as given in Table 7.34, which contains three attributes as follows:

   - *Region*: Region of Great Britain
   - *Alcohol*: Average weekly household spending on alcoholic beverages in pounds
   - *Tobacco*: Average weekly household spending on tobacco products in pounds

   a. Apply the centroid method to perform clustering. Determine how alcohol consumption relates to tobacco consumption in Great Britain.

   b. Apply the *k*-means algorithm with different sets of attributes and determine the relationships among the different attribute pairs. Interpret the results. Is alcohol consumption closely related to tobacco consumption?

■ TABLE 7.34 Alcohol and tobacco consumption

Region	Alcohol	Tobacco
North	6.47	4.03
Yorkshire	6.13	3.76
Northeast	6.19	3.77
East Midlands	4.89	3.34
West Midlands	5.63	3.47
East Anglia	4.52	2.92
Southeast	5.89	3.20
Southwest	4.79	2.71
Wales	5.27	3.53
Scotland	6.08	4.51
N. Ireland	4.02	4.56

    c. Create clusters using the association rules clustering method. Is the method effective in this case?

    d. Compare and contrast the results of (a), (b), and (c).

7. Consider the following maintaining balance database table as given in Table 7.35. The table contains data that gives the amount of forward/backward and side/side sway experienced by two groups of subjects (young and elderly) while taking part in a reaction-time test. The table contains the following attributes:

- *ID*: Number assigned to each subject
- *Forward_backward*: Mean sway range (in millimeters) in the forward-backward plane

■ TABLE 7.35 Maintaining balance

ID	Forward_backward	Side_side	Age_group
1	19	14	elderly
2	30	41	elderly
3	20	18	elderly
4	19	11	elderly
5	29	16	elderly
6	25	24	elderly
7	21	18	elderly
8	24	21	elderly
9	50	37	elderly
1	25	17	young
2	21	10	young
3	17	16	young
4	15	22	young
5	14	12	young
6	14	14	young
7	22	12	young
8	17	18	young

- *Side_side*: Mean sway range (in millimeters) in the side-to-side plane
- *Age_group*: Young or elderly

    a. Apply the density-search algorithm to perform clustering. Select different sets of attributes and threshold values to form clusters. List all the rules that can be generated from the clusters. Give interpretations of each rule generated. Is there any difference in sway range between the elderly and the young?

    b. Determine whether there is a difference between the elderly and the young by rules generated using the association rules clustering method. List any other rules that can be generated by the clustering. Explain the effect of different threshold values used in this clustering.

    c. Use the group-average method to generate clusters. Interpret the results. Do the different age groups affect any sway range?

8. The calcium database table given in Table 7.36 contains results of a randomized comparative experiment to investigate the effect of calcium on blood pressure in African-American men. A treatment group of 10 men received a calcium supplement for 12 weeks, and a control group of 11 men received a placebo during the same period. All subjects had their blood pressure tested before and after the 12-week period. The table contains the following attributes:

- *Treatment*: Whether subject received calcium or placebo
- *Begin*: Seated systolic blood pressure before treatment
- *End*: Seated systolic blood pressure after treatment
- *Decrease*: Decrease in blood pressure (*Begin* − *End*)

    a. Use the graph theory algorithm with the single-link method to determine clusters with different critical values. Give appropriate interpretations of the results of clustering.

    b. Apply the density search algorithm to perform clustering. Select different sets of attributes and threshold values to form clusters. List all the rules that can be generated from the clusters. Give interpretations of each rule generated. Is calcium a determinant factor in reducing blood pressure in African-American men?

    c. Use the association rules clustering algorithm to generate association rules from clusters. Interpret these rules to determine the effect of calcium and placebo in reducing blood pressure in African-American men.

■ TABLE 7.36 Calcium treatment

Treatment	Begin	End	Decrease
Calcium	107	100	7
Calcium	110	114	−4
Calcium	123	105	18
Calcium	129	112	17
Calcium	112	115	−3
Calcium	111	116	−5
Calcium	107	106	1
Calcium	112	102	10
Calcium	136	125	11
Calcium	102	104	−2
Placebo	123	124	−1
Placebo	109	97	12
Placebo	112	113	−1
Placebo	102	105	−3
Placebo	98	95	3
Placebo	114	119	−5
Placebo	119	114	5
Placebo	112	114	2
Placebo	110	121	−11
Placebo	117	118	−1
Placebo	130	133	−3

■ 7.8 SELECTED BIBLIOGRAPHIC NOTES

A basic introduction to data clustering in databases is given in [Dubes 1988], [Everitt 1980], [Balasubramaniam 1990], and [Aggrawal 1998]. [Anquetil 1998] discusses a concept extraction technique from file names. Hierarchical clustering was described in [Bajcsy 1998], [Clerkin 2001], [Fisher 1995], and [Murtagh 1983]. [Barbara 2003], [Huang 1997a], [Judd 1998], and [Zhang 1996] describe clustering techniques for large datasets, whereas multilevel data clustering for large datasets was given in [Babu 1990]. [Han 1998] gives a general introduction to hypergraph based clustering in high-dimensional datasets. Chen presented a technique for clustering in object-oriented databases in [Chen 1996b]. Conceptual clustering techniques for information retrieval were included in [Bhatia 1998], [Biswas 1998], [Ketterlin 1995], [McClean 2001], [Perkowitz 1999], and [Porrata 2000].

[Everitt 1980] and [Everitt 1993] describe non-hierarchical clustering algorithms, also known as partition algorithms or optimization algorithms, which try to find partitions (resulting clusters) that minimize either intra-cluster distances or inter-cluster distances through various algorithms, including k-means. In [Everitt 1980], four types of clustering algorithms (hierarchical, optimization, density-search, and clumping algorithms) are discussed. Other variations such as k-prototype, k-mode, hypergraph, and association rule algorithms were introduced by [Han 1997], [Huang 1997b], and [Kaufman 1990]. The k-means algorithm in Section 7.5.3 was used in [Huang 1997b] to show how to process large databases quickly and produce optimal clusters within a short time interval.

The Taxmap algorithm discussed in Section 7.5.4 for the density search algorithm was proposed and used by Carmichael and Sneath in [Everitt 1980]. Association rule mining using clustering was discussed in [Liu 2001], [Miller 1997], and [Gray 1998]. Spatial data mining is another potential application area of cluster analysis and was discussed in [Ng 1994].

Clustering techniques for web applications include web document categorization and adaptive websites. They were discussed in [Boley 1999], [Perkowitz 1999], and [Zamir 1997]. User query clustering for a search engine for the Web was given in [Wen 2001] and [Wen 2002]. Furthermore, categorical data clustering is described in [Gibson 1998], whereas spatial data clustering is used in [Han 2001]. [Hinnenberg 1998] proposed an efficient process for clustering of data in multimedia databases.

Case clustering for case-based reasoning systems was mentioned in [Cheng 1997]. Ramkumar and Swami describe a technique for data clustering without using distance functions in [Ramkumar 1998]. Sample and subsampling techniques were used for cluster analysis in data mining in [Rocke 2003], whereas the clustering of documents is discussed in [Dengel 1995] and [Deogun 1986]. [Milligan 1996] addressed the issue of clustering validation for applied analyses.

■ 7.9 CHAPTER BIBLIOGRAPHY

[Aggrawal 1998] R. Aggrawal, J. Gehrke, D. Gunopulos, and P. Raghawan: "Automatic Subspace Clustering of High Dimensional Data for Data Mining Applications," *Proceedings of the ACM SIGMOD International Conference on Management of Data*, pp. 94–105, 1998.

[Anquetil 1998] N. Anquetil and T. C. Lethbridge: "Extracting Concepts from File Names: A New File Clustering Criterion," *International Conference on Software Engineering (CSE)*, Kyoto, Japan, April, pp. 84–93, 1998.

[Babu 1990] V. S. S. Babu: "Optimal Number of Levels for a Multilevel Clustering Method," *Pattern Recognition Letters*, Vol. 11, No. 9, pp. 595–599, 1990.

[Bajcsy 1998] P. Bajcsy and N. Ahuja: "Location- and Density-based Hierarchical Clustering Using Similarity Analysis," *IEEE Transactions on Pattern Analysis and Machine Intelligence*, Vol. 20, No. 9, pp. 1011–1015, 1998.

[Balasubramaniam 1990] A. Balasubramaniam, G. Parthasarathy, and B. N. Chatterji: "Knowledge-based Approach to Cluster Algorithm Selection," *Pattern Recognition Letters*, Vol. 11, No. 10, pp. 651–661, 1990.

[Barbara 2003] D. Barbara and P. Chen: "Using Self-Similarity to Cluster Large Datasets," *Data Mining and Knowledge Discovery*, Vol. 7, pp. 123–152, 2003.

[Bhatia 1998] S. K. Bhatia and J. S. Deogun: "Conceptual Clustering in Information Retrieval," *IEEE Transactions on Systems, Man and Cybernetics*, Vol. 28, No. 3, pp. 427–436, 1998.

[Biswas 1998] G. Biswas, J. Weinberg, and D. Fisher: "ITERATE: A Conceptual Clustering Algorithm for Data Mining," *IEEE Transactions on Systems, Man and Cybernetics—Part C: Applications and Reviews*, Vol. 28, No. 2, pp. 219–230, 1998.

[Boley 1999] D. Boley, M. Gini, R. Gross, S. Han, K. Hastings, G. Karypis, V. Kumar, B. Mobasher, and J. Moore: "Partitioning-Based Clustering for Web Document Categorization," *Decision Support Systems*, Vol. 27, No. 3, pp. 329–341, 1999.

[Chen 1996a] M.–S. Chen, J. Han, and P. S. Yu: "Data Mining: An Overview from a Database Perspective," *IEEE Transactions on Knowledge and Data Engineering*, Vol. 8, No. 6, pp. 866–883, 1996.

[Chen 1996b] Y.–H. Chen, J.–K. Lai, and C. Lee: "A Pattern-Based Clustering Strategy for Object-Oriented Databases," *IEEE International Conference on Systems, Man, and Cybernetics*, 1996.

[Cheng 1997] C. H. Cheng, J. Motwani, A. Kumar, and J. Jiang: "Clustering Cases for Case-Based Reasoning Systems," *Journal of Computer Information Systems*, Vol. 38, No. 1, pp. 30–37, 1997.

[Clerkin 2001] P. Clerkin, P. Cunningham, and Conor Hayes: "Ontology Discovery for the Semantic Web Using Hierarchical Clustering," *Proceedings of Workshop on ECML/PKDD*, Germany, 2001.

[Dengel 1995] A. Dengel and F. Dubiel: "Clustering and Classification of Document Structure—A Machine Learning Approach," *Proceedings of 3rd International Conference on Document Analysis and Recognition (ICDAR)*, pp. 587–591, 1995.

[Deogun 1986] J. S. Deogun and V. V. Raghavan: "User-oriented Document Clustering: A Framework for Learning in Information Retrieval," *Proceedings of the 9th Annual International ACM SIGIR Conference on Research and Development in Information Retrieval*, pp. 157–163, 1986.

[Dubes 1988] R. C. Dubes and A. K. Jain: *Algorithms for Clustering Data*, Prentice Hall, 1988.

[Everitt 1980] B. Everitt: *Cluster Analysis*, 2nd Ed., Halsted Press, 1980.

[Everitt 1993] B. Everitt: *Cluster Analysis*, 3rd Ed., Halsted Press, 1993.

[Fayyad 1996] U. Fayyad, G. Piatestky–Shapiro, and P. Smyth: "From Data Mining to Knowledge Discovery in Databases," *AAAI*, 1996.

[Fisher 1995] D. H. Fisher: "Optimization and Simplification of Hierarchical Clusterings," *Proceedings of the 1st International Conference on Knowledge Discovery and Data Mining*, pp. 118–123, 1995.

[Garofalakis 2003] M. Garofalakis and D. Hyun: "Building Decision Trees with Constraints," *Data Mining and Knowledge Discovery*, Vol. 7, pp. 187–214, 2003.

[Gibson 1998] D. Gibson, J. Kleinberg, and P. Raghavan: "Clustering Categorical Data: An Approach Based on Dynamical Systems," *Proceedings of VLDB*, pp. 311–312, 1998.

[Gray 1998] B. Gray and M. E. Orlowska: "CCAIIA: Clustering Categorical Attributes into Interesting Association Rules," *Proceedings of the 2nd Pacific–Asia Conference on Knowledge Discovery and Data Mining (PAKDD)*, pp. 132–143, 1998.

[Han 1997] E. H. Han, G. Karypis, and V. Kumar: "Hypergraph Based Clustering in High-dimensional Datasets: A Summary of Results," *Proceedings of Workshop on Research Issues on Data Mining and Knowledge Discovery*, pp. 1–8, 1997.

[Han 1998] E. H. Han, G. Karypis, V. Kumar, and B. Mobasher: "Hypergraph Based Clustering in High-dimensional Datasets: A Summary of Results," *IEEE Bulletin of the Technical Committee on Data Engineering*, Vol. 21, No. 1, 1998.

[Han 2001] J. Han, M. Kamber, and A. K. H. Tung: "Spatial Clustering Methods in Data Mining: A Survey," *Geographic Data Mining and Knowledge Discovery*, pp. 188–217, 2001.

[Hinnenberg 1998] A. Hinneburg and D. A. Keim: "An Efficient Approach to Clustering in Large Multimedia Databases with Noise," *KDD*, pp. 58–65, 1998.

[Huang 1997a] Z. Huang: "Clustering Large Datasets with Mixed Numeric and Categorical Values," *Proceedings of the 1st Pacific–Asia Conference on Knowledge Discovery and Data Mining*, Singapore, 1997.

[Huang 1997b] Z. Huang: "A Fast Clustering Algorithm to Cluster Very Large Categorical Datasets in Data Mining," *Proceedings of SIGMOD Workshop on Research Issues on Data Mining and Knowledge Discovery*, pp. 311–322, 1997.

[Judd 1998] D. Judd, P. McKinley, and A. Jain: "Large-scale Parallel Data Clustering," *IEEE Transactions on Pattern Analysis and Machine Intelligence*, Vol. 20, No. 8, pp. 871–876, 1998.

[Kaufman 1990] L. Kaufman and P. J. Rousseeuw: *Finding Groups in Data: An Introduction to Cluster Analysis*, Wiley–Interscience Publications, 1990.

[Ketterlin 1995] A. Ketterlin, P. Gancarski, and J. J. Korczak: "Conceptual Clustering in Structured Databases: A Practical Approach," *Proceedings of the 1st International Conference on Knowledge Discovery and Data Mining*, 1995.

[Liu 2001] F. Liu, Z. Lu, and S. Lu: "Mining Association Rules Using Clustering," *Intelligent Data Analysis*, Vol. 5, pp. 309–326, 2001.

[McClean 2001] S. McClean, B. Scotney, K. Greer, and R. Páircéir: "Conceptual Clustering of Heterogeneous Distributed Databases," *Proceedings of the PKDD Workshop on Ubiquitous Data Mining*, Freiberg, Germany, 2001.

[Miller 1997] R. J. Miller and Y. Yang: "Association Rules Over Interval Data," *Proceedings of the 1997 ACM SIGMOD International Conference on Management of Data*, pp. 452–461, 1997.

[Milligan 1996] G. W. Milligan: "Clustering Validation: Results and Implications for Applied Analyses," *Clustering and Classification*, World Scientific Publishing, 341–375, 1996.

[Murtagh 1983] F. Murtagh: "A Survey of Recent Advances in Hierarchical Clustering Algorithms," *The Computer Journal*, Vol. 26, No. 4, pp. 354–359, 1983.

[Ng 1994] R. T. Ng. and J. Han: "Efficient and Effective Clustering Methods for Spatial Data Mining," *Proceedings of VLDB Conference*, pp. 144–155, 1994.

[Perkowitz 1999] M. Perkowitz and O. Etzioni: "Adaptive Web Sites: Conceptual Cluster Mining," *Proceedings of the 16th International Joint Conference on Artificial Intelligence (IJCAI)*, Vol. 1, Stockholm, 1999.

[Porrata 2000] A. Pons–Porrata, J. Ruiz–Shulcloper, and Jose F. Martinez–Trinidad: "Refunion-Generalization-Conceptual Clustering Algorithm," *The 5th Iberoamerican Symposium on Pattern Recognition*, pp. 679–690, 2000.

[Ramkumar 1998] G. D. Ramkumar and A. Swami: "Clustering Data without Distance Functions," *Bulletin of the IEEE Computer Society Technical Committee on Data Engineering*, 1998.

[Rocke 2003] D. M. Rocke and J. Dai: "Sampling and Subsampling for Cluster Analysis in Data Mining: With Applications to Sky Survey Data," *Data Mining and Knowledge Discovery*, Vol. 7, No. 2, pp. 215–232, April 2003.

[Wen 2001] J. Wen, J. Nie, and H. Zhang: "Clustering User Queries of a Search Engine," *Proc. of the 10th International World Wide Web Conference—W3C*, pp. 162–168, 2001.

[Wen 2002] J. Wen, Jian–Yun and H. Zhang. "Query Clustering Using User Logs," *ACM Transactions on Information Systems (ACM TOIS)*, Vol. 20, No. 1, pp. 59–81, 2002.

[Zamir 1997] O. Zamir, O. Etzioni, O. Madani, and R. Karp: "Fast and Intuitive Clustering of Web Documents," *Proceedings of the 3rd International Conference on Knowledge Discovery and Data Mining*, 1997.

[Zhang 1996] T. Zhang, R. Ramakrishnan, and M. Livny: "BIRCH: An Efficient Data Clustering Method for Very Large Databases," *Proceedings of the 1996 ACM SIGMOD International Conference on Management of Data*, pp. 103–114, 1996.

CHAPTER 8

Fuzzy Information Retrieval

■ 8.1 INTRODUCTION

The vast amount of information stored in a database system is permanent data. Information retrieval, knowledge recovery, and data mining are becoming more important than ever in today's business world. To retrieve information from a database system, queries are used to specify datasets that meet specific search criteria. In traditional database management systems, the queries retrieve the data that satisfies crisp criteria. In some cases, this lack of flexibility leads to an empty answer. In other cases, the results of queries may not be a reflection of the abstraction of information stored inside the permanent data. This limitation of traditional database systems results from the database model chosen and its data type constraints.

One challenging aspect of the traditional relational database is how to retrieve fuzzy information from the system. Fuzzy information can provide a very high-level abstraction of problem representation. Fuzzy set theory gives us a tool to link the data stored in the system with a linguistic variable, which can help us represent and retrieve fuzzy information from a relational database system.

In this chapter, basic fuzzy set theory is described. Information retrieval based on a fuzzy set is described as a data-mining example. Furthermore, problem representation with linguistic variables is presented from the viewpoint of fuzzy information retrieval. Problem-solving approaches related to fuzzy information retrieval are also described and reviewed.

■ 8.2 FUZZY SET BASICS

Most of us have some contact with conventional logic, in which a statement is either true or false with nothing in between. Although this principle of true or false has dominated Western logic for the last 2,000 years, the idea that things must be either true or false is nonsense in many cases. For example, is the statement "I am rich" completely true or false? The answer is probably true or false or neither since the question we need to consider is how rich is rich. A man with a million dollars may be rich or not rich depending on the condition of comparison. This idea of gradations of truth is familiar to every one of us who faces decision making of any sort. The breakthrough in the exploration of multivalued logic was made by Professor Lofti Zadeh of the University of California at Berkeley in 1965. In this section, we will consider fuzzy set basics with which a continuous gradation of truth values ranging between true and false can be studied.

A fuzzy subset of some universe U is a collection of objects from the universe in which each object is associated with a degree of membership. The degree of membership is always a real number between 0 and 1. It measures the extent to which an element is associated with a particular set. A degree of membership 0 for an element of a fuzzy set is given to an element that is not in an ordinary set, whereas the membership value 1 is given to the elements that are in an ordinary set. Consider the fuzzy set defined as follows:

$$A = \{1/a, 0.9/b, 0.2/c, 0.8/d, 1/e, 0/g\}.$$

This fuzzy set indicates the following:

1. Members a and e are in the fuzzy set.
2. Member g is not in the fuzzy set.
3. Members b, c, and d are in the fuzzy set with partial membership values of 0.9, 0.2, and 0.8, respectively.

Mathematically speaking, a fuzzy set is said to be a general case of an ordinary set. A fuzzy set is a set without a crisp boundary, which means the transition from "belongs to the set" to "does not belong to the set" is gradual. This gradual transition is characterized by a membership function that gives the fuzzy set flexibility in modeling commonly used linguistic expressions such as "the water is cold" or "the weather is hot." The degree of membership of a fuzzy set depends on the problem that needs to be solved and the information that is to be retrieved. Membership functions can be as simple as any linear relation or as complicated as any mathematically complex function. Furthermore, membership functions can be multidimensional.

Basic operations in fuzzy-set theory include union, intersection, empty, equal, complement, and containment. For example, union ($\cup$) and intersection ($\cap$) are defined by the following formulas, in which m means member-of function, A and B are fuzzy sets, Max( ) returns the largest value, and Min( ) returns the smallest value from the set:

$$C = A \cup B, \text{where } mC(x) = \text{Max}(mA(x), mB(x))$$
$$C = A \cap B, \text{where } mC(x) = \text{Min}(mA(x), mB(x))$$

Extended operations on fuzzy sets include concentration, dilation, normalization, intensification, and fuzzification. An example of concentration (CON) can be defined as follows:

$$\text{CON}(A) = \{A(x) \times A(x) \,|\, x \text{ is an element of } U\}$$

These extended operations on fuzzy sets bear great analogy with fuzzy logic. This correspondence to fuzzy logic enables us to mathematically model and solve natural language representation problems using fuzzy logic. These extended operations, together with basic operations on fuzzy sets, can be used in conjunction with linguistic variables in our approach to data mining in relational database models.

■ 8.3 FUZZY SET APPLICATIONS

Unlike conventional set theory, which uses Boolean values of either 0 or 1, fuzzy sets have a function that admits a degree of membership in the set from complete exclusion (which corresponds to 0) to absolute inclusion (which corresponds to 1). While conventional sets have only two possible values, 0 and 1, fuzzy sets do not have this arbitrary boundary to separate members from nonmembers.

Fuzzy logic can be used to naturally describe our everyday business applications since it presents a flexible method to get a high-level abstraction of problem representation. In the real world, problems are often vague and imprecise, so they cannot be described in conventional two-value (true or false) logic. On the contrary, fuzzy logic allows a continuous gradation of truth values ranging from false to true in the description process of application models. In this section, a number of fuzzy set applications will be presented and reviewed to explain the potential benefits of fuzzy logic in data mining.

■ 8.3.1 Project Management

Fuzzy logic can be used in project management to improve the quality and overall process of project scheduling. Since project characteristics such as estimated project duration and cost can be easily associated with fuzzy sets, fuzzy boundaries can be used to estimate the time expected for each phase of project development. Each phase can be specified with linguistic variables to be estimated with fuzzy boundaries. This use of fuzzy logic can enhance the management of projects through its ability to look deeply into the semantics of a project's governing parameters.

Earl Cox presented applications of fuzzy logic in project management, acquisition analysis, and fraud detection [Cox 1992a]. Figure 8.1 gives an example of the membership function for determining budget costs for project development, which indicates that any project expenditure estimated at less than $0.6M is not be considered absolutely expensive, but rather partially expensive with a degree of confidence.

■ 8.3.2 Data Analysis

Fuzzy boundaries are drawn on the fuzzy world used for data analysis. Based on the fuzzy boundaries drawn for data analysis, queries are specified with

FIGURE 8.1
Project costs

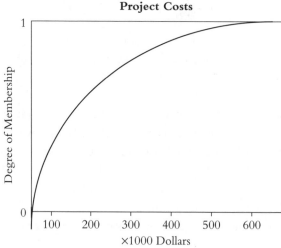

linguistic variables which allow greater flexibility in formulating queries more naturally than traditional queries. These queries will return the results with the composite truth values associated with each record. For example, as a part of the database architecture for the acquisition of a company's credit analysis, fuzzy logic can be used to specify queries with fuzzy linguistic variables for the retrieval, screening, and analysis of data.

Another example of a fuzzy model is an expert system that detects possible fraudulent behaviors of healthcare providers. The normal behavior is created first. The expert system is then used to collect the behavioral patterns of each provider. The fuzzy region is defined and tracked using the fuzzy model to find the variant behaviors.

The interpretation of fuzzy variables is often situation dependent. For example, consider a database containing the scores of Test of English as Foreign Language (TOEFL) tests in different countries. The score distribution of each country will vary depending on various factors. Therefore, to process a query with a fuzzy variable with, say, *high* in it, different standards may have to be used to reflect the factors specific to each country, although this may not be the case for all data. Table 8.1 shows the data in the *high* fuzzy boundary in three different countries.

In Table 8.1, we see that each country is characterized with different distributions. In this case the same vocabulary "high" can be interpreted within different fuzzy boundaries, so it may be possible that a different interpretation

■ TABLE 8.1 Data in the *high* fuzzy boundary in three countries

	Country *c*	Country *b*	Country *a*
Person 1	450	490	530
Person 2	465	531	540
Person 3	470	550	550
Person 4	500	499	573
Person 5	510	550	580
Person 6	495	565	620
Person 7	515	530	610
Person 8	487	523	592
Person 9	525	537	550
Person 10	511	580	587

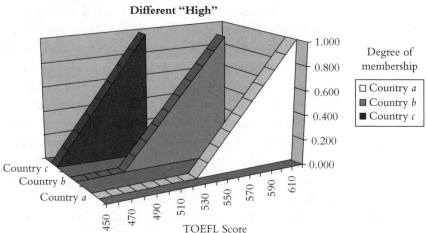

can be given for the same score. For example, if we set the alpha cut at 0.2 for inclusion into the membership of "high" scores, we get the score of 470 for country *c*, 510 for country *b*, and 540 for country *a*, as can be seen in Figure 8.2. This is because the data being considered for each case is based on different environments (i.e., countries).

Another example of fuzzy logic application for data analysis can be found in financial databases. In financial areas, it is often difficult to precisely describe exactly what information needs to be retrieved. For example, to determine which companies meet an operating profile of about $600 million in revenues (Table 8.2), it may not be easy to draw crisp or clear boundary points to search

■ **TABLE 8.2 Revenue table**

Name	P:E ratio	Revenues ($ million)
Company *a*	13.40	500
Company *b*	7.49	570
Company *c*	18.13	587
Company *d*	15.42	650
Company *e*	19.12	800
Company *f*	13.81	900
Company *g*	15.16	1000
Company *h*	15.90	1200
Company *i*	16.02	1280

the information in the database. The simplest approach to the query is to use an SQL query: "select company from revenue table where revenue > $600M." In this case a very crisp boundary was used in the condition clause. However, companies with revenues of $599 million, $580 million, or even $575 million may be excluded but could be of interest to users. Hence, when searching for approximate information in databases, fuzzy reasoning should be used to define boundaries based on fuzzy logic. Fuzzy sets can be used to solve this type of problem by generating a conceptual definition of a selection space.

To identify the list of companies meeting the above-mentioned criteria for revenue, a fuzzy set called HIGH can be defined to map a revenue stream instead of crisp boundary points. The fuzzy set is set to zero below $550 million and is set to unity (1) at $1400 million ($1.4 billion). The query can be written as "SELECT company FROM revenue table WHERE revenue is HIGH." This fuzzy database query requires automatically adding another attribute to it and providing the degree of membership in the fuzzy set HIGH. The companies in the table are attached with the degree of membership to represent the confidence in meeting the selection criteria. Figure 8.3 shows the membership function for the fuzzy set HIGH.

A direct-mailing system is another application system that can be implemented based on fuzzy logic. Since the purpose of this system is to increase the sales profit with a fixed budget, it is important to obtain a dataset of highly potential customers who are likely to buy products at a certain time. More mail flyers are sent with the expectation that more sales will be triggered as a result of the direct-mailing service. From a database of customers, a list of highly potential customers is retrieved based on a fuzzy criteria defined with

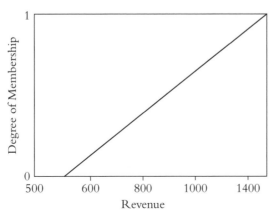

■ **FIGURE 8.3**
Membership function for HIGH revenue

a set of factors that will affect the customer's purchasing decision. The potential benefits of fuzzy logic applications for data analysis become immense as the number of data-mining systems with fuzzy logic grows.

■ 8.3.3 Nuanced Information Systems

Nuanced information systems deal with data with an option for a list of values in which each value is complemented by additional information. The data type of nuanced information can be defined as a list of pairs of (V, N): V is a value that can be precise or fuzzy, while N is a nuance such as very, quite, usually, etc., that can be associated with the value. Examples of nuanced information data types are (25, nearly), (young, quite), (profit_high, very), etc., which mean nearly 25 years old, quite young, and very high profit, respectively.

Nuanced information can also be represented by characteristic functions. In the following example, three types of alloys with different composites are grouped into a fuzzy relationship with the degree of membership corresponding to the percentage of the elements the alloy contains. Each component in the relation can be considered a fuzzy set that can be determined by a characteristic function. In this example, the characteristic function for bronze alloy is shown in Figure 8.4 in an organizational structure form. Notice that the support for this characteristic function is derived from the discrete domain of each component.

For support of a continuous domain, consider nuanced information to evaluate an attribute such as *height of a person*. For example, to evaluate a fuzzy value (165, *around*) of height, the continuous characteristic function shown in Figure 8.5 may be used to include all the neighborhood values of 165 for the *around* nuance. The function indicates that the height values of 165, 166, and 167 all support the fuzzy value (165, *around*) with 100% confidence. Other neighborhood values, such as 163 and 168, support the fuzzy value with partial confidence.

■ **FIGURE 8.4**
Bronze alloy fuzzy
relationship with
the characteristic
function

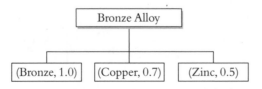

μ(bronze alloy) = {(bronze, 1); (copper, 0.7); (zinc, 0.5)}

■ FIGURE 8.5
A continuous
characteristic
function for μ (165,
around)

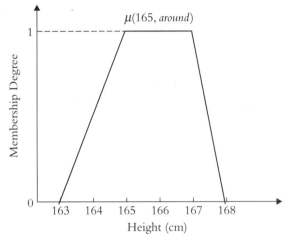

■ 8.4 LINGUISTIC VARIABLES

Linguistic variables are variables whose values are not numbers but words
or phrases, as found in a sentence of natural language. Linguistic variables
are often used to embed fuzzy meaning into fuzzy queries. Since they carry
fuzzy meaning, the interpretation of any linguistic variable requires the identification and application of a fuzzy membership function such as those discussed in the previous section.

The specification of a linguistic variable involves primary terms, connectives, negations, and hedges. Primary terms are the labels of a fuzzy set
associated with the meaning of linguistic variables such as *cheap, medium*, and
expensive. Connectives act as linguistic modifiers such as *and* and *or.* The "*and*"
can be defined as *A and B* = min(A, B), while the "*or*" can be defined as *A or
B* = max(A, B). In either case, *A* and *B* represent the degrees of membership *A*
and *B*, respectively. For example, suppose the degree of *cheap* membership
is 0.3 and the degree of *medium* membership is 0.7. Then the following can
be easily derived:

cheap(0.3) *and medium*(0.7) = min(*cheap*(0.3), *medium*(0.7)) = *cheap*(0.3)

cheap(0.3) *or medium*(0.7) = max(*cheap*(0.3), *medium*(0.7)) = *medium*(0.7)

Negation also acts as a linguistic modifier. It is defined by "*not A* = 1 − *A*,"
where *A* is a degree of membership. For example, *not cheap*(0.6) = 0.4.

Hedges act as linguistic modifiers of primary terms, such as **very, much, more or less, quite**, and **somewhat**. They are used to modify primary terms by applying appropriate formulae to get correct membership values. Suppose that A is a *cheap* membership function. Then, the following formulae may be applied to obtain the membership values of *cheap* modified by **very, more or less, plus**, and **minus**.

$$\textbf{very } cheap = cheap^2$$
$$\textbf{more or less } cheap = cheap^{0.5}$$
$$\textbf{plus } cheap = cheap^{1.25}$$
$$\textbf{minus } cheap = cheap^{0.75}$$

Using the base formulae above, we could create the meaning of other hedges when applied to a primary term. We assume A to be the membership function for the primary term. Synonyms for each hedge are also provided in parentheses.

very (*synonym*: too)
Value: A^2

very very (*synonyms*: extremely, incredibly, especially, awfully, exceedingly, dreadfully, extraordinarily, enormously, fantastically, vastly, completely, wholly, intensely, truly, certainly, really, significantly)
Value: A^4

plus very (*synonyms*: highly, greatly, deeply, seriously, hardly, a bit)
Value: $(A^2)^{1.25}$

more or less (*synonyms*: approximately, about, around, roughly, in the region of, in the order of, something like, relatively, somewhat, slightly, moderately, maybe, negotiable)
Value: $A^{0.5}$

minus more or less (*synonyms*: rather, quite, pretty, fairly, sort of, kind of, actually)
Value: $(A^{0.5})^{0.75}$

■ 8.5   FUZZY QUERY PROCESSING

Since fuzzy queries are specified with linguistic variables, they have to be interpreted with fuzzy membership functions as discussed in the previous section. The fuzzy functions give quantitative meaning to fuzzy queries so

■ **TABLE 8.3 Visitors table**

Country	No. of visitors	Country	No. of visitors	Country	No. of visitors
Argentina	260	Hong Kong	671	Russia	238
Australia	454	India	368	Singapore	389
Austria	389	Ireland	411	South Korea	649
Bahamas	817	Israel	303	Spain	714
Belgium	325	Italy	1271	Switzerland	671
Bermuda	368	Jamaica	1141	Taiwan	562
Brazil	498	Japan	1082	Thailand	303
Colombia	325	Netherlands	822	Trinidad/ Tobago	216
Costa Rica	303	P.R. of China	947	Turkey	519
Greece	433	Peru	260	Venezuela	281
Guatemala	303	Philippines	476		

that appropriate data meeting the fuzzy criteria can be retrieved based on the quantitative criteria. A few examples of fuzzy queries are shown below. All of these queries are specified with linguistic variables such as *high, low, acceptable, somewhat*, and *mostly*. In the following, these queries are processed with appropriate membership functions. The database table used for these queries contains data about the number of American tourists in 32 foreign countries. Table 8.3 shows these data.

Fuzzy queries samples:

SELECT country FROM table WHERE no._of_visitors = *acceptable*

SELECT country FROM table WHERE no._of_visitors = *high* AND *low*

SELECT country FROM table WHERE no._of_visitors = *somewhat high*

SELECT country FROM table WHERE no._of_visitors = *mostly high*

To handle these four fuzzy queries, the two adjectives *high* and *low* must be defined with appropriate fuzzy membership functions. The following two linear formulas are used to interpret the two linguistic variables, respectively:

$$F(x) = mx + c, \text{ where } m = (1 - 0)/(\text{highest} - \text{lowest}) \quad \text{for } high$$
$$F(x) = -mx + c, \text{ where } m = (1 - 0)/(\text{highest} - \text{lowest}) \quad \text{for } low$$

In the formulas, x represents the number of people who travel around the world and c represents a constant. By solving the linear equation, the constant c in both cases can be obtained as follows:

$$c = -1/\text{(highest} - \text{lowest)} \times \text{lowest} \qquad \text{for } high$$

$$c = 1/\text{(highest} - \text{lowest)} \times \text{highest} \qquad \text{for } low$$

Thus, by substituting the values for the constant c and the linear function $F(x)$, the membership function in terms of x is generated as follows:

$F(x)$ $= 1/\text{(highest} - \text{lowest)} \times x - (1/\text{(highest} - \text{lowest)} \times \text{lowest)} \qquad$ for *high*
$F(x)$ $= -1/\text{(highest} - \text{lowest)} \times x + (1/\text{(highest} - \text{lowest)} \times \text{highest)}$ for *low*
$F(x)$ $=$ degree of membership
highest $= 1271$ people (in thousands)
lowest $= 216$ people (in thousands)
x $=$ the number of American visitors in each country

Using these two membership functions, the fuzzy variables *high* and *low* can be interpreted so that data records meeting the fuzzy criteria can be retrieved with the degree of membership. For example, to handle the following fuzzy query, the membership function $F(x)$ for *high* defined above can be used. The retrieved dataset is shown in Table 8.4.

SELECT country FROM table WHERE no._of_visitors = *high*

In Table 8.4, Italy is the country that Americans visit most with 100% confidence. Jamaica and Japan follow Italy with 87% and 82% confidence, respectively. However, if the records are listed backward, they represent the result for the following opposite query:

SELECT country FROM table WHERE no._of_visitors = *low*

Furthermore, the table can be used for handling natural-language queries such as the following:

Is Switzerland the country Americans visit most often?
How often do Americans visit Austria?
Is the Bahamas one of the countries Americans visit frequently?

The two previous queries can be combined with the AND operator as follows:

SELECT country FROM table WHERE no._of_visitors = *high* AND *low*

■ TABLE 8.4 Data for no._of_visitors = *high*

Country	No. of visitors	Membership	Country	No. of visitors	Membership
Italy	1271	1	Ireland	411	0.185
Jamaica	1141	0.877	Austria	389	0.164
Japan	1082	0.821	Singapore	389	0.164
P.R. of China	947	0.693	Bermuda	368	0.144
Netherlands	822	0.574	India	368	0.144
Bahamas	817	0.57	Belgium	325	0.103
Spain	714	0.472	Colombia	325	0.103
Hong Kong	671	0.431	Costa Rica	303	0.082
Switzerland	671	0.431	Guatemala	303	0.082
South Korea	649	0.41	Israel	303	0.082
Taiwan	562	0.328	Thailand	303	0.082
Turkey	519	0.287	Venezuela	281	0.062
Brazil	498	0.267	Argentina	260	0.042
Philippines	476	0.246	Peru	260	0.042
Australia	454	0.226	Russia	238	0.021
Greece	433	0.206	Trinidad/Tobago	216	0

This query requires that data meeting both *high* and *low* criteria be retrieved. In this case, since two opposite criteria are used, the membership function must include both. Figure 8.6 shows the graphical representation of the membership function for *high* and *low* combined. Table 8.5 shows the result of the query satisfying both criteria.

In addition to *high* and *low* linguistic variables that have a linear relation between the degree of membership and the number of visitors, an additional variable such as *acceptable* can be derived using a different membership function. This can be done by building another fuzzy set from the original dataset. A simple fuzzy query specified with *acceptable* is the following:

SELECT country FROM table WHERE no._of_visitors = *acceptable*

■ **FIGURE 8.6**
Membership
function for *high*
and *low* combined

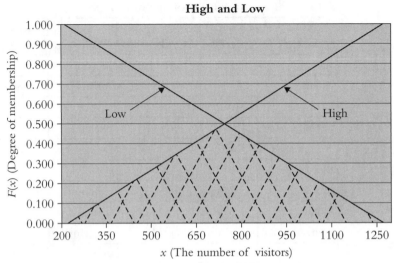

■ TABLE 8.5 Data for no._of_visitors = *high* and *low*

Country	No. of visitors	Membership	Country	No. of visitors	Membership
Spain	714	0.472	Singapore	389	0.164
Hong Kong	671	0.431	Bermuda	368	0.144
Switzerland	671	0.431	India	368	0.144
Bahamas	817	0.43	Jamaica	1141	0.123
Netherlands	822	0.426	Belgium	325	0.103
South Korea	649	0.41	Colombia	325	0.103
Taiwan	562	0.328	Costa Rica	303	0.082
P.R. of China	947	0.307	Guatemala	303	0.082
Turkey	519	0.287	Israel	303	0.082
Brazil	498	0.267	Thailand	303	0.082
Philippines	476	0.246	Venezuela	281	0.062
Australia	454	0.226	Argentina	260	0.042
Greece	433	0.206	Peru	260	0.042
Ireland	411	0.185	Russia	238	0.021
Japan	1082	0.179	Italy	1271	0
Austria	389	0.164	Trinidad/ Tobago	216	0

In this case, the relationship between the number of visitors and the degree of membership is not linear, but a sine curve. The membership function $F(x)$ can be defined with the following sine curve function with max = 1271, min = 216, and x = the number of visitors:

$$F_{acceptable}(x) = 1/2 + 1/2 \times \sin\left[(1.5 + (x - min)/(max - min)) \times \pi\ (\ )\right]$$

Note that from the original definition of function $\sin(x)$, $\sin(0) = 0$, $\sin(\pi/2) = 1$, $\sin(\pi) = 0$, and $\sin(3/2 \times \pi) = -1$, etc. In representing the relationship between the degree of membership and the number of visitors, the shape of the curve is the same as the $\sin(x)$ curve, where x ranges from $3/2 \times \pi$ to $5/2 \times \pi$. Then the curve is shifted to the origin of the X–Y system, where $3/2 \times \pi$ corresponds to the new position of $X = 0$ and $5/2 \times \pi$ corresponds to the new position of π. The minimum value of $\sin(x)$, which is $\sin(3/2 \times \pi)$ $= -1$, corresponds to the minimum value of $F(x)$, which is 0. The maximum value of $\sin(x)$, which is $\sin(5/2 \times \pi) = 1$, corresponds to the maximum value of $F(x)$, which is 1.

In the $F(x)$ function, if the variable x is substituted with min, $\sin[(1.5 + (x-min)/(max-min)) \times \pi(\ ))]$ becomes -1, which sets $F(x)$ to 0. If x is substituted with max, then $\sin((1.5 + (x-min)/(max-min)) \times \pi(\ ))$ becomes 1, which sets $F(x)$ to 1. Hence, the degree of membership $F(x)$ is within the range $[0, 1]$ in terms of x, the number of visitors, which is within the range of $[min, max]$. Accordingly, the membership function graph for *acceptable* can be drawn as shown in Figure 8.7.

■ **FIGURE 8.7**
Membership
function graph for
acceptable

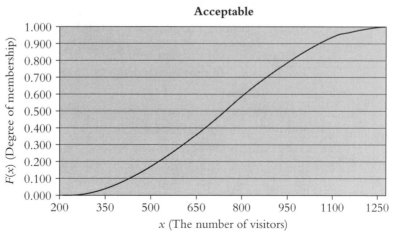

■ TABLE 8.6 Data for no_of_visitors = *acceptable*

Country	No. of visitors	Membership	Country	No. of visitors	Membership
Italy	1271	1	Ireland	411	0.082
Jamaica	1141	0.963	Austria	389	0.065
Japan	1082	0.923	Singapore	389	0.065
P.R. of China	947	0.785	Bermuda	368	0.05
Netherlands	822	0.616	India	368	0.05
Bahamas	817	0.609	Belgium	325	0.026
Spain	714	0.456	Colombia	325	0.026
Hong Kong	671	0.393	Costa Rica	303	0.017
Switzerland	671	0.393	Guatemala	303	0.017
South Korea	649	0.361	Israel	303	0.017
Taiwan	562	0.243	Thailand	303	0.017
Turkey	519	0.19	Venezuela	281	0.009
Brazil	498	0.166	Argentina	260	0.004
Philippines	476	0.143	Peru	260	0.004
Australia	454	0.12	Russia	238	0.001
Greece	433	0.101	Trinidad/ Tobago	216	0

Now consider the following query:

SELECT country FROM table WHERE no._of_visitors = *acceptable*

Using the membership function in Figure 8.7, the result of the query will look like Table 8.6. In the table, Italy is the most acceptable country, followed by Jamaica and Japan.

Another important feature of fuzzy logic is the ability to define "hedges," the modifiers of fuzzy values. Hedges play the same role as adverbs in English, such as "very," "much," and "more or less." They act as linguistic modifiers of primary terms. These modifiers of fuzzy variables maintain close ties to natural language. For example, the fuzzy variable *high* can be modified to **somewhat** *high*, **mostly** *high*, etc. Thus, the result of query processing will be narrower with hedges since adverbs modify the meaning of primary terms. The interpretation of hedges is quite a subjective process and varies from application to application. In this section, the following hedges will be used to illustrate the role of hedges in fuzzy queries:

usually, not, somewhat, very, and **mostly**

Very

The hedge **very** can be used to modify primary terms such as *high* and *low*. It is used to increase the degree of membership. Hence, the result of the query will be more confident. When the hedge **very** is used with a primary term, the linear shape of the membership function will change to a membership function of curved shape since the hedge **very** should increase the confidence of membership. Figure 8.8 shows the graphical representation of the membership functions for **very** *high* and **very** *low*.

The membership functions for **very** *high* and **very** *low* use the functions for *high* and *low*. They show that **very** is obtained by applying the power of two to the primary membership functions.

$$F_{\textbf{very } high}(x) = F^2_{high}(x) \qquad \text{for } high$$
$$F_{\textbf{very } low}(x) = F^2_{low}(x) \qquad \text{for } low$$

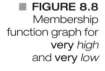

FIGURE 8.8
Membership function graph for **very** *high* and **very** *low*

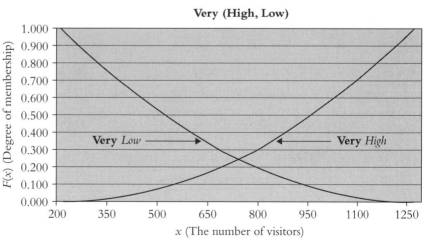

■ **TABLE 8.7** Data for no._of_visitors = **very** *high*

Country	No. of visitors	Membership	Country	No. of visitors	Membership
Italy	1271	1	Ireland	411	0.034
Jamaica	1141	0.769	Austria	389	0.027
Japan	1082	0.674	Singapore	389	0.027
P.R. of China	947	0.48	Bermuda	368	0.021
Netherlands	822	0.33	India	368	0.021
Bahamas	817	0.325	Belgium	325	0.011
Spain	714	0.223	Colombia	325	0.011
Hong Kong	671	0.186	Costa Rica	303	0.007
Switzerland	671	0.186	Guatemala	303	0.007
South Korea	649	0.168	Israel	303	0.007
Taiwan	562	0.108	Thailand	303	0.007
Turkey	519	0.082	Venezuela	281	0.004
Brazil	498	0.071	Argentina	260	0.002
Philippines	476	0.061	Peru	260	0.002
Australia	454	0.051	Russia	238	0
Greece	433	0.042	Trinidad/ Tobago	216	0

Table 8.7 shows the result of the following query, with the hedge **very** applied to the primary variable *high*:

SELECT country FROM table WHERE no._of_visitors = **very** *high*

Similarly, Table 8.8 shows the result of the following query, with the hedge **very** applied to the primary variable *low*:

SELECT country FROM table WHERE no._of_visitors = **very** *low*

Generally, Usually

The hedge "generally" and/or "usually" is used to contrast intensification. It can be interpreted with the following membership function. Function $F(x)$ has the shape of a sine curve with the maximum value of 1 and the minimum value of 0. Its graphical representation is shown in Figure 8.9. From the

■ **TABLE 8.8 Data for no._of_visitors = "*very low*"**

Country	No. of visitors	Membership	Country	No. of visitors	Membership
Trinidad/ Tobago	216	1	Greece	433	0.631
Russia	238	0.959	Australia	454	0.6
Peru	260	0.918	Philippines	476	0.568
Argentina	260	0.918	Brazil	498	0.537
Venezuela	281	0.881	Turkey	519	0.508
Thailand	303	0.842	Taiwan	562	0.452
Israel	303	0.842	South Korea	649	0.348
Guatemala	303	0.842	Switzerland	671	0.323
Costa Rica	303	0.842	Hong Kong	671	0.323
Colombia	325	0.804	Spain	714	0.279
Belgium	325	0.804	Bahamas	817	0.185
India	368	0.733	Netherlands	822	0.181
Bermuda	368	0.733	P. R. of China	947	0.094
Singapore	389	0.699	Japan	1082	0.032
Austria	389	0.699	Jamaica	1141	0.015
Ireland	411	0.664	Italy	1271	0

■ **FIGURE 8.9**
Membership
function graph for
usually *high*

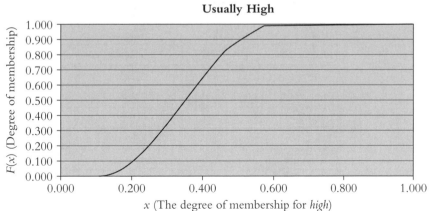

Usually High

figure, it can be observed that the value of min is equal to 0.1 and the value of max is equal to 0.6:

$$F_{\text{usually } high}(x) = 1/2 + 1/2 \times \sin((1.5 + (x - \min)/(\max - \min)) \times \pi(\ ))$$

Every degree of membership in the x-axis over 0.6 yields 1 as the degree of membership $F(x)$ for **usually** *high*. The following query is an example that applies the hedge **usually** to the primary term *high*. The result of the query is partially shown in Table 8.9.

SELECT country FROM table WHERE no._of_visitors = **usually** *high*

■ TABLE 8.9 Data for no._of_visitors = **usually** *high*

Country	No. of visitors	Membership for *high*	Membership for usually *high*
Italy	1271	1	1
Jamaica	1141	0.877	1
Japan	1082	0.821	1
P.R. of China	947	0.693	1
Netherlands	822	0.574	0.994
Bahamas	817	0.57	0.991
Spain	714	0.472	0.847
Hong Kong	671	0.431	0.744
Switzerland	671	0.431	0.744
South Korea	649	0.41	0.685
Taiwan	562	0.328	0.431
Turkey	519	0.287	0.308
Brazil	498	0.267	0.252
Philippines	476	0.246	0.197
Australia	454	0.226	0.148
Greece	433	0.206	0.106
Ireland	411	0.185	0.069
Austria	389	0.164	0.04
Singapore	389	0.164	0.04
Bermuda	368	0.144	0.019
India	368	0.144	0.019

Not

Not is another hedge that is used to define the opposite side of the adjective that follows this word. It means negation or complement and can be defined by the following membership function:

$$F_{not}(x) = \{1 - F(x) \mid x \text{ is in } U\}$$

$F(x)$, the degree of membership, is defined within the range $[0, 1]$. For the tourist example, x is the number of visitors. The hedge **not** can be applied to any fuzzy primary term to define the negation of the term's meaning. If **not** is applied to the primary term *high*, the graphical representation of the membership function will be as shown in Figure 8.10.

The result of the following query is shown in Table 8.10:

SELECT country FROM table WHERE no._of_visitors = **not** *high*

Notice that the result of this query is the same as the query with the *low* fuzzy condition.

Somewhat

Quite or **somewhat** corresponds to fuzzy dilution, which is done by taking the square root of the membership function at each point in the set. This dilution operation modifies the original $F_{high}(x)$ by sharply increasing the degree of membership of the elements that are just barely in the set.

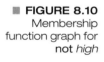

FIGURE 8.10
Membership function graph for not *high*

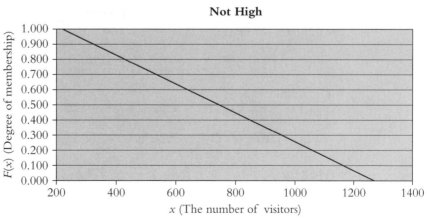

■ **TABLE 8.10 Data for no._of_visitors = not** *high*

Country	No. of visitors	Membership	Country	No. of visitors	Membership
Trinidad/ Tobago	216	1	Greece	433	0.794
Russia	238	0.979	Australia	454	0.774
Argentina	260	0.958	Philippines	476	0.754
Peru	260	0.958	Brazil	498	0.733
Venezuela	281	0.938	Turkey	519	0.713
Costa Rica	303	0.918	Taiwan	562	0.672
Guatemala	303	0.918	South Korea	649	0.59
Israel	303	0.918	Hong Kong	671	0.569
Thailand	303	0.918	Switzerland	671	0.569
Belgium	325	0.897	Spain	714	0.528
Colombia	325	0.897	Bahamas	817	0.43
Bermuda	368	0.856	Netherlands	822	0.426
India	368	0.856	P.R. of China	947	0.307
Austria	389	0.836	Japan	1082	0.179
Singapore	389	0.836	Jamaica	1141	0.123
Ireland	411	0.815	Italy	1271	0

The membership function is shown below and its graphical representation is depicted in Figure 8.11.

$$F_{\text{somewhat } high}(x) = \left(F_{high}^{1/2}(x) \right)$$

The result of the following query with the **somewhat** *high* fuzzy condition is partially shown in Table 8.11.

SELECT country FROM table WHERE no._of_visitors = **somewhat** *high*

Mostly

Mostly is a hedge used to confine the degree of membership to the range 0.5 to 1. Every membership value that has a degree less than 0.5 is assigned 0

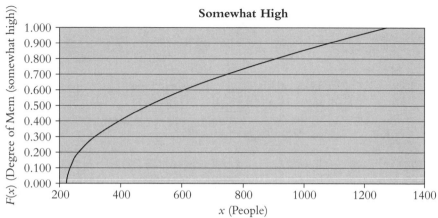

FIGURE 8.11 Membership function graph for **somewhat** *high*

as the degree of membership for **mostly**. The result obtained will be more reliable than just using the primary fuzzy variable. The following function is used to represent the fuzzy membership for **mostly**:

$$F_{\text{mostly } high}(x) = 1/2 + 1/2 \times \sin((1.5 + (x - \min)/(\max - \min)) \times \pi(\ ))$$

TABLE 8.11 Data for no._of_visitors = somewhat *high*

Country	No. of visitors	Membership for *high*	Membership for somewhat *high*
Italy	1,271	1	1
Jamaica	1,141	0.877	0.936
Japan	1,082	0.821	0.906
P.R. of China	947	0.693	0.832
Netherlands	822	0.574	0.758
Bahamas	817	0.57	0.755
Spain	714	0.472	0.687
Hong Kong	671	0.431	0.657
Switzerland	671	0.431	0.657
South Korea	649	0.41	0.641
Taiwan	562	0.328	0.573
Turkey	519	0.287	0.536
Brazil	498	0.267	0.517

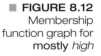

■ **FIGURE 8.12**
Membership
function graph for
mostly *high*

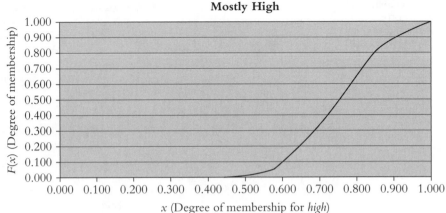

Here the value of min is set to 0.5, and max is set to 1. The x is the degree of membership for primary fuzzy terms such as *high*. The graphical representation for **mostly** *high* is given in Figure 8.12.

The result of the following query with the **mostly** *high* fuzzy condition is partially shown in Table 8.12:

SELECT country FROM table WHERE no._of_visitors = **mostly** *high*

■ **TABLE 8.12 Data for no._of_visitors = mostly *high***

Country	No. of visitors	Degree of membership for *high*	Degree of membership for mostly *high*
Italy	1271	1.000	1.000
Jamaica	1141	0.877	0.857
Japan	1082	0.821	0.715
P.R. of China	947	0.693	0.324
Netherlands	822	0.574	0.054
Bahamas	817	0.570	0.047

■ 8.6   FUZZY QUERY PROCESSING USING FUZZY TABLES

The most ideal property of any query processing system for efficient information retrieval is the ability to handle regular queries in the form of either quantitative or qualitative queries and fuzzy queries that are expressed with ambiguous and/or fuzzy terms. Any queries into which fuzzy or ambiguous terms are embedded are called fuzzy queries. The part of the query processor that handles the fuzzy queries is called the fuzzy modulator, which applies the concept of fuzzy logic to handle the ambiguous terms used in query expressions. To make the query processor correctly respond to the fuzzy queries, fuzzy logic is applied.

A relational database used by the query processor to interpret fuzzy expressions generally contains multiple quantitative data instances. These quantitative data tuples in the database will be the basis for the interpretation of fuzzy expressions. Thus, the relational database needs to be converted into a fuzzy table from which the interpretation of the fuzzy terms can be more straightforward. In the following sections, converting a relational database into a fuzzy database using a fuzzy table is described.

■ 8.6.1   Convert Raw Data to Fuzzy Member Functions

For the sake of simplification, a book database is used to consider the *price* attribute of books, focusing on three value categories: *cheap, medium*, and *expensive*. Defining the exact boundaries between *cheap* and *medium* and between *medium* and *expensive* is subjective, fuzzy, and interpretation dependent. Hence, the prices of all the books in the database need to be considered when determining distribution characteristics of the prices. In order to determine the range of each value category and interpret the relative meaning of *cheap, medium*, and *expensive*, we use standard deviation and mean to solve the fuzzy boundary problem.

Standard deviation (SD) is a statistical measurement used to show how tightly all the data points are clustered around the value representing the mean of the dataset. This method is based on normal distribution of data, where most of the data values in a given set are close to the average value, while a relatively small number of data values tends to one extreme or the other. In this chapter, however, SD is used for a different purpose and does not require exploitation of the normal distribution. The SD and the mean

▮ **TABLE 8.13 Book transaction table**

Book ID	Price
1	10.00
2	60.50
3	100.00
...	...
1000	30.50

are defined by the following formulae, where n is the total number of datasets with $1 \leq i \leq n$. The mean is the average of the data values in the population. It equals the sum of the data values divided by the total number of values:

$$SD = \sqrt{\sum (X_i - \bar{X})^2/(n-1)} \quad \text{and} \quad \bar{X} = \sum X_i/n$$

Creating a Crisp Dataset

Suppose we have a transaction table as shown in Table 8.13.

The transaction table is used to plot a graph of a crisp dataset in which the transaction volume of the attribute being considered is depicted. In this example, the vertical line of the graph shows the number of people who purchased the book for a particular price and the horizontal line shows the price range. The following is the four simple steps used to determine the crisp set of data values:

Step 1: Find the mean of the data values.
Step 2: Determine the SD to find the medium category.
Step 3: Consider the left of the medium area as below the medium category.
Step 4: Consider the right side of the medium area as above the medium category.

After applying these steps to the book table, a graph can be drawn as shown in Figure 8.13. Using a carefully selected SD measure, a medium range can be determined. The remaining areas, one below the medium area and the other above the medium area, are designated as the two extreme categories, respectively. In the book example, the low extreme is designated as the *cheap* category and the high extreme as the *expensive* category as shown in Figure 8.13. The SD measure is used to set the boundaries between the categories

FIGURE 8.13
Crisp dataset

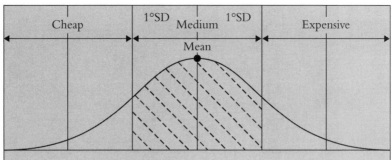

and can be adjusted as needed to reset the boundaries. For illustration purposes in the discussion to follow, let the *low, medium*, and *high* extremes be called category 1 (C_1), category 2 (C_2), and category 3 (C_3), respectively.

To be able to handle fuzzy terms in query processing, the crisp dataset needs to be transformed into the corresponding fuzzy dataset. This process is done through the fuzzy membership functions that will be shown in the next section. These membership functions will enable the construction of a fuzzy table from which the interpretation of fuzzy terms on the crisp dataset is made feasible.

Membership Functions for Categories C_1 and C_3

For category C_1, the low extreme of the crisp dataset, the mean value (C_{1mean}) of the area is used to determine the membership function. The membership function Y is dependent on an attribute, say X, in concentration. Y may be considered for two cases: (1) when X is less than C_{1mean} and (2) when X is between C_{1mean} and C_{2mean}. Then, the handling of each case in the C_1 category for the membership function Y can be done as follows:

Case 1: For $0 \leq X \leq C_{1mean}$, $Y = 1$.
Case 2: For $C_{1mean} < X < C_{2mean}$, $Y = mX + b$, where $Y =$ degree of membership, $X =$ price, $m =$ slope $[(Y_2 - Y_1)/(X_2 - X_1)]$, $b =$ Y-axis intercept, $X_1 = C_{1mean}$, $Y_1 = 1$, $X_2 = C_{2mean}$, and $Y_2 = 0$.

Applying this principle to our book table, the membership function is depicted as shown in Figure 8.14.

The same principle can be applied to category C_3 as illustrated by case 3 and case 4 following. Here, C_{2mean} and C_{3mean} are used instead. Y may be considered for two cases: (1) when X is greater than C_{3mean} and (2) when X is between

■ **FIGURE 8.14**
Membership
function for the
cheap category

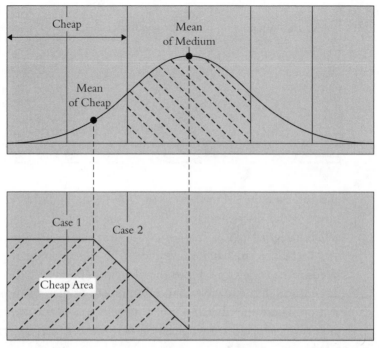

■ **FIGURE 8.15**
Membership
function for
the *expensive*
category

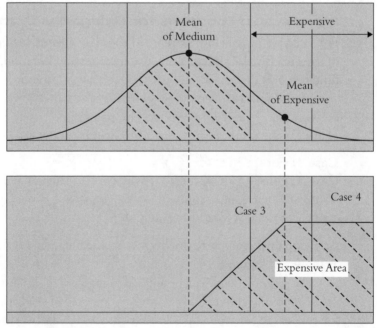

■ **FIGURE 8.16**
Membership
function for the
medium category

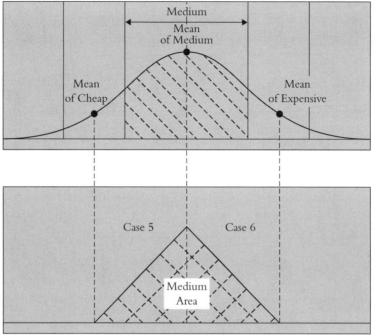

C_{2mean} and C_{3mean}. The membership function depicted in Figure 8.15 is obtained after applying this principle to the book table.

Case 3: For $C_{2mean} < X < C_{3mean}$, $Y = mX + b$, where Y = degree of membership, X = price, m = slope $[(Y_2 - Y_1)/(X_2 - X_1)]$, b = Y-axis intercept, $X_1 = C_{2mean}$, $Y_1 = 0$, $X_2 = C_{3mean}$, and $Y_2 = 1$.
Case 4: For $X > C_{3mean}$, $Y = 1$.

Membership Function for Category C_2

The membership function for category C_2 is formulated on the medium range obtained after excluding the two extremes, the C_1 and C_3 categories. In this case, all three measures C_{1mean}, C_{2mean}, and C_{3mean} are considered as is shown in cases 5 and 6. The graphical representation of the membership function derived from the book table is given in Figure 8.16.

Case 5: For $C_{1mean} < X < C_{2mean}$, $Y = mX + b$, where Y = degree of membership, X = price, m = slope $[(Y_2 - Y_1)/(X_2 - X_1)]$, b = Y-axis intercept, $X_1 = C_{1mean}$, $Y_1 = 0$, $X_2 = C_{2mean}$, and $Y_2 = 1$.

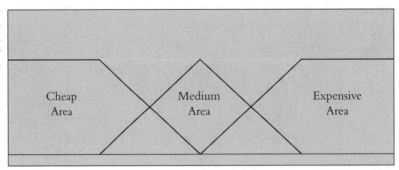

Case 6: For $C_{2mean} < X < C_{3mean}$, $Y = mX + b$, where $Y =$ degree of membership, $X =$ price, $m =$ slope $[(Y_2-Y_1)/(X_2 - X_1)]$, $b = Y$-axis intercept, $X_1 = C_{2mean}$, $Y_1 = 1$, $X_2 = C_{3mean}$, and $Y_2 = 0$.

The membership function for any attribute being concentrated is obtained by combining all the membership functions covering each category of the attribute values. In the book table, combining all the membership functions representing all three categories (C_1, C_2, and C_3) enables the formulation of the complete fuzzy membership function of the attribute *price* as shown in Figure 8.17. This function covers a complete fuzzy set for *cheap, medium*, and *expensive* categories of the price attribute of the books.

■ 8.6.2 Fuzzy Table

Once we create the complete fuzzy membership function for an attribute, a fuzzy table can be constructed from the original crisp transaction table. In building the table, all of those categorical fuzzy functions covering each category are considered in representing the degree of membership of a certain value to each category. In the books example, each of the categorical fuzzy functions corresponding to *cheap, medium*, and *expensive* categories of the *price* attribute is evaluated to create the fuzzy table from the original transaction table. This is done by applying the formula of each categorical membership function to the price values in the transaction table. Hence, the original transaction table yields the fuzzy table in Table 8.14 using the previously derived categorical membership functions. The last three columns correspond to the different categories of price values. The quantitative values under each column represent the degree of membership of each value to the corresponding category. This fuzzy table is used to generate answers to fuzzy queries. This process is further discussed in Section 8.6.3 where the fuzzy search engine is discussed.

■ **TABLE 8.14 A fuzzy table with a basic fuzzy quantifier**

Book ID	Cheap	Medium	Expensive
1	0.8	0.2	0.0
2	0.0	0.7	0.3
3	0.0	0.0	1.0
…	…	…	…
1000	0.4	0.6	0.0

■ 8.6.3 Fuzzy Search Engine

The handling of fuzzy queries is processed in two parts. One part deals with parsing of the query in terms of hedges, connectives, and primary terms. Once parsed, these terms are interpreted using the fuzzy numbers in the fuzzy databases. In the other part of the search, the traditional database is converted into fuzzy databases in which all data are represented in terms of the degree of fuzziness. Figure 8.18 depicts both parts, which merge a constructed fuzzy table with a parsed fuzzy query to produce search results. The fuzzy table is very crucial for interpreting the fuzzy query because it provides an essential foundation needed to match between the raw data and

■ **FIGURE 8.18**
Fuzzy search
diagram

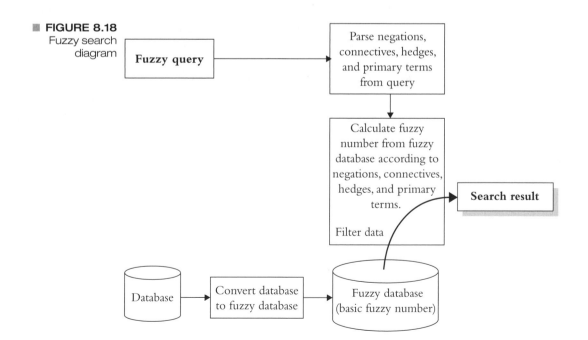

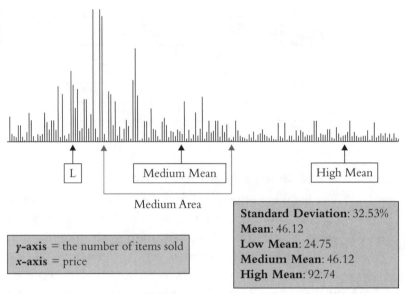

FIGURE 8.19
Data distribution in
transaction table

L

Medium Mean

High Mean

Medium Area

y-axis = the number of items sold
x-axis = price

Standard Deviation: 32.53%
Mean: 46.12
Low Mean: 24.75
Medium Mean: 46.12
High Mean: 92.74

the fuzzy meaning of the primary terms. The fuzzy meaning of the primary terms can be further fuzzified with connectives and hedges.

To understand the necessity and motivation behind the fuzzy table, take a look at the data distribution illustrated in Figure 8.19. The data distribution in the figure represents the relationship between price and number of copies sold in the book database.

■ 8.6.4 Fuzzy Table Construction

From the transaction table in Table 8.15, a distribution graph shown in Figure 8.19 can be generated. The *x*-axis covers the values ranging from

TABLE 8.15 Transaction table

TID	Book ID	Price
1	1565924150	10.25
2	0201758660	28.95
3	186100527X	70.95
4	0735614237	42.95
...	...	...
1683	0764545647	109.25

FIGURE 8.20
A fuzzy set graph

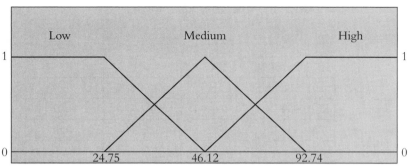

$0 to $369.50. The mean, SD, mean of *cheap* (*low*) area, mean of *medium* area, and mean of *expensive* (*high*) area can be determined accordingly. By applying the formulae discussed in Section 8.6.1, the fuzzy set graph shown in Figure 8.20 can be obtained.

Using the fuzzy set generated, each record in the transaction table can be converted to fuzzy numbers to obtain a fuzzy table as shown in Table 8.16.

■ 8.6.5   Fuzzy Query Processing

In this section, the handling of three fuzzy queries is illustrated. The results of the queries are generated using fuzzy graphs and fuzzy tables.

Fuzzy Query 1: List the Books That Are Very Cheap

In this case, each degree of membership listed in each record of the fuzzy table is applied to the **very** formula. The resulting **very** fuzzy table is shown in Table 8.17.

The result of the query, the list of **very** *cheap* books, is shown in Figure 8.21. In this figure, the alpha-cut value of 0.3 was used as the threshold. This way

TABLE 8.16 Fuzzy table with a basic fuzzy number

Book ID	Cheap	Medium	Expensive
1565924150	1.0	0.0	0.0
0201758660	0.8	0.2	0.0
186100527X	0.0	0.3	0.7
0735614237	0.1	0.9	0.0
...	...	...	...
0764545647	0.0	0.0	1.0

■ TABLE 8.17 The **very** fuzzy table

Book ID	Very *cheap*	Very *medium*	Very *expensive*
1565924150	1.0	0.0	0.0
0201758660	0.64	0.04	0.0
186100527X	0.0	0.09	0.49
0735614237	0.01	0.81	0.0
...	...	...	...
0764545647	0.0	0.0	1.0

■ FIGURE 8.21
Very *cheap* books

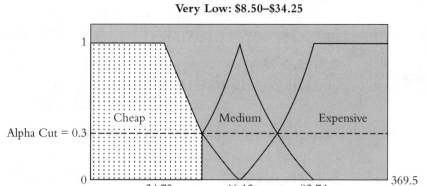

Very Low: $8.50–$34.25

Book ID	Price
0596000669	8.5
0890066604	10.0
0201708981	12.75
0072131403	19.5
0596001320	21.5
0672321580	22.95
0596000278	30.5
...	...
0079136788	34.25

the query processor will list the books that satisfy the degree of *cheap* membership equal to or greater than 0.3.

Fuzzy Query 2: List the Books That Are Medium- and High-Priced

In a similar manner as the previous query, the list of *medium*-and-*high* priced books is shown in Figure 8.22 using the same alpha-cut threshold.

Fuzzy Query 3: List the Books That Are Cheap or Medium-Priced

The result of the query, the list of *cheap-or-medium-priced* books, is shown in Figure 8.23. The alpha-cut threshold of 0.3 was used as depicted in the fuzzy set graph.

■ **FIGURE 8.22**
Medium- and *high*-priced books

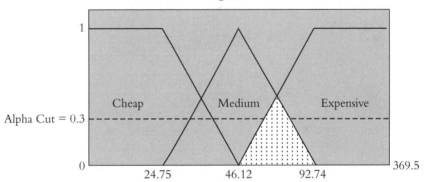

Book ID	Price
1558604677	46.5
0201633469	48.95
1558601694	50.5
0130183806	53.5
0130950696	68.5
0130129399	74.95
089006606X	81.5
…	…
0471491845	90.5

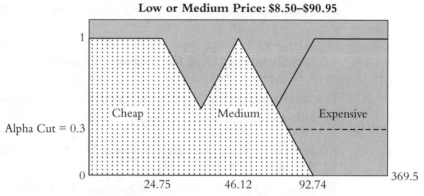

Low or Medium Price: $8.50–$90.95

Book ID	Price
0596000669	8.5
0890066604	10.0
0201708981	12.75
0072131403	19.5
1558604677	46.5
0201633469	48.95
1558601694	50.5
0130183806	53.5
0130950696	68.5
0130129399	74.95
089006606X	81.5
...	...
0471491845	90.95

■ 8.7   ROLE OF RELATIONAL DIVISION FOR INFORMATION RETRIEVAL

Since conventional relational databases contain data that is crisp, most data manipulation operations are centered on the retrieval of data based on non-fuzzy selection
criteria. However, the need for specifying queries with fuzzy terms has increased
as users focus more of their attention on the retrieval of information rather
than data. A solution to the fuzzy query representation problem is to store fuzzy
information in a database, for example, storing the fact that a student is a middle-
aged man with a high GPA who has a modest number of friends. Storing data
with fuzzy values, however, does pose a number of potential problems.

One problem is that the information would be meaningless for some analytical programs because of the fuzziness of the data. Another possible problem is that the contents of certain attributes such as age or GPA would change on a regular basis. This is because any really useful information is either volatile or perishable. Thirdly, data interpretation may not be consistent. Since databases are shared by many departments, students with a high GPA conceived by the graduate school might be considered average to the computer science department. Because of these potential problems, it is more natural to treat the facts in a fuzzy manner than to store fuzzy information in a database. Also, in this way, database conversion is not necessary since we have the facts in the database.

Applying fuzzy logic for the qualification of information from a database system of tables and objects is a very crucial part of interpreting data in a fuzzy manner.

■ 8.7.1 Information Retrieval through Relational Division

In this section, we will consider the relational division operator as a way to handle fuzzy query processing. For the simplicity of illustration, a relation of degree two will be used to divide a relation of degree one. First, the definition of relational division will be given. Then the extension of relational division with degrees of certainty, called fuzzy relational division, will be presented with an example. The proposal used for extending the relational division operator is Mouaddib's [Mouaddib 1994].

Let $R(X, Y)$ and $S(Y)$ be two relations with attributes X and Y, respectively. The relation division $R \div S$ yields a new relation $D(X)$ with sole attribute X such that every value x of $D(X)$ appears as a value of $R[X]$, which is the relational projection of R on X, and the pair (x, y) appears in R for all values y in S. The relation $D(X)$ can be written as $D(X) = \{x \mid x \in R[X], \forall y \in S[Y], (x,y) \in R[X,Y]\}$. Another definition of relational division can be given in terms of projection (π), selection (σ), and intersection ($\cap$). If we let n be the number of elements in S, $D(X)$ can be deduced from the following three formulae:

1. $R_i'(X, Y) = \sigma_{Y=y_i}(R)$;
2. $_i(X) = \pi_X R_i'(X, Y)$;
3. $D(X) = \cap R_i(X)$, where $y_i \in S$ and $i \in [1, n]$.

■ **TABLE 8.18** Relation D(puppy) = $R \div S$

R		S	D
Puppy	**Color**	**Color**	**Puppy**
p1	White	White	p1
p1	Yellow	Yellow	
p1	Red		
p2	Red		
p2	Brown		
p3	Whitish		
p3	yellow		

For example, consider Table 8.18 for relations R and S. The result of dividing R by S is the set of puppies having both colors in S, white and yellow. Hence, the resulting relation D(puppy) = $\{p1\}$.

■ 8.7.2 Information Retrieval through Fuzzy Relational Division

In this section, the relational division operation is extended to process fuzzy queries. For this purpose, a new definition for fuzzy division needs to be given so that it can be applied to a fuzzy database whose attribute values could be fuzzy.

Let $R(X, Y)$ and $S(Y)$ be two fuzzy relations. Let D_X and D_Y be the domains of the X and Y attributes, respectively. Then the fuzzy division operator $\div_f$ can be defined by the following three steps with $y_i \in S$ and $i \in [1, n]$. In the formulae below, $\cap^f$ the fuzzy intersection operator, π^f the fuzzy projection operator, and σ^f is the fuzzy selection operator:

1. $R_i'(X, Y) = \sigma^f_{Y=y_i}(R)$
2. $R_i(X) = \pi^f_X R_i'(X, Y)$
3. $R \div_f S = \cap^f R_i(X)$

Fuzzy relations R_i', R_i, and $R \div_f S$ resulting from the above formulae can be represented by the following characteristic functions, where $x \in D_X$, $y \in D_Y$, and $u \in R_i'$. The $u.\alpha$ in formula (4) indicates the membership grade of u in R.

4. $\mu_{R_i}(u) = \min(u.\alpha, \max_y \min(\mu_{Y_i}(y), \mu_{u.Y}(y)))$

5. $\mu_{R_i}(x) = \max_{u.X=x} \mu_{R_i}(u)$

6. $\mu_{R \div_f S}(x) = \min(\mu_{R_i}(x))$

For illustration purposes, the relation R in Table 8.18 can be extended to the fuzzy relation R shown in Table 8.19. The values in the α column indicate the degree of certainty with which a puppy has the associated color. Suppose that we want to find puppies that are *whitish* AND *yellowish*. In this case relation S in Table 8.19 can be used to process the query with relational division.

The characteristic functions for the color of the puppies are defined in Table 8.20. Each line of the table determines a characteristic function with each coefficient indicating the membership degree. The characteristic function of $R \div_f S$ can be calculated as follows by applying the formulae (4), (5), and (6) given above.

Let $u1, u2, u3, u4, u5, u6$, and $u7$ be the seven tuples in R. Then

$$\mu_{R_i}(u1) = \min(1, \max_y \min(\mu_{whitish}(y), \mu_{white}(y))) = 0.8$$

$$\mu_{R_i}(u2) = \min(0.8, \max_y \min(\mu_{whitish}(y), \mu_{yellow}(y))) = 0$$

$$\mu_{R_i}(u3) = \min(0.7, \max_y \min(\mu_{whitish}(y), \mu_{red}(y))) = 0$$

■ TABLE 8.19 Fuzzy relations *R* and *S*

Puppy	*Color*	α
p1	White	1
p1	Yellow	0.8
p1	Red	0.7
p2	Red	1
p2	Brown	0.7
p3	Whitish	0.6
p3	Yellow	1

Color	α
Whitish	1
Yellowish	1

■ TABLE 8.20 Characteristic functions for puppy colors

	White	Whitish	Brown	Yellow	Yellowish	Red
White	1	0.8	0	0	0	0
Whitish	0.8	1	0	0	0	0
Brown	0	0	1	0.2	0.4	0
Yellow	0	0	0.2	1	0.8	0
Yellowish	0	0	0.4	0.8	1	0
Red	0	0	0	0	0	1

$$\mu_{R_1'}(u4) = \min(1, \max_y \min(\mu_{whitish}(y), \mu_{red}(y))) = 0$$

$$\mu_{R_1'}(u5) = \min(0.7, \max_y \min(\mu_{whitish}(y), \mu_{brown}(y))) = 0$$

$$\mu_{R_1'}(u6) = \min(0.6, \max_y \min(\mu_{whitish}(y), \mu_{whitish}(y))) = 0.6$$

$$\mu_{R_1'}(u7) = \min(1, \max_y \min(\mu_{whitish}(y), \mu_{yellow}(y))) = 0$$

Hence, we deduce

$$\mu_{R_1}(p1) = \max(\mu_{R_1'}(u1), \mu_{R_1'}(u2), \mu_{R_1'}(u3)) = 0.8$$

$$\mu_{R_1}(p2) = \max(\mu_{R_1'}(u4), \mu_{R_1'}(u5)) = 0$$

$$\mu_{R_1}(p3) = \max(\mu_{R_1'}(u6), \mu_{R_1'}(u7)) = 0.6$$

In the same manner, we can obtain the following:

$$\mu_{R_2'}(u1) = \min(1, \max_y \min(\mu_{yellowish}(y), \mu_{white}(y))) = 0$$

$$\mu_{R_2'}(u2) = \min(0.8, \max_y \min(\mu_{yellowish}(y), \mu_{yellow}(y))) = 0.8$$

$$\mu_{R_2'}(u3) = \min(0.7, \max_y \min(\mu_{yellowish}(y), \mu_{red}(y))) = 0$$

$$\mu_{R_2'}(u4) = \min(1, \max_y \min(\mu_{yellowish}(y), \mu_{red}(y))) = 0$$

$$\mu_{R_2'}(u5) = \min(0.7, \max_y \min(\mu_{yellowish}(y), \mu_{brown}(y))) = 0.4$$

$$\mu_{R_2'}(u6) = \min(0.6, \max_y \min(\mu_{yellowish}(y), \mu_{whitish}(y))) = 0$$

$$\mu_{R_2'}(u7) = \min(1, \max_y \min(\mu_{yellowish}(y), \mu_{yellow}(y))) = 0.8$$

Similarly, we can deduce

$$\mu_{R_2}(p1) = \max(\mu_{R_2'}(u1), \mu_{R_2'}(u2), \mu_{R_2'}(u3)) = 0.8$$

$$\mu_{R_2}(p2) = \max(\mu_{R_2'}(u4), \mu_{R_2'}(u5)) = 0.4$$

$$\mu_{R_2}(p3) = \max(\mu_{R_2'}(u6), \mu_{R_2'}(u7)) = 0.8$$

Finally, we can obtain

$$\mu_{R+_fS}(p1) = \min(\mu_{R_1}(p1), \mu_{R_2}(p1)) = 0.8$$
$$\mu_{R+_fS}(p2) = \min(\mu_{R_1}(p2), \mu_{R_2}(p2)) = 0$$
$$\mu_{R+_fS}(p3) = \min(\mu_{R_1}(p3), \mu_{R_2}(p3)) = 0.6$$

Therefore, we can conclude that puppy $p1$ is *whitish* AND *yellowish* with 80% certainty, while puppy $p3$ is so with 60% certainty. Furthermore, we conclude that puppy $p2$ is neither *whitish* nor *yellowish* at all.

■ 8.8 ALPHA-CUT THRESHOLDS

An alpha-cut threshold defines a minimum degree of membership value. Without it, the amount of information retrieved by the query processor may be enormous. It minimizes the amount of unnecessary information since any membership value less than the threshold will be excluded from the candidate list. A restricted set of more reliable information is obtained by establishing an appropriate alpha-cut threshold to define a boundary between useful and useless information.

■ **TABLE 8.21 Alpha cut 0.2 applied to both *high* and *low***

| Country | No. of visitors | Degree of Membership | | |
		high	*low*	*high & low*
Spain	714	0.472	0.528	0.472
Hong Kong	671	0.431	0.569	0.431
Switzerland	671	0.431	0.569	0.431
Bahamas	817	0.570	0.43	0.43
Netherlands	822	0.574	0.426	0.43
South Korea	649	0.410	0.590	0.410
Taiwan	562	0.328	0.672	0.328
China	947	0.693	0.307	0.31
Turkey	519	0.287	0.713	0.287
Brazil	498	0.267	0.733	0.267
Philippines	476	0.246	0.754	0.246
Australia	454	0.226	0.774	0.226
Greece	433	0.206	0.794	0.206

In the case when a conjunctive operator (AND) or a disjunctive operator (OR) is used, the alpha-cut threshold is applied to both operands. The threshold is then applied again to the composite truth value of the complete "where" clause, which may contain many fuzzy propositions. Hence, the alpha-cut threshold acts as a hurdle for inclusion in the candidate set. For example, Table 8.21 shows the result of applying the alpha-cut threshold value of 0.2 to the following query:

SELECT country FROM Table X WHERE no._of_visitors = *high* AND
no._of_visitors = *low*

To handle this query, only the countries with the number of visitors both *high* and *low* with at least 0.2 membership values are considered. Then the alpha-cut threshold is applied again to the table that is the result of applying the AND operator to both the high and low number of visitors as shown in Table 8.21.

Without applying the alpha-cut threshold, the resulting table looks like Table 8.22, which contains many more records. If most of the records are not

■ TABLE 8.22 Tourist table without applying an alpha-cut threshold

Country	No. of Visitors	Degree of Membership (high & low)	Country	No. of Visitors	Degree of Membership (high & low)
Spain	714	0.472	Singapore	389	0.164
Hong Kong	671	0.431	Bermuda	368	0.144
Switzerland	671	0.431	India	368	0.144
Bahamas	817	0.430	Jamaica	1141	0.123
Netherlands	822	0.426	Belgium	325	0.103
South Korea	649	0.410	Colombia	325	0.103
Taiwan	562	0.328	Costa Rica	303	0.082
P.R. of China	947	0.307	Guatemala	303	0.082
Turkey	519	0.287	Israel	303	0.082
Brazil	498	0.267	Thailand	303	0.082
Philippines	476	0.246	Venezuela	281	0.062
Australia	454	0.226	Argentina	260	0.042
Greece	433	0.206	Peru	260	0.042
Ireland	411	0.185	Russia	238	0.021
Japan	1082	0.179	Italy	1271	0.000
Austria	389	0.164	Trinidad/ Tobago	216	0.000

useful for making certain decisions in terms of *high* AND *low* criteria, then an appropriate alpha-cut threshold will help eliminate unnecessary tuples as shown in Table 8.21. A high alpha-cut filters out records that are not highly compatible with the intention of the query, while a low alpha cut allows records even weakly compatible with the query intent.

Even when adverbs and adjectives of the hedge method are used, the alpha-cut threshold can be used for filtering the results of queries. But it is not necessary to apply the alpha-cut threshold to each adverb or adjective. The alpha-cut threshold is applied to the result only once instead of being applied to each adverb and adjective and then combined together. For instance, an alpha-cut threshold can be applied to **somewhat** and *high* in the query below.

■ **TABLE 8.23 Alpha-cut threshold 0.4 applied to somewhat *high***

Country	No. of Visitors	Degree of Membership (*high*)	Degree of Membership (somewhat *high*)
Italy	1271	1.000	1.000
Jamaica	1141	0.877	0.936
Japan	1082	0.821	0.906
P.R. of China	947	0.693	0.832
Netherlands	822	0.574	0.758
Bahamas	817	0.570	0.755
Spain	714	0.472	0.687
Hong Kong	671	0.431	0.657
Switzerland	671	0.431	0.657
South Korea	649	0.410	0.641
Taiwan	562	0.328	0.573
Turkey	519	0.287	0.536
Brazil	498	0.267	0.517
Philippines	476	0.246	0.496
Australia	454	0.226	0.475
Greece	433	0.206	0.454
Ireland	411	0.185	0.430
Austria	389	0.164	0.405
Singapore	389	0.164	0.405

Then, Table 8.23 shows the result after applying an alpha-cut threshold equal to 0.4.

SELECT country FROM table WHERE people = **somewhat** *high*

For the result shown in Table 8.23, **somewhat** is combined with *high* before applying the alpha-cut threshold because **somewhat** does not hold a joint relation with *high*. The **somewhat** is an adverb of the hedge that is added on to *high*. That is why some records with the degree of membership of *high* below 0.4 are still included in the resulting relation shown in the table.

Without the alpha-cut threshold, the size of the resulting table is much larger than Table 8.23. Note, however, that the setting of an alpha-cut threshold to a specific value highly depends on the purpose of the fuzzy query and the type of information being sought.

■ 8.9 CHAPTER SUMMARY

A fuzzy set is a set without a crisp boundary, which means the transition from "belongs to the set" to "does not belong to the set" is gradual. This gradual transition is characterized by a membership function that gives the fuzzy set flexibility in modeling commonly used linguistic expressions. The membership degree of a fuzzy set depends on the problem that needs to be solved and the information that is to be retrieved. Membership functions can be as simple as any linear relation or as complicated as any mathematically complex function. Furthermore, membership functions can be multidimensional.

Fuzzy logic can be used to naturally describe everyday business applications since it presents a flexible method of getting a high-level abstraction of problem representation. In the real world, problems are often vague and imprecise and cannot be described with conventional, two-valued (true or false) logic. On the contrary, fuzzy logic allows a continuous gradation of truth values ranging from false to true in the description process of application models.

Linguistic variables are variables whose values are not numbers but are words or phrases, as found in a natural-language sentence. Linguistic variables are often used to embed fuzzy meaning into fuzzy queries. Since they carry fuzzy meaning, the interpretation of any linguistic variable requires the identification and application of a fuzzy membership function.

Since fuzzy queries are specified with linguistic variables, they have to be interpreted with fuzzy membership functions. Membership functions give quantitative meaning to fuzzy queries so that an appropriate dataset meeting the fuzzy criteria can be retrieved based on the quantitative criteria. Examples of fuzzy queries specified with linguistic variables, such as *high, low, acceptable, somewhat*, and *mostly*, have been processed with appropriate membership functions. The part of the query processor that handles fuzzy queries is called the fuzzy modulator, which applies the concept of fuzzy logic to handle the ambiguous terms used in query expressions. To make the query processor correctly respond to the fuzzy queries, fuzzy logic is applied.

Relational division is another way to handle fuzzy query processing. A relation of a certain degree is divided by a relation of smaller degree. The relational division operator is extended to the fuzzy division operator to process fuzzy queries. An alpha-cut threshold defines a minimum degree of membership value. Without it, the amount of information retrieved by the query processor can be enormous. It minimizes the amount of unnecessary information since any membership values less than the threshold are excluded from the candidate list. A restricted set of more reliable information is obtained by establishing an appropriate alpha-cut threshold to define a boundary between useful and useless information.

■ 8.10   EXERCISES

1. The fish price database table shown in Table 8.24 contains data on prices in cents per pound received by fishermen and vessel owners for various species of fish and shellfish in California in 1970 and 1980.

   The table contains the following three attributes:
   - *Fish type*:   Species of fish
   - *Price* (1970):   Price in cents per pound in 1970
   - *Price* (1980):   Price in cents per pound in 1980

      a. Compose fuzzy queries with the following linguistic variables: *acceptable, high*, and *low*.

      b. Apply the following hedges to the queries composed in (a): **usually, not, somewhat, very**, and **mostly**.

      c. Apply all the queries composed in both (a) and (b) to Table 8.24.

2. *Fortune* magazine publishes a list of billionaires annually. The following list (shown in Table 8.25) includes 60 individuals or families. Their *wealth, age*, and *geographic location* (Asia, Europe, Middle East, United States, or Other) are reported as follows:

   - *Wealth*: Wealth of family or individual in billions of dollars
   - *Age*: Age in years (for families it is the maximum age of family members)
   - *Region*: Region of the world (Asia, Europe, Middle East, United States, and Other)

■ TABLE 8.24 Fish prices

Fish Type	Price (1970)	Price (1980)
Cod	13.1	27.3
Flounder	15.3	42.4
Haddock	25.8	38.7
Menhaden	1.8	4.5
Ocean Perch	4.9	23
Salmon, Chinook	55.4	166.3
Salmon, Coho	39.3	109.7
Tuna, Albacore	26.7	80.1
Clams, Soft-Shelled	47.5	150.7
Clams, Blue Hard-Shelled	6.6	20.3
Lobsters, American	94.7	189.7
Oysters, Eastern	61.1	131.3
Sea Scallops	135.6	404.2
Shrimp	47.6	149

  a. Compose fuzzy queries with the following linguistic variables: *rich, young*, and *old*.

  b. Apply the following hedges to the queries composed in (a): **not, somewhat, very**, and **mostly**.

  c. Apply all the queries composed in both (a) and (b) to Table 8.25.

  d. Apply an appropriate alpha-cut threshold value to the queries in (c) to generate more than three possible answers.

3. Consider Table 8.26, which contains information on alcohol and tobacco consumption over several different regions in Great Britain.

  The table contains the following three attributes:

  • *Region*: Region of Great Britain
  • *Alcohol*: Average weekly household spending on alcoholic beverages in pounds
  • *Tobacco*: Average weekly household spending on tobacco products in pounds

■ **TABLE 8.25 Billionaires in 1992**

Wealth	Age	Region	Wealth	Age	Region	Wealth	Age	Region
37	50	M	4.0	62	M	1.8	47	E
24	88	U	4.0	69	E	1.8	86	U
14	64	A	4.0	49	A	1.8	67	A
13	63	U	3.9	64	A	1.7	54	U
13	66	U	3.9	83	A	1.7	77	E
11.7	72	E	3.8	41	A	1.7	61	U
10.0	71	M	3.8	78	A	2.0	60	E
8.2	77	U	3.6	80	A	2.0	74	O
8.1	68	U	3.5	68	O	1.9	48	U
7.2	66	E	3.4	67	U	1.9	60	E
7.0	69	M	3.4	71	O	1.8	86	U
6.2	36	O	3.4	54	A	1.8	67	A
5.9	49	U	3.3	62	E	1.7	54	U
5.3	73	U	3.3	69	A	1.7	77	E
5.2	52	E	3.3	58	U	1.7	61	U
5.0	77	M	3.2	71	U	1.4	52	A
5.0	73	M	3.2	55	O	1.4	73	A
4.9	62	A	3.0	66	E	1.3	83	U
4.8	54	U	3.0	65	E	1.3	64	E
4.7	63	U	3.0	50	U	1.3	71	O

  a. Identify the regions where alcohol consumption is **very** *high*.

  b. Identify the regions where tobacco consumption is **somewhat** *high*.

  c. Identify two regions where alcohol consumption is *high* and tobacco consumption is *low*.

  d. Identify the three regions where both alcohol and tobacco consumption are *low*.

4. Table 8.27 contains a Montana outlook poll which asked a random sample of Montana residents whether their personal financial status was *worse*, the *same*, or *better* than a year ago, and whether they thought the state economic outlook was better than a year ago. This table contains

■ TABLE 8.26 Alcohol and tobacco consumption

Region	Alcohol	Tobacco
North	6.47	4.03
Yorkshire	6.13	3.76
Northeast	6.19	3.77
East Midlands	4.89	3.34
West Midlands	5.63	3.47
East Anglia	4.52	2.92
Southeast	5.89	3.20
Southwest	4.79	2.71
Wales	5.27	3.53
Scotland	6.08	4.51
North Ireland	4.02	4.56

■ TABLE 8.27 Montana outlook poll

Age	Sex	Inc	Pol	Area	Fin	Stat
3	0	2	2	1	2	1
2	0	3	3	1	3	1
1	0	2	*	1	2	1
3	1	2	1	1	1	0
3	1	3	3	3	2	*
1	0	2	1	3	3	*
3	1	1	3	3	1	1
1	0	1	3	2	1	0
3	1	*	3	3	2	0
1	0	*	1	1	2	1
2	1	2	3	1	2	*
3	1	1	3	2	2	0
2	0	2	1	3	3	0
3	0	*	3	2	2	0
3	0	3	3	3	3	1
3	0	3	1	3	1	1
1	1	2	1	3	3	*
3	1	2	1	3	2	1
3	1	2	3	3	1	0
2	0	3	3	3	3	1

these items and accompanying demographics about the respondents. It also contains results for every other person included in the poll. The table contains the following attributes:

- *Age*: 1, under 35; 2, 35–54; 3, 55 and over
- *Sex*: 0 male, 1 female
- *Inc*: yearly income: 1, under $20K; 2, 20–35K; 3, over 35K
- *Pol*: 1, Democrat; 2, Independent; 3, Republican
- *Area*: 1, Western; 2, Northeastern; 3, Southeastern Montana
- *Fin*: Financial status, 1, worse; 2, same; 3, better than a year ago
- *Stat*: State economic outlook, 0, better; 1, not better than a year ago

  a. Which area of Montana has the most male residents whose financial status was better than a year ago?
  b. Which age group of Montana residents had the view that the state economic outlook was better than last year?
  c. Which income group of female Republicans has a worse financial status and believes the state economic outlook has gotten worse?

5. Table 8.28 contains data about six apples in terms of *color* and *place of product*. Using either relational division or fuzzy relational division, answer the following queries. Create and use appropriate subtables to perform relational division to generate answers for queries (a) through (d). Convert Table 8.28 into a fuzzy relation and create other fuzzy relations to answer queries (e) through (g).

   a. Which apples have both green and yellow colors?
   b. Which apples are produced in both California and Washington?
   c. Which apples are both golden and green?
   d. Which apples are produced in both Japan and California?
   e. Which apples are both greenish and yellowish?
   f. Which apples are reddish?
   g. Which apples are both golden and yellowish?

6. Consider Table 8.29, which contains data on the average salaries for professors at the top 26 universities in the Association of American Universities. Salaries of full, associate, and assistant professors at these universities are provided. Using the table, answer the following fuzzy queries. Determine appropriate alpha-cut threshold values to limit the number of

▮ **TABLE 8.28** Apples with multiple colors

Apple	Color	Place of Product
A1	Green Red Yellow	California Washington Japan
A2	Green Yellow Golden	California Japan
A3	Red Yellow	Washington
A4	Green Golden	Washington California
A5	Green Yellow	California Japan
A6	Green Golden Yellow	Washington Japan California

generated answers to between three and five. Note that the salaries are in units of thousand dollars. The able contains the following attributes:

- *University*: Name of the university
- *Average salary*: Average salary for all professors at the university in 1992
- *Full prof. salary*: Average salary for full professors at the university in 1992
- *Assoc. prof. salary*: Average salary for associate professors at the university in 1992
- *Asst. prof. salary*: Average salary for assistant professors at the university in 1992

  a. Which universities have *low* full professor salaries?
  b. Which universities have **very** *high* assistant professor salaries?
  c. Which universities have *acceptable* assistant professor salaries?
  d. Which universities have *high* full professor and *low* assistant professor salaries?
  e. Which universities have **mostly** *high* associate professor salaries?
  f. Which universities have **generally** *high* full, associate, and assistant professor salaries?
  g. Which universities do not have **very** *low* average faculty salaries?

■ **TABLE 8.29 Faculty salaries**

University	Average salary	Full prof. salary	Assoc. prof. salary	Asst. prof. salary
Duke	64.47	83.00	57.50	46.10
Vanderbilt	59.20	78.90	49.70	42.50
Washington Univ.	58.77	75.40	51.40	43.80
Tulane	55.94	70.20	50.80	41.50
Cal Tech	75.54	93.30	70.00	56.40
Carnegie Mellon	63.01	79.30	55.00	49.40
Cornell	57.65	70.96	52.35	44.86
Virginia	54.91	71.60	47.80	39.50
Texas	54.01	70.30	45.70	40.80
Rochester	58.94	75.50	51.70	43.90
Nebraska	51.33	63.50	46.00	40.30
Univ. of Iowa	55.86	69.50	50.40	42.80
Stanford	71.09	91.20	64.40	50.00
Colorado	53.69	64.90	49.60	42.40
Univ. of Penn.	72.33	90.50	64.10	56.20
Michigan	59.05	73.10	54.00	44.80
Princeton	66.53	92.70	54.90	43.00
Iowa State	53.95	67.10	49.70	40.00
Purdue	54.71	70.20	47.90	40.70
Univ. of Chicago	67.16	86.90	57.30	50.90
Yale	64.69	90.20	52.30	43.20
Wisconsin	53.55	65.50	48.40	42.60
Penn State	54.48	68.80	49.10	40.30
Cal Berkeley	66.80	79.80	53.70	44.80
Illinois	53.94	67.10	48.40	41.70
Minnesota	53.45	66.50	47.60	41.80

■ 8.11   SELECTED BIBLIOGRAPHIC NOTES

General introductions to fuzzy database systems can be found in [Vamos 2003], [Cox 1992a], [Cox 1992b], [Leung 1989], [Vamos 2003], [Tashiro 1993], [Buckles 1995], and [Nakajima 1996]. An information-theoretic fuzzy approach to knowledge discovery in databases is described in [Maimon 1998]. [Vila 1994] gives a logic approach to fuzzy relational databases. [Zhang 1997] presents a methodology for integrating a fuzzy relational database system with a multidatabase system, whereas [Nemati 2002] discusses the issue of architectural integration of knowledge management, decision support, artificial intelligence, and data warehousing. [Au 2005], [Kuok 1998], and [Chan 2002] discuss the application of fuzzy data mining in association rule generation. [Wan 2004] focuses on the issue of mining association rules from XML data, whereas [Smith 2002] deals with fuzzy spatial data mining. The application of fuzzy data mining for database access, query, and retrieval is discussed in [Cox 1995], [Smith 1998], and [Chung 1998]. [Chung 1998] deals specifically with accident databases.

[Au 2001] shows how a classification method can be supported by a fuzzy approach to determine the degree of membership. Fuzzy representation and mining of functional dependencies are discussed in [Bosc 1994], [Raju 1988], and [Wang 2000]. In addition, fuzzy application on decision support is provided in [Castro–Schez 2005]. A fuzzy approach to uncertainty management in image databases is included in [Chianese 2004]. [Chiang 2000] shows the role of a fuzzy linguistic system for the mining of time series data, whereas [Dockery 1989] gives a general introduction to fuzzy linguistic databases.

[Groenemans 1997] describes a fuzzy database model based on quasi–order relations, whereas [Galindo 2002] shows how to apply fuzzy databases to the management of a tourism database. A system named "Gefred" in [Medina 1994] is a generalized model of fuzzy relation databases. [Ferrari 1996] describes an ASIC chip set for parallel fuzzy database mining and [Hopper 2003] gives an improved method for fuzzy partitions for fuzzy regression models. An object-oriented fuzzy database model is detailed in [Gyseghem 1995] with a focus on fuzzy behavior and relationships. The study of fuzzy application on web mining and fuzzy identification in fuzzy databases is provided in [Mitra 2004] and [Mouaddib 1994].

■ 8.12 CHAPTER BIBLIOGRAPHY

[Au 2001] W.-H. Au and K. C. Chan: "Classification with Degree of Membership: A Fuzzy Approach," ICDM 2001, pp. 35–42, 2001.

[Au 2005] W.-H. Au and K. C. Chan: "Mining Changes in Association Rules: A Fuzzy Approach," *Fuzzy Sets and Systems*, Vol. 149, No. 1, pp. 87–104, 2005.

[Bosc 1994] P. Bosc, D. Dubois, and H. Prade: "Fuzzy Functional Dependencies: An Overview and a Critical Discussion," *Proceedings of the 3rd IEEE International Conference on Fuzzy Systems*, pp. 325–330, 1994.

[Buckles 1995] B. P. Buckles and F. E. Petry: "Fuzzy Databases in the New Era," SAC, pp. 497–502, 1995.

[Castro–Schez 2005] J. J. Castro–Schez, L. Jimenez, J. Moreno, and L. Rodriguez: "Using Fuzzy Repertory Table-based Technique for Decision Support," *Decision Support Systems*, Vol. 39, No. 3, pp. 293–307, 2005.

[Chan 2002] K. C. Chan, W.-H. Au, and B. Choi: "Mining Fuzzy Rules in a Donor Database for Direct Marketing by a Charitable Organization," IEEE ICCI, pp. 239–246, 2002.

[Chianese 2004] A. Chianese, A. Picariello, L. Sansone, and M. L. Sapino: "Managing Uncertainties in Image Databases: A Fuzzy Approach," *Journal of Multimedia Tools and Applications*, Vol. 23, pp. 237–252, 2004.

[Chiang 2000] D.-A. Chiang, L. R. Chow, and Y. F. Wang: "Mining Time Series Data by a Fuzzy Linguistic Summary System," *Fuzzy Set and Theory*, Vol. 112, No. 3, pp. 419–432, 2000.

[Chung 1998] P. W. Chung and M. Jefferson: "A Fuzzy Approach to Accessing Accident Databases," *Applied Intelligence*, Vol. 9, No. 2, pp. 129–137, 1998.

[Cox 1992a] E. Cox: "Applications of Fuzzy System Models," *AI Expert*, Vol. 7, No. 2, pp. 34–39, 1992.

[Cox 1992b] E. Cox: "Solving Problems with Fuzzy Logic," *AI Expert*, Vol. 7, No. 3, pp. 28–37, 1992.

[Cox 1995] E. Cox: "Relational Database Queries Using Fuzzy Logic," *AI Expert*, Vol. 10, No. 1, pp. 23–29, 1995.

[Dockery 1989] J. T. Dockery and E. Murray: "Fuzzy Linguistic Databases: An Application," *Information Systems*, Vol. 14, No. 6, pp. 501–505, 1989.

[Ferrari 1996] A. Ferrari, A. Bellettini, R. Guerrieri, and G. Baccarani: "An ASIC Chip Set for Parallel Fuzzy Database Mining," *IEEE Micro*, Vol. 16, No. 6, pp. 60–67, 1996.

[Galindo 2002] J. Galindo, M. Carmen Aranda, J. L. Caro, A. Guevara, and A. Aguayo: "Applying Fuzzy Databases and FSQL to the Management of Rural Accommodation," *Tourism Management*, Vol. 23, No. 6, 2002.

[Groenemans 1997] R. Groenemans, E. E. Kerre, G. De Cooman, and E. Van Ranst: "Fuzzy Database Model Based on Quasi-Order Relations," *Journal of Intelligent Information Systems*, Vol. 8, No. 3, pp. 227–243, 1997.

[Gyseghem 1995] N. Van Gyseghem and R. De Caluwe: "Fuzzy Behaviour and Relationships in a Fuzzy OODB-Model," *Proceedings of the ACM Symposium on Applied Computing*, pp. 503–507, 1995.

[Hopper 2003] F. Hopper and F. Klawonn: "Improved Fuzzy Partitions for Fuzzy Regression Models," IJAR, Vol. 32, pp. 85–102, 2003.

[Kuok 1998] C. M. Kuok, A. W. C. Fu, and M. H. Wong: "Mining Fuzzy Association Rules in Databases," *ACM SIGMOD Record*, Vol. 27, No. 1, pp. 41–46, 1998.

[Leung 1989] K. S. Leung, M. H. Wong, and W. Lam: "A Fuzzy Expert Database System," *IEEE Transactions on Data & Knowledge Engineering*, Vol. 4, No. 4, pp. 287–304, 1989.

[Maimon 1998] O. Maimon, A. Kandel, and M. Last: "Information-Theoretic Fuzzy Approach to Knowledge Discovery in Databases," *Proceedings of the 3rd Online World Conference on Soft Computing in Engineering, Design and Manufacturing* (WSC3), 1998.

[Medina 1994] J. M. Medina, O. Pons, and M. A. Vila: "Gefred: A Generalized Model of Fuzzy Relational Databases," *Information Sciences*, Vol. 76, No. 1–2, pp. 87–109, 1994.

[Mitra 2004] S. Mitra and H. Legind Larsen: "Special Issue on Web Mining Using Soft Computing," *Fuzzy Sets and Systems*, Vol. 148, No. 1, pp. 1–3, 2004.

[Mouaddib 1994] N. Mouaddib: "Fuzzy Identification in Fuzzy Databases: The Nuanced Relational Division," *International Journal of Intelligent Systems*, Vol. 9, No. 5, pp. 461–473, 1994.

[Nakajima 1996] H. Nakajima: "Fuzzy Logic and Data Mining," *Software Computing in Intelligent Systems and Information Processing*, Proceedings of the Asian Fuzzy Systems, IEEE, 1996.

[Nemati 2002] H. R Nemati: "Knowledge Warehouse: An Architectural Integration of Knowledge Management, Decision Support, Artificial Intelligence and Data Warehousing," *Decision Support Systems*, Vol. 33, No. 2, pp. 143–161, 2002.

[Raju 1988] K. V. S. V. N. Raju and A. K. Majumdar: "Fuzzy Functional Dependencies and Lossless Join Decomposition of Fuzzy Relational Database Systems," *ACM Transactions on Database Systems*, Vol. 13, No. 2, pp. 129–166, 1988.

[Smith 1998] M. H. Smith, S. Rubin, and L. J. Trajkovic: "Fuzzy Data Mining for Querying and Retrieval of Research Archival Information," The 17th International Conference of the NAFIPS, 1998.

[Smith 2002] G. B. Smith and S. Bridges: "Fuzzy Spatial Data Mining," *Proceedings of the North American Fuzzy Information Processing Society Conference* (NAFIPS), New Orleans, LA, 2002.

[Tashiro 1993] H. Tashiro, N. Ohki, T. Nomura, T. Yokoyama, and Y. Masushita: "Managing Subjective Information in Fuzzy Database Systems," ACM Conference on Computer Science, pp. 156–161, 1993.

[Vamos 2003] T. Vamos: "Why Fuzzy in Data Mining?" *The 4th International Symposium on Uncertainty Modeling and Analysis* (ISUMA), 2003.

[Vila 1994] M. A. Vila, J. C. Cubero, J. M. Medina, and O. Pons: "A Logic Approach to Fuzzy Relational Databases," *International Journal of Intelligent Systems*, Vol. 9, No. 5, pp. 449–461, 1994.

[Wan 2004] J. W. Wan and G. Dobbie: "Mining Association Rules from XML Data Using XQuery," *Proceedings of Australian Workshop on Data Mining and Web Intelligence* (DMWI), Vol. 32, pp. 169–174, 2004.

[Wang 2000] S.-L. Wang, J.-S. Tsai, and T.-P. Hong: "Mining Functional Dependencies from Fuzzy Relational Databases," SAC, Vol. 1, pp. 490–493, 2000.

[Zhang 1997] W. Zhang, E. Laun, and W. Meng: "A Methodology of Integrating Fuzzy Relational Databases in a Multidatabase System," *Proceedings of the 5th International Conference on Database Systems for Advanced Applications* (DASFAA), pp. 401–410, 1997.

Data Mining Products and Applications

■ XpertRule Miner

- Developer: Attar Software Ltd.
- URL: www.attar.com
- Techniques Used: Decision trees, rules
- Platforms: ODBC, Windows
- Domain: Any
- Key Benefits: XpertRule Miner can be exported to a Knowledge Builder application, supports CRISP DM KDD development process and multi-tier client server architecture.
- Special Features: Association rules, classification, clustering
- Overview: XpertRule Miner supports the complete KDD process through the use of an iconic click and drag GUI interface. It supports the CRISP DM KDD development process. Visualization of results includes various 2D and 3D graphs and figures. XpertRule Miners supports multitier client–server architecture. Access to any database supported by an ODBC connection is allowed. Attar provides a companion product to XpertRule Miner. XpertRule Knowledge Builder provides a data flow development environment for KDD applications. The output from XpertRule Miner can be exported to a Knowledge Builder application.

■ STATISTICA Data Miner

- Developer: StatSoft, Inc.
- URL: www.statsoft.com/dataminer.html

- Techniques Used: ARIMA, decision trees (CART, CHAID), exponential smoothing, neural networks (Back-propagation, MLP, RBF, SOM), regression
- Platforms: Windows
- Domain: Any
- Key Benefits: Greatly increases the performance when data repositories are very large.
- Special Features: Classification, clustering, prediction
- Overview: STATISTICA Data Miner provides a comprehensive set of statistical methods to solve data mining problems. It offers a point and click iconic-based GUI to create a workflow description of the KDD and data mining tasks to be performed. Created Visual Basic code can be used to update or modify the tasks at a later date. Extended versions of traditional neural network techniques, association rule algorithms, CART and CHAID, and a wide variety of other techniques are included. The application offers options to process remote databases "in place" (without creating local copies), which greatly increases the performance when data repositories are very large.

■ Quadstone

- Developer: Quadstone
- URL: www.quadstone.com
- Techniques Used: Decision trees, regression
- Platforms: Unix (Solaris, HP, IBM AIX) and Windows NT
- Domain: Any
- Key Benefits: Deploys customer selections, models and scores in real-time or batch modes.
- Special Features: Prediction, profiling, segmentation.
- Overview: Quadstone System is a comprehensive analytical CRM software tool that includes tools to create customer-oriented datasets; segment, profile, and model customer data with advanced data mining algorithms; and deploy customer selections, models and scores in real-time or batch modes. A sophisticated GUI interface and graphical visualization tools are provided.

■ Partek

- Developer: Partek Incorporated
- URL: www.partek.com
- Techniques Used: Genetic algorithms, neural networks, regression
- Platforms: Unix, Windows
- Domain: Any
- Key Benefits: Supports many normalization and scaling transformation techniques.
- Special Features: Clustering, prediction
- Overview: Partek actually consists of several companion products designed to perform pattern recognition, exploratory data analysis, statistical inference, and predictive modeling. The pattern recognition product, Partek Pro, contains over 20 predefined similarity measures. Partek can access data imported from flat files, ODBC databases, and web servers. Many normalization and scaling transformation techniques are supported. The Pattern Visualization System contains many tools to graphically view the data mining results.

■ Mantas

- Developer: Mantas, Inc.
- URL: www.mantas.com
- Techniques Used: Decision trees, neural networks
- Platforms: Unix, Windows
- Domain: Financial services industry
- Key Benefits: Identifies potential money laundering risks relating to enterprise products and transaction services.
- Special Features: Association rules, classification, clustering, link analysis, prediction, sequence analysis, time series.
- Overview: Mantas, Inc., a spin-off from SRA International in May 2001, provides knowledge discovery solutions for the global financial services industry. The Mantas Knowledge Discovery Platform provides an extensible foundation that proactively collects, analyzes, highlights, and disseminates relevant, actionable information. The Mantas product suite includes five products. Mantas Best Execution is used to analyze brokerage trading

and identify opportunities to improve execution quality. Mantas Equities Trading Compliance monitors trading behavior to ensure adherence to industry rules and regulations. Mantas Brokerage Fraud and Anti-Money Laundering monitor security and monetary transaction for potential fraud and money laundering activities. Mantas Brokerage and Investor Protection monitors broker and investor behavior and trading activity to identify potential risks to both the investor and the firm. Mantas Enterprise Anti-Money Laundering is used to identify potential money laundering risks relating to enterprise products and transaction services.

■ KnowledgeSTUDIO

- Developer: ANGOSS Software Corporation
- URL: www.angoss.com/analytics_software/KnowledgeSTUDIO.php
- Techniques Used: Decision trees (CHAID), expectation-maximization, K-means, neural networks (MLP, RBF), regression (linear, logistic)
- Platforms: Windows, Server (Solaris, Windows)
- Domain: Any
- Key Benefits: Creates a client–server architecture and helps to access data directly in relational databases.
- Special Features: Classification, clustering, prediction, rules
- Overview: KnowledgeSTUDIO is a complete data mining workbench that performs many different tasks. It reads data from all major statistical packages and can import data from relational databases using ODBC. The optional KnowledgeSTUDIO Software Development Kit can be used to create in-house data mining applications. Application code can be generated for Visual Basic, PowerBuilder, Delphi, C++, and Java and then embedded into user code. KnowledgeSERVER can be used to create client–server architecture. It also can be used to access data directly in relational databases.

■ Enterprise Miner

- Developer: SAS Institute Inc.
- URL: www.sas.com/products/miner

- Techniques Used: Decision trees (CART, CHAID), K nearest neighbors, regression (linear, logistic), memory-based reasoning, neural networks (Kohonen, MLP, RBF, SOM)
- Platforms: Client(Windows), Server (Unix, Windows)
- Domain: Any
- Key Benefits: Creates a process flow to be performed by the data mining task.
- Special Features: Association rules, classification, clustering, prediction, time series
- Overview: Enterprise Miner from SAS implements the complete KDD process using their own process model called SEMMA (Sample, Explore, Modify, Model, and Assess). An icon-based, point and click GUI (not unlike Clementine) creates a process flow to be performed by the data mining task. In addition, Enterprise Miner contains many tools for bagging and boosting, sampling, visualization, imputation, filtering, transformations, and model assessment. An experiment text mining feature is also available. Enterprise Miner generates the complete scoring formula for all stages of model development in the form of SAS, C, and Java for subsequent model deployment and scoring.

■ Data Mining Suite

- Developer: Information Discovery, Inc.
- URL: www.datamining.com/dmsuite.htm
- Techniques Used: Rule induction
- Domain: Any
- Key Benefits: Mines large relational databases
- Special Features: Association rules, forecasting, prediction, rules
- Overview: The Data Mining Suite is designed to mine large relational databases. The suite of tools actually consists of six different modules, each targeted to different data mining functions. Incremental data mining is supported, as are multidimensional mining and ROLAP. The results of all data mining are viewed as patterns or rules. The most unique feature of the Data Mining Suite is the fact that generated patterns are stored and are accessible using the Pattern Query Language (PQL).

■ Clementine

- Developer: SPSS Inc. (formerly Integral Solutions, Ltd.)
- URL: www.spss.com/clementine
- Techniques Used: Apriori, BIRCH, CARMA, Decision trees (C5.0, C&RT a variation of CART), K-means clustering, neural networks (Kohonen, MLP, RBFN), regression (linear, logistic) rule induction (C5.0, GRI)
- Platforms: HP/UX, IBM AIX, Sun Solaris, Windows NT
- Domain: Any
- Key Benefits: Supports common web usage mining applications
- Special Features: Association rules, classification, clustering, factor analysis, forecasting, prediction, sequence discovery
- Overview: Perhaps the most unique feature of Clementine is its GUI approach to data mining, which Clementine pioneered in 1994. Through the use of descriptive icons, a user creates a data flow description of the functions to be performed. Each icon represents a step in the overall KDD process. Included are icons for such functions as accessing data, preparing data, visualization, and modeling. By dragging and dropping the icons onto the Clementine desktop, a stream of functions is created. Through the use of predefined templates of streams, Clementine provides support for common web usage mining applications. To assist in the creation of sequences, Clementine uses Capri. Clementine mines large data sets using a client/server model. When applicable, the server converts data access requests into SQL queries, which can then access a relational database. Clementine supports a wide variety of data formats. Clementine solutions are exported and deployed outside of Clementine using Clementine Solution Publisher.

■ AI Trilogy

- Developer: Ward Systems Group, Inc.
- URL: www.wardsystems.com
- Techniques Used: Genetic algorithms, jackknife estimation, neural networks
- Platforms: Windows
- Domain: Any
- Key Benefits: Includes a utility for training neural networks to run in Excel and user programs.

- Special Features: Classification, forecasting, prediction
- Overview: AI Trilogy is a suite of three products: NeuroShell Predictor, Neuroshell Classifier, and GeneHunter. ASCII, CSV, and Excel files are supported. The NeuroShell Run-Time Server is also included as a utility for trained neural networks to run in Excel and user programs.

■ BrainMaker

- Developer: California Scientific Software
- URL: www.calsci.com
- Techniques Used: Neural networks
- Platforms: Macintosh, Windows
- Domain: Any
- Key Benefits: Helps to choose best network and best training data.
- Special Features: Forecasting
- Overview: BrainMaker is neural network software that can be used with many different data sources, including Lotus, Excel, dBase, ASCII, or binary. It is one of the most popular NN software tools. A companion product, NetMaker, is included to assist in the construction of the neural networks. An optional package, Genetic Training Option (GTO), uses a genetic algorithm to create several possible neural nets. Through several iterations of training and genetic evolution, the best network can be chosen. This process also helps to choose the best training data.

■ DBMiner

- Developer: DBMiner Technologies Inc.
- URL: www.dbminer.com
- Techniques Used: Decision trees, K-means
- Platforms: Windows
- Domain: Any
- Key Benefits: MS SQL server, GUI interface
- Special Features: Association rules, classification, clustering
- Overview: DBMiner accesses data from many sources, including Microsoft SQL Server, Excel, OLEDB, and other relational databases through ODBC. Users can use either a DMSQL interface or a GUI interface.

Interface through MS SQL server's OLAP allows a cube view of data. There actually are three different products: DBMiner AX 2000 targets association rules, DBMiner SX 2000 performs sequential mining, and DBMiner GX 2000 targets OLAP mining.

■ GainSmarts

- Developer: Urban Science
- URL: www.urbanscience.com/main/gainpage.htm
- Techniques Used: Bayesian classification, decision trees (AID, CHAID), genetic algorithms, K-means, neural networks, regression (linear, logistic)
- Platforms: SAS, Windows
- Domain: Any
- Key Benefits: SAS, ACCESS, Collaborative filtering
- Special Features: Classification, clustering, prediction
- Overview: GainSmarts is a comprehensive product that supports all steps in the KDD process. It is flexible in the data sources that are supported, including any supported by SAS or ACCESS. Collaborative filtering and survival analysis are also supported.

■ Intelligent Miner

- Developer: IBM Corporation
- URL: www.software.ibm.com/data/iminer
- Techniques Used: Decision trees (modified CART), K-means, neural networks (MLP, back-propagation, RBF), regression (linear)
- Platforms: Windows, Solaris, AIX, OS/390, OS/400
- Domain: Any
- Key Benefits: DataJoiner, GUI Interface
- Special Features: Association rules, clustering, classification, prediction, sequential pat-terns, time series
- Overview: DB2 Intelligent Miner for Data performs mining functions against traditional DB2 databases or flat files. It also has capabilities to access data in other relational DBMSs using ODBC. However to do this IBM's DataJoiner must be used. It is implemented using a client–server approach with a straightforward GUI interface provided to assist the user in choosing data mining functions. Several visualization techniques are

used. There are two other products in the IBM Intelligent Miner family. Intelligent Miner for Text performs mining activities against textual data, including e-mail and web pages. It consists of text analysis tools, a search engine, NetQuestion Solution, and a web crawler package. The text analysis tools include the ability to cluster, classify, summarize, and extract important features from a document. NetQuestion Solution is a set of tools to facilitate indexing and searching web documents. DB2 Intelligent Miner Scoring allows SQL applications the ability to request data mining applications against a DB2 or Oracle database. It is a user-defined extension to DB2. It can be used to determine the actual score that a record has with respect to user-defined ranking criteria.

■ JDBCMine

- Developer: Intelligent Systems Research
- URL: www.intsysr.com/JDBCMine.htm
- Techniques Used: Decision trees (C4.5)
- Platforms: Windows, Java
- Domain: Any
- Key Benefits: Classifies JDBC and ODBC database
- Special Features: Classification
- Overview: JDBCMine performs classification against JDBC and ODBC databases using C4.5. The decision trees created can be visually browsed, printed, or saved as JPEG files.

■ KnowledgeSEEKER

- Developer: ANGOSS Software Corporation
- URL: www.angoss.com/analytics_software/KnowledgeSEEKER.php
- Techniques Used: Decision trees (CHAID, XAID, entropy-based algorithms)
- Platforms: Windows, Unix (AIX, HP-UX, IRIX, Digital Alpha, Sinux, Solaris, SCO, LINUX)
- Domain: Any
- Key Benefits: GUI interface
- Special Features: Classification
- Overview: KnowledgeSEEKER has a graphically based GUI and supports decision tree classification algorithms.

■ LOGIT

- Developer: Salford Systems
- URL: www.salford-systems.com
- Techniques Used: Regression (logistic)
- Platforms: DOS, MacOS, Unix
- Domain: Any
- Key Benefits: Regression tool
- Special Features: Forecasting, hypothesis testing
- Overview: LOGIT is a logistic regression tool. As with MARS, DBMS/Copy allows the use of many different data formats.

■ Magnum Opus

- Developer: RuleQuest Research Pty Ltd
- URL: www.rulequest.com/MagnumOpus-info.html
- Techniques Used: Opus
- Platforms: Windows, Unix (Solaris, Linux)
- Domain: Any
- Key Benefits: Lift, coverage, support
- Special Features: Association Rules
- Overview: Magnum Opus generates association rules using the measures of leverage, lift, strength, coverage, and support. Only rules that satisfy the desired measurement constraints are generated. Filtering of rules is also performed. Association rules can be generated for market basket–type data as well as other attribute values. Numeric attributes are automatically partitioned into sub ranges.

■ Minotaur

- Developer: Neural Technologies
- URL: www.neuralt.com
- Techniques Used: Neural networks
- Domain: Any
- Key Benefits: Neural networks, financial applications
- Special Features: Classification, prediction, rules

- Overview: Minotaur and Minotaur Transcure are neural network products targeted to support financial applications. Minotaur is aimed at fraud detection analysis in the telecommunications industry. Minotaur Transcure targets improving the efficiency of credit card transaction processing.

■ Re:order

- Developer: Lumio Limited
- URL: www.lumio.com/products.reorder
- Domain: Any
- Key Benefits: PMML
- Special Features: Sequential patterns
- Overview: The Re:order software product targets the efficient discovery of sequences. Sequences may or may not be required to be contiguous in time. Through the use of templates, users indicate the type of sequences to be detected. Templates may include temporal constraints as well as information about required or optional items to appear in the sequence. Capri uses the Predictive Modeling Mark-Up Language (PMML) to represent sequences.

■ S-Plus

- Developer: Insightful Corporation
- URL: www.insightful.com
- Techniques Used: ARIMA, correlation (Pearson), decision trees, hierarchical clustering (agglomerative, divisive), K-means, regression (linear, logistic, nonlinear, polynomial), statistical techniques (Jackknife, Monte Carlo)
- Platforms: Unix, Windows
- Domain: Any
- Key Benefits: Handle missing data and analysis with outliers
- Special Features: Classification, clustering, hypothesis testing, prediction, time series analysis
- Overview: The S-Plus data mining tool has versions for UNIX (including Linux) and Windows, as well as client–server versions. S-PLUS can import or export data from ASCII, SAS, SPSS, MATLAB, Excel and Lotus spreadsheets,

and other formats. S-PLUS can also import data from databases via ODBC or directly from Oracle on Solaris. S-PLUS is extensible: analytics are created using the object-oriented "S" language, and user-defined C, C++, FORTRAN, or Java code can be incorporated into S routines. A GUI is provided on both Windows and UNIX, and S-PLUS supports over 80 different charting types. Techniques are provided to handle missing data and for analysis of data with outliers.

■ SuperQuery

- Developer: AZMY Thinkware, Inc.
- URL: www.azmy.com
- Techniques Used: Rule induction
- Platforms: Windows
- Domain: Any
- Key Benefits: SuperQuery
- Special Features: Rules
- Overview: There are two main versions of SuperQuery. The Office edition is designed to work with Excel and Access data files, whereas the Discovery edition can be used to access many different types of data sources, including Access, xBASE, Borland Paradox, Excel, text files, and ODBC databases.

■ WebAnalyst

- Developer: Megaputer Intelligence Inc.
- URL: www.megaputer.com/products/wa/index.php3
- Platforms: Windows
- Domain: Any
- Key Benefits: Client-server architecture
- Special Features: Web mining (prediction, patterns)
- Overview: WebAnalyst provides web usage mining functions in a client–server architecture. WebAnalyst not only analyzes web usage logs, but also can be used to make real-time predictions as to the future behavior of a website visitor. These can then be used to dynamically personalize pages for the user.

■ WizWhy

- Developer: WizSoft
- URL: www.wizsoft.com/Why.html
- Techniques Used: Rule induction
- Platforms: Windows
- Domain: Any
- Key Benefits: Deviate from rules
- Special Features: Prediction, rules (if-then and if-and-only-if)
- Overview: WizWhy is a rule induction data mining tool that can be used for (1) analyzing the data, (2) issuing predictions, and (3) revealing unexpected cases that deviate from the rules. WizWhy accesses many different types of data, including dBase, MS Access, MS SQL, Oracle, OLE databases, ODBC, and ASCII.

■ BLAST

- Developer: NCBI (National Center for Biotechnology Information)
- URL: www.ncbi.nlm.nih.gov/Tools/
- Techniques Used: Nucleotide Sequence Analysis–Basic Local Alignment Search Tool (BLAST)
- Platform: Windows
- Domain: Health Care
- Key Benefits: BLAST can be run locally as a full executable and can be used to run BLAST searches against private, local databases, or downloaded copies of the NCBI databases.
- Special Features: The BLAST programs have been designed for speed, with a minimal sacrifice of sensitivity to distant sequence relationships.
- Overview: BLAST (Basic Local Alignment Search Tool) is a set of similarity search programs designed to explore all of the available sequence databases regardless of whether the query is protein or DNA.

■ CGAP

- Developer: NCI (National Cancer Institute)
- URL: www.ncbi.nlm.nih.gov/ncicgap/

- Techniques Used: Collaborating on public cancer data
- Platform: Windows
- Domain: Health Care
- Key Benefits: CGAP develops profiles of cancer cells by comparing gene expression in normal, precancerous, and malignant cells from a wide variety of tissues.
- Special Features: NCBI designed to maintain an internal database that tracks CGAP samples, libraries and clones used in the generation of EST and SAGE data.
- Overview: The Cancer Genome Anatomy Project (CGAP) aims to decipher the molecular anatomy of cancer cells. CGAP develops profiles of cancer cells by comparing gene expression in normal, precancerous, and malignant cells from a wide variety of tissues.

■ Electronic-PCR

- Developer: NCBI (National Center For Biotechnology Information)
- URL: www.ncbi.nlm.nih.gov/sutils/e-pcr/
- Techniques Used: Electronic PCR
- Platform: Windows.
- Domain: Health Care
- Key Benefits: Improved search sensitivity and reverse searching
- Special Features: Electronic PCR compares the query sequence against data in NCBI's UniSTS, a unified, non-redundant view of STSs from a wide range of sources.
- Overview: Electronic PCR allows you to search your DNA sequence for sequence tagged sites (STSs) that have been used as landmarks in various types of genomic maps. It compares the query sequence against data in NCBI's UniSTS, a unified, non-redundant view of STSs from a wide range of sources.

Index

Practical Applications of
DATA MINING

Sang C. Suh
Texas A&M University—Commerce

JONES & BARTLETT
LEARNING

World Headquarters
Jones & Bartlett Learning
40 Tall Pine Drive
Sudbury, MA 01776
978-443-5000
info@jblearning.com
www.jblearning.com

Jones & Bartlett Learning
Canada
6339 Ormindale Way
Mississauga, Ontario L5V 1J2
Canada

Jones & Bartlett Learning
International
Barb House, Barb Mews
London W6 7PA
United Kingdom

Jones & Bartlett Learning books and products are available through most bookstores and online booksellers. To contact Jones & Bartlett Learning directly, call 800-832-0034, fax 978-443-8000, or visit our website, www.jblearning.com.

Substantial discounts on bulk quantities of Jones & Bartlett Learning publications are available to corporations, professional associations, and other qualified organizations. For details and specific discount information, contact the special sales department at Jones & Bartlett Learning via the above contact information or send an email to specialsales@jblearning.com.

Production Credits
Publisher: Cathleen Sether
Senior Acquisitions Editor: Timothy Anderson
Senior Editorial Assistant: Stephanie Sguigna
Production Director: Amy Rose
Associate Production Editor: Tiffany Sliter
Associate Marketing Manager: Lindsay White
V.P., Manufacturing and Inventory Control: Therese Connell
Cover and Title Page Design: Kristin E. Parker
Composition: Glyph International
Cover Images: Globe with code: © Hannu Viitanen/Dreamstime.com; Abstract road map: © Gallowen/Dreamstime.com
Printing and Binding: Malloy, Inc.
Cover Printing: Malloy Inc.

Library of Congress Cataloging-in-Publication Data
Suh, Sang C.
    Practical applications of data mining / Sang C. Suh.
        p. cm.
    Includes index.
    ISBN-13: 978-0-7637-8587-1 (pbk.)
    ISBN-10: 0-7637-8587-3 (ibid)
    1. Data mining. I. Title.
    QA76.9.D343S686 2010
    006.3—dc22

                        20100235006048

6048

Printed in the United States of America
15 14 13 12 11   10 9 8 7 6 5 4 3 2